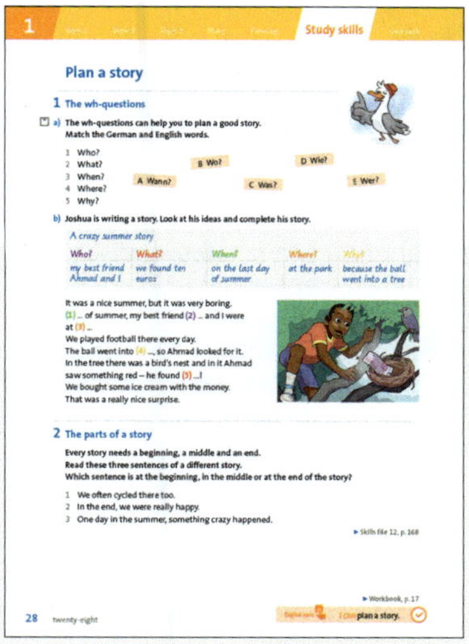

1 Study skills

Plan a story

1 The wh-questions

2 The parts of a story

28 twenty-eight

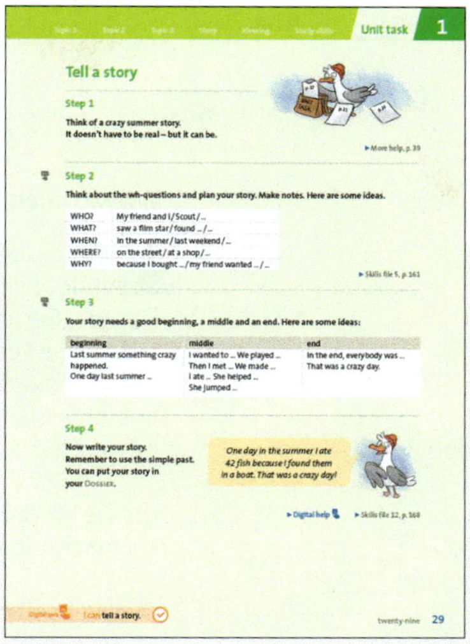

Unit task 1

Tell a story

Step 1

Step 2

Step 3

Step 4

twenty-nine 29

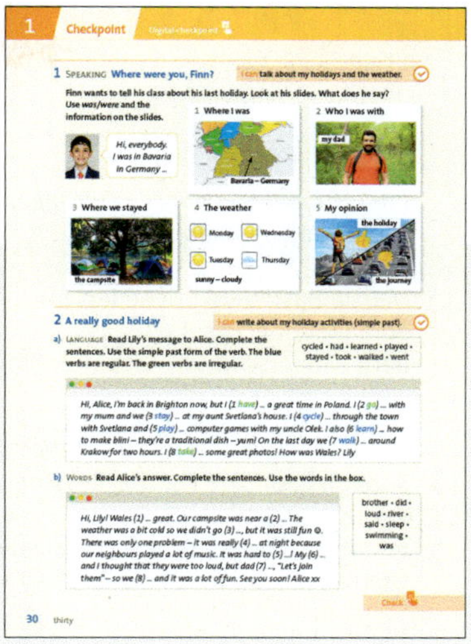

1 Checkpoint

1 Speaking Where were you, Finn?

2 A really good holiday

30 thirty

Lern- und Arbeitstechniken

Auf der *Study skills*-Seite übst du wichtige Lern- und Arbeitstechniken, z. B. wie du neue Wörter am besten lernst.

Eine Aufgabe am Unit-Ende

In der *Unit task* erstellst du ein größeres Produkt, z. B. eine Präsentation. Dabei wendest du das Gelernte aus der Unit an.

Im *Checkpoint* wiederholst du

Hier überprüfst du, wie gut du die Lernziele der Unit schon erreicht hast.

Nach Units 2 und 4 findest du ein *Text file* mit interessanten Texten zum Thema der Unit.

Diese Verweise führen dich in die *Diff bank* am Ende der Unit

▶ More help	▶ Parallel exercise	▶ More practice
Hilfen zu den Aufgaben	einfachere Variante einer Übung	weitere Übungen

Diese Lernangebote findest du im hinteren Teil des Buches

▶ Skills file	▶ Language file	▶ Wordbank
eine Übersicht über die Lern- und Arbeitstechniken	die wichtigsten Sprachregeln	zusätzliche Wörter zu bestimmten Themen

Let's talk	Vocabulary	Dictionary
Redewendungen nach wichtigen Themen und Situationen geordnet	eine Liste der neuen Vokabeln einer Unit mit hilfreichen Tipps	alphabetische Wörterlisten zum Nachschlagen (Englisch–Deutsch, Deutsch–Englisch)

BASIC lighthouse 2

Im Auftrag des Verlages herausgegeben von
Ulrike Rath, Aachen
sowie
Martin Bastkowski, Schellerten;
Sonja Mahne, Basel;
Berit Schaarschmidt, Aschaffenburg

Erarbeitet von
Olivia Wintgens, Würselen; Rebecca Robb Benne, Kopenhagen; Zoe Thorne, Royston
sowie
Jennifer O'Hagan, Bristol (*Checkpoints*);
Ursula Fleischhauer, Hannover (*Vocabulary*)

In Zusammenarbeit mit der Englischredaktion
Klaus Unger (Projektleitung),
Silvia Wiedemann (koordinierende Redakteurin),
Kathrin Spiegelberg
Ingrid Raspe, Düsseldorf (*Vocabulary, Dictionary E–D*)

Beratende Mitwirkung
Sabine Bay, Cloppenburg; Armin Düpmeier, Warendorf; Lina Hein-Gehrmann, Wuppertal; Daniel Henn, Frankfurt/Main; Tobias Pfeifer, Dossenheim
sowie
Vertr.-Prof. Dr. Christian Ludwig, Berlin; Prof. Dr. Bernd Rüschoff, Essen; Prof. Dr. Michaela Sambanis, Berlin

Medienmanagement
Silke Kirchhoff

Illustrationen
Harald Ardeias, Schelklingen; Irina Zinner, Hamburg

Fotos
Anja Poehlmann, Brighton
Für die freundliche Unterstützung danken wir der *Varndean School, Brighton*

Umschlaggestaltung
Rosendahl, Berlin

Layoutkonzept
Klein & Halm, Berlin

Designberatung
Ungermeyer, Berlin

Layout und technische Umsetzung
designcollective, Berlin
Straive

Druck
Mohn Media Mohndruck, Gütersloh

PEFC
PEFC/04-31-1033

PEFC zertifiziert
Dieses Produkt stammt aus nachhaltig bewirtschafteten Wäldern und kontrollierten Quellen.

www.pefc.de

www.cornelsen.de

Soweit in diesem Lehrwerk Personen fotografisch abgebildet sind und ihnen von der Redaktion fiktive Namen, Berufe, Dialoge und Ähnliches zugeordnet oder diese Personen in bestimmte Kontexte gesetzt werden, dienen diese Zuordnungen und Darstellungen ausschließlich der Veranschaulichung und dem besseren Verständnis des Buchinhaltes.

Dieses Werk berücksichtigt die Regeln der reformierten Rechtschreibung und Zeichensetzung.

Die Webseiten Dritter, deren Internetadressen in diesem Lehrwerk angegeben sind, wurden vor Drucklegung sorgfältig geprüft. Der Verlag übernimmt keine Gewähr für die Aktualität und den Inhalt dieser Seiten oder solcher, die mit ihnen verlinkt sind.

Die Cornelsen App ist eine fakultative Ergänzung *zu Lighthouse*, die die inhaltliche Arbeit begleitet und unterstützt. Als solche unterliegt sie nicht der Genehmigungspflicht.

Alle Drucke dieser Auflage sind inhaltlich unverändert und können im Unterricht nebeneinander verwendet werden.

ISBN 9783060357697 broschiert
1. Auflage, 1. Druck 2023

ISBN 9783060357703 gebunden
1. Auflage, 1. Druck 2023

ISBN 9783060345830 E-Book

BASIC
lighthouse 2

Cornelsen

Inhalt

Unit 2 Friends and heroes

L Listening · R Reading · S Speaking · W Writing · M Mediation · V Viewing · IC Intercultural competence · MK Medienkompetenz · LS Life skills · Voc Vocabulary · G Grammar

Unit 3 Activities and games

Unit 4 Celebrate!

L Listening · R Reading · S Speaking · W Writing · M Mediation · V Viewing · IC Intercultural competence · MK Medienkompetenz · LS Life skills · Voc Vocabulary · G Grammar

Inhalt

Unit 5 Getting ready for the future

L Listening · R Reading · S Speaking · W Writing · M Mediation · V Viewing · IC Intercultural competence · MK Medienkompetenz · LS Life skills · Voc Vocabulary · G Grammar

Anhang

Skills file 156

Language file 170

Die Angebote des Schulbuchs sind nicht obligatorisch abzuarbeiten. Die Auswahl der Übungen und Übungsteile richtet sich nach den Schwerpunkten des schulinternen Curriculums.

Hello again!

The last day of the holidays

1 LISTENING AND SPEAKING Ready for school

a) **Listen. Who is happy to go back to school? Choose the correct answer.**

1 Zane and Lily are / aren't happy.
2 Noah is / isn't happy.
3 Sunita is / isn't happy.

b) WALK AROUND **Are you happy to be back at school? Tell different partners.**

I'm	happy to be back at school • not happy to be back at school • ...
I want to	see my friends again • have more free time • ...
The summer holidays are	too short • too long • boring • the best • ...

▶ Workbook, p. 6

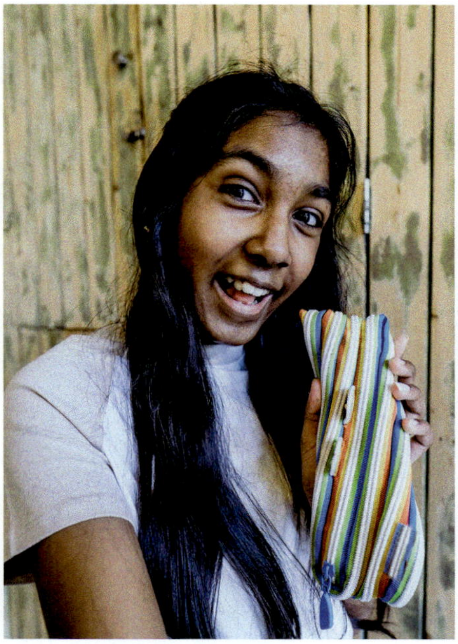

2 LISTENING AND SPEAKING A day at Brighton beach

a) Lily and Zane are at the beach. Imagine you're there too. Close your eyes and listen.

b) Listen again. Draw a picture of you at the beach.

c) Show your picture to a partner and talk about it.

I'm	sitting on the beach • walking on the pier • looking at the sea • eating ice cream • ...
I can see	the water • the sun • the beach • the pier • seagulls • people • ...
I can hear	the sea • the wind • seagulls • kids • families • music • ...
People are	playing • swimming • eating • walking • ...

▸ Workbook, p. 7

Digital quiz   I can talk about summer activities.

Unit 1
Travel and holidays

I was at home in Brighton.

I was in Spain, in a hotel near the beach.

I was in Poland with my mum.

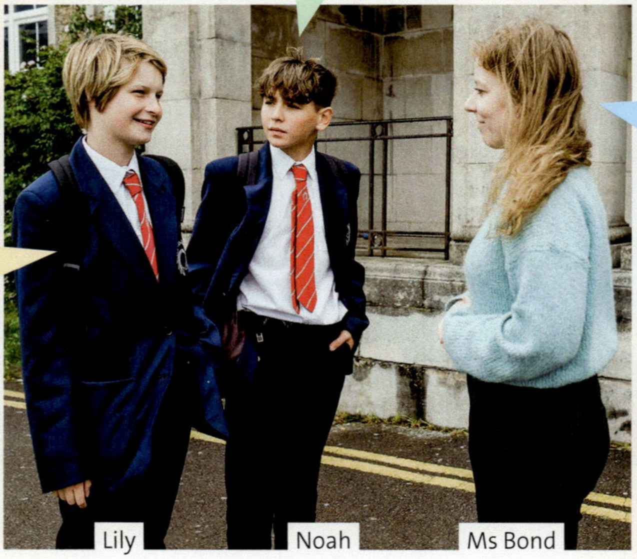

1 LISTENING Where were they?

a) BEFORE YOU LISTEN **Look at the speech bubbles and photos on** **pages 12 and 13****. Write where each person was.** *Ms Bond: ... Lily: ... Noah: ... Sunita: ... Zane: ... Alice: ...*

b) **Listen and find out: Who says what? Write the names.**

1 It was really hot, but it was a great holiday.
2 It was fun, but it was cold.
3 We were often in our garden.
4 There were a lot of tourists.
5 It was nice to see my family.
6 I was with my parents and my little sister.

c) **Listen again and check.**

Nach dieser Unit kann ich ...

- über meine Ferien sprechen
- über Ferienaktivitäten schreiben
- über das letzte Wochenende sprechen
- von neuen Erfahrungen berichten

Unit task

- eine Geschichte erzählen

My mum, my brother Nish and I were in Prague.

I was in France, in a holiday apartment.

I was on a campsite in Wales.

2 SPEAKING Where were you?

a) **What about your summer holidays? Write two sentences.**

I was I wasn't We were We weren't	at home. at the beach / by the sea. in a holiday apartment / hotel. in Germany / Austria / Turkey. on a campsite.	It was It wasn't	🙂 amazing / cool / fun / great. boring / 😣 horrible. sunny / hot / cold / rainy / windy.

b) WALK AROUND **Ask and answer these questions: Where were you? How was it?**

▶ Workbook, p. 8 ▶ More practice 1+2, p. 34 ▶ Language file 1, p. 174 ▶ Countries, p. 266

Digital quiz I can **talk about my holidays and the weather.**

Holiday stories

1 SONG My summer holiday

a) Listen. Where was the singer? Was it a good holiday?

b) Listen again and choose the correct words.

1 She was on holiday with her dad and her brother / sister.
2 They stayed in a hotel / holiday apartment.
3 The weather was rainy / hot.
4 They watched a football match / dancers.
5 They danced and moved their feet / hands.
6 The food was good / bad.

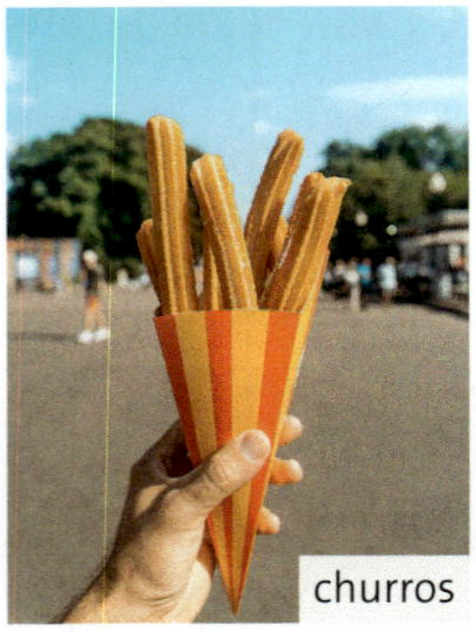
churros

► More help, p. 35

2 LOOKING AT LANGUAGE The simple past (regular verbs)

Erklär-film

The singer talks about the past. Look at the blue words and complete the rule.

We watched flamenco dancers in the street.
We listened and danced and moved our feet.

► Language file 2, p. 174

Wenn du über die ... sprichst, verwendest du das *simple past*.
Bei regelmäßigen Verben hängst du ... an das Verb an.

3 Emma's holiday plans

Pick the correct verb.

1 My big sister and I presented / wanted to stay on a campsite this year. It's our dream holiday.
2 We talked / listened about it with our parents.
3 My mum moved / liked the idea.
4 My dad enjoyed / wanted a campsite with a shower.
5 So we used / looked for different campsites online.
6 My sister phoned / answered one campsite and asked / talked our questions ... and the campsite was perfect! My sister and I were happy – finally, we can have our dream holiday!

4 Noah's summer in Brighton

Complete his sentences with words from the box.

brushed • liked • played • stayed • travelled • watched • ~~worked~~

1 My parents *worked* some days.
2 Buddy and I often ... ball in our garden.
3 I ... Buddy every day. He looks really nice now!
4 One day I ... to see my grandma in Portsmouth.
5 In the evening I ... TV with my parents.
6 We ... in Brighton this summer – and I ... it!

5 Zane's holiday in France

Complete the sentences. Use verbs from the box and change them into the simple past.

cycle • help • love • start • stay • talk • use

1 We ... in a holiday apartment. It was small, but the pool was nice.
2 My sister and I ... that pool every day! We ... it.
3 Every morning, my dad and I ... into town for bread on our bikes.
4 I ... in French with people at the shops – it was hard, but they were nice to me.
5 Sometimes I ... my mum with dinner.
6 I was sad when we ... our journey back to Brighton. Maybe we can come back next summer!

▶ Parallel exercise, p. 35 ▶ More practice 3, p. 35

6 GAME Last summer

Work in groups. The first student says a sentence about last summer. The next student repeats it and adds a sentence.

A Last summer, I played table tennis.
B Last summer, I played table tennis and I learned to skateboard.
C Last summer, I learned to skateboard and I ...

Ideas
- *cycled in the park / in my street / ...*
- *helped my parents / my grandparents / ...*
- *learned to code / skateboard / ...*
- *played table tennis / cards / with my pet / ...*
- *watched lots of films / a football match / ...*

▶ Workbook, p. 9

7 Reading A holiday story

a) Before you read **Can you remember: Where was Sunita on holiday? Was it a good holiday?**

b) **Read Sunita's story. Check your answers from a).**

My holiday was great! Mum, my brother Nish and I were in Prague.
We went by plane and stayed in a hotel. We did lots of fun activities together and saw a lot of sights.

One evening we went on a scary tour in the old town. Our guide looked like a vampire! He told us horrible stories and we were all a bit scared.

I had to ask Nish a question, so I moved over to him and said, "Nish?"
But I scared him ... and he jumped! Everybody in the group laughed.

c) **Copy the table. Look at Sunita's story and find the simple past forms of the verbs.**

be	was / were
go	went
do	d...
see	s...
tell	t...
have	
say	

Einige *simple past*- Formen sind unregelmäßig. Diese musst du lernen. Du findest eine Liste auf S. 271.

► More practice 4, p. 36 ► Language file 2, p. 174

8 An afternoon in Prague

Pick the correct verb.

After the tour we did / went to the river. We had / told lunch in a nice little restaurant and said / saw a lot of boats on the river. So we said / did a boat trip too – that was fun. Finally we visited the old castle and the guide told / saw us a lot of things about the history of Prague. Nish said / went it was boring, but mum liked it.

9 Nish's favourite day in Prague

Complete the sentences with words from the box.

did • had • said • saw • told • went

The next day Nish (1) ... an ad for minigolf. He (2) ... his mum and Sunita about it. Sunita liked the idea too, so Meera (3) ..., "Let's go this afternoon." They (4) ... by bus and were surprised when they arrived. It was in a big, modern building, and they (5) ... different activities for people to do: video games, trampolining, a cinema – and minigolf! Later, they travelled back to the hotel. "That was my favourite day," said Nish. "We (6) ... a lot of fun activities – but not everything. Let's go again!"

10 WORDS Travel and holiday words

a) **Read the umbrella words and the three phrases. Can you write them under the correct umbrella?**

- ... saw a lot of sights
- ... in a hotel
- ... train

I stayed ... | *I went by ...* | *I ...*

b) **Collect more words and phrases from pages 12–16 for the umbrella words.**

▸ More help, p. 36 ▸ More practice 5, p. 36 ▸ Skills file 1, p. 157

My task

11 My summer holidays

Read the message from your friend and write an answer. You can use your words from ex. 10.

Hi!
How were your summer holidays? Where were you? I was in London with my parents. We went by train and we stayed in a hotel. We saw a lot of sights! I liked the food too.
Tell me all about your summer activities!
Bye for now
Cameron

Hi, Cameron!

London is cool!
I was at home. /
I was in ... We went there by ...
We stayed ...
I saw my friends / went to the pool / ...

Bye!

▸ Digital help
▸ Countries, p. 266 ▸ Wordbank 1, p. 185

▸ Workbook, pp. 10–11

Digital quiz I can write about my holiday activities.

At home in the holidays

1 Get ready for the *Brighton Pride* parade

Brighton Pride **is the city's biggest event – 160,000 people visit it every year. Lily, Zane, Noah and Sunita want to see the parade together. Complete the sentences with words from the box.**

was • did • ~~got up~~ • had • looked for • said • texted • told • wanted • went (2x)

The morning before *Pride* was busy for everybody!
Zane (1) *got up* early and (2) ... breakfast with his mum.
Noah (3) ... his headphones, so he and his dad (4) ... them everywhere in the house. Finally, Noah (5) ... his dad, "It's OK! They're here."
Lily (6) ... her *Pride* make-up. Then she (7) ... to Brighton Station to meet her friends.
Sunita (8) ... goodbye to her mum and (9) ... to Preston Park to take the train to Brighton Station. When she (10) ... on the train, she (11) ... Lily.

2 LISTENING Waiting for Sunita

a) BEFORE YOU LISTEN **Lily, Zane and Noah are at Brighton Station. Where's Sunita? Guess.**

1 At the parade.
2 On a train.
3 At Brighton Station.

b) **Listen and check.**

c) **Copy the table. Then listen to the station announcements and complete it.**

from	arrival time	platform
Cambridge	*9.55*	...
Eastbourne	...	*8*
London Victoria	*10.06*	...
Portsmouth	...	*2*
Bristol	*10.22*	...

► Skills file 6, p. 162
► Workbook, p. 12

3 VIEWING Buying a ticket

a) **Lots of tourists visit Brighton and they often travel by train. Watch the video and choose the correct buttons on the ticket machine.**

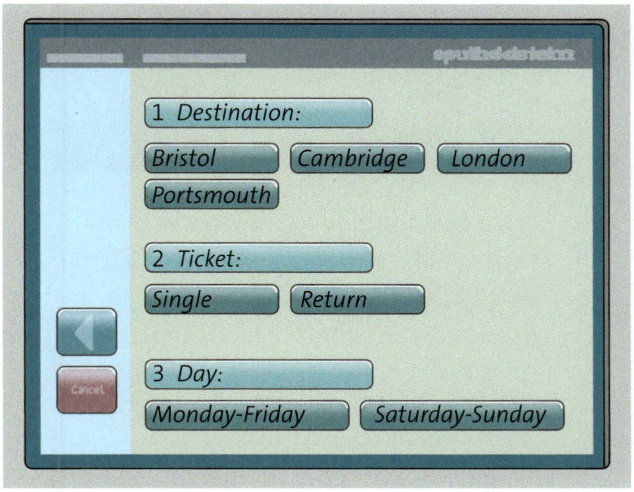

Good to know

In the UK the money is pounds (£) and pence (p). £1 is 100 pence.

You write:	You say:
50p	fifty p
£1.50	one pound fifty
£32.50	thirty-two pounds fifty

b) **Look at these tickets A–E and say the prices.**

Ticket A costs ... Ticket B ...

▶ More practice 6+7, p. 37

▶ Workbook, p. 13

4 READING *Brighton Pride*

Read Lily's three messages to her aunt Svetlana about *Pride* and complete the information.

1 Lily went to *Pride* with her ...
2 Noah wore his ...
3 Lily loved ... and ...
4 In the parade they saw ...
5 They ate ...
6 They listened to ...

Pride was amazing! 😃 *I went with my friends. Sunita bought a Pride flag* 🏳️‍🌈*, but I didn't buy a flag because I made my own decorations. Noah wore his headphones* 🎧*, so he didn't have a problem with the music. We all wore Pride make-up.*

We watched the parade. It was so fun, and everybody was really happy! I loved 😍 *all the colours* ❤️🧡💛💚💙💜 *and rainbow* 🌈 *clothes. We saw Willow in the parade with her girlfriend, but they didn't see us.*

Then we went to the family Pride area and ate rainbow cake 🍰 😋*. We didn't go to the concert after the parade, but we listened to street musicians* 🎸 *. We had a great time!*

5 LOOKING AT LANGUAGE
The simple past: negatives

Erklär-film

a) Read Lily's messages again and look at the list of top *Pride* activities. Tick (✓) the things Lily that did and cross (×) the things that she didn't do.

Top things to do at *Brighton Pride*:
1 wear *Pride* make-up
2 watch the parade
3 go to the concert
4 buy a *Pride* flag
5 eat rainbow cake

b) Write all the simple past negatives in Lily's messages. Then answer the question.

I didn't ...
Noah ...
Willow and her girlfriend ...
We ...

Welches Wort brauchst du immer in verneinten Sätzen im *simple past*?

► Language file 3, p. 175

► Workbook, pp. 13–15

6 A message from Lily's aunt

Lily's aunt Svetlana texted her back. Complete her text with the negative simple past of the words in the box.

× bring • × eat • × ~~enjoy~~ •
× play • × stay • × want

▸ More practice 8, p. 37
▸ More practice 9, p. 38

*I love your photos, Lily! It looks like you had a great time!
We went to a music festival this summer, but there were some problems. First, I (1) didn't enjoy the music! The bands (2) … my kind of music, so I (3) … to dance. Then your uncle Olek said, "I don't like the food here!" So he (4) … anything and was hungry. Finally, I remembered something – I (5) … my phone! So we (6) … very long and went home.*

My task

7 My town in the holidays

a) **Write five sentences about your activities in the holidays: some true, some false.**

I went to	a concert / a parade / a film festival / a music festival / a show / …	in my town / … with my friends / family / …
It was	amazing / great / OK / boring / horrible / …	
I We	ate bought watched / listened to / saw / … wore loved / enjoyed / liked / …	hot dogs / ice cream / … presents / a cap / … a band / dancers / a film / … fun clothes / a special T-shirt / … the music / the food / …
I didn't We didn't	eat / buy / watch / listen to / see / wear / like / enjoy / …	

b) **Swap with your partner. Guess the false sentences and tell your partner.**

I went to a film festival in my town.

You didn't go to a film festival.

▸ Digital help

Digital quiz I can **talk about a special day in my holidays.**

A weekend project

1 Listening Welcome, Finn!

a) Before you listen Look at the title of this exercise and the photo. Who do you think Finn is?

He's cool –
he likes
coding too!

b) Copy the table. Listen and complete it. You don't need to understand everything.

name	*Finn Demir*
from	...
pet	...
likes (two things)	...

c) Listen again and check.

2 Mediation A clean-up party

a) Ms Bond tells class 8C about a class activity on Saturday. Read the brochure. What do you do at a clean-up party on the beach?

Come to our clean-up party on Brighton Beach

Collect plastic bags, bottles and other rubbish. Help make the beach and the water clean for people and sea animals.
- Sing, dance and clean up.
- Wear funny clothes and listen to music.
- We have rubbish bags and gloves for everybody.

b) During dinner at home Finn tells his mum about the clean-up party in German. His mum asks questions. Act out the conversation with a partner.

Finn	Am Samstag wollen wir ...
Mutter	Das klingt interessant. Was macht ihr genau?
Finn	...
Mutter	Was sollst du anziehen?
Finn	...
Mutter	Sollst du etwas mitbringen?
Finn	...

► Skills file 8, p. 164

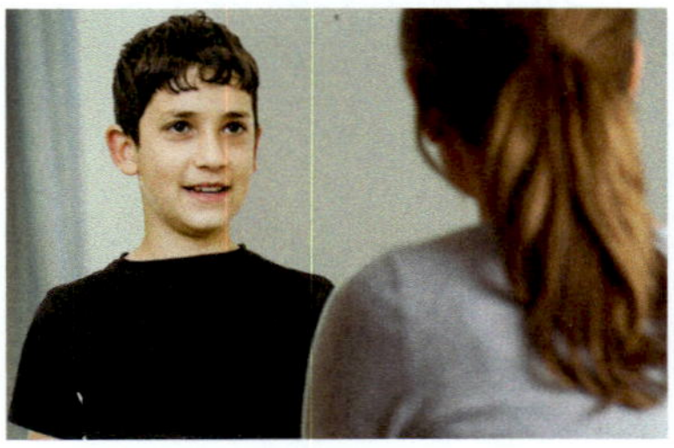

3 Listening On Monday

a) After the clean-up party Ms Bond talks to the class. Look at the pictures and listen. There's one thing that they didn't find – what is it?

b) Listen again. Write who found each thing.

Sunita found a …
Noah …

A
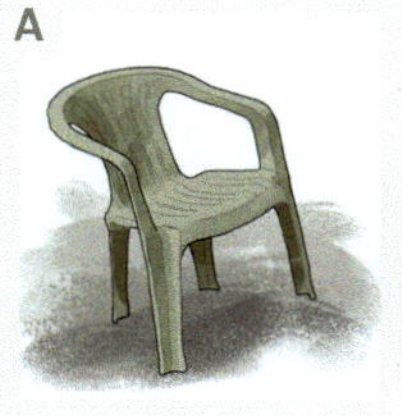
B
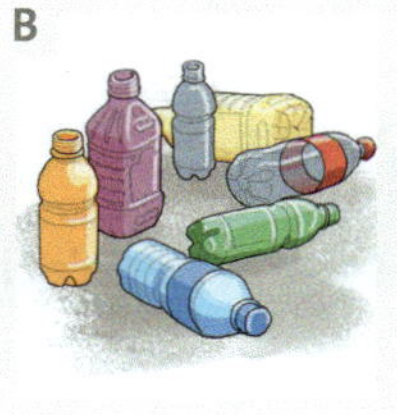
C
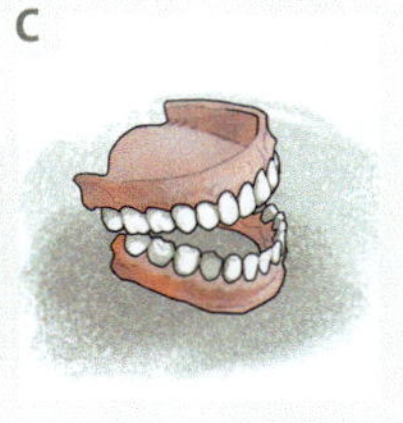
D
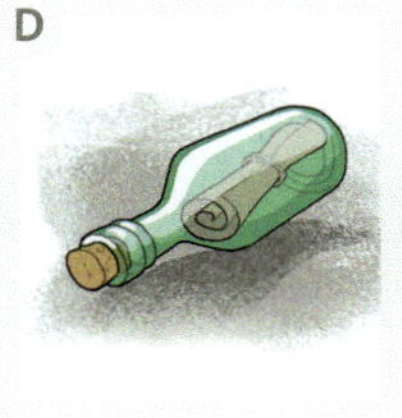
E
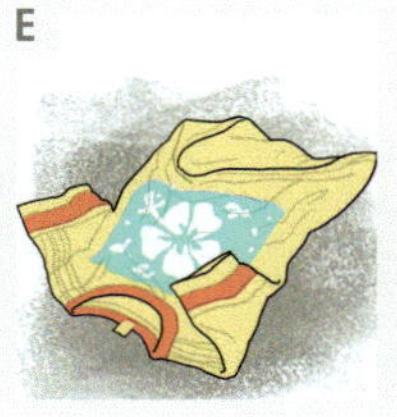
F

My task

4 Last weekend

a) **In the break the kids talk about the rest of their weekend. Match numbers 1–5 to Finn, Lily, Noah, Sunita and Zane.**

1 At lunchtime on Saturday I cooked spaghetti for my mum and my sister Holly.

2 Last weekend I helped my mum with all the animals.

3 On Sunday morning I went to the beach with dad and Buddy.

4 On Sunday afternoon my mum and I went to Brighton Pier for the first time.

5 Yesterday I had a parkour class.

b) Speed dating **What about you? Tell different partners about your last weekend.**

Last weekend	I played football / basketball / table tennis / handball / video games / …
Yesterday	I did yoga / judo / my homework / a school project / …
On Saturday morning	I went running / skateboarding / shopping / …
At lunchtime on Saturday	I went to the library / the market / the sports centre / my friend's house / …
In the afternoon / evening	I cleaned my room / my bike / the bathroom / …
On Sunday morning	I had a pizza / a barbecue / a karaoke night / …
…	
It was great / exciting / cool / amazing / boring / hard / scary / …	

► More practice 10, p. 38

► Workbook, p. 16

Digital quiz I can talk about last weekend.

Noah's journey

1 Reading Noah's ticket

Before you read **Look at Noah's ticket and complete the sentences.**

1 Noah travelled on ...
2 He travelled from ... to ...
3 He travelled at ...
4 He travelled by ...

2 Reading What happened?

a) **Read the story.**

b) **Put what happened in the correct order.**

A Buddy swam in the sea.
B Sunita asked Noah about travelling alone.
C Sunita, Lily and Zane helped Noah.
D Noah got on the right train to Brighton.
E Noah got on the wrong train.
F Noah got on the train to Portsmouth.

Saturday 5th October

1 Today I travelled to my grandma's house alone for the first time. I love seeing my grandma, but she lives in Portsmouth and my parents are busy, so I don't see her often. Last week, Sunita asked me, "Do you want to see her alone? You can go by bus or train." I thought about it and I was a bit scared at first.

2 But then I thought, "I'm twelve now. I want to try!"
So I asked mum and dad. They said *yes!*
So this morning dad bought a ticket for me and Buddy and I got on the train at Brighton station. I had a wonderful day with grandma in Portsmouth. It was sunny and we went to the beach. We had a picnic and Buddy swam in the sea – he was so happy in the water! Grandma and I were happy too.

3 In the afternoon grandma and I were tired, so grandma took me to Portsmouth station. I got on the train alone because you need a ticket to go to the platforms.

4 But there was a problem – I got on the wrong train! I was really scared at first, and I didn't know what to do!

5 Then Buddy put his head on me and looked at me. He was very calm and he helped me to feel calm too. I texted Sunita, Lily and Zane and they helped me find the right train back to Brighton.

6 I texted mum and dad too and I told them what happened. They were very happy when I arrived at Brighton station. They were really proud of me for trying something new. I was proud too!

3 Feelings in the story

Copy the table. Write the feelings and the names from the story.

Part	Feeling			Name
1		=	*scared*	*Noah*
2		=	...	...
3		=	...	...
4		=	...	...
5		=	...	
6		=		

► Skills file 7, p. 163

4 Who said it?

Which person in Noah's story maybe said these sentences?

1 OK Noah, you can go by train to Portsmouth alone.
2 Welcome to Portsmouth, Noah! It's so nice to see you!
3 Goodbye, Noah. Have a good journey to Brighton!
4 Oh no, I'm on the wrong train! I don't know what to do!
5 Don't worry, Noah. Get off the train at the next station.
6 We're so proud of you, Noah – that was scary, but you did it!

5 What a day!

Match the sentence halves.

1 I travelled ...
2 Dad bought ...
3 Grandma and I had ...
4 I got on ...
5 Buddy helped me ...
6 I arrived ...

A a ticket.
B the train.
C at Brighton station.
D to my grandma's house.
E a picnic.
F to feel calm.

6 LIFE SKILLS Try new things

a) **Different things are scary to different people. How scary are the activities in the box to you?**

Singing to other people Picking up a snake Travelling by plane Watching a thunderstorm Talking to new people Riding a horse	is	very scary. OK. not scary.

b) **Talk to your partner. What's the same? What's different?**

Travelling by plane is very scary.

Really? For me it's picking up a snake.

That's the same for me.

c) **What do you want to try this year? Use the list or your own ideas. Pick one thing and write:**

I want to try ...

d) **Put it in an envelope and give it to your teacher. Your teacher keeps it for you, but doesn't read it. You can open it at the end of the school year!**

► Workbook, p. 17

Digital quiz I can **talk about new experiences.**

Brighton stories: Summer holidays

1 Before you watch Holidays

Write words for the topic "summer holidays" on a piece of paper.

swimming, eating ice cream, going to the beach, …

2 Viewing Three holiday experiences

a) Watch the video to minute 7.08. Can you see any words from 1 in the video? Tick (✓) them.

b) Which holiday do you think was the best?

c) Now watch the ending. Which holiday did Joe think was the best?

d) Put the pictures in the correct order.

A

B

C

D

E

F

3 Now you

Think of a summer holiday activity with a partner. Find pictures, props, or mime the activity. Present your activity to the class. The class guesses the name of the activity.

– I think it's surfing!
– Yes, it is! / No, it isn't. Guess again!

▸ Wordbank 1, p. 185

Plan a story

1 The wh-questions

a) **The wh-questions can help you to plan a good story.
Match the German and English words.**

1 Who?
2 What?
3 When?
4 Where?
5 Why?

A Wann? B Wo? C Was? D Warum? E Wer?

b) **Joshua is writing a story. Look at his ideas and complete his story.**

A crazy summer story

Who?	What?	When?	Where?	Why?
my best friend Ahmad and I	we found ten euros	on the last day of summer	at the park	because the ball went into a tree

It was a nice summer, but it was very boring.
(1) ... of summer, my best friend (2) ... and I were at (3) ...
We played football there every day.
The ball went into (4) ..., so Ahmad looked for it.
In the tree there was a bird's nest and in it Ahmad saw something red – he found (5) ...!
We bought some ice cream with the money.
That was a really nice surprise.

2 The parts of a story

**Every story needs a beginning, a middle and an end.
Read these three sentences of a different story.
Which sentence is at the beginning, in the middle or at the end of the story?**

1 We often cycled there too.
2 In the end, we were really happy.
3 One day in the summer, something crazy happened.

▶ Skills file 12, p. 168

Digital quiz I can plan a story.

Tell a story

Step 1

Think of a crazy summer story.
It doesn't have to be real – but it can be.

▸ More help, p. 39

Step 2

Think about the wh-questions and plan your story. Make notes. Here are some ideas.

WHO?	My friend and I / Scout / ...
WHAT?	saw a film star / found ... / ...
WHEN?	in the summer / last weekend / ...
WHERE?	on the street / at a shop / ...
WHY?	because I bought ... / my friend wanted ... / ...

▸ Skills file 5, p. 161

Step 3

Your story needs a good beginning, a middle and an end. Here are some ideas:

beginning	middle	end
Last summer something crazy happened. One day last summer ...	I wanted to ... We played ... Then I met ... We made ... I ate ... She helped ... She jumped ...	In the end, everybody was ... That was a crazy day.

Step 4

Now write your story.
Remember to use the simple past.
You can put your story in your DOSSIER.

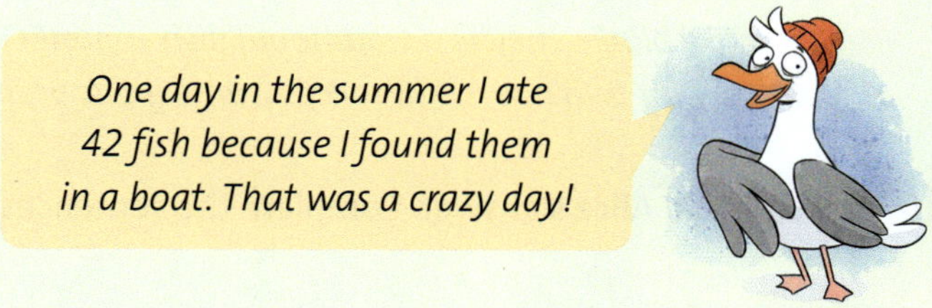

One day in the summer I ate 42 fish because I found them in a boat. That was a crazy day!

▸ Digital help ▸ Skills file 12, p. 168

Digital quiz I can tell a story.

1 Speaking Where were you, Finn?

I can talk about my holidays and the weather.

Finn wants to tell his class about his last holiday. Look at his slides. What does he say? Use *was/were* and the information on the slides.

Hi, everybody. I was in Bavaria in Germany …

1 Where I was

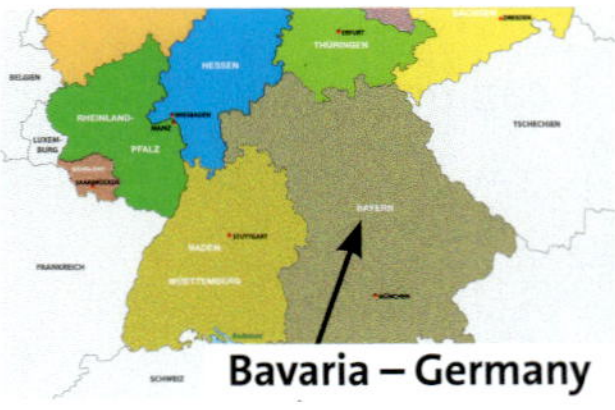

2 Who I was with

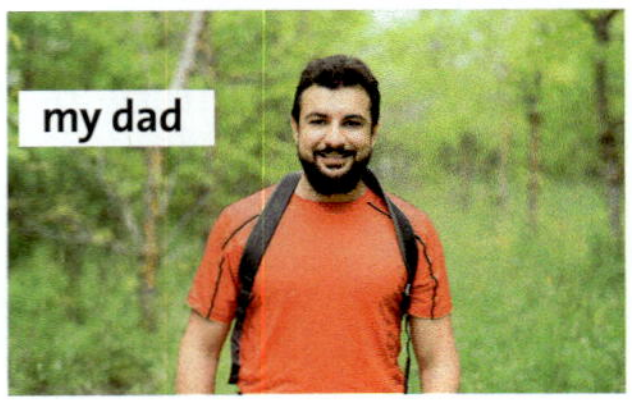

3 Where we stayed

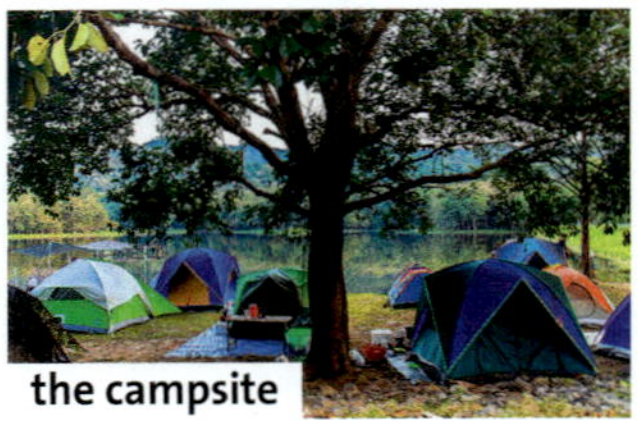

4 The weather

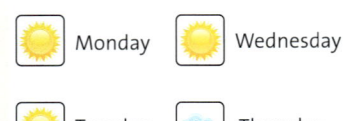

Monday
Wednesday
Tuesday
Thursday

sunny – cloudy

5 My opinion

2 A really good holiday

I can write about my holiday activities (simple past).

a) Language Read Lily's message to Alice. Complete the sentences. Use the simple past form of the verb. The blue verbs are regular. The green verbs are irregular.

cycled • had • learned • played • stayed • took • walked • went

Hi, Alice, I'm back in Brighton now, but I (1 have) … a great time in Poland. I (2 go) … with my mum and we (3 stay) … at my aunt Svetlana's house. I (4 cycle) … through the town with Svetlana and (5 play) … computer games with my uncle Olek. I also (6 learn) … how to make blini – they're a traditional dish – yum! On the last day we (7 walk) … around Krakow for two hours. I (8 take) … some great photos! How was Wales? Lily

b) Words Read Alice's answer. Complete the sentences. Use the words in the box.

Hi, Lily! Wales (1) … great. Our campsite was near a (2) … The weather was a bit cold so we didn't go (3) …, but it was still fun ☺. There was only one problem – it was really (4) … at night because our neighbours played a lot of music. It was hard to (5) …! My (6) … and I thought that they were too loud, but dad (7) …, "Let's join them" – so we (8) … and it was a lot of fun. See you soon! Alice xx

brother • did • loud • river • said • sleep • swimming • was

Check

3 LANGUAGE An interesting day

I can talk about a special day in my holidays (simple past: negatives).

Read Noah's conversation with his mum. Complete the sentences with the negative simple past of the words in the box.

× ~~eat~~ • × like • × walk • × want • × watch • × wear

Mum Hi, Noah, how was your day at *Pride*?
Noah It was really interesting. It wasn't like other Saturdays!
Mum Which things were interesting?
Noah Well, I (1) *didn't eat* sandwiches, I ate rainbow cake. I (2) ... my grey T-shirt, I wore lots of colours. I (3) ... TV, I watched a parade. And people (4) ... in the streets, they danced!
Mum Wow, that really sounds different! Did you enjoy it?
Noah Well, I liked the cake, but I (5) ... all the people. And I wore my headphones because I (6) ... to listen to the loud music.
Mum OK. Well, we can have a quiet Saturday next week!

4 LISTENING The first day of my holidays

a) **Read the sentences. Then listen to Zane. Which sentences are true? Choose three.**

1 Zane ate sausages for breakfast.
2 In the morning the weather was good.
3 There were lots of people at Dover.
4 Zane was worried on the ferry.
5 After the ferry journey he read a book.
6 When they arrived, he went swimming.

b) **Listen again and write the time for each picture:** *1: 6.00*

Check

5 READING Evie's journal

I can talk about last weekend.

Read about Evie's weekend.

Monday, 14th September

1 Wow, what a busy weekend! On Saturday morning I took Jimmy for a walk on the beach. There were three other dogs there. Jimmy enjoyed it a lot and I took some cute pictures of them. It was fun!

2 But when I got home, my phone wasn't in my bag. It was a big problem because I use my phone every day and I have a lot of very special photos on there.

3 I wanted to go back to the beach, but then I saw my cousin Charlie at the door. I thought, "That's weird, why is Charlie here on a Saturday morning?"

4 "Hi, Evie, I just got a message from a Varndean student," said Charlie. "He was at the beach clean-up and he found your phone there! His name is Noah." Charlie had a big smile on his face.

5 I relaxed again and thanked him. "Great news!" I said. "Where does he live? And when can I come to his house?"

6 I went to his house yesterday evening. I gave Noah some chocolate to say thank you. Then I went home to check all my new messages!

a) **Put Evie's day in the correct order:** *1: D*

A Evie's phone wasn't in her bag.
B Charlie told her some good news.
C Evie got her phone back.
D Evie went to the beach.
E Charlie arrived at Evie's house.
F Evie asked Charlie for more information.

b) **How did Evie feel? Write a feeling word for paragraph 1–6. Use the words in the box.**

calm • happy (2 x) • surprised • worried

1 ... 2 ... 3+4 ... 5 ... 6 ...

6 WRITING Last weekend

Imagine you found something last weekend. Write a message to your British friend. Say what you found, where you found it and what you did next. You can use the ideas in the boxes.

Hi, Kyle, guess what happened last weekend?! I found ... Then ... In the end ... See you!

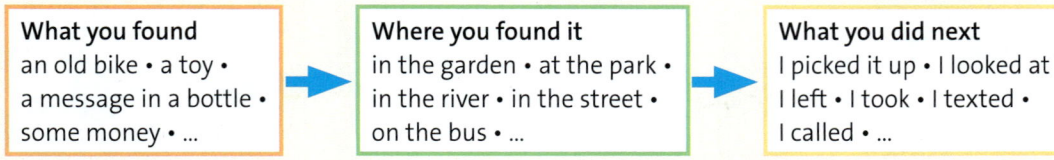

What you found
an old bike • a toy • a message in a bottle • some money • ...

→

Where you found it
in the garden • at the park • in the river • in the street • on the bus • ...

→

What you did next
I picked it up • I looked at it • I left • I took • I texted • I called • ...

Check

7 Mediation An interview with Finn

I can talk about new experiences.

Read a part of the interview in the school's online magazine.
Finn's grandpa asks him some questions on the phone. Complete Finn's answers.

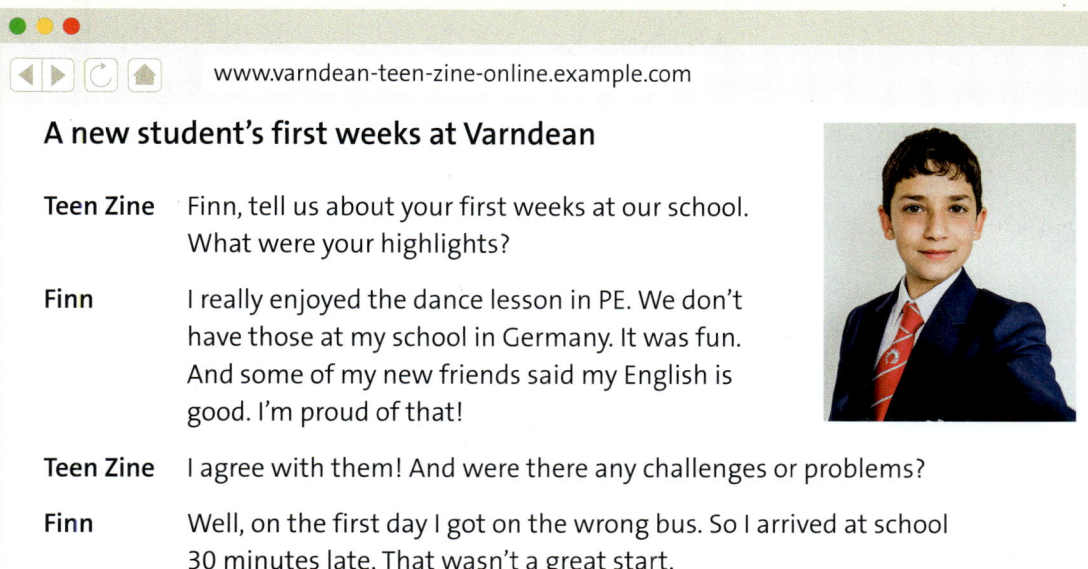

www.varndean-teen-zine-online.example.com

A new student's first weeks at Varndean

Teen Zine Finn, tell us about your first weeks at our school. What were your highlights?

Finn I really enjoyed the dance lesson in PE. We don't have those at my school in Germany. It was fun. And some of my new friends said my English is good. I'm proud of that!

Teen Zine I agree with them! And were there any challenges or problems?

Finn Well, on the first day I got on the wrong bus. So I arrived at school 30 minutes late. That wasn't a great start.

Opa Gestern hast du mir ja dieses Interview mit dir geschickt. Worum ging es da?
Finn Es ging um ...
Opa Und was hat dir bis jetzt am besten gefallen?
Finn ...
Opa Es war aber bestimmt nicht alles einfach, oder?
Finn Nein, zum Beispiel ...

8 Study skills Lena's story

I can plan a story.

Read Lena's sentences for her scary story.

a) **Which sentence is the beginning? Which sentence is the end?**

A And the door opened, but nobody was there!
B I saw a cute cat with big, green eyes near an old house.
C It was a dark night in November.
D So I walked over to the cat.
E I ran away and never went there again.
F Then I heard a loud noise from inside the house.

b) **Now put the sentences (A–F) in the correct order.**

Diff bank

▸ Page 13

More practice 1 Where were you yesterday?

a) Make a list of different places on the board.
- *swimming pool*
- *supermarket*
- *...*

b) Make a circle. Throw a ball and say where you were yesterday.

I was at the swimming pool. Where were you?

I was at the supermarket. Where were you?

More practice 2 Beni's holidays

a) Complete the conversation with *was* or *were*.

Lily Where were you in the summer holidays?
Beni I (1) ... in France with my family. We (2) ... at my grandparents' house. We (3) ... there for three weeks.
Lily How was it?
Beni It (4) ... great to see my grandparents! And we (5) ... lucky because the weather (6) ... nice.

b) Practise the conversation.

▸ Page 14

More help 1 SONG My summer holiday

I had a wonderful holiday last summer
I went to Spain with my dad and my big brother
We stayed in a hotel in Granada
And the weather, oh, it was hot, hot, hot!

We went to Spain and we went by train
And we swam and sunbathed every day
It was so cool in the swimming pool
It was the best ever holiday! ¡Olé!

We watched flamenco dancers in the street
We listened and danced and moved our feet
I loved eating churros, hot and sweet,
And the tapas, oh, they were oh so good!
We went to Spain ...

▸ Page 15

Parallel exercise 5 Zane's holiday in France

Complete the sentences. Put the verbs in brackets into the simple past.

1 We (stay) ... in a holiday apartment. It was small, but the pool was nice.
2 My sister and I (use) ... that pool every day! We (love) ... it.
3 Every morning, my dad and I (cycle) ... into town for bread on our bikes.
4 I (talk) ... in French with people at the shops – it was hard, but they were nice to me.
5 Sometimes I (help) ... my mum with dinner.
6 I was sad when we (start) ... our journey back to Brighton. Maybe we can come back next summer!

More practice 3 *-ed* sounds

Listen and repeat.

stayed, used, loved, cycled, talked, helped, started

▸ Page 16

More practice 4 Sunita and Zane's summer

Look at the holiday pictures. Some captions are wrong. Correct them.

I think caption 1 is right. – I agree. / I think it's wrong. The correct caption is ...

1 We went to Prague by bus.

2 A guide showed us the old town.

3 We had some sandwiches by the river.

4 My family travelled to France by train.

5 I loved our pool.

6 I went on holiday with my little brother.

▸ Page 17

More help 10 WORDS Travel and holiday words

b) **Write these words and phrases under the correct umbrella.**

at my dad's flat • went to the pool • at my grandparents' house • bus • went shopping • car • in a holiday apartment • visited fun places • in a hotel • liked the food • on a campsite • plane • saw my friends • train • went to the zoo

More practice 5 What's the word?

1 It's a kind of transport. It isn't a car, but it goes on the road.
2 It's a place to stay – it's a flat, but it isn't your home and you pay for it.
3 It's an activity. You do it when you move your feet to music.
4 It's a place to stay. It's outside and not as expensive as a hotel.
5 It's a kind of transport. It's very fast. You need a station for it.

▸ Skills file 11, p. 167

▸ Page 19

More practice 6 WORDS At the station

Complete the sentences with the words from the box. Sometimes there are two answers.

arrive • destination • leave • platform • return ticket • single ticket • ~~station~~ • ticket machine

1 Brighton has a big train *station*.
2 The train's ... is London.
3 What time does the train ... / ...?
4 There's the ... – but can I pay by card?
5 My train is on ... three.
6 I need a ... / ... to Eastbourne.

More practice 7 VIEWING Buying a ticket

ROLE-PLAY **Read and act out the dialogue with a partner.**

Mo Excuse me. Hi!
Jarek Oh, hello.
Mo Do you need any help?
Jarek Yes, please! I want to buy a ticket, but I don't understand the ticket machine.
Mo No problem, I can help you. Where are you going?
Jarek I need a ticket to London.
Mo OK. And do you want a single ticket or a return?
Jarek I'm coming back tomorrow, so I would like a return ticket, please.
Mo OK. It says that a return ticket to London costs £34.90.
Jarek Oh, that's expensive!
Mo Yeah, trains to London are quite expensive ... And this is a cheap ticket because it's the weekend! How do you want to pay – cash or card?
Jarek Can I pay by card?
Mo Yes, just put it on the machine there.
Jarek Thank you for your help. Oh, when is the next train to London?
Mo It's in ten minutes. It's at 11.27. And it's a direct train.
Jarek Great! So I don't need to change trains?
Mo No.
Jarek Thank you so much!
Mo You're welcome. Have a nice day.

▸ Page 21

More practice 8 They didn't do it!

a) **Write five sentence starters with verbs in the negative simple past. Use the names of friends or people in your class. Swap with your partner.** *Julia didn't play ... Amir didn't watch ...*

b) **Write endings for your partner's sentences, then swap again.**
Example: *Julia didn't play football last weekend. Amir didn't watch TV yesterday.*
Who has the best sentences?

▸ Page 21

☒ More practice 9 **No, I didn't!**

Blue Bird thinks that Scout did some bad things at *Pride*, but Scout says she didn't do them. Write what Scout says.

Blue Bird	You ate all the chips!
Scout	(1) No, I *didn't eat* all the chips.
Blue Bird	You played bad music on the beach!
Scout	(2) No, I ...
Blue Bird	You wore my *Pride* cap! Now it's dirty.
Scout	(3) ...
Blue Bird	You talked loudly at the concert!
Scout	(4) ...
Blue Bird	You ate a girl's piece of cake.
Scout	(5) ...
Blue Bird	You went to bed too late after *Pride*!
Scout	(6) ...

OK, maybe I ate all the chips.

▸ Page 23

More practice 10 **Time phrases**

a) **Look at the time phrases. Get in a group. Each student has one of the time phrases. Stand in a line in the correct order. Start with *today* at the front and go back in the past.**

today | last year | yesterday | last weekend | last week | last month

b) **Copy the timeline. Write the phrases from a) in the correct order.**

PAST ? | ? | ? | ? | ? | *today* **PRESENT**

▸ Page 29

More help UNIT TASK **Tell a story**

Steps 1–4

Think of a crazy summer story.
Read Scout's story below. Change the words in blue and write your own story.
You can write some more sentences if you like.

A crazy summer story

It was the last day of summer.
My best friend George and I were at the beach.
We wanted to find some food there.
Then my friend saw something weird – a pink elephant!
It was very big and dirty.
I didn't know what to do, so I just said *hello* and waved.
The elephant looked at me.
"I think she likes you!" said George.
That was a crazy day!

Unit 2
Friends and heroes

A

B
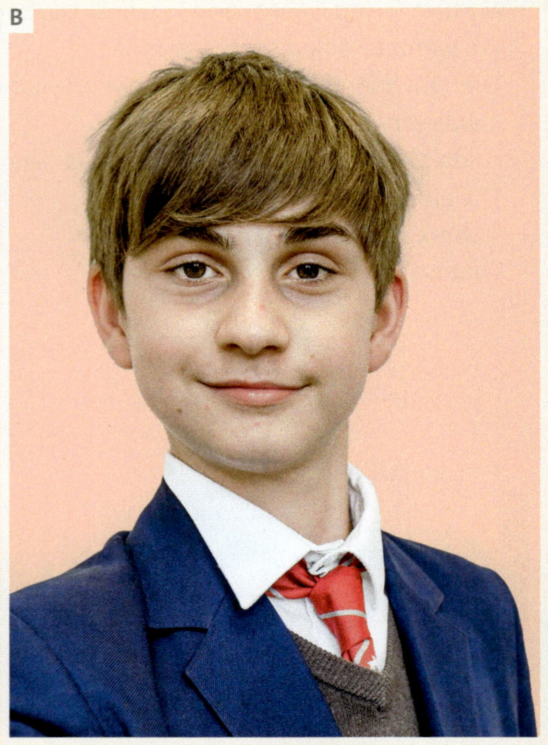

1 LISTENING The head students

a) BEFORE YOU LISTEN Look at pictures A–D. Which colours can you see? Write a colour word in the air. Your partner guesses.

b) Listen and find the correct photo for each head student. *Mihai is ... Sofia ... Jodie ... Faye ...*

c) Listen again and check. Then talk about the head students with your partner.

He She	has	brown • curly • dark-blond • long • short • straight	hair.
		braces.	
	is wearing	glasses • a blue-green / ... tie	

Nach dieser Unit kann ich ...

- Aussehen beschreiben
- die Persönlichkeit meiner Freundinnen und Freunde beschreiben
- über meine Vorbilder sprechen
- einen Superhelden oder eine Superheldin beschreiben
- über Zusammenarbeit sprechen

Unit task

- Informationen recherchieren und ein Quiz erstellen

C

D

2 SPEAKING Who is it?

GAME **One student describes another student in class, but doesn't say the name. Who is it – do you know? Stand up and say the name.**

I'm thinking of a girl with long, brown hair. She's wearing a red sweatshirt and white shoes.

I think it's Sarah.

That's right.

Good to know

Many British schools have head students. They're students in year 11 and they help other students.

▸ Wordbank 2, p. 186
▸ Workbook, p. 24

Digital quiz I can describe what someone looks like.

My friends

1 Reading **Profiles**

a) Before you read **What's a good friend like? Collect words with the class.**

A good friend is kind and ...

b) **Read the two profiles. Guess who they describe: Lily, Zane, Sunita or Noah?**

COMPETITION

Write a profile about your best friend. The best profile wins a prize!

My best friend

- *My best friend is amazing!*
- *He's kind and he helps his family.*
- *He's very confident and funny!*
- *He's also good at sports.*
- *We often ride our bikes together.*
- *He's my best friend because he's always there for me.*

My best friend

My best friend is very clever – she's really good with computers.

She's my best friend because she's very fair, and she's always honest. I often don't feel very confident – but when I'm with her, I feel brave!

c) **Listen and check your answers.**

d) **Make a mind map in your** Vocab file **with words to describe a person. Use the words from p. 40 and the profiles.**

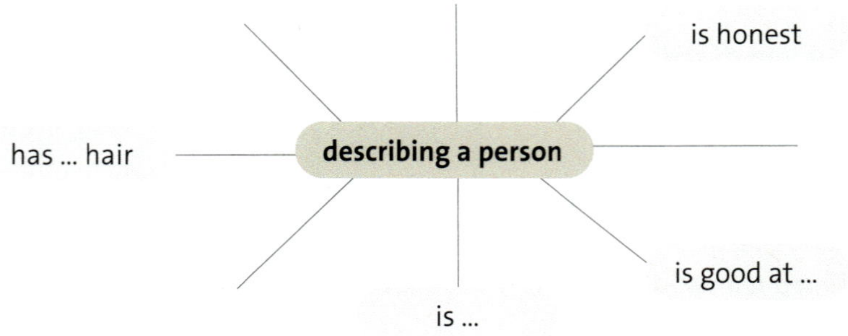

▶ More practice 1, p. 65 ▶ Wordbank 2, p. 186

2 Speaking I think you're ...

a) Think of things that you like about students in your class.
Make notes.

Paula: funny
Fatih: helpful
...

Ideas

brave • clever • confident • fair • funny • good at ... • helpful • honest • kind

b) Walk around Say something nice to different students in your class.

3 Words What's important

a) What's important to you in a friend? Choose your top three from the box in ex. 2.
Then discuss in your group.

b) What's important to you in a teacher, a head student, a sportsperson or a pop star?
Choose your new top three.

▶ Workbook, p. 25

4 SONG My best friend

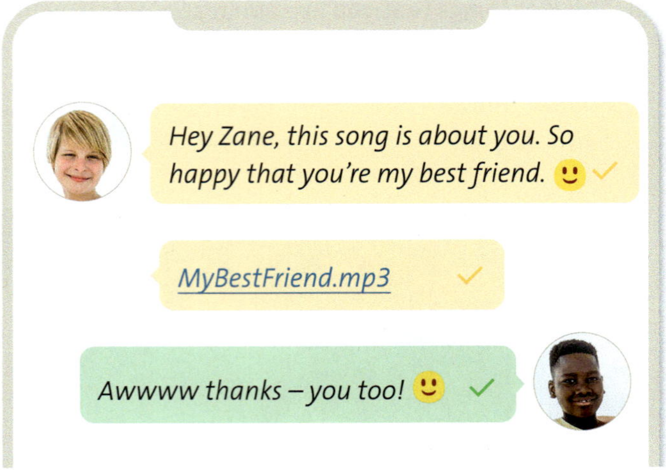
Hey Zane, this song is about you. So happy that you're my best friend.
MyBestFriend.mp3
Awwww thanks – you too!

My best friend

I want to tell you that you're my buddy.
You're always funny and (1) ...
And people know that when they see you
I'm never far behind.

'Cause I'm the bread and you're the (2) ...
You can't have one without the other.

You're left, I'm (3) ....
You're (4) ... , I'm night.
You're the milk, I'm the (5) ...
It's always you and me.

I'm so glad that you're my best (6) ...
There's no one else like you!

a) BEFORE YOU LISTEN Look at the song text. Complete the gaps 1–6 with the words in the box.

butter • day • friend • kind • right • tea

b) Listen and check.

c) Can you find more pairs like in the song? Use the words below or your own ideas.

morning and ...
table and ...
chicken and ...
question and ...

▸ More help, p. 65

d) Listen to the song again and sing.

5 MEDIATION **Finn's friends**

a) **Read Finn's messages. Who are they for?**

b) **Look at Sunita's questions. Help her understand the German message.**

A message from Finn!
But it's in German.

Hi, Suri, wie geht's dir?
Ich habe schon viele Freunde
an meiner neuen Schule.
Neben mir sitzt Noah.
Klug und total nett.
Er hat einen Hund, der heißt
Buddy und ist sehr süß.
In meiner Klasse ist auch ein
cooles Mädchen. Sie heißt
Sunita und ist sehr witzig.
LG Finn
???
Sorry, Sunita, that message
wasn't for you! It was for
a friend in Germany.

1 Freunde means friends, I think.
  What does he say about friends?
  He says that he has … at his new school.
2 He writes something about Noah.
  What does he say about him?
3 I can see he talks about Buddy.
  Does he like him?
4 He talks about me too!
  What does he say about me?
  He says that you are …

c) **Check with a partner.**

▸ Skills file 8, p. 164

My task

6 My favourite person

Write a short profile of your favourite person. Don't say who it is!
It can be your best friend, someone at school, someone in your family or a different person.
Use the profiles in 1b) and your mind map from 1d) on p. 42 to help you.
You can also draw a picture.

My favourite person is amazing. He's / She's always …
He's / She's also good at …
We often … together.
I want to be like him / her because he's / she's always …

▸ Digital help

▸ Workbook, p. 26

Digital quiz **I can describe my friend's personality.**

My hero, your hero

1 LISTENING Lily's neighbour

a) BEFORE YOU LISTEN **Lily is at her neighbour Li-Jun's flat after school. Describe the picture.**

b) **Lily asks Li-Jun about the article. Listen and complete the sentences.**

Li-Jun saved (1) ... when he fell into the water at (2) ...
The boy's dad called (3) ... to say *thank you* to Li-Jun.

c) **Match Li-Jun's answers A–F to Lily's questions 1–6. Then listen again and check.**

1 Did you do something important?
2 Did it happen at Brighton beach?
3 Did the boy get hurt?
4 Did his dad see what happened?
5 Did they go home right away?
6 Did you call the newspaper?

A Yes, he did.
B No, he didn't.
C Yes, it did.
D No, I didn't.
E Yes, I did.
F Yes, they did.

d) **Take turns to read a question and answer.**

2 LOOKING AT LANGUAGE Simple past: *yes/no*-questions and short answers

Erklär-film

Look at the questions and answers. Complete the explanation.

Did you do something important? – Yes, I did.
Did the boy get hurt? – No, he didn't.

Fragen ohne Fragewort im *simple past* fangen meistens mit ... an.
! Das Verb steht dann in der Grundform (*help, hurt, go, do, ...*).

► Language file 4, p. 175

► Workbook, pp. 27–29

3 Speaking About Li-Jun

a) **Partner B: Look at** p. 64.
Partner A: Read about Li-Jun. Answer partner B's questions: *Yes, he did. / No, he didn't.*

b) **Ask partner B these questions:**

1 Did Li-Jun get married?
2 Did he have any children?
3 Did he always live on the Whitehawk Estate?
4 Did he enjoy his work?

Li-Jun Chen
- was born in a village in China and lived there when he was a child
- didn't want to leave China, but he wanted to help his family
- lived in London, and then in Brighton
- first was a sports trainer, later became a teacher

4 When you were five years old

a) **Put the words in the correct order to make questions in the simple past.**

1 you / to school? / go / Did
2 you / Did / a pet? / have
3 like / Did / football? / you
4 Did / a bedroom? / share / you
5 your flat or house / have / Did / a garden?
6 near you? / your grandparents / live / Did

b) **Can you remember when you were five? Think about answers to the questions in** a)**.
Then ask and answer the questions with a partner:** *Yes, I did. / No, I didn't.*

► More practice 2, p. 65

5 Lily's school day

Li-Jun and Lily talk in the evening. Complete Li-Jun's questions with the words from the box.

How • What • ~~When~~ • Where • Who • Why

1 ... did you leave school? – At 15.05, like every Monday.
When did you leave school?
2 ... did you come back late? – There was a problem with my bike.
3 ... did you get home? – I took the bus.
4 ... did you leave your bike? – At school. It's OK there.
5 ... did you do at school today? – We did a science project.
6 ... did you do the project with? – Noah. He helped me a lot.

► Parallel exercise, p. 66

6 Looking at language Simple past: questions with question words

Erklärfilm

Look at the questions from 5 **again. Which word do you need after the question word?**

► More practice 3, p. 66 ► Language file 5, p. 175

7 Listening Our heroes

a) Before you listen **What kind of people are heroes for you? Add more ideas to the box.**

activists • influencers • singers • ...

b) **Lily talks to four students about their heroes. Listen and put the pictures in the correct order.**

A 
Sierra Evans

B 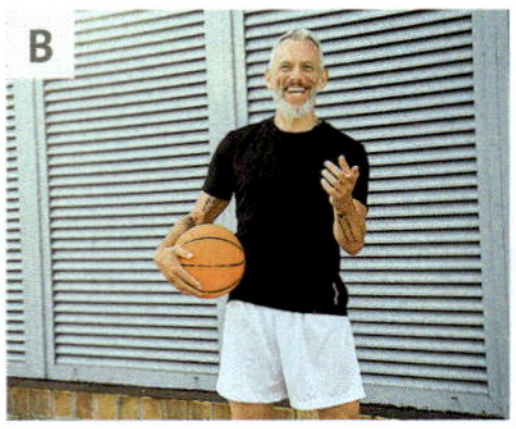
Otis King

C 
Jozef Krupa

D 

Jade Woods

c) **Read sentences 1–4. Then listen again and match persons A–D to the sentences.**

This person ...
1 doesn't have favourites in the team.
2 wants to help save our planet.
3 gives money to animal charities.
4 works long hours and helps many people.

▸ Skills file 6, p. 162

8 Words Opposites

a) Word building **Read the box. What are the opposites of words 1–6? Write pairs.**

When we add un- to the start of some adjectives, it means 'not'.
Now the words have the opposite meaning.

1 cool	4 happy
2 kind	5 helpful
3 friendly	6 lucky

b) **Sometimes there are new words for the opposites. Match these opposites.**

1 tidy	A boring
2 interesting	B scared
3 quiet	C horrible
4 nice	D messy
5 brave	E loud

▸ More practice 4, p. 66 ▸ Skills file 1, p. 157

fair

unfair

9 SPEAKING Two student heroes

a) **Partner B:** Look at p. 64.
Partner A: Read the article about Destiny. Answer partner B's questions about her.

b) Partner B has information about Jonah, another student. Ask partner B questions and find out about him.

1 Why did Jonah stay in hospital for a long time?
2 What did people say about Jonah?
3 What did Jonah want to do?
4 How did he do this?

Destiny
Destiny's school football team needed money for new sports clothes. So Destiny skateboarded for 10 kilometres in funny clothes! Her parents and friends gave her money for every kilometre. Her team was very happy with its new football clothes!

My task

10 Interviews about heroes

a) THINK Do you have a hero? It can be somebody in your family or a friend, or it can be a famous person. Look at the questions and make notes.

- Who is your hero? *My hero is ...*
- What's he or she like?
- What did he or she do? Think of one thing that this person did:
  My hero ...
  – planned a great birthday party
  – did something brave
  – helped a friend / neighbour / animals / the planet / somebody on the street / ...
  – had a great idea
  – worked hard when he or she had a big problem
  – ...

► Skills file 5, p. 161

b) PAIR Ask your partner about his or her hero. Ask the three questions from a). Make notes.

c) SHARE Tell the class about your partner's hero.

Adar's hero is his cousin Rashid. He's very kind and clever. He collected phones and gave them to families for free.

► Digital help

► Workbook, p. 29

Digital quiz I can ask and answer questions about my hero.

Superheroes

1 Reading Who is it?

a) Before you read Lily, Sunita, Noah and Zane drew and described their own superheroes. Guess and match the names to the pictures A–D.

I think Noah's superhero is ... because he likes ...

b) Make groups of four students. Each student reads about one superhero on p. 51. Was your answer in a) correct?

c) Read about your superhero again. Copy and complete the table. Then tell your group.

name	*born in*	*born on*	*superpower*

d) Listen to the other group members and complete your table.

Good to know

You say years in dates like this:
1960 nineteen sixty
2006 two thousand and six
2022 twenty twenty two

A

B

C
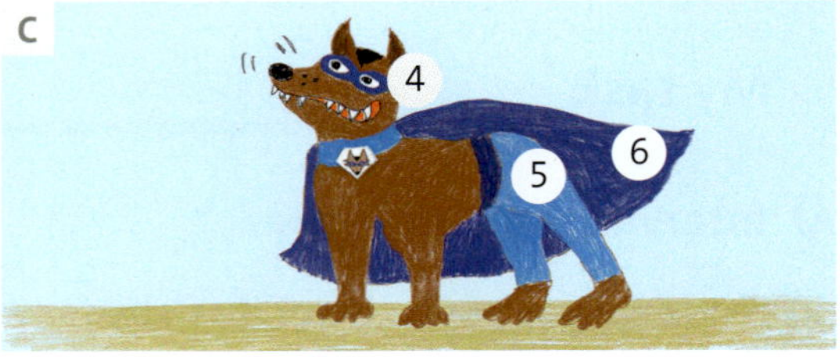

D

▸ More practice 5, p. 67

2 Words Clothes

a) Read the last sentences of all the superhero descriptions on p. 51. Write the words for the clothes 1–7 in the pictures. *1 dress, 2 ...*

b) Make a page in your Vocab file for clothes. You can make a mind map, draw pictures or write sentences. Add the words from these pages and other clothes words.

▸ More practice 6, p. 67 ▸ Wordbank 3, p. 187

▸ Workbook, pp. 30–31

My name is *ComputerGirl*.
I was born in 2006 on planet Voria. I'm very clever and I can get into any computer. But I only use my power to help people.
I wear long black boots and a silver helmet.
Sunita

I'm *Superdog*. I was born in 2002 on earth.
One day a weird dog barked at me ... and I became a dog! I have very strong teeth and a good nose.
I wear a blue cape, blue trousers and a blue eye mask.
Noah

DolphinMan here! I was born in the sea in 2008. When people put chemicals in the water in 2020, I became part man, part dolphin. I can swim very fast and stay in water for a long time.
I wear a silver swimsuit.
Zane

I'm *The Climber*. I can climb everywhere!
I was born in 1960 on planet Octo.
When bad snakes killed my family, I had to leave, so I came to earth.
I have eight arms. They're very handy!
I wear a purple dress and a purple cape.
Lily

▶ More practice 7, p. 68

My task

3 I'm a superhero!

a) **Think of a superhero and make notes: name, story, superpower, clothes.**
▶ More help, p. 68 ▶ Wordbank 3, p. 187 ▶ Skills file 5, p. 161

b) **Write a paragraph about yourself as a superhero. Look at the texts above for help.**
My name is … / I'm … / … here!
Tell your superhero story. How did you become a superhero? Use the simple past.
I was born in …
I became a superhero when I ate … / I fell into chemicals / …
What's your superpower?
I can …
What do you wear?
I wear …
You can put your text in your DOSSIER.

c) **Present your superhero to a partner. Say what you think of your partner's superhero.**
Your superhero looks cool / weird / strong / …!
▶ Digital help

▶ Workbook, p. 32

Digital quiz I can write about superheroes.

A great team!

1 READING An accident

a) BEFORE YOU READ **Look at the pictures in the story and say what you think happened.**

I think Finn …

b) **Read the story and check your ideas from a).**

Last Saturday the four friends and Finn were at Lily's estate. They were bored. Finn asked about the friends' free time activities.

Finn I know you like coding, Sunita. What about you, Lily? What do you do in your free time?

Lily I do parkour. Do you know what that is?

Finn It's the same word in German, but I'm not sure what people do.

Lily Let me show you. I can walk on the wall like this. Then I can jump down … and land on my feet like this!

Finn Wow, that was cool, Lily. I'm surprised how easy it looks. Let me try …

Lily No, Finn! It looks easy, but it isn't.

But Finn didn't listen …

Lily Get down, Finn! It's dangerous.

Finn No, it's OK. I'm really good at jumping!

Finn jumped ... and fell. The kids were really worried. Finn's face was very white.

Lily Finn, are you OK?

Finn My ankle hurts – and my head too.

Sunita OK, let's call 999. ... Hello, I need an ambulance please. Yes, my name's Sunita Chandra. My friend Finn fell. His head and ankle hurt. ... Yes, Finn Demir, he's twelve. ... We're on the Whitehawk Estate in Brighton. ... Yes, thanks.

Sunita Don't move your legs, Finn. But you must stay warm, and you can't sleep.

Noah We need to stay calm. I can help.

Noah showed everybody some breathing exercises. Then Lily got a warm blanket.

Zane I can talk to Finn, so he doesn't fall asleep.

Zane told Finn some jokes and Finn tried to be brave. Sunita called Finn's mum.

Finn Is the ambulance coming? I feel bad.

Noah The ambulance is here. It's OK, Finn.

Man Hello Finn, I need to check you out. Right ... now let's get you in the ambulance!

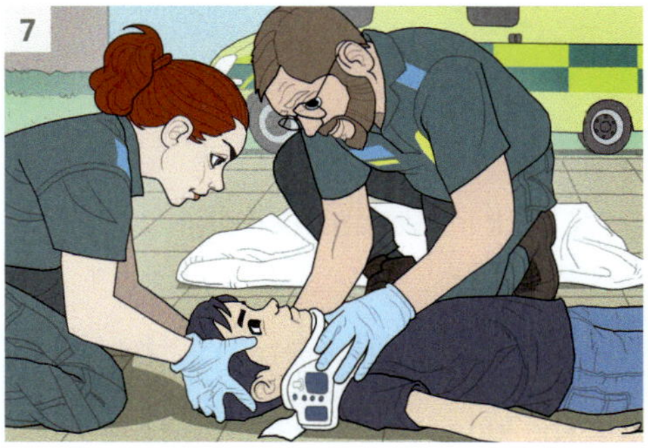

Then Finn's mum arrived. She looked worried. She talked to Finn in the ambulance. Finally Finn's mum and the four tired friends got in her car and went to the hospital.

2 What happened?

Choose the correct summary A, B or C.

A The friends helped Finn after he fell. He needed to go to hospital.
B Finn's friends helped him after an accident. His arm was hurt.
C Finn had an accident. The friends helped him and he wasn't hurt.

► Skills file 7, p. 163

3 What did they do?

Read the story again. Say who did what.

1 ... called 999 and Finn's mum.
2 ... showed the others some breathing exercises.
3 ... got a warm blanket.
4 ... told funny stories.
5 ... tried to be brave.

4 How did they feel?

bad • bored • surprised • tired • worried (2x)

Complete the sentences.

1 At first the kids were ...
2 Finn saw Lily's jump and was ...
3 When Finn fell, the four friends were ...
4 Finn felt ... after he fell.
5 When Finn's mum arrived, she was ...
6 In the car the four friends felt ...

5 Words Parts of the body

a) **Write the words for 1–8 in your exercise book. Most of them are in the story.**

1	2	3	4	5	6	7	8
		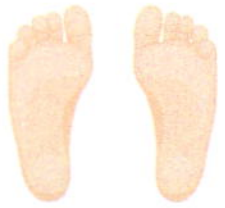		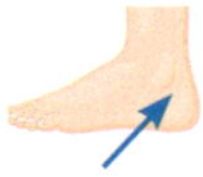		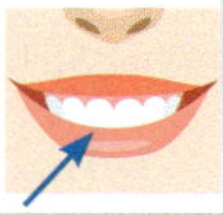	
f___	*h___*	*f___*	*l__*	*a____*	*a__*	*t____*	*h___*

b) **Check in Wordbank 4 on p.188.**

► More practice 8, p. 69

6 Listening The end of the story

The kids are in the waiting room at the hospital. Listen. True or false?

1 Finn feels fine.
2 He has a broken ankle.
3 He doesn't want to see his friends.
4 Lily feels sorry that she showed Finn parkour.
5 Finn thinks they were a great team.
6 Finn thought Zane's jokes were funny.

7 Life skills Teamwork

The kids worked as a team when Finn had an accident. When is teamwork important? Think of situations at school, in sports and hobbies or with your family.

Teamwork is important when you do a school project. – That's right. And when ...

► Workbook, p. 33

Digital quiz I can understand a story about working in a team.

Brighton stories: Special people

1 BEFORE YOU WATCH The people in the video

Who can you see in the picture?
What do you think they are doing?

I can see ...
I think they are ...ing ...

2 VIEWING Gloria's present

a) **Watch the video. Match Daisy, Emir, Gloria and Joe to their roles.**

1 plays the girlfriend
2 plays the uncle
3 films the video
4 holds the props[1]

A

B

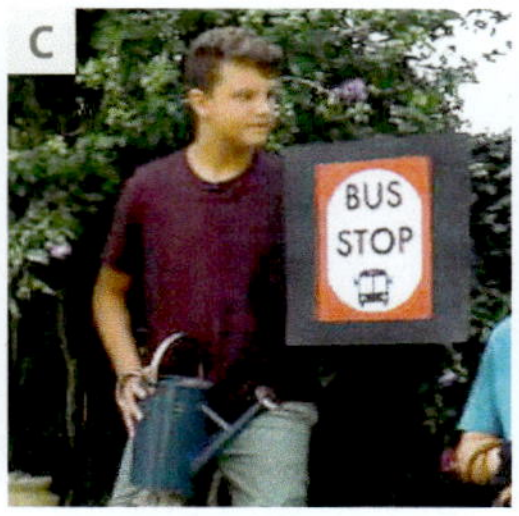

C

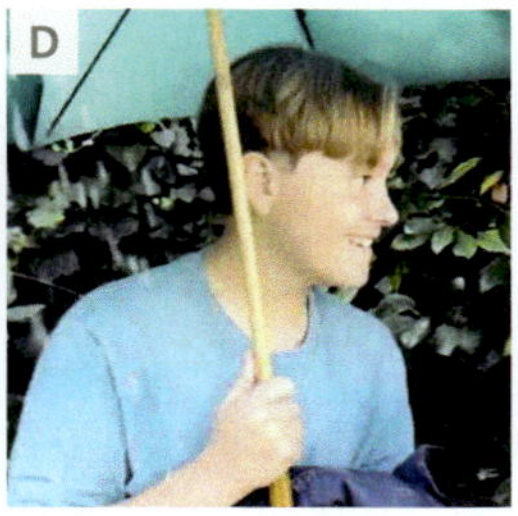
D

b) **Watch again. Read the sentences. True or false?**

1 Gloria needs a present for her cousin Tim's wedding[2].
2 Tim is going to marry Claire, his girlfriend.
3 Gloria thinks the story of how they met is boring.
4 Tim and Claire met at a bus stop.
5 Tim hit Claire with his umbrella[3].
6 Claire was angry at Tim.
7 Claire and Tim shared the umbrella.
8 Daisy, Emir, Gloria and Joe are happy with the video.

3 Now you

a) **Did uncle Tim and aunt Claire like the video? What did they write to the kids?**

They liked / didn't like ... They laughed / felt ...

b) **Does Gloria want to act out the video at Christmas?**

[1] **props** *die Requisiten* [2] **wedding** *die Hochzeit* [3] **umbrella** *der Regenschirm*

Work out meaning

1 Use word families

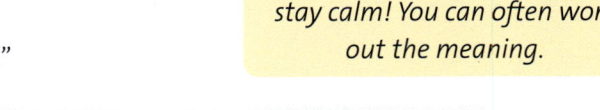

When you don't know a word, stay calm! You can often work out the meaning.

a) Read the sentences. What do the blue words mean in German?

1 Finn had a party for his friends. It was a nice surprise.
2 He said: "Thank you for your kindness!"
3 Then, with great care, Finn started to walk.
4 His friends watched in amazement.
5 They said: "This is great! What luck!"

b) Copy and complete the table with the blue words in a).

ADJECTIVE	NOUN
surprised	...
kind	...
careful	...
amazing	
lucky	

2 Use German and other languages

**a) Finn speaks German, Turkish and English.
He understands a lot of English words because they're like German: English:** *arm* **– German:** *Arm*
Some English words aren't like German, but they're like Turkish: English: *ambulance* **– German:** *Krankenwagen* **– Turkish:** *ambulans*

Some words look the same in some languages and have the same meaning.

Say what the words below in blue mean. Use German or other languages to help you.

1 Finn has a German and a Turkish passport.
2 In Germany Finn loves to buy cakes from the bakery.
3 Finn's favourite sea animals are whales.
4 He doesn't like worms!

b) Sometimes Finn makes mistakes in English. Choose the correct words from the box to correct his mistakes.

a kind of • bathroom • get • good • phone • so

1 I ~~become~~ money from my dad every month.
2 Does our hostel room have a ~~bad~~?
3 I felt horrible, ~~also~~ I went to bed.
4 I can hear my ~~handy~~. Do you know where it is?
5 A mango is ~~an art of~~ fruit.
6 Buddy is a very ~~brave~~ dog. He always listens to Noah.

False friends look the same in some languages, but they have a different meaning.

► Skills file 2, p. 158

Digital quiz

I can work out the meaning of new words.

Make a quiz

Step 1: Choose a famous person

Make teams. Together, think of famous people from the past. The box can help you. Agree on one person.

Ideas

- Muhammad Ali
- Albert Einstein
- Mahatma Gandhi
- Astrid Lindgren
- Nelson Mandela
- Rosa Parks
- Sophie Scholl
- Mother Theresa

Step 2: Find information

Learn more about your person. Use the internet to find information.

When was this person born? *Muhammad Ali was born in …*
When did this person die? *He died in …*
What did this person do / win / discover / …? *He was … and won …*

► More help, p. 69 ► Skills file 4, p. 160

Step 3: Write quiz questions

a) **Write four questions about your person.**

When Where	was	…	born?
When	did	…	die?
What	did	…	do? discover? fight against? write?
Where	did	…	go to school?
What sport	did	…	do?
What prizes	did	…	win?

b) **For each question write two answers: one is correct, one is wrong.**

When was Einstein born?
A in 1979 ✗ B in 1879 ✓

Step 4: Do the quiz

Do the quiz in two teams. The teams take turns to ask and answer questions. Each team gets two points for a correct answer.

Digital quiz

I can research information and make a quiz.

1 Speaking Who is it?

I can describe what someone looks like.

Describe a Varndean student, but don't say his or her name. Your partner says who it is. Take turns. Tip: Think about hair, braces, glasses and tie colour.

This student has long, black hair.

That's Sunita!

2 Listening A group project

I can describe my friend's personality.

Noah, Sunita, Lily and Zane are working on a presentation about the history of Brighton. Copy the table. Listen. Write the correct job (A–D) for each student.

name	Noah	Sunita	Lily	Zane
job	...	...		

Check

3 LANGUAGE Sports heroes

I can ask and answer questions about my hero (simple past).

a) **Read Lily's message to her friends. Then write their questions in the simple past.**

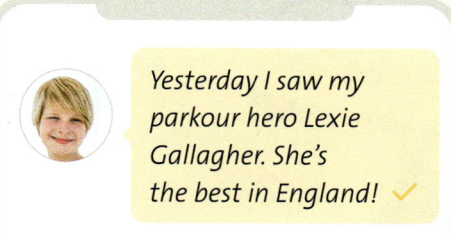

Yesterday I saw my parkour hero Lexie Gallagher. She's the best in England!

1 … / see her / in Brighton / you / ?
Did you see her in Brighton?
2 have / … you / a good time / ?
3 … / take / some photos / you / ?
4 … / with you / she / talk / ?
5 any new skills / show you / … she / ?
6 … / do / you / some parkour together / ?

b) **Now write Lily's short answers to her friends' questions.**

1 Yes, *I did.* 2 Yes, I … 3 Yes, … 4 Yes, … 5 No, she … 6 No, we …

c) **Read Zane's message. Complete his friends' questions with the correct question word.**

I saw my heroes too – Albion FC!

1 Why / When did you see them?
– On Saturday afternoon.
2 Where / Who did you see them?
– At the Amex, of course!
3 How / Where did they play?
– They were great. We won!
4 Who / Why did you watch the game with?
– With Holly.
5 What / Who did you do after the game?
– I went swimming.

4 WORDS Noah's hero

Some words on Noah's poster are wrong. Complete the sentences with the correct word.

My hero

This is my uncle Chris. He's my **(1) ohre!** He lives in Hove with my **(2) tuna** Sarah and my **(3) sucoins** Amy and Joe.

My uncle works for the police. Last year, after an accident, he helped people who were **(4) urth**.

And when a family looked for their dog in the **(5) karp**, Chris helped them to **(6) nifd** him.

I really like to **(7) sitiv** him. He has lots of **(8) hiebbos** and interests – he's always **(9) suby**.

Check

5 WRITING Finn's superhero

I can write about superheroes.

Look at Finn's notes and picture for his art project. Then write a paragraph about RoboGull.
You can use the phrases in the table and your own ideas.

name:	RoboGull
born:	Brighton, 2022
story:	was hungry
	ate a phone
	...
description:	four feet
	...
superpowers:	play music with feet
	...

His / Her	name / ... is ... eyes / feet / ... are ...
He / She	was born in ... became a superhero when ... ... can / has / is / wears / ...

6 MEDIATION A message from Suri

Read the message from Finn's friend Suri in Dresden. Answer Zane's questions in English.

Hi, Finn!
Dein RoboGull klingt witzig! Ich habe mir auch mal eine Superheldin ausgedacht. SkateGirl heißt sie. Sie hat zu viel Zeit im Skatepark verbracht und sich eines Tages in SkateGirl verwandelt. Sie sieht aus wie jedes Mädchen, aber anstelle von Füßen hat sie ein Skateboard. Sie kann superschnell fahren und sehr hoch springen.
LG, Suri

Zane Hey, Finn, you look happy. What's your message about?
Finn My friend Suri wrote to me about ...
Zane Cool. How did SkateGirl become a superhero?
Finn She was ... so long that she became ...
Zane What does she look like?
Finn She looks like any girl, but she doesn't have ... – she has ... at the end of her legs.
Zane And what can she do?
Finn She skates everywhere and she can ... fast and ... very high.

Check

7 READING An interview

I can understand a story about working in a team.

Read an interview with the head students in the school's online magazine.

www.varndean-teen-zine-online.example.com

A busy week for our head students!

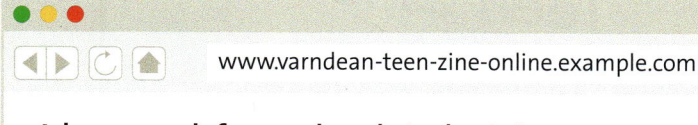

Teen Zine Mihai, can you tell us how your week started?
Mihai Well, we heard about Jake in assembly. Jake is in year 7 and he's in hospital at the moment.
Teen Zine And you wanted to help him?
Jodie Yes. So we talked at lunchtime and made a plan.
Sofia The next day Jodie and I made a big card. Over a hundred students wrote something in it and some teachers did too.
Mihai And then Faye had a great idea ...
Faye Yes. I like to play the guitar and write songs. So I wrote a song for Jake.
Mihai And then we thought: Let's sing this in assembly.
Faye It was amazing. All the students singing Jake's song together.
Teen Zine I was there too. It sounded great. And Mihai, what did you do?
Mihai I made a video of the song and took it to Jake in hospital with the card.
Teen Zine I'm sure Jake was very happy. Well done, guys! We're proud of you!

a) Choose the correct summary.

A A student was ill. Some students and teachers went to the hospital to see him.
B The head students planned a special present for a Varndean student in hospital.
C A student was ill. He went to a special assembly at school and then felt better.

b) Say who did what.

1 ... collected messages on a big card.
2 ... wrote a song for Jake.
3 ... recorded the song.
4 ... went to the hospital.

8 STUDY SKILLS Instructions at Varndean

I can work out the meaning of new words.

What are the blue words in German? You know words that look like that.

1 Don't run on the stairs! It's unsafe.
2 Always be polite, even if you disagree.
3 Help other people if they have a problem. Kindness is important.
4 Read your teacher's corrections. They can help you learn.
5 Cyclists – please leave your bikes in a safe place.

Check

VARNDEAN Teen Zine

Our school magazine: by students for students

This month's topics: friends and heroes

My favourite friend poem

Hug O'War *by Shel Silverstein (1930–1999)*

I will not play at tug o'war.
I'd rather[1] play at hug o'war,
Where everyone hugs
Instead[2] of tugs[3],
Where everyone giggles
And rolls on the rug[4],
Where everyone kisses,
And everyone grins,
And everyone cuddles,
And everyone wins.

I love this poem. Do you like it?
Silas

tug o'war

hugs

giggles

grins and cuddles

For some people, their favourite friend is their pet! What about you?

This is our top ten list of the things that we like to do with our friends!

1 have a sleepover[5]
2 chat online
3 look at videos on our phones
4 have a film night
5 listen to music
6 play video games
7 play card games
8 have a picnic in the park
9 play mini golf
10 prank[6] each other

Send us your top ten lists!

[1] **rather** *lieber* [2] **instead** *anstatt* [3] (to) **tug** *ziehen* [4] **rug** *der Teppichläufer* [5] **sleepover** *die Übernachtungsparty*
[6] (to) **prank each other** *sich gegenseitig Streiche spielen*

Heroes

October is *Black History Month* and *Teen Zine* wants to celebrate it! Here are two of our favourite heroes. Do you know more?

Lewis Hamilton
Formula 1 driver

Lewis Hamilton was born in the UK in 1985. He has won many prizes and is one of the best drivers of all time! But some people are racist[1] – they insult[2] him and treat[3] him badly. Lewis is brave and doesn't let it go. He says it is time for people to change – and not just talk about it!

Doreen Lawrence
anti-racist activist

Doreen Lawrence came to the UK from Jamaica when she was a little girl. In 1993 Doreen's son Stephen was killed[4] in a racist attack[5] when he was 18 years old. Doreen has worked very hard for justice[6] for her son and has won many prizes for her work.

E-postcard from the USA

Lea from Varndean is on a school exchange[7] in the USA.

Hi from San Francisco!

My school exchange is great so far, but I miss you all at Varndean! I'm lucky because I have made some new friends here. It's easy to make friends because there are a lot of clubs: dance, climbing, photography, cooking, computers ... everything! I'm in the science club and the film club.

One of my best friends is Luisa. She was born in the USA, but her parents are from Mexico and they speak Spanish at home. Luisa is teaching me some Spanish – it's a very important language in the USA. A lot of people in the USA have family in Cuba, Mexico, Puerto Rico and other Latin American countries.

Have a good day!
Lea

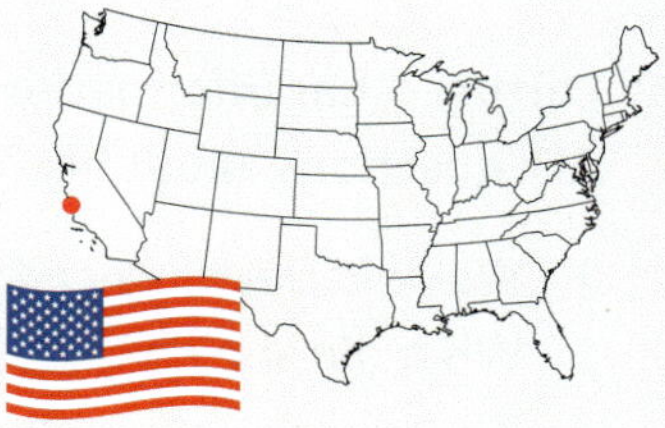

[1] **racist** *rassistisch* [2] (to) **insult** *beleidigen* [3] (to) **treat sb. badly** *jdn. schlecht behandeln*
[4] **he was killed** *er wurde getötet* [5] **attack** *der Angriff* [6] **justice** *die Gerechtigkeit* [7] **exchange** *der Austausch*

Partner page

▸ Page 47

3 Speaking About Li-Jun

Partner B

a) **Ask partner A these questions about Li-Jun.**

1 Did Li-Jun live in China when he was a child?
2 Did he want to leave China?
3 Did he always live in Brighton?
4 Did he only have one job in Britain?

b) **Read about Li-Jun. Then answer partner A's questions:** *Yes, he did. / No, he didn't.*

Li-Jun Chen
- got married to Betty
- didn't have any children
- moved to the Whitehawk Estate in 2020
- enjoyed his work a lot

▸ Page 49

9 Speaking Two student heroes

Partner B

a) **Partner A has information about Destiny. Ask questions about her.**

1 Why did Destiny need money?
2 What did she do?
3 Who did she get money from?
4 How did her team feel?

b) **Now read the article about Jonah. Answer partner A's questions about him.**

Jonah

When Jonah was 10 years old, he was very ill and stayed in hospital for a long time. People said he was always kind to everybody.
Jonah loved magic tricks. When he left the hospital, Jonah wanted to say *thank you* to everybody there. So he did a magic show in the hospital.

Diff bank

▸ Page 42

More practice 1 Who is it?

Think of a person that you and your partner both know. Describe this person. You can use the words in the box. Your partner guesses.

brave • clever • confident • good at sports • good with computers • helpful • kind

She's friendly and she's honest.
Is it Blue Bird?
Yes, you're right!

▸ Page 44

More help 4 SONG My best friend

fish and chips
macaroni and cheese
shoes and socks
sun and moon
summer and holidays
the weekend and fun

I'm the fish ...
... and I'm the chips!

▸ Page 47

More practice 2 Noah and Buddy

Write Lily's questions about Buddy.

Lily	(1 you get) ... Buddy when he was small?
	Did you get Buddy when he was small?
Noah	No, we didn't. He was a year old.
Lily	(2 he come) ... from another home?
Noah	No, he didn't. He had training before we got him.
Lily	(3 he learn) ... to be so good and quiet?
Noah	Yes, he did. He's never scared or mean.
Lily	(4 you choose) ... Buddy?
Noah	No, I didn't. My parents did.
Lily	(5 you love) ... him when you got him?
Noah	Yes, I did. He's so cute and friendly!

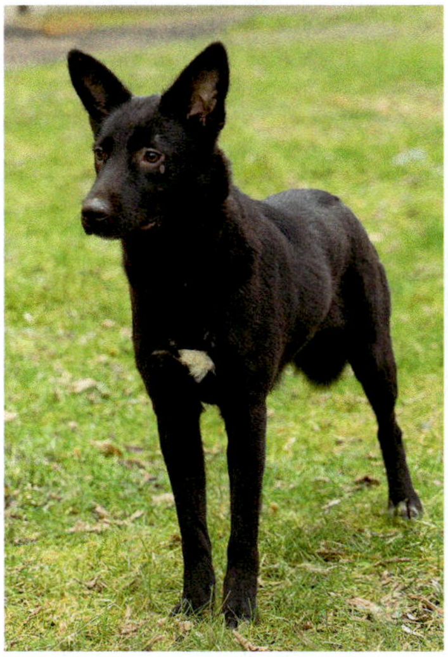

▸ Page 47

Parallel exercise 5 Lily's school day

Li-Jun and Lily talk in the evening. Complete Li-Jun's questions with the correct question words.

1 When / What did you leave school? – At 15.05, like every Monday.
2 How / Why did you come back late? – There was a problem with my bike.
3 Where / How did you get home? – I took the bus.
4 Where / Who did you leave your bike? – At school. It's OK there.
5 What / When did you do at school today? – We did a science project.
6 Why / Who did you do the project with? – Noah. He helped me a lot.

More practice 3 Five questions

a) **Copy and complete the questions with *how, what, when, where* and *who*. Then check the correct questions in class.**

1 ... did you get up yesterday?
I got up at ...
2 ... did you go to school yesterday?
I went to school by ... / I walked to school.
3 ... did you see on the way to school?
I saw ... on the way to school.
4 ... did you go after school yesterday?
I went ... after school.
5 ... did you have for dinner yesterday?
I had ... for dinner.

b) WALK AROUND
Ask different students the five questions. Write the names and the answers.

c) **Tell the class about one student.**

Slava got up at six a.m. yesterday.

▸ Page 48

More practice 4 Say something nice

a) **Write two sentences to describe Lily, Sunita, Noah, Zane and Scout.**

Lily is ... She isn't ...

b) **Compare your sentences with a partner.**

For Lily, I have: ...

Say something nice about me.

▸ Page 50

More practice 5 Years and dates

a) Listen and say the dates. Take turns.

1 6th June
2 12th September
3 20th May
4 3rd July
5 22nd February
6 21st March
7 5th May
8 19th November

The first day of the year is the first of January. The last day of the year is the thirty-first of December. My favourite day is the first of April – I was born then!

b) Listen and check how to say the dates.

c) Now say the years. Take turns.

2022 1968 1750 1895 1999 2009 2015 1983

d) Listen and check how to say the years.

More practice 6 Lady Cool and Mr Brave

Describe the superheroes and what they're wearing.

Lady Cool is wearing a red ...

Mr Brave is wearing ...

▸ Page 51

☒ **More practice 7** ## A hard life

a) **Link the two sentences. Start with *when*.**

1 I was a kid. I lived on planet Oolala.
When I was a kid, I lived on planet Oolala.
2 The Zoogs killed my parents. They took me to planet Zoog.
3 I lived there. I worked for the Zoogs.
4 It got really hard. I left.

b) **Link the two sentences with *when* in the middle.**

1 I was happy. I came to earth. *I was happy when I …*
2 I changed my body. I saw that people looked different!
3 I became a superhero. People needed my help.
4 I used my superpowers. I helped people.

▸ Page 51

More help ## 3 My Task I'm a superhero!

Story

I was born	on planet … in …
I came to earth	in … when …
I became a superhero when I	ate a special fish. drank a chemical. …

Clothes

I wear	long red boots. a silver cape. a red helmet. a black eye mask. …

Superpowers

I'm	very clever. fast. strong. …
I have	good eyes. a good nose. …
I can	become a different person or animal. move things when I look at them. read thoughts. see through things and people. swim underwater. travel in time. …
I can't	get hurt. …

▸ Page 54

More practice 8 What is it?

Write the correct parts of the body.

1 It's at the end of your arm.
2 They're part of your feet, on the right and left.
3 It's at the top of your body.
4 You hear with them.
5 You see with them.
6 You brush them every morning.
7 It's the front of your head.
8 You put shoes on them.

▸ Page 57

More help UNIT TASK Make a quiz

Choose one person from history.

Muhammad Ali

- was born on 17 January 1942 in Louisville, Kentucky, USA
- died on 3 June 2016
- was a famous boxer
- was champion (three times) and won an Olympic gold medal

Albert Einstein

- was born on 14 March 1879 in Ulm, Germany
- died on 18 April 1955
- discovered important information about science
- won the Nobel Prize in 1921

Astrid Lindgren

- was born on 14 November 1907 in Vimmerby, Sweden
- died on 28 January 2002
- wrote famous books for children: *Ronja, Räubertochter* and *Pippi Langstrumpf*

Sophie Scholl

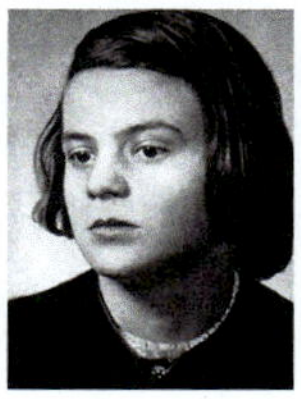

- was born on 9 May 1921 in Forchtenberg, Germany
- died on 22 February 1943
- was a student in Munich
- fought against Nazi Germany

Unit 3
Activities and games

www.activities-in-Brighton.example.com

A

Watch a show at Bright Theatre

♥ 5

- *Beauty and the Beast* – a panto for all the family!
- 19–23 January
- Full of great songs, jokes and fun!
- Tickets £8–£10

B

Have fun at The Beach Zip!

♥ 3

- Ride our zip wire at Brighton beach.
- Tickets £10– £18

1 Listening A family activity

a) Before you listen **Look at the four activities in Brighton. Say which activity you want to do and why.**

Good to know

In Britain, a pantomime or panto is a funny show with music. Everybody in the theatre sings the songs and talks to the actors.

I want to	...	because	I like	cooking • exciting activities • making things • songs • ...
			it looks	creative • delicious • exciting • fun • ...

b) **Zane and his family want to do a family activity at the weekend. Listen. Say which activity A–D they choose together.**

Nach dieser Unit kann ich ...

- über Aktivitäten und Uhrzeiten sprechen
- Pläne machen und darüber sprechen
- Musik, Shows, Filme und Spiele vergleichen
- einen Weg beschreiben
- darüber sprechen, wie lange ich online bin
- meine Meinung äußern

Unit task

- Aktivitäten für einen besonderen Tag an der Schule planen und vorstellen

EN

C

Learn to cook Thai food!

2

- Make delicious food and take it home!
- 19 January
- Cost: £40

D

Get creative and make your own insect hotel!

0

- You can also see lots of different insects in special boxes.
- A fun, free family activity!

c) Listen again. Are the sentences true (T) or false (F)?

1 Zane's dad looks at the "What's on in Brighton" page.
2 Zane's mum thinks pantos are always fun.
3 The Brighton Zip costs only £10 if you live in Brighton.
4 Holly is too small for the zip wire.
5 The cooking course is too expensive.
6 Zane's mum doesn't like insects.

▶ More practice 1, p. 93

▶ Workbook, p. 40

Digital quiz

I can talk about family activities.

What are your plans?

1 Reading School activity week in year 8

a) Before you read **This is the programme for activity week next month. Look at the activity titles and the photos. Which activity sounds fun to you?**

Activity Week – a week of fun and new skills!

Dungeons and Dragons
Play this wonderful role-playing game at school. Everyone can try it!

Knitting
You can knit a toy animal or a blanket and make amazing decorations. Classes are at school.

Karate
Practise karate with a trainer in Varndean's sports hall. You are going to learn a lot!

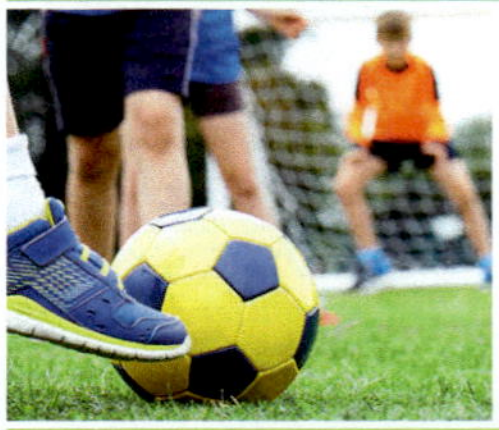

Football club
Practise with great trainers here at school and visit a real football stadium.

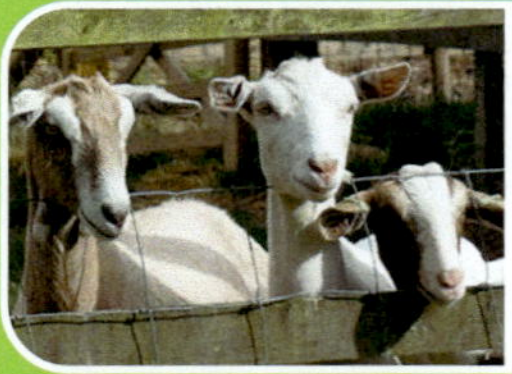

Goats and other animals
Meet our school goats! We are also going to visit a farm and see more animals there.

Photography
Learn new photography skills. Take photos at school and of street art in Brighton.

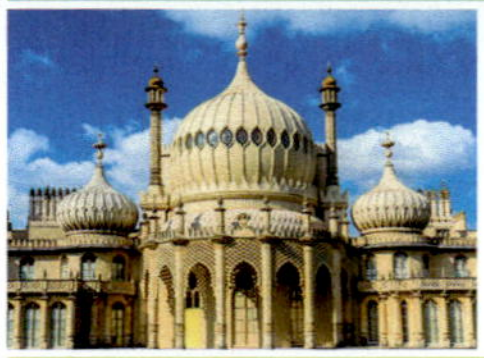

History in Brighton
Learn more about Brighton's amazing history and visit lots of places in Brighton.

Tea party and show
Plan a summer tea party at Varndean and prepare a show with singing and acting.

b) **Now read about the activities. Which activities ...**

1 are creative?
2 are good if you like sports?
3 do you do with a partner or team?
4 only happen at school?
5 happen at school and other places in Brighton?

2 LISTENING What are you going to choose?

a) BEFORE YOU LISTEN **Which activity is best for Lily, Noah, Sunita and Zane? Why?**

The best activity for Lily is karate because ...

The best activity for	Lily Noah Sunita Zane	is	...	because he/she	likes sport • animals • games • cooking • singing • ...
					is brave • creative • confident • ...

b) **After class, the four friends talk about activity week. Listen and complete the correct activities. Were your ideas in a) correct?**

1 Lily: I'm going to choose ...
2 Noah: I'm going to choose ...
3 Zane: I'm going to choose ...
4 Sunita: I'm going to choose ...

c) **Listen again. First complete the activities that the students aren't going to choose. Then choose the correct reasons.**

goats and other animals • history in Brighton • karate • photography

1 Lily: I'm not going to choose ... because I already do a lot of sport / games.
2 Noah: I'm not going to choose ... because I know all those places / people.
3 Zane: I'm not going to choose ... because the camera on my phone is too old / terrible.
4 Sunita: I'm not going to choose ... because there are so many animals at school / home!

d) WALK AROUND **Tell different partners your top activity and what you aren't going to do.**

I'm going to choose 'Tea party and show' because I'm good at singing. I'm not going to choose 'Goats and other animals' because I don't like them. What about you?

I'm going to choose 'Dungeons and Dragons' because I'd like to try something new. I'm not going to choose 'Knitting' because I think it's boring.

▸ Workbook, p. 41

3 Listening **Weekend plans**

a) Before you listen **Can you remember: What is Zane going to do at the weekend?**

b) **Listen to the conversation between Zane and Lily after school on Friday. When can Zane go to the film?**

c) **Read the tip.**

Sometimes people say the time like this:

quarter past twelve (12.15)	half past twelve (12.30)	quarter to one (12.45)

Now write the times.

1 	2 	3 	4 	5 
It's ... past five.	It's half ...	It's quarter ...	It's ...	It's ...

4 Zane's weekend

a) **Read the sentences and write the times.**

1 Holly and dad are going to take the bus at quarter past ten. *10.15*
2 I'm going to swim in a competition at quarter to three.
3 Mum and dad are going to meet in front of the restaurant at quarter to seven.
4 Grandma is going to make dinner for us at quarter past six.
5 I'm going to make lunch at half past twelve.
6 We're going to watch a show at half past two.

b) **Listen and check.**

► Parallel exercise, p. 93 ► More practice 2, p. 93

► Workbook, p. 43

Digital quiz I can **say at what time activities happen.**

My task

5 Make plans for the weekend

a) **Read and practice the conversation between Zane and Lily from ex. 3 with a partner.**

Lily What are you going to do on Sunday, Zane? I'm going to watch the new superhero film. Do you want to come with me?
Zane When do you want to go?
Lily It starts at quarter past three.
Zane Sorry, I can't. I'm going to see *Beauty and the Beast* with my family at half past two.
Lily OK, what about Saturday evening? It starts at quarter to seven.
Zane Good idea! Let's meet at the cinema at half past six.
Lily Great, see you then!
Zane OK, bye!

b) **Now find a time to meet your partner.**

Partner B: Look at p. 92.
Partner A: Look at your phone's calendar. You start.

Saturday
visit grandpa 11.00

Sunday
go swimming with Charlie 10.45

Partner A Hi! What are you going to do on Saturday afternoon? Can we play football?
Partner B Sorry, I can't. I'm going to ... What about Saturday morning?
Partner A Sorry, I can't. I'm going to ... What about Sunday afternoon?
Partner B Good idea! Let's meet at ...
Partner A Great! See you then!
Partner B OK, bye!

▶ Digital help

▶ Language file 7–9, pages 176–177 (rezeptiv)

Digital quiz I can make plans and talk about them.

Music, films and shows

1 LISTENING What kind of music do you like?

a) BEFORE YOU LISTEN Look at the kinds of music in the box.

A classical	B acoustic	C pop	D rap	E rock	F electro

What are the words in German? Tell your partner.

Rap is the same in German.

b) Listen to six music clips (1–6). Match them to the kinds of music (A–F) in a).

c) Listen to the conversation at Noah's house.
Who is it:
Lily (L),
Noah (N),
Sunita (S)
or Zane (Z)?

1 Who loves rock?
2 Who doesn't like rock?
3 Who listens to classical music?
4 Who likes rap?
5 Who doesn't like pop (two people)?

d) Which kinds of music do you like? Who's your favourite band or singer? Tell your partner. Use the words in 1a) or your own ideas.

▸ Skills file 6, p. 162

2 It's louder!

Read these sentences from the conversation in 1. Then copy and complete the pairs 1–6.

It's louder than their last album!
Can you play something quieter?
Classical music is slower than rock.
Rap is cooler than rock.
Pop is faster and happier than classical music.

1 loud → louder
2 quiet → ...
3 slow → ...
4 cool → ...
5 fast → ...
6 happy → ...

Erklär-film

3 Looking at language Rap is cooler than pop

a) Listen to the rest of the conversation. Who is it: Lily (L), Noah (N), Sunita (S) or Zane (Z)?

1 Who thinks classical music is as bad as pop?
2 Who likes acoustic?
3 Who likes electro?
4 Who thinks rap is worse than classical music?
5 Who thinks rap is better than electro?

b) Read these sentences from the conversation in a). Then copy and complete the pairs 1–3.

Acoustic is more relaxing than pop.
Electro is more energetic than acoustic.
Rap is more interesting than electro.

1 relaxing → more relaxing
2 energetic → ...
3 interesting → ...

c) Complete the rule.

Personen und Dinge kann man miteinander vergleichen.
Bei kurzen Adjektiven hängst du ... ans Ende des Adjektivs.
Bei langen Adjektiven setzt du ... vor das Adjektiv.
Ausnahmen: *good – better*
bad – worse
Wenn zwei Sachen gleich sind, sagst du:
Classical music is as bad as pop.

▶ Language file 10, p. 178

4 Comparing music

Walk around Compare two kinds of music. Find a partner and say a sentence. If your partner agrees, high five. If he/she doesn't agree, shake your head.

I think	classical music acoustic music pop rap rock electro	is	faster slower quieter louder more interesting more relaxing more energetic cooler better worse	than	...

▶ More practice 3 + 4, p. 94

▶ Workbook, pp. 44–45

5 Reading What do you want to watch?

a) Before you read **The kids want to watch something online. What kind of film or show can they watch? Is A–C an action film, a cartoon or a sci-fi film?**

A

Dex 3000 is the worst robot in town – but he's also the kindest. All that he wants is a real friend.

B

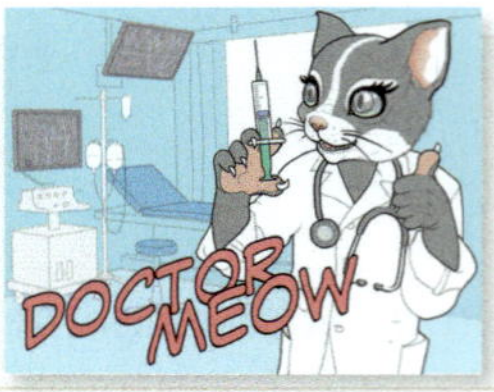

The funniest show of the year! Doctor Meow is the cleverest cat in town – but Doctor Woof thinks he's cleverer …

C

It's going to be Agent Green's most exciting job ever! This time she's going to the most dangerous place on the planet.

b) **Which film or show is the best for Zane, Lily and Sunita?** *I think the best film / show for … is …*

I want to watch something funny. I don't like action films.

I don't like cartoons – I want to watch something really exciting!

I love films about space or robots – like my robot Robbie!

6 Looking at language The coolest and most exciting film

Erklär-film

a) **Look at the table on the right and fill in the missing words from ex. 5a).**

good	better	best
bad	worse	worst
funny	funnier	…
clever	cleverer	…
exciting	more exciting	…
dangerous	more dangerous	…

b) **Complete the rule.**

Möchtest du sagen, was du am coolsten, am aufregendsten, am besten findest?
Bei kurzen Adjektiven hängst du … ans Ende des Adjektivs.
Bei langen Adjektiven setzt du … vor das Adjektiv.

► Language file 11, p. 178

7 Speaking The best film

Which film from 5a) do you like best and why? Tell your partner. Use the words in 6a) and change the words in blue: *I like Dr Meow best because it's the funniest film.*

► More practice 5, p. 95
► Workbook, p. 46

8 VIEWING Film time

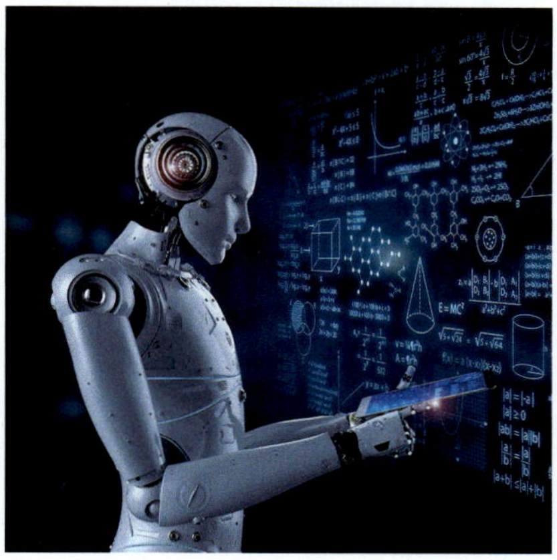

a) The kids watched one of the films from 5a).
Watch the film trailer. Which film did they choose?

b) Watch the trailer again and choose the correct answers.

1 The main character is an agent / a robot / a doctor.
2 He's friendly / clever / fast.
3 The film takes place in Brighton / Liverpool / London.
4 The film is about friends / heroes / space.
5 The film is scary / sad / funny.
6 It has good actors / special effects / music.

My task

9 A film trailer

a) Work in a small group. Choose a film that you all like.

b) Write sentences for a film trailer. You can use these ideas to help you. ▶ Digital help

This is	an action film a cartoon a sci-fi film	about	animals • friends • music • space • superheroes • ...
It takes place in	London • New York • a school • space • ...		
The main character is	a dog • a footballer • a robot • a singer • a superhero • a ...		

c) Add more information and compare your film with another film.

It's the	best coolest funniest most exciting ...	film	this summer. this year. ever. ...
It's	better cooler funnier more exciting ...	than	'Spiderman'. ...

▶ Wordbank 5, p. 189

'SuperScout' is the best action film this year. She's cooler than all the other superheroes!

d) Record your sentences. Play your trailer to your class.

e) Compare your trailers. Which trailer was the funniest or the most exciting or the best?

Digital quiz I can compare music, shows and films.

Gaming

1 What do you think?

Your teacher reads a sentence.
Stand up if you agree,
remain seated if you don't.

1 Video games are boring.
2 Computer gaming is better than console gaming.
3 Puzzle games aren't real games.
4 Adventure games are the best.

2 LISTENING Where do I go next?

a) BEFORE YOU LISTEN Finn and Sunita are playing an online game. Look at the game map. Tell your partner what you can see.

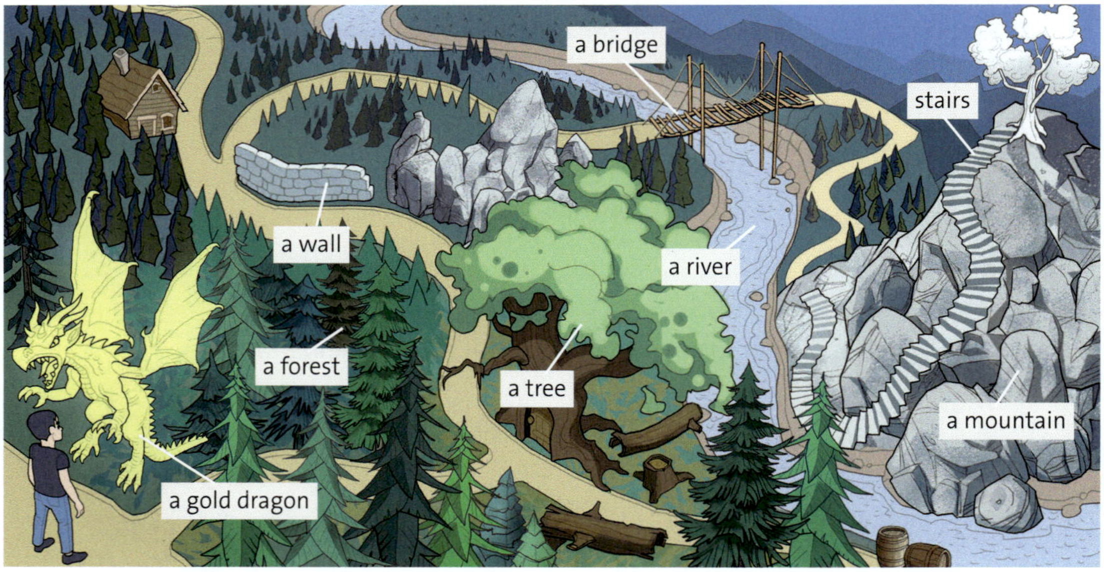

b) Sunita is helping Finn with the game. Where does he need to go? Listen and complete the directions. Use the words in a).

To find the key, Finn must go through the (1) ... and turn left at the big (2) ...
He goes straight on, past a small (3) ... and then turns (4) ...
He goes across the (5) ... and then up the (6) ... on the (7) ...

▶ Parallel exercise, p. 95

c) Listen again and check. Where's the key? Describe it or point.

▶ More practice 6 + 7, p. 96

3 READING Sunita's trophies

a) **Read Sunita's chat with Finn and point to the trophies that they talk about.**

b) **Read the descriptions of some of Sunita's other trophies. Write the letter of the trophy.**

1 It's the one to the right of the sun trophy.
2 It's the one on the top left.
3 It's the one above the eye trophy.
4 It's the one between the lion trophy and the cloud trophy.
5 It's the one under the money trophy.

c) **Choose a trophy and describe it. Your partner guesses.**

It's the big / small / round / long / blue / red / yellow / ... one.
It's the one above / under / next to / between ...
It's the one to the right / left of ...

▶ More practice 8, p. 96

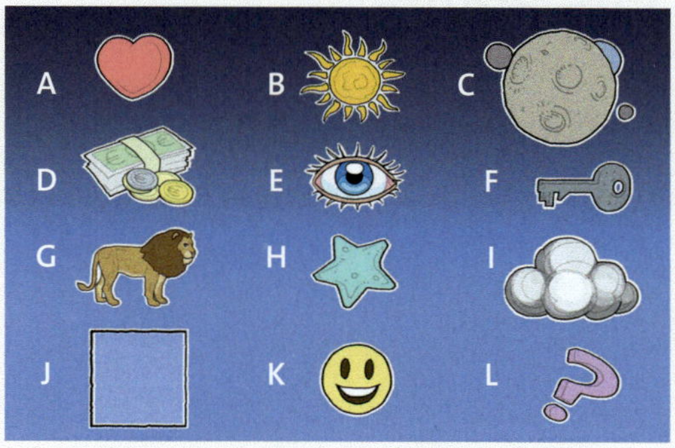

FinnD	Oh wow, you have so many trophies!
SuperNita	Haha, thx!
FinnD	What's the big blue one for?
SuperNita	You mean the one next to the smiley face? That's for a perfect score.
FinnD	Coooooool ... And what about the one on the bottom right?
SuperNita	I got that one when I found a secret level!
FinnD	😍😍😍
SuperNita	😊

My task

4 Game designer

a) **Draw a game map like the one in 2. Add lots of different places.** ▶ More help, p. 97

b) **Where does the character start? Write directions to a secret place on the map.**

Go	left at • right at • straight on at • past	the	house • forest • tree • ...
	across		bridge • river
	down • up		mountain • river • stairs
	into • through		castle • forest • river

c) **Swap with your partner and follow their directions to find their secret place.**

▶ Digital help

▶ Workbook, pp. 47–48

Digital quiz

I can **understand and give directions.**

Zane online

1 READING Too much of a good thing?

a) BEFORE YOU READ **Tell a partner how much time you spend online every day and what you do.**

How much time do you spend online?

I usually spend about … minutes / hours every day.

What do you do?

I chat with friends / play games / send messages / watch videos / …

▶ Wordbank 6, p. 190

b) **Look at the pictures. What can you see? What do you think the story is about?**

c) **Now read the story. Check your answers from b).**

"Oh, I'm so bored!" thought Zane. "What am I going to do all day?" It was Friday, but Zane was at home because he was ill. He had a bad cough and a headache. "I can't go out. I can't talk to my friends because they're at school. And I can't do homework because my head hurts!" Zane opened a video app and watched a video. "Why not?" thought Zane. The video was really funny. Zane laughed out loud. He clicked on the next one … and the next one … Then it was lunch time.

"Your dad is going to get Holly from school today," said Zane's mum. "And I have a meeting in town. Are you going to be OK?" "Sure, Mum," said Zane.

After lunch Zane watched videos again. When his dad came home with Holly, Zane was still on his phone. He was tired and his headache was worse. "No more screen time today, Zane!" said his dad. "You know the rules – one hour a day!" The next week Zane went back to school, but he watched videos every evening on his phone – sometimes until very late.

"You look tired, Zane," his mum said on Thursday. "What's wrong?"
Zane smiled. "I'm just tired from when I was ill."
"Hmm," said his mum. "You have a maths test on Monday – it's on the calendar. Do you need help?"
"No, I don't need help, thanks. Everything is fine."

The next weekend, his friends went swimming, but Zane didn't go.
"Sorry," he said to Lily on the phone. "I need to study for the maths test."
"I can help you," said Lily.
"Thanks, but my mum is going to help me," Zane said. "I must go now. Bye!"

Lily was surprised. Zane always went swimming with them.
"Something is wrong," she said. "Zane didn't come for brunch at Noah's house last weekend, and he didn't do his history homework. Noah told me. Zane always does his homework!"
"Finn said Zane watches lots of videos now," answered Sunita.
"Right," said Lily. "I'm going to visit Zane."

Lily went to Zane's house.
"Good to see you Lily," Zane's mum said. "Zane is in his room."
Zane was surprised and not very happy.
"I told you I was busy."
"Too busy for your friends, Zane?" asked Lily.
Zane looked angry. "Please go, Lily."

2 Zane's problem

Read the story again. Match the sentence parts. *1 B, 2 ...*

1 Zane watched ...
2 His dad told him ...
3 The next week he ...
4 His mum was worried and ...
5 Lily knew that ...
6 Lily went to see Zane, but ...

A something was wrong.
B videos all day when he was ill.
C she asked Zane if he needed help.
D watched videos every evening.
E he didn't want to see his friend.
F to remember the rule about screen time.

► Skills file 7, p. 163

3 The story ending

a) Read the three different story endings. Which one do you like best?

I think A / B / C is the best.

A	B	C
Lily looked sad. She went out of the door. "Wait, Lily!" Zane said. "I'm sorry, I can't stop. I think I need help."	Then Lily stopped. "No, Zane! I'm worried about you. Don't you think friends are more important than videos?"	"OK, Zane. But I don't want to be your friend any more," said Lily. "But, Lily ...," Zane looked surprised.

b) Talk about the different endings with a partner. Say what you think about each one.

I think	A B C	is	the best ending the worst ending	because	Zane tells Lily how he feels. Lily tells Zane how she feels. Lily / Zane is mean. ...

► More practice 9, p. 97

4 LIFE SKILLS Screen time

a) Look at the tips in the box and discuss the questions.

1. How do you feel when you spend too much time online?
   I feel OK / tired / bored / great / ...
2. Which tip is best for Zane?
   I think tip number ...
3. Do you know any other good tips?
   A good tip is ...
4. Do your parents have rules about screen time? What rules?
   We have these rules:
   – *screen time is one hour a day,*
   – *no screens after 7 p.m.,*
   – *no phone in the bedroom,*
   – *no phones at dinner time for everyone.*

> 1 Go outside.
> 2 Meet your friends.
> 3 Go swimming.
> 4 Sing with your band.
> 5 Cook something nice.
> 6 Put your phone in the living room at night.

b) Plan your screen time for next week and tell a partner.

I'm going to spend / use / ...   I'm not going to ...

Digital quiz   I can talk about screen time.

Brighton stories: After-school fun

1 Before you watch After-school activities

**Which of the activities would you like to do?
Tell your partner and say why.**

I'd like to do ... because I like plants / clothes / ...
I think ... is creative / exciting / fun / relaxing / ...

gardening

photography

sewing

street dancing

2 Viewing A group activity

a) **Watch the video. Is it Joe, Daisy, Gloria or Emir? There can be more than one answer.**

1 ... likes gardening.
2 ..., ... and ... don't like gardening.
3 ... wants to teach the others how to dance.
4 ... is super tired at the end.
5 ... learned the most.
6 ... is the winner.

b) **Watch the video again. Who says what? Match pictures A–D to sentences 1–4.**

1 "Let me guess: The best dancer wins?"
2 "I'm a natural talent!"
3 "Let's try again."
4 "Let's do some more!"

A
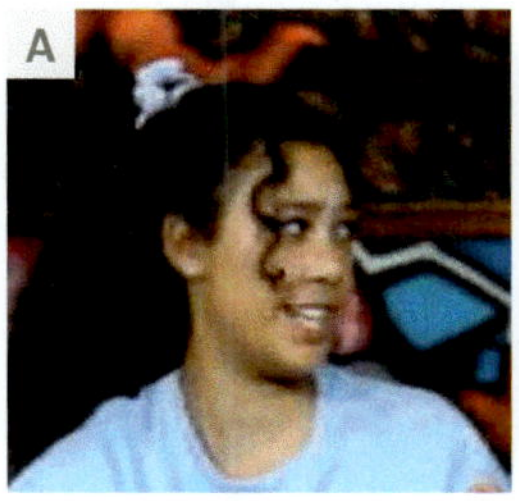
B
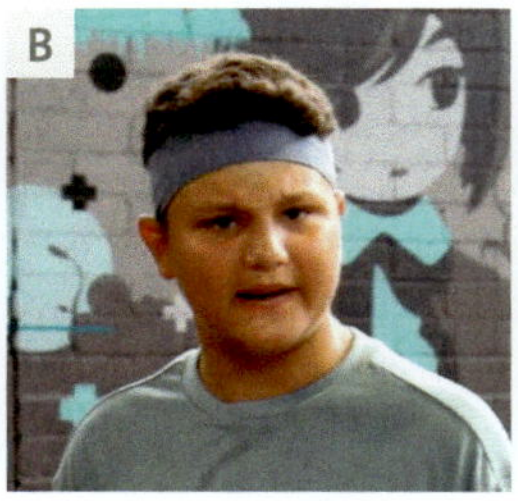
C

D
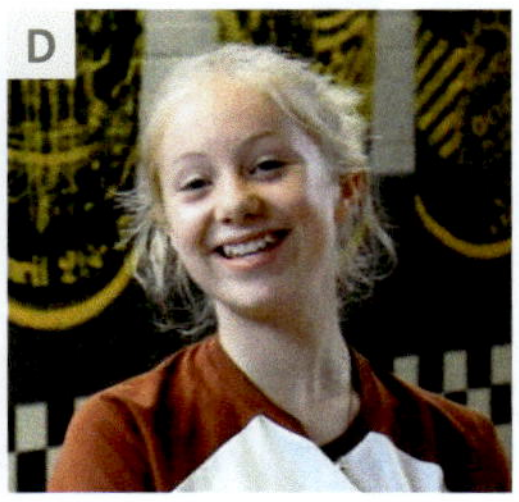

3 Now you

Joe says who wins at the end of the video. Do you agree? Why or why not?

I agree. I think ... is the best dancer because she has the best moves / ...
I don't agree. In my opinion ... is the best dancer because he / she looks amazing / ...

▸ Workbook, p. 49

Give your opinion

1 Reading **What do you think?**

a) There's a new show called 'Scout's World'. Who likes it? Who doesn't like it?

Zane I think 'Scout's World' is the best show ever! It's so funny.
Lily That isn't true. In my opinion, it isn't funny at all!
Sunita Really, Lily? I agree with Zane. It's a great show. I love it! What do you think, Finn?
Finn You're right Sunita. It's a cool show. Noah, do you like it?
Noah No, I don't. I don't agree with Zane. It's boring!

b) Copy and complete the table with the blue phrases in a).

give an opinion	ask for an opinion	agree	don't agree

2 Speaking **I think ...**

Look at the topics and the adjectives. Choose a topic and give your opinion. What does your partner think? Then swap roles. Each partner gives three opinions.

Topics
cats • cold weather • dogs • football • gaming • mice • pizza • school • school uniforms • the colour pink • shopping • vegetables • vegetarian food • ...

Adjectives
boring • cool • cute • delicious • easy • exciting • fun • hard • horrible • interesting • nice • scary • ...

I think cats are horrible!

I don't agree. Cats are really cute! I think cold weather isn't nice.

3 Opinion line **Stand in a line!**

What do you think: Is learning English easy? Stand in a line. Then count the students.

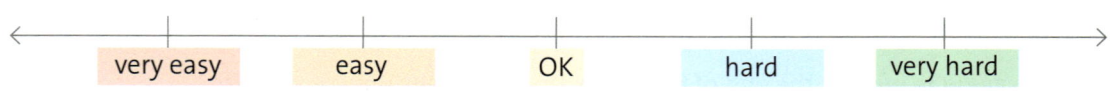

very easy — easy — OK — hard — very hard

Talk about your results: *Three students think that English is hard.*

► Skills file 10, p. 167

Digital quiz — I can ask for opinions and give my opinion.

Plan and present an activity day

Step 1: Think of ideas

You're going to plan an activity day at school in your group. First brainstorm activities with a partner and make a list. The ideas in the box can help you.

Ideas

- sports and games (a match or a competition)
- a party or a show (a musical, concert or disco)
- sell books, food or clothes for charity
- ...

Step 2: Discuss your ideas

Join another pair. Compare and discuss your ideas. Agree on your best ideas.

You have some great ideas! I think a fun run is the best activity.
I think a table tennis competition is more exciting than a concert.
I agree. / I don't agree. I think ...

► Skills file 10, p. 167

Step 3: Plan your day

a) **Make a plan with activities, times and places.**

b) **Make a poster for your day.**

A table tennis competition

Do you like table tennis?
Join our competition!
It's going to be a great day!

Where: in the sports hall
When: Saturday, January 18th, at 10.30
Cost: It's free!

Step 4: Present your day

a) **Tell another group or the class about your activity day.**

We're going to have a table tennis competition. It's going to be at our school, on Saturday, January 18th. It's going to start at half past ten. It's going to be a lot of fun!

b) **Give the group feedback on their poster.**

I like your poster.

Good ideas.

Great job!

► Digital help

► Let's talk, Feedback phrases, p. 199

Digital quiz I can plan and present an activity day.

1 Speaking At the family Arts Centre

I can talk about family activities.

a) Look at the posters. Which two activities do you want to do?

b) Agree on two activities. Say when and where.

IN THE GARDEN

9.15 – 9.45
Meet our new fish and give them some breakfast!

10.30 – 11.30
Go on an insect tour.

IN THE ARTS ROOM

9.30 – 10.30:
Make an insect hotel for your garden.

10.45 – 11.30:
Design a tree house for our centre. Prizes for the best designs!

IN THE CAFE

9.00 – 9.30:
Hungry? Try some eggs from our chickens.

10.15 – 11.15:
Decorate a cake (and then eat it for free!).

At quarter past nine I want to ... in the ...

Good idea! It ends at ..., so we can ... at ...

OK then, let's first ... and then ...

2 Language After school

I can make plans and talk about them.

Read the conversation. Look at Sunita and Finn's calendars and complete the sentences.

Finn What a long day! What are you going to do after school?

Sunita I'm going to have dinner with my family, and then I'm going to (1) ... online. After that, Nish is going to help me with my (2) ..., I hope! What about you?

Finn It's my grandpa's birthday, so we're going to have a (3) ... with him and watch him open our present. Then we're going to (4) ...
And after that I'm going to (5) ... too!

Sunita Great – see you online later.

have dinner	6.00
play games	7.00
French homework	8.00

video call with grandpa	5.30
make pizza	6.00
play games	7.00

3 Language Lily's trip

Lily is going to go to Scotland for the weekend. Put Zane's questions in the correct order.

1 going to travel / by car? / Are you
2 going to read / Are you / on the journey? / a book
3 cold? / Is the weather / going to be
4 Are you / skiing? / going to go

Check

4 Reading Comments about a new song

I can compare music, shows and films.

Read the online comments about a new song.

a) Choose the correct text for each person.

1 PopQueen
2 Calm_Cal
3 Electro*Guy
4 Rock_4eva

www.what's-new-in-rock-music.example.net

A Oh, no. My favourite band isn't cool any more. Their last album was amazing, but this song is ... not good at all. It's their worst song. Rock music needs to be louder than this! I think I'm going to fall asleep.

B What a great song! I don't usually listen to rock music (pop is my thing), but this sounds so good. It's much cooler than my dad's old rock songs. I love the video too. I'd like a house on the beach like that.

C Interesting lyrics, but the guitars are too loud for me. Songs sound so much better when you can hear what the singer is saying! I'm going to listen to some acoustic music now – it's a bit quieter and more relaxing. See you!

D Cool song! I'm not really a fan of rock music because sometimes I think it sounds angry. I usually listen to electro. But this is perfect for me: It's energetic and when I hear it, I want to dance.

b) Choose the correct answer.

1 The new song is than the band's other songs.	A quieter	B louder	C more exciting
2 The music video shows a	A family	B pop band	C home near the sea.
3 The words in the song are	A relaxing	B interesting	C loud.
4 The song doesn't sound	A cool	B energetic	C angry.

5 Language Which show do you want to see?

a) Look at the posters and choose the correct words.

Mary Poppins is louder / funnier than *Oliver!*
Oliver! is more energetic / more relaxing than *Mary Poppins*.
Mary Poppins is shorter / longer than *Billy Elliot*.

BILLY ELLIOT
A boy wants to dance!
90 minutes | Tickets: £20

OLIVER!
A musical with lots of energy.
120 minutes
Tickets: £15

Mary Poppins
A funny show for all the family.
75 minutes
Tickets: £12

b) Complete the sentences with the words in the box.

longest • most expensive • shortest

Oliver! is the ... show.
Billy Elliot is the ... show.
Mary Poppins is the ... show.

Check

6 LISTENING Noah's new computer game

I can understand and give directions.

a) Listen to the conversation. Where do Noah, Sunita and Finn find the trophies? Write the correct place (A–D) for each trophy (1–3). You don't need one of the places.

	Place
Trophy 1	...
Trophy 2	...
Trophy 3	

b) Listen again. Who is it: Noah (N), Sunita (S) or Finn (F)?

1 ... chooses a character that is fast.
2 ... chooses a character that can see better than other characters.
3 ... tells the other players what to do.
4 ... goes into the castle.
5 ... climbs a tree.
6 ... doesn't find a trophy.

7 WORDS A secret level

Sunita tells Finn how to find a secret level in the computer game. Look at the pictures and complete her sentences with the correct word from the box.

above
across
between
past
right
straight

1 Go ... the silver bridge.

2 When you're on the other side, turn ...

3 Go ... on.

4 Go ... the castle.

5 Stop ... the two weird trees.

6 The key is ... your head in a gold bag.

Check

8 WRITING Sunita's screen time

I can talk about screen time.

For her computing homework, Sunita needs to write about her screen time last week. Look at her notes and write her text. You can start like this:

On Monday I spent 45 minutes on the computer. I was gaming.
On Tuesday I didn't use ...

~~Monday – computer – gaming – 45 min~~
Tuesday – no screen time
Wednesday – computer – did homework – 30 min
Thursday – no screen time
Friday – phone – watched videos – 25 min
Saturday – no screen time
Sunday – phone – chatted with friends – 30 min

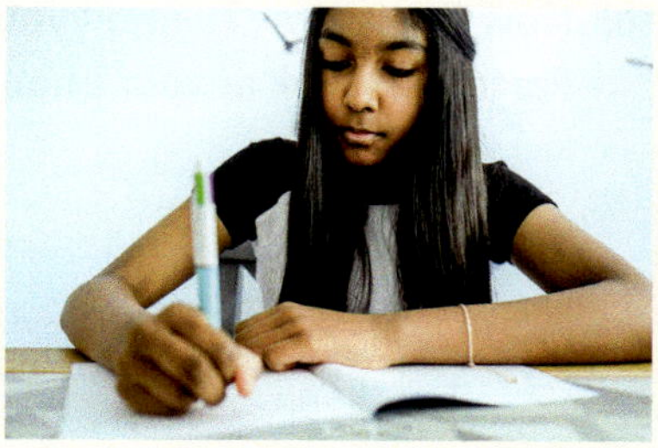

9 STUDY SKILLS Talking about films

I can ask for opinions and give my opinion.

You're talking to your British friend about films. Say what you think. Use the phrases in the box.

Example for 1:

I don't agree. In my opinion action films are the best.

I think ...
In my opinion ...
For me ...

You're right.
I agree.

I don't think so.
I don't agree.

I think sci-fi films are the best.

1 ...

Action films are good – they are often exciting.

2 ...

I think scary films are better than cartoons.

3 ...

I think films about robots are really boring!

4 ...

Check

Partner page

▸ Page 75

5 Make plans for the weekend

Partner B

b) **Now find a time to meet your partner.**
Partner B: Look at your phone's calendar. Partner A starts.

Saturday	
go shopping	
with dad	3.00
Sunday	
watch a film	
at the cinema	10.30

Partner A	Hi! What are you going to do on Saturday afternoon? Can we play football?
Partner B	Sorry, I can't. I'm going to … What about Saturday morning?
Partner A	Sorry, I can't. I'm going to … What about Sunday afternoon?
Partner B	Good idea! Let's meet at …
Partner A	Great! See you then!
Partner B	OK, Bye!

Diff bank

▸ Page 71

More practice 1 A family activity

Read these sentences. What's correct: A, B or C?

1 *Beauty and the Beast* is on from the 19th to the 23rd of
A November B December C January.
2 Tickets for the panto cost A £8–10 B £80 C £18.
3 Tickets for The Beach Zip cost A £8 B £40 C £10–18.
4 At the cooking course, you learn how to cook
A Thai food B Chinese food C British food.
5 The cooking course costs A £18 B £24 C £40.
6 At the free activity you can make your own
A insect hotel B special boxes C Thai food.

▸ Page 74

Parallel exercise 4 Zane's weekend

a) **Read the sentences. Match the correct times in the box to the sentences.**

12.30 • 6.45 • ~~10.15~~ • 6.15 • 2.45 • 2.30

1 Holly and dad are going to take the bus at quarter past ten. *10.15*
2 I am going to swim in a competition at quarter to three.
3 Mum and dad are going to meet in front of the restaurant at quarter to seven.
4 Grandma is going to make dinner for us at quarter past six.
5 I am going to make lunch at half past twelve.
6 We are going to watch a show at half past two.

b) **Listen and check.**

More practice 2 Find the correct time!

- Your teacher writes some digital times on the board.
- Make two teams. One student from each team stands near the board.
- Your teacher says a time on the board: *half past four*.
- Which of the two students near the board can touch the correct time on the board first? That team gets one point.
- Then the next two students stand near the board.

▸ Page 77

More practice 3 Scout's favourite band

Compare the people in the picture.

1 Ellis has (long) ... hair than Alex.
2 Alex is (tall) ... than Sam, but (short) ... than Charlie.
3 Ellis is (popular) ... than Charlie.
4 Sam's guitar is (small) ..., but (colourful) ... than Charlie's guitar.
5 Charlie's guitar is (expensive) ... than Sam's guitar.
6 Alex is (strong) ... than Ellis.

More practice 4 The singer and the guitar player

Look at the pictures. Copy and complete the sentences. Use *as ... as* and the correct word from the box.

~~cool~~ • fast • happy • loud • strong • tall

1 The singer is *as cool as* the guitar player.

2 The singer is ... the guitar player.

3 The singer is ... the guitar player.

4 The guitar player is ... the singer.

5 The guitar player is ... the singer.

6 The guitar player is ... the singer.

▸ Page 78

More practice 5 **Good, better, best!**

Write three sentences and compare the kinds of music, films and shows.
The words in the box can help you.

bad • boring • cool • exciting • fast • good • interesting • relaxing • slow

A classical rock electro

I think electro is cooler than classical, but rock is the coolest.

B acoustic pop rap
C action films cartoons sci-fi films

▸ Page 80

Parallel exercise **2** LISTENING **Where do I go next?**

b) Sunita is helping Finn with the game. Where does he need to go?
Listen and choose the correct words.

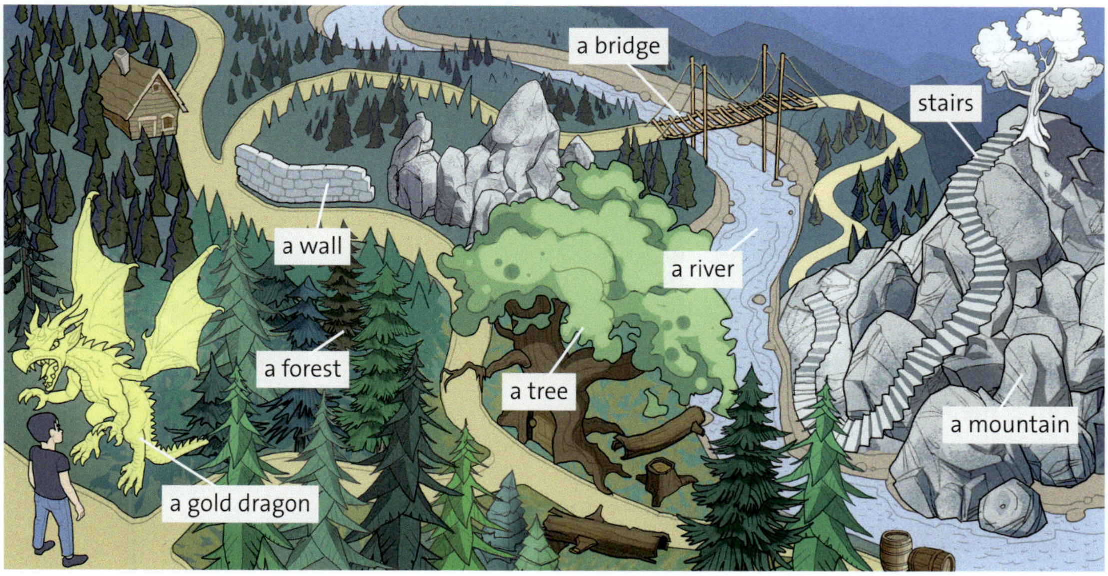

To find the key, Finn must go through the (1) house/forest and turn left at the big (2) tree/bridge. He goes straight on, past a small (3) house/wall and then turns (4) left/right. He goes across the (5) forest/bridge and then up the (6) stairs/tree on the (7) mountain/wall.

▸ Page 80

More practice 6 Scout's sandwich

Help Scout get to the sandwich. Complete the directions.

Scout, you need to go (1) ... and then turn (2) ... at the grey bin. Go (3) ... the family with the dog, turn (4) ... at the sandcastle and it's (5) ... the green bin.

More practice 7 Where do I go?

Match the prepositions in the box to the pictures.

across • down • into • past • through • up

1 ... the stairs

2 ... the stairs

3 ... the tree

4 ... the road

5 ... the forest

6 ... the shop

▸ Page 81

More practice 8 At a shop

Finn wants to buy some more gaming equipment. Make his conversation better. Change repeated nouns to *one* or *ones*.

Finn Look at these gamepads! Which gamepad do you like best, Sunita?
Sunita I think the black gamepad looks cool, but I like the big grey gamepad too.
Finn Me too. That's my favourite gamepad. And I need some headphones! Which headphones do you have?
Sunita I have blue headphones, but I really want some red headphones.

More help 4 MY TASK Game designer

a) Use this map for your game.

▸ Page 84

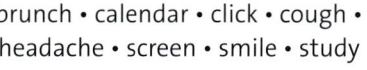

More practice 9 Words in the story

brunch • calendar • click • cough • headache • screen • smile • study

Write the words for the pictures.

Unit 4
Celebrate!

1 Listening Celebrations in Britain

a) Before you listen **Choose a photo. What can you see? Your partner guesses: A–D.**

I can see	different colours • fireworks • food • a parade • ...
People are	eating • throwing powder • wearing masks • ...

b) **Listen and match the names 1–4 to the photos A–D.**

1 Notting Hill Carnival
2 Holi (Festival of colours)
3 Eid al-Fitr (Festival of breaking the fast)
4 Guy Fawkes Night

► More practice 1, p.123

Nach dieser Unit kann ich ...

- über Feste sprechen
- ein Festessen beschreiben
- über Festvorbereitungen und Familienfeiern sprechen
- Präsentationen planen und üben

Unit task

- ein Fest präsentieren

C

D

2 SPEAKING Celebrations where you live

a) THINK **First think of different celebrations. Choose one.**

b) PAIR **Tell a partner about your celebration.**

My celebration is ...	Easter • Halloween • Hanukkah • Christmas • ...
People	wear special clothes • eat nice food • go to a parade • sing songs • ...
There are ...	biscuits • candles • decorations • fireworks • lights • sweets • ...

c) SHARE **Tell the class.**

► More practice 2, p. 123

► Workbook, p. 56

Digital quiz I can **talk about celebrations.**

Special meals

1 Reading Ramadan and Eid al-Fitr

a) Read the conversation and find out: What's Zane's idea?

Noah Hi, Zane! What are you doing this evening?
Zane We're going to have a late dinner. You know, for the month of Ramadan.
Noah I see you aren't fasting.
Zane No, dad fasts, but mum and Holly and I don't fast.
Noah Ah, OK. Can I ask you – is it hard for your dad?
Zane Ha, that's what everyone asks! But it's important to him. And he eats in the morning and at night.
Noah Do you all celebrate Eid al-Fitr?
Zane Yes, we all go to the celebration meal. It's great!
I have an idea – maybe you want to come?
Noah Yes, I'd love to! But Eid al-Fitr isn't just about food, right?
Zane No, it isn't. Dad prays and thanks Allah and he gives money to charity. And children usually get presents from their parents and grandparents.

b) Are these sentences true or false? Correct the false sentences.

1 Zane and his sister don't fast.
2 Fasting is important to Zane's dad.
3 During Ramadan Zane's dad can't eat or drink anything at night.
4 Zane enjoys the celebration meal.
5 Eid al-Fitr is just about food.
6 Children usually get presents from their teachers.

▸ Parallel exercise, p. 123

c) Match the definitions A–E to the words 1–5.

1 dinner	A when you're not sure
2 (to) fast	B (to) talk to god
3 (to) celebrate	C (to) have fun on a special day
4 maybe	D the meal in the evening
5 (to) pray	E when you don't eat food for some time

2 Mediation An invitation to Eid al-Fitr

Read Zane's invitation and complete Finn's message to his dad.

Hi, Lily, Sunita, Noah and Finn!
I'd like to invite you to celebrate Eid al-Fitr with my family and other people in our neighbourhood.
Date: *Sunday 1st May*
Time: *1 p.m.*
Place: *The garden behind the mosque*
We're going to say 'Eid Mubarak' and eat an amazing meal together.
I hope you can come!
Zane

Hallo Papa!
Zane hat mich zum ... eingeladen!
Er feiert mit ...
Das Fest findet am ... um ... im ... statt.
Wir werden ...
Ich freue mich schon darauf!
Grüße aus Brighton
Dein Finn

► Skills file 8, p. 164

3 Listening Before the celebration

a) **Listen. What three topics do Zane and his friends talk about? Choose from the box.**

charity • clothes • food • games • Zane's invitation

b) **Listen again and choose the correct answers.**

1 Don't bring some / any food.
2 There isn't some / any pork.
3 The vegetarian dish is rice with some / any vegetables in it.
4 There are salads, bread and some / any cake too.
5 People can buy some / any food or toys or clothes.

4 Looking at language *some / any*

Erklär-film

Look at these sentences and the picture. Choose the correct words in blue and find the rule.

People can buy some toys. Don't bring any food.

Du benutzt *some*
– in bejahten / verneinten Sätzen,
– wenn du jemandem etwas anbietest,
– wenn du um etwas bittest.
In bejahten / verneinten Sätzen verwendest du *any*.

► More practice 3 + 4, p. 124 ► Language file 12, p. 179

Would you like some chips?
Yes, please. Can I have some fish too?

► Workbook, p. 57

5 Reading At the cafe

a) Before you read What kind of food and drink do you have at a cafe?

b) Zane is helping his dad with a shopping list for his cafe.
Match Zane's answers A–F to his dad's questions 1–6.

1 OK, Zane. How much coffee is there?
2 What about cake?
How much cake is there?
3 OK. And how much sugar is there?
4 How many lemons do we have?
5 How many packets of bread are left?
I sold lots of sandwiches yesterday.
6 OK, and finally, how many bottles of milk?

A There's only a little sugar left, Dad.
B Let's see – one, two three. Only a few, Dad!
Three lemons.
C Milk? Only a few bottles of milk left, Dad.
You need to buy almost everything!
D There's only a little coffee, Dad.
Put that on the list.
E There's only a little cake left.
Wait! Here are four more cakes.
There's a lot of cake, Dad.
F Only a few packets.
It looks like two packets of bread.

c) What do they have a lot of at the cafe?

► More practice 5, p. 125 ► Language file 13, p. 179

6 Speaking What would you like?

a) Everyone is at the Eid al-Fitr meal and Zane is giving food to Noah.
Complete the conversation with words from the box.

enjoy • have • here • of • please • some • thanks

Zane Would you like (1) ... potato curry?
Noah Yes, (2) ...
I'd like some rice and some yoghurt too.
Zane OK, (3) ... you are.
Would you like a lamb kebab?
Noah No, (4) ...
Could I have a little salad please?
Zane (5) ... course. What about some fruit?
Noah Yes, please. May I (6) ... some melon?
Zane Yes, here you are. (7) ... your meal!

b) Listen and check.

c) Practise the conversation.
Then change the words in blue and practise it again.

► More practice 6, p. 125 ► Wordbank 7, p. 191

► Workbook, p. 58

My task

7 An invitation to a special meal

a) **Read the invitation. What kind of meal is it?**

Hi Charlie!
I'd like to invite you to dinner at my home
for a special German meal.
We're going to have some 'Käsespätzle' –
it's a kind of pasta dish. There's a lot of cheese
with onions in it. We eat it with salad.
For dessert we're going to eat apple cake
with cream. It's my grandma's recipe.
I hope you can come!
Sasha

b) **You want to invite an English exchange student to a special meal at your home. Change the words in blue in the invitation. You can use the ideas in the box or your own ideas. Look up new words in a dictionary.**

It's a kind of	pasta • rice • vegetable • meat • ...	dish.	
It's a	hot • cold • German • vegetarian • ...	meal • dish.	
There's	a little • a lot of • ...	cheese • cream • fruit • sauce • ...	in it.
We eat it with	bread • cheese • potatoes • rice • salad • yoghurt • ...		
It's	my favourite food • a family recipe • ...		

▸ Wordbank 7, p. 191

c) **Check your writing.**

– Does your invitation have all the information?
– Are your descriptions of the food clear?
– Is your spelling correct? (You can check in the *Dictionary* on pages 234–249 or in an online dictionary.)

d) GALLERY WALK **Put all the invitations on the wall or on your desks and read them. Which meal sounds best? Tell the class.**

▸ Digital help ▸ Skills file 3, p. 159

Digital quiz I can describe a special meal.

Meera ♥ Ben

1 LISTENING A big celebration

a) BEFORE YOU LISTEN **Look at the title of this topic. Who are Meera and Ben? What celebration do you think Sunita and Lily are discussing?**

a birthday • Christmas • a festival • a new job • a new pet • a wedding

b) **Listen and check your idea.**

c) **Listen again. Choose the correct answers.**

1 Sunita has / doesn't have new clothes for the celebration.
2 Lily, Zane and Noah can / can't come to the celebration.
3 Sunita is / isn't going to ask her mum if Finn can come.
4 Sunita wants an idea for decorations / a surprise for her mum and Ben.
5 Lily talks about the presentation / song on Zane's birthday.
6 Lily, Zane and Noah can help with the wedding / presentation.

2 READING Sunita's surprise

a) BEFORE YOU READ **Can you remember what Sunita's surprise for Ben and Meera is?**

I think her surprise is ...

b) **Read Sunita and Willow's conversation. Sunita needs to do two things. What are they?**

Willow How's your present for Meera and dad?
Sunita Good! I've thought of some nice stories, and I've found photos of mum and Ben.
Willow Have you made the slide show?
Sunita Yes, I have. But I still haven't found any good music. And I'm feeling nervous because I haven't practised the presentation.

3 Getting ready

a) Partner B: You're Nish. Look at p. 122.
Partner A: You're Sunita. Tell Nish what you've done.

I haven't found any clothes for the wedding yet.
And I haven't finished my presentation.
I've invited my friends.
But I haven't got the invitations from mum yet.
I've bought a present for mum and Ben.
But I haven't made a card yet.

b) Your partner is Nish and tells you what he has done.

c) Now compare the sentences one by one. Take notes.
What have Sunita and Nish done?

Sunita and Nish have …

4 Have you ever …?

a) Choose four of these questions.

Have you ever	been to Turkey? eaten chips with cheese? had an amazing dream? seen a lion? met a famous person? given money to charity? swum in the sea? won a competition?

Have you ever …?
Yes, I have.
No, I haven't.

b) Ask your partner your questions and take notes.
Answer your partner's questions.

c) Tell the class one thing about your partner:

Sofia has swum in the sea.

Behzad has met a famous person.

► More practice 7 + 8, p. 126
► Language file 14–15, pp. 180–181

► Workbook, pp. 59–60

5 Reading Sunita's family

a) **Willow calls Sunita. Who is at Sunita's house?**

Willow Hi, Sunita. Have your grandparents arrived from India?
Sunita Yes, they have. They've just got here. They're very tired.
Willow Has your family from Birmingham come too?
Sunita Yes, my aunt and uncle and cousins are here. Our house is full of people!
Willow Isn't that nice?
Sunita Well, I can't watch TV. There are too many people in the living room. And Nish and I have to help mum with the chores. But I have to finish my presentation soon! I still have to find one more story about mum.
Willow You can ask your grandparents. But they mustn't tell your mum about the surprise.
Sunita Good idea! Oh, my cousins want to play with me again. Don't laugh, Willow! They're going to be your cousins soon.

b) **Complete the sentences with words from the box.**

Birmingham • grandparents • India • isn't • tired • Willow

1 Sunita's grandparents have arrived from ...
2 It's a long trip and they're ...
3 Sunita's aunt, uncle and cousins have arrived from ...
4 Sunita ... happy that her house is full.
5 Sunita's ... can give her one more story for the presentation.
6 ... is going to have more people in her family soon.

► Parallel exercise, p.126

6 Lots of chores

With so many guests in the house, there's a big list of chores for Meera, Sunita and Nish.

I have to do it. = *Ich muss es tun.*
I don't have to do it. = *Ich brauche es nicht zu tun.*
! I mustn't do it. = *Ich darf es nicht tun.*

a) **Read the list and complete the sentences with *has to* or *have to*.**

1 Nish and Sunita ... tidy their rooms.
2 Nish ... help mum with the cooking.
3 Sunita ... vacuum the living room.
4 Meera ... make the beds.

b) **Now complete the sentences with *doesn't have to* or *don't have to*.**

1 Nish and Sunita ... clean the bathroom.
2 Sunita ... take out the rubbish.
3 Nish and Sunita ... go shopping.
4 Nish ... set the table.

Nish
- tidy his room
- help mum with the cooking
- play with his cousins
- take out the rubbish

Sunita
- tidy her room
- vacuum the living room
- set the table
- play with her cousins

Meera
- go shopping
- make the beds
- clean the bathroom

► Workbook, pp. 61–62

7 Reading A small family

a) **Read Willow's diary. What's the best heading? Pick A, B or C.**

A Getting married B Big and small families C I don't like my family

When I was little, I had a small family. It was just me, my mum and my dad. Small families are OK, I guess. You have to enjoy being alone sometimes. It can be very quiet and you may be lonely sometimes, but at least you don't have to share things with your family. But you mustn't think that it's all bad! I like being alone, and I can spend all day in my own room alone.
But soon my dad is going to get married. Then Meera, Sunita and Nish and all their aunts, uncles and cousins are going to be my family too. No more small family for me!

b) **True or false?**

1 When Willow was a child, she had a big family.
2 She thinks small families are OK.
3 Willow has her own room.
4 She doesn't like being alone.
5 Willow's dad is going to get married next year.
6 Sunita is going to be Willow's stepsister soon.

My task

8 Speaking Big and small families

a) **What's better: Living in a big or a small family? Talk about it with your group.**

A big family A small family	is good isn't so good	because	you're never alone. it's lonely / boring. it's always quiet / loud. you have to share the TV / ... you can't talk to different people. ...
In a big family In a small family		you	mustn't use the bathroom for too long. may be lonely sometimes. can spend more time with your parents. can't have your own room.

b) **What about your family: Is it big or small? What's good or bad about it? Write at least four sentences. You can put your text in your Dossier.**

My family is ... I think a ... family is good because ...

▶ Digital help

▶ Workbook, p. 62

Digital quiz I can talk about big and small families.

Family celebrations

1 Listening Ben and Willow's song

a) Before you listen **It's the day before the wedding. What can you see in the picture? Tell your partner.**

I can see ...
Ben is playing ...
... are listening.
... is smiling.

b) **Listen to the song and answer the questions.**

1 What are Ben and Willow singing about?
2 Is it a happy or a sad song?

c) Words **Look at the song text and find:**

1 three family members
2 three words that mean 'really good'
3 three pairs of words that rhyme

d) **What do you think about the song? Tell your partner.**

I think it's boring / cool / fun / ...
I like / don't like the music / rap / words / ...

► Skills file 6, p. 162

The day that I've waited for

I have something to say, but it isn't easy.
I hope it doesn't sound too cheesy,

but I'm feeling over the moon
'cause we're getting married soon.
And I don't think that anyone
could be a better stepdaughter or stepson.
And someone amazing is gonna be my wife,
so that's why this is gonna be
the best day of my life!

It's the day that I've waited for.
I have everything I want and more.
There's nowhere else I wanna be
than right here with my new family
on this day that I've waited for.

Is everyone ready to throw that confetti?
I feel like I've joined the family already.
I can't wait to celebrate this awesome date.
Dad, don't be late!
Ha, don't worry – it's gonna be great!

It's the day that I've waited for ...

2 At the sangeet celebration

Later that evening Sunita told her friends what happened at the sangeet. Choose the correct words.

Today was sangeet, the first day of the wedding celebrations. It's a tradition for many Indian families. (1) Everyone / Anything did a song, poem or dance. It was so fun! After Ben's song (2) someone / everywhere from his family gave a nice talk. I didn't want to sing (3) someone / anything, but I prepared my robot Robbie to do a special dance! After that, (4) everybody / everything ate Ben's delicious meal. Then our parrot George flew onto the table! He knocked (5) everything / everywhere over – there was food (6) everywhere / everybody! I think this was my favourite family party! What about you?

► Language file 16, p.181 ► More practice 9, p.127

My task

3 Family parties

a) **Think of a family party (or a dream party) from the past. Make notes.** ► Skills file 5, p.161

b) **Write about your party. Answer the questions below and write at least five sentences.**

What kind of party was it?
It was a barbecue / garden party / disco / ...
What did the party celebrate?
We celebrated my father's birthday / my sister's new school / my mother's new job / my aunt's wedding / Christmas / ...
Where was at the party?
It was at home / in a hall / at a restaurant / at my grandma's house / ...
What did you do?
Everyone danced / ate cake / watched fireworks / played games/ sang karaoke / wore special clothes / ...
How was it? – *I had a great time / It was so fun! / It was the best party ever! / ...*

► More help, p.127

c) WALK AROUND **Hang up the texts in the classroom. Walk around and read the texts. Which party sounds the most fun to you? Put a post next to your favourite party.**

Your party sounds great!

► Digital help

► Workbook, pp.63–64

Digital quiz I can **talk about family celebrations.**

The big day

1 Reading What's going to happen?

a) Before you read **Look at these questions and say what you think.**

- Are clothes important at a wedding?
- Is it important to be on time for a wedding or is it OK to be late?
- Who feels calm at a wedding? Who feels excited?

b) **Now read the story and find out: Was Ben on time for the wedding?**

It's 9 o'clock on Saturday morning and everyone is excited because it's Ben and Meera's big day!

Sunita is helping her mum put on her beautiful red wedding dress.

"Mum," says Sunita, looking worried. "Have you talked to Ben today? You know he's often late."

Meera smiles. "Yes, I have. Don't worry, Sunita. It's all going to be fine." "OK," says Sunita.

Willow is helping her dad put on his tie. "Do I look OK?" he asks. "I haven't worn a suit and a tie for a long time!"

"OK, I'm almost ready," says Ben. "I just need to put on my shoes."

"Great, Dad," smiles Willow. "I have a surprise for you. Look out of the window."

Ben looks down at the street. "You've decorated our bikes! Oh, Willow, they're perfect, thank you!" But then two men walk over to their bikes.

"What are they doing with our bikes?" asks Willow.

You look amazing!

You look amazing!

"Hey! Stop!" Ben says. They run down the stairs, but the men have left – with the bikes!

"They've taken our bikes!" says Willow.

Just then, they hear the front door close behind them.

"The door!" says Ben. "My keys are still in the flat. We can't go back in. Our phones are still in the flat too, so we can't call for help."

Willow looks down at Ben's feet. "And that's not all, Dad – your shoes are in the flat too. You're still wearing your slippers!"

"And it's half past nine! We need to go now, or we're going to be late," says Ben.

As they walk, Ben says sadly, "This is terrible! It's a very important day and I'm wearing my slippers. Meera isn't going to be happy ..."

"It's OK, Dad. We're not late!" says Willow. "Look, here's the bandstand. And look at Meera!"

Ben feels happy again when he sees Meera smiling at him. She finds it amazing that he looks so smart – and then she laughs when she sees his slippers!

"Sorry," says Ben. "I can explain later ..."

"Don't worry," laughs Meera. "I'm still going to marry you – in your slippers!"

2 What happened?

Complete the sentences.

1 Sunita was worried that Ben could be ...
2 Ben and Meera looked ...
3 Two men took the ...
4 Ben and Willow left their keys and ... in the flat.
5 Ben wore ...
6 When Meera saw Ben, she ...

► Parallel exercise, p. 127 ► Skills file 7, p. 163

3 Words in the text

Find the words in the story with these meanings.

1 a jacket and trousers (line 14)
2 you use them to go from the ground floor to the top floor (line 27)
3 the things that you need to open doors (line 32)
4 shoes that you wear inside (line 37)
5 what people look like when they are wearing very nice clothes (line 47)

► Skills file 11, p. 167

4 A multicultural wedding

Choose a person in the picture and describe them. Your partner points.

– *She's wearing a yellow and blue sari. / She's wearing a yellow dress and a red scarf. / He's wearing a purple shirt.*
– *That's Meera / Sunita / this man here / ...*

5 LIFE SKILLS Sharing things from all over the world

a) **Meera and Ben share Indian and British traditions in their wedding.**
Do you share things from different countries and cultures in your life?

I eat Turkish and Chinese food. I listen to American music. I watch Japanese cartoons.

Ideas
- food
- music
- celebrations
- films
- clothes
- ...

b) **Compare your ideas with the class.**

► Workbook, p. 65

Digital quiz I can talk about different cultures in my life.

Brighton stories: Family and heritage[1]

1 Before you watch What's a lie?

A lie is when you don't tell the truth. Have you ever told a lie? Tell your partner about an example from your life.

I told a lie last week / month / ... It was about a party / a friend / a test / ...

2 Viewing Two truths and a lie

a) **Watch the first part of the video. Look at the sentences for Gloria, Emir and Daisy. Which sentence is a lie?**

Gloria
1 Her dad is from Jamaica.
2 Her parents met in a skating club.
3 Her mum is a hairdresser[2].

Emir
1 His sister only eats yellow foods.
2 His mum has a tattoo on her foot.
3 His dad is Kurdish.

Daisy
1 Her great-great-grand-mother's name was Daisy.
2 Daisy and her mum both have blue eyes.
3 All her family have always lived in Brighton.

b) **Watch the ending again. Put the pictures in the correct order.**

A

a boat

B

a fish and chip shop

C
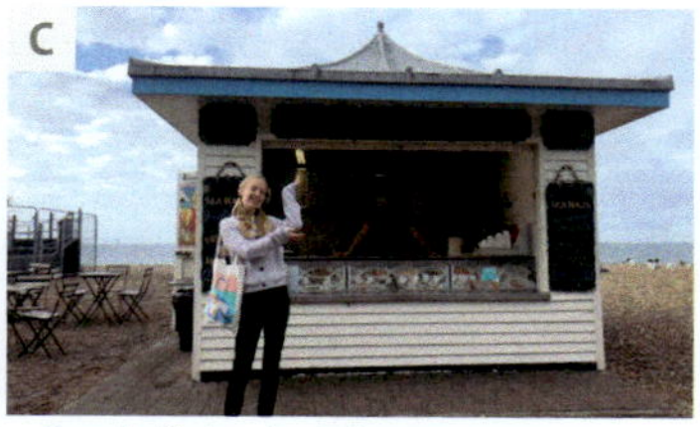
a fresh fish store[3]

D

a sweet shop

E

a museum

F

Pavilion Gardens

3 Now you

a) **Play the *Two truths and a lie*-game. Write three sentences about your family for your partner. One must be a lie.** *My family are ... My sister's hobby is ... My brother's favourite sport is ...*

b) **Read out your sentences to your partner. He or she guesses the lie!**

[1] **heritage** *die Herkunft, das Erbe* [2] **hairdresser** *der Friseur/die Friseurin* [3] **fresh fish store** *das Fischgeschäft*

Prepare and practise a presentation

1 Collect ideas

Finn has collected these ideas for a presentation. What is it about?

every summer in and around Dresden · along the River Elbe · tickets not too expensive · lots of exciting activities, shows, music concert · big festival (Elbhangfest) · great food

2 Prepare your slides

a) **Look at Finn's slides and read Scout's tip. Why is slide 1 better than slide 2?**

Write short notes and a big title.
Choose big pictures.

1 *Elbhangfest*
- big festival
- every summer
- in and around Dresden
- along the River Elbe

2
- There are lots of exciting activities, shows and great music concerts.
- You can eat lots of great food too.
- Tickets are not too expensive.

b) **Make a new slide 2 for Finn.**

3 Make cards with short notes for each slide

Match Finn's notes to slides 1 and 2 and write his two cards.

on three days · all kinds of music: rock, pop, punk, classical, jazz · art markets · free tickets if you're under 18 · on the streets, in churches, parks and in castle Pillnitz · theatre shows, street dance competitions, parades · food from all over the world

4 Practise, practise, practise

a) **Read the tips in the box. Which four tips are helpful?**

b) **Present Finn's two slides. Try to talk freely. Practise with a partner and take turns. Give your partner feedback.**

Great job. Try to speak loudly and clearly.

Ideas
1 Make cards with notes for each slide.
2 Look at your cards all the time.
3 Speak loudly and clearly.
4 Don't smile.
5 Practise in front of a mirror at home.
6 Record your presentation and watch it.

▸ Wordbank 8, p. 192 ▸ Skills file 9, pp. 165–166
▸ Let's talk: Giving feedback, p. 199

Digital quiz I can prepare and practise a presentation.

Present a celebration

Step 1: Think of a celebration

Think of a celebration.
The ideas in the box can help you.

a family birthday • your birthday • Christmas • a festival • a school party • Halloween

Step 2: Plan

Make a list of ideas for your presentation.
Then put them in order for your slide show.

It's a festival. We celebrate it every year at … /

What? • Where? • When? • special clothes • decorations • food • music • traditions

Step 3: Your slides and cards

a) Make your slides, then write your cards with short notes.

b) Check this list. Have you …

- put pictures on your slides?
- put a big title on each slide?
- used short notes on your slides and cards?
- checked the spelling?

► Wordbank 8, p. 192 ► Skills file 9, pp. 165–166

Step 4: Practise your presentation

Practise your presentation with a partner. Give feedback.

*Great job!
But the pictures are very small.*

I liked your slides, but please don't just read your text. Talk freely.

Step 5: Present your celebration

Think of the feedback in step 4 and present your celebration in a group.

► Digital help

Digital quiz I can present a celebration.

1 Listening A winter celebration

I can talk about celebrations.

a) Before you listen Look at Zane's photo. What is he celebrating?

Halloween | Bonfire night | a birthday

b) Now listen. What do Finn and Zane talk about? Choose three topics from the box.

clothes • food • games • history • music • weather

c) Listen again. Choose the correct answers.

1 Zane's photo is from A October B November.
2 Finn A doesn't know anything B knows quite a lot about Bonfire Night.
3 Zane A always B sometimes celebrates at the same park.
4 Zane usually celebrates with A his friends B his mum, dad and sister.
5 When the weather is really cold, Zane A stays at home B still celebrates.

d) Speaking What do you celebrate in the winter? Tell your partner about it. You can use the ideas below.

I celebrate Christmas / Diwali / my dad's birthday / ... • We eat ... • I wear ...

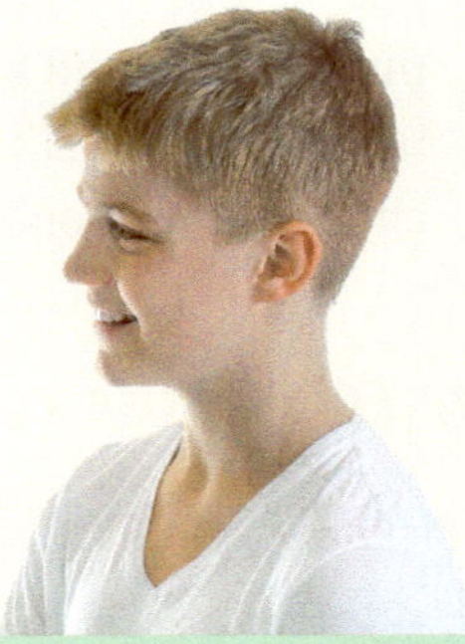

I don't celebrate ..., but I celebrate ... • I also celebrate ... • We eat ... • I wear ...

2 Language On the phone

I can describe a special meal (some and any).

Complete the sentences with *some* and *any*.

Caller Hi, we'd like (1) ... pizzas, please: one four cheeses, two vegetarian and two ham and tomatoes. Please can we also get (2) ... chips?
Restaurant Sure! Would you like (3) ... sauces? And would you like (4) ... drinks?
Caller We don't want (5) ... drinks, thank you. But we'd like (6) ... mayo.
Restaurant Great. You can pick it up in half an hour.

3 MEDIATION A message from Leon

Read the message from Finn's friend Leon in Dresden. Answer Sunita's questions in English.

Hey Finn, tut mir leid, aber ich kann heute doch nicht mit dir und Sunita am Computer spielen. Meine Familie organisiert ein besonderes Essen für meine Schwester, da sie für einen Monat nach Frankreich fährt. Wir machen ein Picknick mit all ihren Lieblingsgerichten – ein Hühnercurry, ein Salat (ohne Tomaten!), verschiedene Käsesorten und Brot. Danach gibt's Obst mit Joghurt. Morgen Abend habe ich Zeit, oder am Wochenende. Wie sieht's bei euch aus? Bis dann, Leon

Sunita	Is Leon going to play with us tonight?
Finn	He can't any more because his family is organizing (1) ...
Sunita	Ah, OK. Is it his sister's birthday?
Finn	No, his sister is going (2) ...
Sunita	What are they going to eat?
Finn	They're going to have a picnic with (3) ...
Sunita	Sounds nice! Can he play another time?
Finn	Yes, he can play (4) ...

4 LANGUAGE A conversation about families

Complete the conversation. Choose the correct verb.

I can talk about big and small families (can / have to / mustn't).

Teacher	Today we're talking about big and small families. What's good about them? And what do you think is bad? Tell me your ideas.
Zadie	Small families are quieter than big families. I don't like it when it's too loud, because then I (1) can / can't relax!
Sunita	OK, but in a big family, you (2) have to / don't have to worry about being alone because you (3) can / can't always find somebody to talk to.
Zadie	That's true, but in a big family, you (4) have to / don't have to share everything! Your room, your clothes, the TV, the bathroom ...
Pratik	And in a big family you (5) have to / mustn't put chocolate or sweets on your desk You (6) have to / don't have to eat it before your brothers and sisters do!

5 Reading Welcome to Brighton!

I can talk about family celebrations.

1 LILY *Hey, guys. I've had a busy afternoon. Check out the garden area near our flat.*

SUNITA *Love it!! 😍 Are you having a party?*

2 LILY *Yes, my aunt and uncle are coming to stay with us, so we're having a surprise welcome party. Their last visit was years ago because they live in Poland. My family is going to be there and we want to invite some neighbours too.*

ZANE *That's really cool. Surprise parties are the best. How are they going to find out about the party?*

3 LILY *Well, dad is going to meet them at the train station and then he's going to take them back to the flat. Then he's going to say, "Oh no, I can't find my key! I think I left it in the garden area." When they get there, we're going to jump up and say, "Welcome to Brighton!" I hope we don't scare them too much!*

ZANE *Great! You should take a photo of that moment!*

NOAH *Have you made a cake, Lily?*

4 LILY *My sister Chloe is going to make a cake. My job is to decorate the garden. And I need to find some good music.*

SUNITA *Oh, for a disco?*

5 LILY *Yes! We're going to have a quiet disco. We want to dance, but our party should be quiet!*

NOAH *Have a great time, Lily!*

a) Read the messages about Lily's party. True, false or not in the text?

1 Lily's aunt and uncle have never been to Brighton.
2 Lily's dad is going to tell them about the party.
3 The party is going to be in the flat.
4 Noah doesn't like surprise parties.
5 Lily is going to choose some songs.
6 Lily's party is going to be very loud.

b) Words Complete the sentences with words from Lily's messages (1–4).

1 When someone doesn't know about a party, it's a ... (message 2)
2 When you ask someone to come to a party, you ... him/her. (message 2)
3 When you don't know where something is, you can't ... it (message 3)
4 When you make someone feel shocked and worried, you ... him/her. (message 3)
5 When you make a place look nice, you ... it. (message 4)

6 Writing A special thing

I can talk about different cultures in my life.

Your English class is doing a project about different countries and cultures.
Write a short text for the project about a special thing from another country.

a) Make notes. You can use the ideas in the boxes.

What is it?
a book • a letter • a photo • a magazine • a song • a T-shirt • ...

Where's it from?
America • England • France • Japan • Poland • Turkey • ...

Why is it special?
beautiful • expensive • old • a present • ...

b) Write your post. You can start like this:

I'd like to tell you about a special thing ...

7 Study skills My dream festival

I can prepare and practise a presentation.

Zeynep has made the first slide and a card with keywords for her presentation.

1 FunFest
• small garden party
• 1st August
• cool activities
1
– about 40 people (friends and family)
– under trees – perfect when hot
– on (!) the (!) first of (!) August
– We usually do these activities:
– dance competition ("competISCHen")
– yoga
– henna design

a) Present Zeynep's first slide to your partner. Then swap roles.

b) Give feedback. You can use the ideas below.

You looked ...	at me.	at your cards.
You ...	smiled.	didn't smile.
You talked ...	clearly / loudly.	too quietly / fast / slowly.
Your pictures ...	were very good.	were too small.

VARNDEAN Teen Zine

Our school magazine: by students for students

This month's topics: celebrations and food

Burning[1] the clocks

Every year there's a special celebration in Brighton: the *Burning the Clocks* festival.

It's on 21st December, the shortest day of the year. From now on the days will be longer and there will be more light. People celebrate this with paper lanterns. There are parades and music, and lots of people wear special clothes too.

Kieron in 8B says, "It's so much fun to go with my friends. I love the lights and, of course, drinking hot chocolate to keep warm!"

What's the best part of the festival? At the end everybody goes to the beach and puts their lanterns on a big fire. Then there's an amazing firework show.

Don't forget to send us your photos this year!

English breakfasts

Check out this video.
What's your favourite breakfast?

[1] (to) **burn** *(ver)brennen*

Varndean students' special meals

Sarah: *For Hanukkah my grandma makes these amazing latkes – they're special potato pancakes and we eat them with apple sauce.*

Mei-Lin: *My dad is a great cook. He makes the best Chinese food! His special rice with chicken, egg and vegetables is the best!*

Joke time

B Knock knock!
A Who's there?
B Donut!
A Donut who?
B I donut know! You tell me!

Languages at Varndean

What languages do Varndean students and teachers speak?

Turkish
Hindi
French
Urdu
Spanish
Polish
English
Arabic
Romanian
German
Mandarin
Bengali

Can you make a language cloud for your class?

E-postcard from the USA

This month Lea writes about American food.

Hi, everyone! I miss British food sometimes (especially fish and chips on the beach), but wow – the food here is amazing! People eat food from lots of different cultures – not just burgers! I think my favourite is Mexican food. There's a small restaurant near our house which sells the best tacos and guacamole ever!

American restaurants are a bit different to British ones. When you walk in the restaurant, you have to wait until they show you your table. You usually get free water with lots of ice. And it's very important to give the waiter or waitress some extra money, called a 'tip'.

Have a good day!
Lea

Partner Page

▸ Page 105

3 Getting ready

Partner B

a) You're Nish. Listen to Sunita.

b) Now tell Sunita what you've done.

I've found some nice clothes for the wedding.
But I haven't got a tie yet.
I've invited my girlfriend.
But I haven't talked to her about it yet.
I've found some great music for the wedding.
I've bought a present for mum and Ben.

c) Now compare the sentences one by one.
What have Sunita and Nish done?

Sunita and Nish have ...

Diff bank

▸ Page 98

More practice 1 Which celebration is it?

Listen again and complete the sentences with the names in ex. 1b) on p. 98.

1 ... celebrates the start of spring.
2 After Ramadan people celebrate ... with a big meal.
3 The ... has an amazing parade every year.
4 On ... people celebrate a special day in British history.

▸ Page 99

More practice 2 Celebration words

balloons • candle • flags • fire • fireworks • parade • present • special clothes

a) **Match the pictures A–H to the words in the box.**

A

B

C

D

E

F

G

H

b) **Start a 'celebrations' page in your VOCAB FILE. Decide how to organize it: You can make lists, a mind map or write example sentences. Add more words from the unit.**

▸ Page 100

Parallel exercise 1 READING Ramadan and Eid al-Fitr

b) **Complete the sentences.**

1 Zane and his sister do / don't fast.
2 Fasting is important to Zane's dad / mum.
3 During Ramadan Zane's dad can't eat or drink anything at night / during the day.
4 Zane enjoys / doesn't enjoy the celebration meal.
5 Eid al-Fitr is / isn't just about food.
6 Children usually get presents from their teachers / family.

▸ Page 101

☒ More practice 3 **Ready for Eid al-Fitr**

Zane and his family are getting ready for the Eid al-Fitr meal. Choose the correct words.

Mum Zane, would you like (1) some / any water?
Zane No, thanks, Mum. I still have (2) some / any juice.
Holly Mum, can I have (3) some / any chocolate?
Mum No, you can't have (4) some / any food before the meal, Holly.
Zane Dad, I don't have (5) some / any money.
Dad I can give you (6) some / any money, Zane.

☒ More practice 4 **Thanks, Black Bird!**

Look at the picture. What does Scout say to Black Bird? Choose the correct words.

What would you like, Scout?

1 I'd like some / any sausages – not many, two or three.
2 I'd like some / any orange juice, please.
3 I don't want some / any salad. I don't like salad.
4 The fruit looks nice – I'd like some / any strawberries. A lot of strawberries, please.
5 And can I have a some / any cheese? Not much.
6 And I'd like some / any cake – lots of cake! I love cake!

▸ Page 102

More practice 5 How much ... is there?

Read the conversation again. Then complete the table with the words from the box.

Dad OK, Zane. How much coffee is there?
Zane There's only a little coffee, Dad. Put that on the list.
Dad What about cake? How much cake is there?
Zane There's only a little cake left. Wait! Here are four more cakes. There's a lot of cake, Dad.
Dad OK. And how much sugar is there?
Zane There's only a little sugar left, Dad.
Dad How many lemons do we have?
Zane Let's see – one, two three. Only a few, Dad! Three lemons.
Dad How many packets of bread are left? I sold lots of sandwiches yesterday.
Zane Only a few packets. It looks like two packets of bread.
Dad OK, and finally, how many bottles of milk?
Zane Milk? Only a few bottles of milk left, Dad. You need to buy almost everything!

a little	a few
coffee	
...	

bottles of milk • cake • ~~coffee~~ • lemons • packets of bread • sugar

More practice 6 Zane's dad is buying some cake

What is Zane's dad buying today? One student starts. The next student repeats the first thing and adds another thing. Add more and more things – as many as you can!

Zane's dad is buying some sugar.
Zane's dad is buying some sugar and coffee.
Zane's dad is buying some sugar, coffee and ...

▸ Page 105

More practice 7 Run and say

a) Your teacher has put some sentences on the walls. Partner A runs to a sentence, tries to remember it and then tells Partner B. Partner B writes the sentence on a piece of paper. Go on with the next sentence and take turns with each sentence.

b) Together, put the sentences in the correct order and then practise the conversation.

That's a cool activity! You can cut the paper into pieces and move the sentences around!

More practice 8 Have you ever ever …?

Look at the words of a traditional English children's song.
Listen and sing.

Have you ever, ever, ever,
in your long-legged life,
Seen a long-legged sailor
with a long-legged wife?
No, I've never, never, never
in my long-legged life,
Seen a long-legged sailor
with a long-legged wife.

▸ Page 106

Parallel exercise 5 READING Sunita's family

b) Choose the correct answers.

1 Sunita's grandparents have arrived from Birmingham / India.
2 It's a long trip and they're tired / sad.
3 Sunita's aunt, uncle and cousins have arrived from Birmingham / India.
4 Sunita is / isn't happy that her house is full.
5 Sunita's grandparents / cousins can give her one more story for the presentation.
6 Willow / Sunita is going to have more people in her family soon.

▸ Page 109

More practice 9 I've looked everywhere!

Choose the correct words to complete Scout's story.

Oh no, I've looked (1) everywhere / somebody, but I can't find my invitation to the party. (2) Someone / Anything must have seen it! It must be here (3) somewhere / someone. Maybe (4) somebody / everybody has taken it? You see, (5) someone / everywhere has invited me to a party, but I can't remember where it is. And I still need to buy a present! I've looked in lots of shops (6) everywhere / everybody in town, but I couldn't find a good present.

More help 5 Family parties

b) **Read the examples for ideas for your text.**

My sister Chloe had a great barbecue last month. We celebrated the beginning of summer. It was in her garden. Everyone sang karaoke and watched fireworks. I had a great time!

My favourite party was my clown party last year. It was the best birthday party ever! We celebrated in the park. Everyone wore clown clothes and I juggled for everyone.

My family had a disco a few years ago, when my dad opened his cafe. We celebrated in a hall. Everyone danced and ate cake. It was so fun!

▸ Page 111

Parallel exercise 2 What happened?

Match the sentences parts.

1 Sunita was worried that Ben could be ...
2 Ben and Meera looked ...
3 Two men took the ...
4 Ben and Willow left their keys and ... in the flat.
5 Ben wore ...
6 When Meera saw Ben, she ...

A amazing.
B bikes.
C laughed.
D phones
E slippers.
F late.

Unit 5
Getting ready for the future

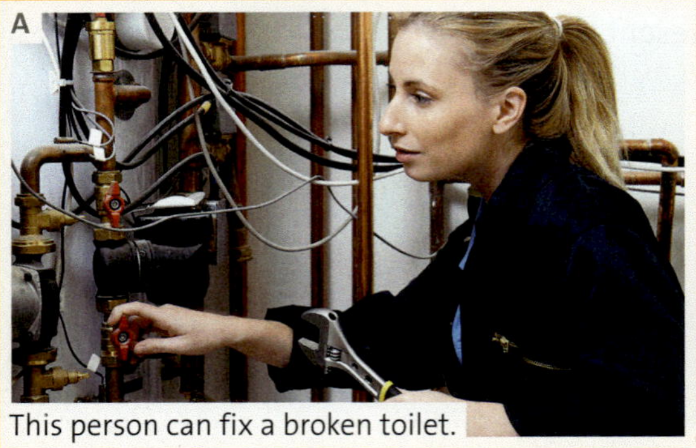

A
This person can fix a broken toilet.

B
This person cuts people's hair.

C
This person stops fires and saves people's lives.

D
This person creates websites, apps or games.

1 Listening **Jobs assembly**

a) Before you listen **Some Varndean parents talked about their jobs at the Year 8 assembly. Look at the photos and read the sentences. Match the jobs to photos A–H.** *A: plumber, ...*

artist • cook • firefighter • hairdresser • mechanic • nurse • plumber • programmer

b) **Listen to the conversation. Put photos A–H in the order that you hear them.**
1 C, 2 ...

▶ More practice 1, p. 151

Nach dieser Unit kann ich ...

- über verschiedene Berufe sprechen
- meine Zukunft beschreiben
- über Arbeiten im Haushalt sprechen
- über Geld und Einkaufen sprechen
- geschriebene Texte überprüfen

Unit task

- Spaß-Horoskope schreiben

E

This person works in a hospital and helps sick people.

F
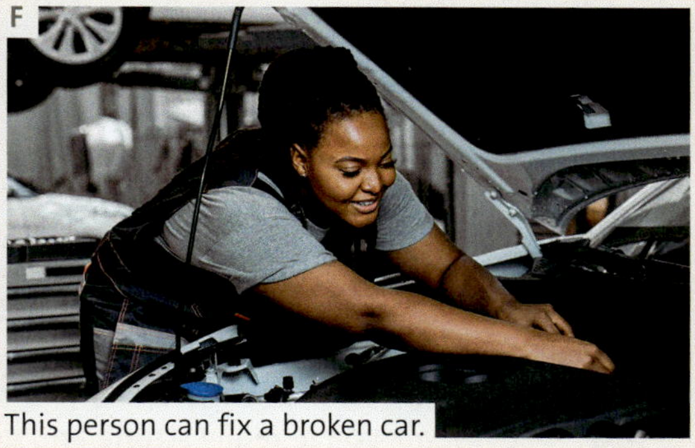
This person can fix a broken car.

G

This person works in a restaurant or cafe and makes delicious food.

H
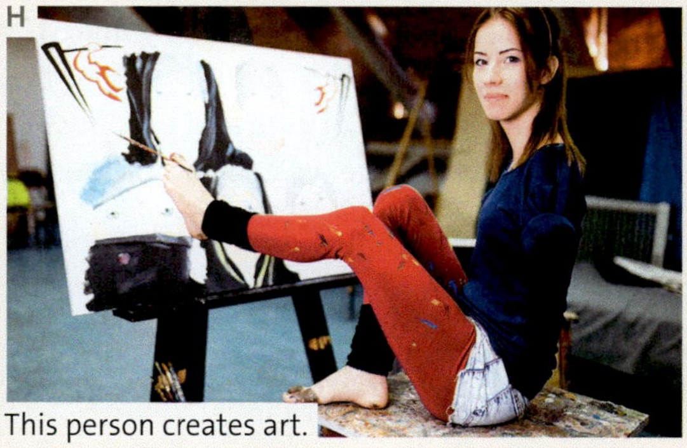
This person creates art.

2 Speaking Jobs

a) **Who do you know with any of the jobs? Tell your partner.**

I know a ...
My cousin / neighbour / ... is a ...
My uncle / friend works in a ...
I don't know anybody with one of these jobs.

Always use *a* or *an* with jobs:
My cousin is a cook.
My mum is an artist.

b) Game **Play in small groups. One student acts out a job. The others guess.**

Are you a ...? Do you work as a ...? – Yes, that's right! / No, that's wrong.

▶ Workbook, p. 72

Digital quiz I can **talk about jobs.**

Future jobs and plans

1 Reading At break

a) **The kids are talking to their friend Ava at school. What do you think they are talking about?**

1 Their parents' jobs
2 The Year 8 assembly about jobs
3 Jobs that they want to do

Lily Hey Ava, how's it going? We're just talking about jobs and the future. What do you want to do?
Ava I think that I want to work for an animal charity. What about you?
Lily I haven't made up my mind yet, but I think I want to be a firefighter like my aunt.
Ava Oh yeah, you're really strong and good at climbing! And you, Noah?
Noah I want to be a vet because I love animals – especially my dog.
Sunita It's a lot of work – ask my mum! I want to be a gamer, so I can play games all day.
Zane Cool! Well, it's no surprise that I want to be a cook. Perhaps I can have my own restaurant or cafe and be a business owner too.
Sunita Well, I hope we can eat for free in your restaurant, Zane!

b) **Read the text again and choose the correct person for each question.**

1 Who wants to work for a charity?
2 Who wants to do the same job as somebody in her family?
3 Who loves his dog?
4 Who knows that being a vet is hard work?
5 Who wants to cook?

2 Words Your future job

a) **What job do you want to do in the future? Look in the Wordbank or in a dictionary for more job words. Copy and complete a secret sentence on a piece of paper:**

I think I want to be a …

▸ Wordbank 9, p. 193 ▸ Skills file 3, p. 159

b) **Your teacher collects all the papers and reads one out. Guess who wrote the sentence. Were you right? Read the next sentence. Were you wrong? Someone else guesses.**

– *I think / Maybe that is …*
– *Yes, you're right. It's me! / No, it's not me. Guess again!*

3 Song Hey, world!

a) Before you listen
Look at the icons and the incomplete words. What are the jobs?

1 *architect*
2 …

a _ _ _ _ _ _ _ t	*bu _ _ _ _ _ s owner*	*f _ _ _ _ _ _ _ _ _ r*

m _ _ _ _ _ _ c	*v _ _*	*wr _ _ _ r*

b) **Listen to the song and write the correct job from a) for each number.**

c) **Look at the song text. Choose the best new title for the song.**

1 I know what I want to be
2 I can do anything
3 I'm scared about my future

d) **True or false?**

The singer …
1 is thinking about the future.
2 doesn't have any friends.
3 is strong.
4 is bad at maths.
5 doesn't want to be an architect.

► Skills file 6, p. 162

Good to know

Lots of jobs end in -er:
(to) sing ► singer
(to) game ► gamer
(to) teach ► teacher

In English you usually use the same words for jobs for men and women.
She's a firefighter.
He's a firefighter.

Hey, world!

In the future maybe I'll be a (1) …
My friends, they won't believe it
when I'm a famous (2) …?
Maybe I'll be a star!
If I work hard, I'll go far.
Or maybe I'll be a (3) … –
I haven't made my mind up yet.

But I'll be, yeah,
I'll be anything I want to be.
So you'll see:
Hey, world – look out for me!

Oh, the girl who's cool
and rules the school –
she'll show me respect
When I'm a (4) … or an (5) …
I'm also strong and good at maths –
I'll make a great (6) …
And if things go wrong sometimes,
I won't panic, no.

'Cause I'll be, yeah,
I'll be anything
I want to be.
Everyone, they'll see:
Hey, world – look out for me!

► Workbook, p. 73

Erklär-
film

4 Looking at language The will-future

a) **Listen to the song from 3 again. Put up your hand when you hear the words *I'll*.**

b) **Look again at these lines from the song in 3. Complete the rules.**

Maybe I'll be a star
I'll be anything I want to be
So you'll see

She'll show me respect
Everyone, they'll see
They won't believe it

Du verwendest das *will-future* um zu sagen, was in der ... wahrscheinlich geschehen wird:
Perhaps Zane will be a cook.

Die Kurzform von *will* ist ... : *You'll see.*

Du bildest diese Zeitform mit ... oder der Kurzform ... und der Grundform des Verbs *(show, see, etc.)*

Wenn du sagen möchtest, was in der Zukunft **nicht** geschehen wird,
verwendest du ... *(= will not)* und die Grundform des Verbs: *They won't believe it.*

!

I will go	=	Ich werde gehen
I *won't* go	=	Ich werde nicht gehen
I want to go	=	Ich will gehen

▶ More practice 2, p. 151 ▶ Language file 17, p. 182

5 Crazy predictions

a) **Write an example of:**

1 a job
2 a city
3 a number
4 a day of the week
5 a name or person
6 a colour

1 firefighter 2 ...

b) **Add your answers to this text and read it to your partner. Who has the funniest prediction?**

You'll be a (1) ... in (2) ... and
you'll earn (3) ... euros an hour.
You won't work on (4) ...
Your boss will be (5) ... and
you'll wear a (6) ... uniform at work.

▶ More practice 3, p. 151 ▶ Wordbank 9, p. 193

▶ Workbook, pp. 74–75

6 Reading Finn's poster

a) Class 8C made posters about their dream future. Complete Finn's poster. Use *'ll* or *won't*.

My dream future (by Finn Demir)

A

I (1) ... be a programmer and
I (2) ... work in an office.
I (3) ... make cool robots!

B

I (4 not) ... live with my parents any more!
I (5) ... live in a modern flat in Los Angeles and
I (6) ... have a really big computer for playing games.

C

Maybe I (7) ... get married and have children. And I (8) ... see my friends every day.

D

I (9) ... go to the cinema in Hollywood at weekends or I (10) ... surf at the beach. It will be so cool!

E

I (11) ... be confident, hard-working and happy.

b) Match the headings to the correct letters in Finn's poster: *A job, B ...*

Family and friends | Hobbies | Home | Me | ~~Job~~

My task

7 A poster about my dream future

a) Make a poster about your dream future like Finn's poster in 6.
Write headings, sentences and draw pictures. You can put the poster in your Dossier.

I'll Maybe I'll I think I'll I won't	be	famous • happy • married • hard-working • rich • successful • ...
	live	alone • in a big house • in London • with my family • ...
	work in	a different country • a hospital • an office • ...
	have	children • lots of friends • a sports car • ...
	go	dancing • mountain biking • snowboarding • surfing • ...

b) Gallery walk Look at all the posters.
Write feedback and positive comments on sticky notes.

Great poster! *I think you'll be successful.* *I love the drawings.*

► Digital help

Digital quiz I can make predictions about my future.

Jobs at home

1 LISTENING Look at this room!

a) BEFORE YOU LISTEN **Look at the picture. What's the problem?**

b) **Listen to the conversation between Sunita and Willow. Who says what?**

1 "I like sharing a room with you."
2 "I don't notice when things are untidy."
3 "I can't find my clothes."
4 "We all do jobs at home."
5 "You don't do anything!"
6 "Let's listen to some music and tidy up our room."

c) **Listen again. Who does what? Write S (Sunita), B (Ben) or N (Nish).**

1 ... vacuums Sunita and Willow's room.
2 ... takes out the rubbish.
3 ... cleans the bathroom.
4 ... does the washing.
5 ... folds the clean clothes.
6 ... looks after the family's pet.

2 WORDS More chores

Complete each chore with the correct verb from the box.

babysit • empty • make • set • vacuum

1 ... my little sister
2 ... my bed
3 ... the table
4 ... the dishwasher
5 ... the floors

► More practice 4 + 5, p. 152

1
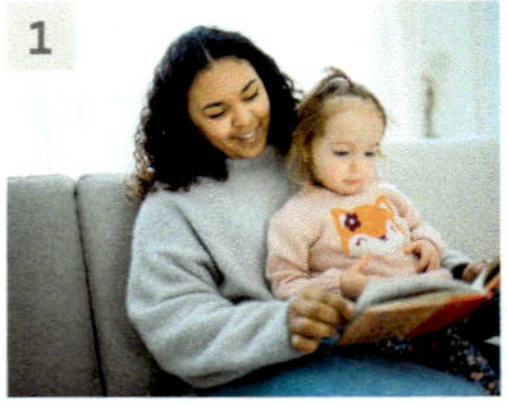
2

3

4

5

► Workbook, p. 76

3 SPEAKING Chores in class 8C

a) Look at the chart.
What does it show?

b) How many students have to do each chore?

28 students make their bed.
28 students …
Two students fold clean clothes.
Two students …

c) There are 30 students in 8C.
How many students don't do each chore?

Two students don't make their beds.
…

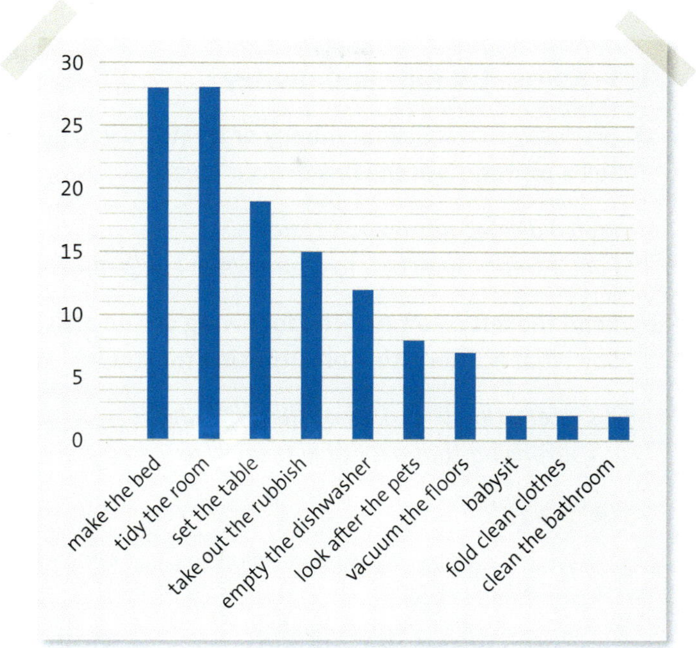

My task

4 My chores

a) Write three chores that you have to do. *I have to …*
Write three chores that you don't have to do. *I don't have to …*

▸ Wordbank 10, p. 194

b) Tell a partner about your chores at home. Use your sentences from 4a).

I have to …
I don't have to …

c) Make groups. Tell your group what chores are OK and what chores you hate.

I have to empty the dishwasher, but that's OK.
I have to take out the rubbish. I hate that!

d) Agree on the top three chores in your group. What's the least favourite chore?
Tell the class.

The three top chores in our group are …
The least favourite chore in our group is …

▸ Digital help

▸ Workbook, p. 77

Digital quiz

I can talk about chores.

Spend or save?

1 Reading UK kids and money

a) Before you read **What money or treats do you get? Tell a partner. Use the box or your ideas.**

I sell old video games and trainers.
I get a treat like tickets to a film when I help my dad.

Ideas
- get birthday money
- sell old things
- do chores
- babysit for neighbours
- get pocket money
- get extra screen time
- can stay up late sometimes

b) **Read the left column of the following online article. Say what is interesting or surprising for you.**

It's interesting that a lot of kids buy / shop ...
It's surprising that a lot of kids save / use ...

www.pocket-money.co.uk.example.com

Top 3 things that UK kids (4–14) buy

1 video / online games 

2 sweets & chocolates 

3 books and magazines 

How UK kids shop

- online with parents
- in shops

Pocket money apps

61% of UK kids use a pocket money app.

Molly's money (14)

My parents put pocket money for me on a card every month. I use the card to pay for stuff online, and I also use it to get cash at a cash machine.

I can see what I spend on the card's app. I buy a lot of chips and drinks. I also spend money on gifts for my friends or online games. My parents say, "It's your money, but you mustn't spend it all!"

So I save some money in a savings account at the bank and I also put some coins in a piggy bank at home.

Sources: https://roostermoney.com/pocket-money-index-uk (10.11.2022)
https://thefintechtimes.com/61-of-uk-children-use-an-app-to-manage-pocket-money (10.11.22)

c) **Read the part about Molly. True or false?**

1 Molly gets pocket money.
2 She uses a card to pay for things.
3 She buys a lot of magazines.
4 She spends money on online games.
5 Molly only saves money in a piggy bank.

d) Words **Find all the money words in the article:** *buy, save ...*
Make a 'money' page in your Vocab file.

▶ More practice 6 + 7, p. 153

▶ Workbook, p. 78

2 Looking at Language **The word order**

Put these sentences in the correct order.

1 loves / clothes. / Molly
2 She / lots of money. / spends
3 because Molly / some money. / saves / Her parents are happy
4 tips about money. / give her / Molly's parents
5 when you / things online." / buy / "Be careful
6 spend it all / "You mustn't / to save!" / because it's important

Die Wortstellung im Englischen ist:	*s* *subject*	*v* *verb*	*o* *object*
Das gilt für Hauptsätze:	*Molly*	*gets*	*pocket money.*
und Nebensätze:	*She*	*spends*	*lots of money because she loves clothes.*

► Language file 18, pp. 182–183

3 Words **Shops and shopping**

a) **You buy shoes at a 'shoe shop' and fish and chips at a 'fish and chip shop'. What are the shops for the things in the box?**

bikes • books • pets • toys • sweets

b) **Now match pictures 1–6 to the shops in the box.**

~~bakery~~ • charity shop • clothes shop • electronics shop • gift shop • newsagent's

1

2

3
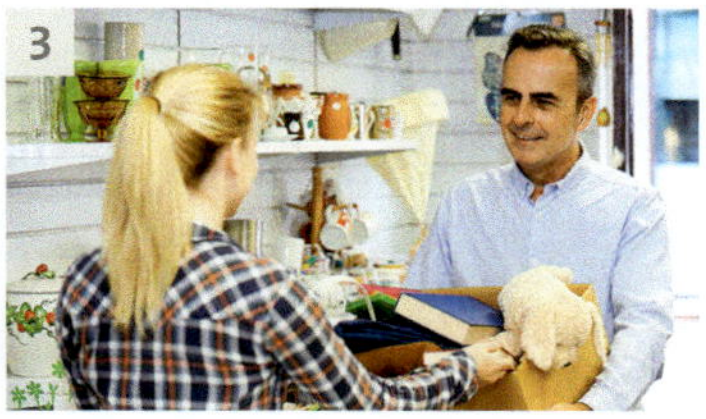
4

5

6

bakery: 6, charity shop: ...

c) **Choose the best words and phrases for you in sentences 1–5. Tell your partner:**

1 I go to shops every week / every month.
2 I like / I don't like shopping.
3 I often / never go shopping with my friends.
4 I / My parents choose my clothes.
5 I often / never buy something at the bakery after school.

► Workbook, p. 79

4 Viewing Shopping

a) Before you watch **Read Scout's speech bubble. Then take turns and say prices A–F.**

A £9.99 B £12.95 C £4.50
D 32p E £6.75 F £38.99

That donut is sixty-five pence – or sixty-five 'p'. And that sandwich is two pounds twenty.
£2.20
65p

b) **Lily's cousin Theo is looking for a T-shirt in a charity shop in Brighton. Watch the video and choose the correct size and price.**

Size: A small B medium C large
Price: A £8 B £10 C £18

c) **Write down sentences 1–6 in the correct order. Watch the video again and check.**

1 I'm just looking.
2 Here's your change.
3 I'll take this.
4 Would you like to pay by card or cash?
5 Hello, can I help you?
6 How much are those trainers over there?

d) **Who says each sentence in c)? Is it the customer or the assistant? Write C or A next to each number.**

5 Speaking That T-shirt is too big

On his way out, Theo sees another T-shirt and trainers in front of the shop and goes back. Complete his questions with the words in the box.

size • that • these • this • trainers

1 What ... is ... T-shirt?
2 Can I try on ... trainers?
3 How much is ... orange T-shirt over there?
4 Do you have those ... over there in black?

► More practice 8, p. 153

This T-shirt is your size. *These* trainers are £15.
£15
£30
That T-shirt is too big. *Those* trainers are £30.

► Workbook, p. 80

6 Mediation and speaking

In a gift shop

Finn is helping a German tourist in a shop in Brighton. Complete the conversation.

Assistant	Hello, can I help you?
Tourist	Hallo – ich meine *hello*. Erm ...
Finn	Kann ich Ihnen helfen? Ich spreche Englisch.
Tourist	Danke, gern. Ich hätte gern dieses T-Shirt, aber in einer kleineren Größe, in S.
Finn	She'd like to buy ...
Assistant	We only have this T-shirt in medium and large.
Finn	Sie haben ...
Tourist	Wie viel kostet das T-Shirt?
Finn	How much ...
Assistant	It's £14.99.
Finn	Es kostet ...
Tourist	Alles klar. Dann nehme ich es in M. Ich möchte gern mit Karte bezahlen.
Finn	That's fine. She'll take it in medium and she'd like to ...

▶ Skills file 8, p. 164

My task

7 Speaking How much is this?

Partner B: Look at p. 150.
Partner A: You're an assistant in a gift shop. Talk to partner B (the customer). You start.

You	Say hello and ask if you can help.
B	...
You	Say the pens cost 40p each or 3 for £1.
B	...
You	Say one T-shirt costs £16.10. Ask what size.
B	...
You	Say you're sorry, you don't have orange T-shirts in medium. You have size medium in red.
B	...
You	Ask if the customer wants anything else.
B	...
You	Say the price for the three pens and T-shirt is £17.10. Ask how the customer wants to pay.
B	...
You	Give the customer's card back. Say "Have a nice day" and "Goodbye".

▶ More practice 9, p. 154

Digital quiz   I can **talk about money and shopping.**

Goodbye, everybody!

1 READING Ava's great idea

a) BEFORE YOU READ **Look at the photos and make notes: Which students can you see? What are they doing? What's Ava's great idea?**

In photo 1 / 2 / ... I can see ...
Ava and Noah are ... Ava is ...
I think Ava's great idea is to ...

▶ Skills file 5, p. 161

b) **Read the story. Check your ideas from a).**

Ava wants to make money for an animal charity. But what can she do? She's creative and good at baking, so she wants to sell cupcakes. Noah and his friends will help her.

On Saturday they arrive at the park and Ava starts to sell the cupcakes. A friendly woman in a blue dress buys two.

It's me, Ava! When are you coming?
What? I can't hear you. Can you say that again?
OK, Dad. See you in five minutes!

After an hour Ava has already sold a lot of cupcakes. Her dad is bringing some more, but he's late.

Finn comes to say goodbye. He says that he's sad to leave his Brighton friends. Sunita and Ava are sad too, especially Sunita.

5

Lily's dad has a new job in London, so her family has to move. Lily is feeling sad, so Ava tells Lily that she will miss her and gives her a big hug.

6

Sunita and Lily say goodbye. They will miss each other too. Sunita has an idea: Maybe she can go to London for a visit?

7

Zane buys a cupcake from Ava. He's happy because his mum is feeling well and his dad has got some help at the cafe.

8

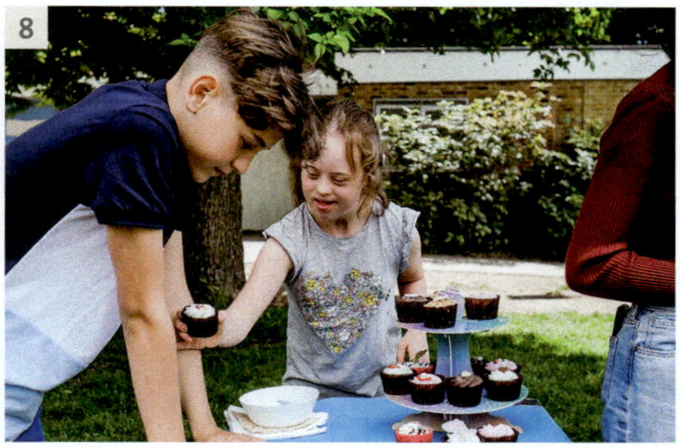

Noah's parents are waiting for him. He's unhappy because he can't do anything alone! Noah talks to Ava about his problem. Ava tells him her parents worry about her too.

9

The friendly woman in the blue dress gives Ava £100 extra for her charity project. She gives Ava her business card and asks if Ava would like to do work experience at her bakery.

10

Ava made £137.20 for the charity! She is feeling very proud today. The kids all say goodbye. It's the start of the summer holidays soon. What will happen next?

▸ Skills file 7, p. 163

2 The students in the story

a) **Match the five students in the box to the correct sentences.**

1 ... has to move to a new city.
2 ... wants to do things alone.
3 ... is happy because his mum is feeling well.
4 ... wants to help a charity.
5 ... will miss two good friends.

Ava • Lily • Noah • Sunita • Zane

b) **Complete Ava's phone call with her dad. Use picture 3 on p. 140 to help you. Then read it with your partner.**

Ava Hi, Dad. ...
Dad Hi, Ava. I'll be there in about five minutes.
Ava What? ...
Dad I'll be there in about five minutes, Ava.
Ava OK, Dad.

▸ More practice 10, p. 154 ▸ More practice 11, p. 155

Ideas

When you make a phone call
Say hello and who you are:
Hi / Hello! It's ...
If the call is bad, say:
I can't hear you. / Can you hear me?
Ask the other person to repeat something:
Can you say that again please?
Say goodbye:
Bye! See you soon! See you later!

3 What will they do?

Make predictions about the students in the story.

1 How will Sunita and Finn stay in contact?
I think they'll email / call / ...
2 How will Lily feel at her new school in London? Will her Brighton friends visit her?
Maybe Lily will ... I think her friends will ...
3 Will Noah talk to his parents about his problem?
I think Noah will ...
4 Will Ava call the woman? What will Ava say?
I'm sure that Ava will ... She'll say ...

▸ Parallel exercise, p. 155

4 LIFE SKILLS Know your strengths

Ava is creative and good at baking. On a piece of paper, make a list of things that you are good at. You can use a dictionary or an online dictionary.

I'm	brave • clever • fair • friendly • funny • helpful • honest • kind • smart • ...
I'm good at	helping people • listening to people • solving problems • ...
I'd like to work with	animals • children • computers • money • numbers • ...

Digital quiz I can understand and talk about people's strengths.

Brighton stories: Chores

1 Before you watch Chores

Write down all the chores that you can remember in two minutes. Which group has the most?

2 Viewing Two competitions

a) Watch the video to minute 3.27 and complete the notes.

Problem: Emir has to finish his ...

Gloria's idea: His friends will ... Emir.

Who will help: Joe and ... will fold the family's clothes.

How they can win: be the ... folder.

The winner is: ...

b) Watch the ending. Read the questions and use the answers in the box. You don't need two answers.

1 What chore is Joe now doing? He's ...
2 What chore is Daisy doing? She's ...
3 What does Emir think would be another good competition?

- doing Emir's homework
- drying the dishes[1]
- making Emir's bed
- taking out the rubbish
- washing up[2]

3 My opinion

Daisy, Emir, Gloria and Joe did three competitions: summer holiday activities (p. 27), street dancing (p. 85) and chores (p. 143). Talk about them with a partner.

I think the	holiday dance chore	competition	was the most interesting. was the funniest. was the best / the worst. was the most boring. was the silliest. ...
I want to try the			because it looks like fun. I'm good at dancing / at competitions. I have a good idea for it. ...

[1] (to) **dry the dishes** *das Geschirr abtrocknen* [2] (to) **wash up** *abwaschen*

▶ Workbook, p. 81

Check writing

1 Use a checklist

a) Finn is back in Germany. Read his letter to Sunita. What will Finn miss in Germany?

b) There are ten mistakes in Finn's letter. Use the checklist to correct the mistakes.

CHECKLIST

- Is the word order correct? ▸ Language file
  I just got ~~last night home~~.
  ▸ I just got home last night.
- Is the spelling correct? ▸ Dictionary
  I've missed german food.
  ▸ I've missed German food.
- Are the tenses correct? ▸ Language file
  ~~I ask~~ my mum.
  ▸ I'll ask my mum.

25th June

Dear Sunita

How are you? (1) I just got last night home. (2) I'm happy my dad to see. I've missed him a lot.

I've missed (3) german food. I'm looking forward to that!

I'll miss (4) fisch and chips. I'll miss Brighton beach (5) to. I'll miss lots of things in (6) england. I won't miss the school uniform!

Most of all, I'll miss my English (7) frends. I think (8) I ask my mum when our next trip will be. I'm (9) shure that it (10) be soon.

Take care
Finn

2 Use linking words

a) Finn wrote very short sentences in his letter. Make them sound better by linking them.

1 I'm happy to see my dad again because / but I've missed him a lot.
2 I've missed German food, but / so I'm looking forward to that!
3 I'll miss fish and chips and / because I'll miss Brighton beach too.
4 I'll miss lots of things in England, because / but I won't miss the school uniform!

b) Read Sunita's answer. Link her sentences with *because, but, so*. Use each word twice.

Hi, Finn! Thanks for writing me.
1 You were in England for a long time, ... of course you're happy to be home!
2 I hope your next visit will be very soon ... I miss you too.
3 Fish and chips are OK, ... German food sounds better to me.
4 Yesterday a tourist asked me a question, ... I couldn't understand her!
5 It was a problem ... she didn't speak English.
6 I learned that she was from Germany, ... I thought of you!
Take care, Sunita

▸ More practice 12, p. 155 ▸ Skills file 13, p. 169

Digital quiz — I can check my writing.

Write fun horoscopes

Step 1: Read about star signs

What's your star sign? Look at the chart and tell your partner.

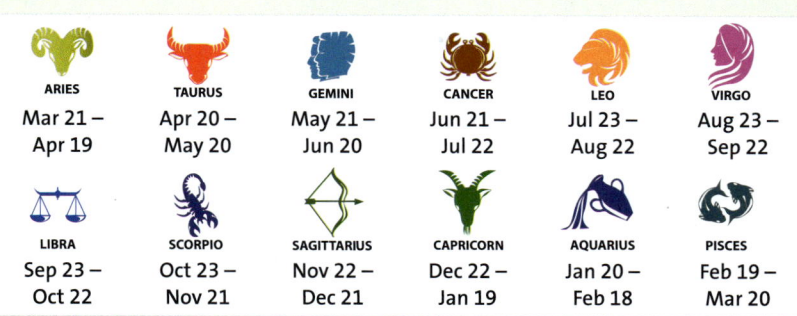

ARIES	TAURUS	GEMINI	CANCER	LEO	VIRGO
Mar 21 – Apr 19	Apr 20 – May 20	May 21 – Jun 20	Jun 21 – Jul 22	Jul 23 – Aug 22	Aug 23 – Sep 22
LIBRA	**SCORPIO**	**SAGITTARIUS**	**CAPRICORN**	**AQUARIUS**	**PISCES**
Sep 23 – Oct 22	Oct 23 – Nov 21	Nov 22 – Dec 21	Dec 22 – Jan 19	Jan 20 – Feb 18	Feb 19 – Mar 20

Step 2: Write predictions

Write 6–8 <u>positive</u> horoscope predictions for your partner's star sign for next week.

You	'll	meet an amazing / interesting person. go on a wonderful trip. have a lucky day / learn something new / … find something important / useful / … get a surprise / a present / a phone call / …
	'll have to	help a good friend / … be kind to your family / pet / … be careful with your money / work hard / …

Step 3: Check!

a) Check your own sentences.
Then check another student's sentences. ► Skills file 13, p. 169

b) Rewrite your predictions on a piece of paper. Put them on a wall in the classroom.

Step 4: Read and give feedback

a) GALLERY WALK Read the predictions for your own star sign.

b) Read out a prediction and give feedback on it to the class.

I think this prediction will / won't happen.

I liked / didn't like this prediction because it's funny / creative / realistic / …

► Digital help

Digital quiz I can write fun horoscopes.

1 Words What do you want to be?

I can talk about jobs.

Some Varndean students are talking about their dream jobs. Complete the sentences with the correct jobs from the box. There are two extra jobs.

architect • firefighter • footballer • gamer • mechanic • plumber • programmer • train driver

Lewis I want to be a (1) ... because I love coding and I want to make websites.
Evie That sounds cool. I want to work with computers too, but I want to be a (2) ... because I'm great at playing games.
Sam That's not a real job! It's too fun. I want do so something with cars – perhaps I'll be a (3) ...
Shakiel I love designing houses, so I want to be an (4) ...
Alex I can help you with that, Shakiel, because I want to be a (5) ... like my uncle! He's strong and really practical.
Mia I don't have a dream job yet. I just know that I want to help people.
Lewis There are lots of jobs for you then! Perhaps a (6) ... or a nurse?
Mia Perhaps!

2 Language My dream home

I can make predictions about my future (will-future).

a) **Sunita is writing to Finn about her dream home. Complete the sentences with the correct words from the box.**

'll do • 'll get up • 'll need • 'll play • will have • 'll swim • will visit • will be • won't leave • won't be

to Finn
from Sunita

Hi, Finn!
You asked me about my dream home. Well, my future home (1) ... in Brighton, but it (2 not) ... like other houses! It (3) ... ten bedrooms, a swimming pool and a cinema. I (4 not) ... . my house at the weekend because all of my friends (5) ... me. On Saturdays we (6) ... in the pool and watch films together. On Sundays we (7) ... yoga in my beautiful studio and then we (8) ... computer games. On Mondays I (9) ... early and go to work. I (10) ... to have a good job to pay for this house!
Best wishes from Sunita

b) Writing **Write a message to your British friend about your dream home. Use the will-future. The text from a) can help you.**

3 Mediation Finn's friends in Germany

I can talk about chores.

Finn wants to tell his class about the chores that kids in Germany do.
He asked ten of his friends what they have to do at home. Look at the chart.
Then complete Finn's sentences.

1 I asked my friends in Germany about …
2 Everybody has to …
3 Most people have to … and …
4 Some people have to … and …
5 Nobody …

4 Speaking The worst chores!

a) Look at the pictures. Who has to do what?

b) Who has the worst chores?
Tell your partner.

I think …

5 LISTENING A shopping trip

I can talk about money and shopping.

a) Lily and her dad are doing some shopping. Which shops are they going to? Listen and put the pictures in the correct order. There's one extra picture.

A gift shop

B newsagent's

C electronics shop

D clothes shop

E bakery

b) The receipts have rain on them. Listen again. Copy and complete the missing information.

Product:	**Product:**	**Product:**	**Product:**
j_____	c_____	_____ cleaner	chocolate ____
Price: £19.__	Price: £_.45	Price: £__.00	Price: £8.__

6 SPEAKING In the second-hand shop

Partner A: You're the shop assistant. Write a price between 50p and £6 for each thing, but don't show your partner.
Partner B: You have £10. Choose three things that you want to buy. Ask for the price and decide what you want to buy. Then swap roles.

Partner A (assistant): You start.
Hello. Can I help you?
The ... costs / cost ... What about this / these ...
Thank you very much. ...

Partner B: Yes, please.
How much is / are the ...
That's great / too expensive.
I'll buy the ... and the ...

trainers

jacket

skateboard

robot

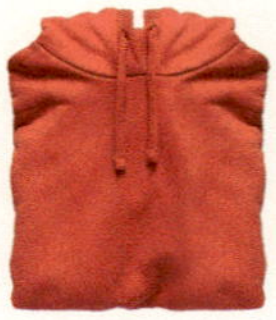
hoodie

headphones

rucksack

basketball

helmet

7 READING Finn's garage sale

I can understand and talk about people's strengths.

Finn is getting ready to go back to Germany but there's a problem: He has too many things! Finn's mum goes into his room and says, "Finn! We can't take all of this back to Germany." A few hours later he has an idea. He sends a message to his friends. "Hi, guys. I want to have a garage sale at the weekend. Do you want to help me? Finn 🙂"

On Saturday morning, Lily and Noah arrive early. Noah tidies the garage and finds some tables. Lily finds some nice paper to put on the tables. She also draws the price labels.

The first people arrive at 9 a.m. Zane answers all of their questions and helps them to choose what to buy. At 3 p.m., everything is gone. Sunita has some good news. She says, "OK guys, I have counted the money. Finn, you now have £53!"
Finn smiles at Sunita and says, "Thanks Sunita, but that money isn't for me. I have surprise for you – it's for our pizzas!

a) Read the story. Who is it? Write the correct name or names.

1 ... has to find a solution for a problem.
2 ... help with the preparations.
3 ... talks to the customers.
4 ... knows how much Finn has earned.
5 ... are going to have a special meal.

b) What are the kids' strengths? Match the correct sentence parts.

1 Noah is good at ...
2 Zane is good at ...
3 Lily is good at ...
4 Sunita is good at ...
5 Finn is good at ...

A decorating.
B maths.
C talking to people.
D surprising his friends.
E tidying up.

8 STUDY SKILLS Mina's weekend plans

I can check my writing.

a) Read Mina's message to her British friend Arlo. Correct the underlined parts. You can use the checklist for language on p. 144.

b) Write a message to your British friend about your weekend plans. The text from a) can help you. Check your text and / or a partner's text.

Hi, Arlo!
How are you? I'm really happy because it finally Friday is (1) 🙂. I have some exciting plans for the Weekend (2). Tomorrow I'm going to see a film at the cinema with some frends (3). Then I go (4) to visit my cousins. They lives (5) near the sea. What are your weekend plans? Will you in Brighton be (6)? I hope you have a great weekend!
Mina

Partner page

▸ Page 139

7 Speaking How much is this?

Partner B

You're a customer in a gift shop. Talk to partner A (the shop assistant). Partner A starts.

A	...
You	Say "Yes, please." Ask how much the pens cost.
A	...
You	Say you'd like three pens. Ask how much the orange T-shirts in the window cost.
A	...
You	Say you'd like size medium.
A	...
You	Say that's fine. You'd like a red T-shirt in size medium.
A	...
You	Say thank you, that's all for today.
A	...
You	Say that you want to pay by card. Give the assistant your card.
A	...
You	...

▸ Page 154

More practice 9 Game Buy and sell

You're the seller.

a) **Choose one card.**
Decide how much each thing at your shop costs.

- *a hat*
- *a guitar*
- *a banana*

- *a swimsuit*
- *a robot*
- *a bottle of water*

- *a skateboard*
- *a packet of biscuits*
- *a poster*

- *a drone*
- *a bike helmet*
- *a cushion*

b) **Stand at a desk.**
Customers will come and ask for things at your shop.
Sell them to the customers. Say:

Hello. Yes, I have that. /
Sorry I don't have that.
It's ...
Sorry, that isn't enough. How about ...?
Yes, that's OK.
Goodbye.

c) **To win, you must sell everything and make the most money of all the sellers.**

Diff bank

▸ Page 128

More practice 1 Jobs assembly

Listen and choose the correct answer A, B or C.

1 Sunita liked the ...
- A firefighter.
- B hairdresser.
- C cook.

2 Lily thinks that firefighters ...
- A have a boring job.
- B have a dangerous and hard job.
- C don't make a lot of money.

3 Noah's hairdresser is ...
- A the hairdresser in assembly.
- B his neighbour.
- C Zane's uncle.

4 Lily's mum is a ...
- A hairdresser.
- B programmer.
- C nurse.

5 The plumber ...
- A has a lot of customers.
- B made a lot of money right away.
- C doesn't like her job.

6 Zane's dad is a ...
- A nurse.
- B plumber.
- C cook.

▸ Page 132

More practice 2 Next weekend

What will happen next weekend? Write three sentences.

Scout Black Bird George	will won't	go to the beach. eat some fish. go swimming. go shopping. sleep in. fly to Portsmouth. ...
I He / She We / You	'll won't	

More practice 3 Scout's friends

Complete Scout's sentences.
Use *will*, *'ll* or *won't* and a verb from the box.

eat • listen • look • sing • walk (2x)

Tomorrow, I think I (1) ... to Hove beach with Blue Bird and maybe we (2) ... to the street musicians. Then we (3) ... for some lunch. Blue Bird (4) ... lots of chips and then she (5) ... really badly – I don't have that problem, of course! In the afternoon, I (6) ... home because I have a date with Black Bird!

▸ Page 134

☒ More practice 4 **A robot for chores**

a) Sunita's robot Robbie is cool, but he can't do chores. Imagine a robot that can do chores. Make notes:

My robot
Name:
Colour:
Looks like:
Can do:

b) Tell a partner about your robot.

My robot's name is ...
It's brown and it looks like a dog. It has four legs and a cute face.
It can tidy my room, ...

More practice 5 **Chores**

Write the chores.

1

s _ _ the table

2

v _ _ _ _ m the floors

3

t _ _ e o _ _ the rubbish

4

f _ _ d clean clothes

5

e _ _ _ y the dishwasher

6

m _ _ e the bed

7

t _ _ y the living room

8

d _ the washing

9

c _ _ _ n the bathroom

▸ Page 136

More practice 6 Money

Complete the conversation with the words in the box.

app • buy • cash • cash machine • bank • pocket money • save • savings account • sell • spend

Sunita Do you get (1) ... from your parents, Noah?
Noah Yes, I do. I get £10 every week.
Sunita That's a lot! I don't get that much. But I (2) ... old video games for extra money.
Noah Well, I have to (3) ... some money. I put some money in a (4) ... at the bank and I put coins in my piggy (5) ...
Sunita Good idea! I use a pocket money (6) ... It's really cool because I get a card and I can (7) ... things with that. I can get money from the (8) ... at the bank with the card too.
Noah My parents give me the money in (9) ... But they say I mustn't (10) ... it all on things like burgers and chips.

More practice 7 SPEAKING Your money

a) THINK **What do you do with your money?**

I spend money on	cafes / the cinema / magazines / snacks / things for my sport / sweets / ...
I save money in	a piggy bank / a savings account / ...
I mustn't spend	(too much) money on fast food / snacks / ... all my money every month.

b) PAIR **Tell a partner. Listen to your partner and take notes.**

c) SHARE **Tell the class one thing that your partner spends money on.**

▸ Page 138

More practice 8 In a clothes shop

Look at the pictures. Complete the conversation with *this*, *that*, *these* or *those*.

Lily Do you like (1) ... white shoes?
Zane They're OK. But I like (2) ... black shoes better.
Lily Yeah, they're nice, but I want white ones.
Zane Oh, right. Oh, (3) ... red hoodie is cool.
I like red – (4) ... red T-shirt is my favourite.
Lily I like red too. The hoodie looks good with (5) ... yellow jeans.
Zane Mm, I don't like yellow. I usually wear black or blue jeans – or white jeans like (6) ... ones.

▸ Page 139

More practice 9 GAME **Buy and sell**

a) Make two groups: buyers and sellers.
Sellers: Go to p. 150.

b) Buyers: Choose one shopping list. You only have £30. Go to one of the sellers and say:

Hello. Excuse me.
Do you have …?
How much is it?
Sorry, that's too expensive.
I'll give you …
The price is OK. I'll take it.

- *a hat*
- *a guitar*
- *a banana*

- *a swimsuit*
- *a robot*
- *a bottle of water*

- *a skateboard*
- *a packet of biscuits*
- *a poster*

- *a drone*
- *a bike helmet*
- *a cushion*

c) The buyer with all three things on their list and the most money left wins.

▸ Page 142

More practice 10 **Ava's phone call**

Read the first part of the phone call. Put the rest in the correct order: *1 H, 2 …*
Then read the call together.

Sara Hello, this is Sara Osman.
Ava Hello, Ms Osman. This is Ava Burt. You gave me your card at the park.

A **Ava** Sorry, I can't hear you. Can you say that again please?

B **Sara** Great! Can you come to my bakery after school on Tuesday?

C **Ava** I'm fine, thank you. I'm calling about doing work experience at your bakery.

D **Sara** OK, see you on Tuesday. Bye, Ava.

E **Sara** I said, can you come to my bakery after school on Tuesday?

F **Ava** Goodbye.

G **Ava** Yes, I can. Tuesday is fine.

H **Sara** Yes, I remember. Hello, Ava. How are you?

More practice 11 Your phone call

You want to meet your partner.
Think of an activity, a time and a place.
Look at the boxes for ideas.

see a film • ride our bikes • play video games • ...

this afternoon • tomorrow evening • Saturday morning • ...

the cinema • the park • my / your house • ...

Now phone your partner. You're going to plan to meet. You can use these phrases:

You	Hello!
Partner	Hi, ...! Can you hear me?
You	Yes, I can. Let's ... Are you free ...?
Partner	Yes, I am. / No, I'm not.
You	Can you say that again, please?
Partner	...
You	OK, what about ...? Let's meet at ...
Partner	OK! It'll be fun!
You	Bye!
Partner	See you later!

Parallel exercise 3 What will they do?

Make predictions about the students in the story. Match A–D to 1–4.

1 I think Sunita and Finn will email each other.
2 Maybe Lily will feel good at her new school.
3 I think Noah will talk to his parents.
4 I'm sure that Ava will call the woman.

A She'll ask to do work experience.
B I think her Brighton friends will visit her soon.
C Maybe they'll play games online together.
D He'll ask them to go places alone.

▸ Page 144

More practice 12 Write your letter

a) **Write a letter to Sunita, Noah, Zane or Lily about the summer.**

I think this summer will be	good / great / amazing / fun / boring / terrible / ...
I'll go / I won't go	to the beach / swimming / on holiday with my family / ...
I'll / I won't	eat ice cream / see my friends / ride my bike / play games / ...

b) **Swap letters with a partner and check your partner's letter. Use the checklist.**

CHECKLIST Does the letter ...
– have the date at the top? ✓
– start correctly? *(Dear / Hello ...)* ✓
– end correctly? *(Take care / Your friend ...)* ✓
– have your partner's name at the bottom? ✓

Auf den ***Skills file***-Seiten findest du Methoden und Tipps, die dir helfen, z. B. Wortschatz zu lernen, Informationen zu sammeln, Seiten zu gestalten oder kleine Vorträge zu halten.

Inhalt

Die mit diesem Symbol gekennzeichneten Abschnitte enthalten Hinweise und Tipps, die dir dabei helfen, elektronische Medien beim Englischlernen einzusetzen.

Erklär-film Dieses Symbol zeigt dir, dass du einen Erklärfilm zu diesem Thema in der App findest.

Lösungen der Merkaufgaben

SF 2, Merkaufgabe:

a) *ähnliches Wort im Deutschen: Ozean; Wörter aus anderen Sprachen: océan, océano, okean, okyanus*

b) *Wortfamilie und Wortbildungsgesetze: (to) speak + Nachsilbe -er: Sprecher/in*

c) *Wortfamilie und Wortbildungsgesetze: sure + Vorsilbe un-: unsicher*

SF 3, Merkaufgabe:

a) *die Etage*

b) *der Fußboden*

SF 4, Merkaufgabe:

b) *school + routine + UK*

SF 7, Merkaufgabe:

Es geht um eine Woche mit Freizeitaktivitäten, z. B. Fußball, Karate und Fotografieren.

SF 8, Merkaufgabe:

a) *Hier kann man für unterschiedliche Tage Hin- und Rückfahrkarten in verschiedene Städte kaufen.*

SF 9, Merkaufgabe:

(zwei Tipps von diesen): Sortiere vor dem Vortrag deine Kärtchen.; Übe deinen Vortrag, lies nicht alles ab.; Schaue das Publikum an.; Sprich laut und deutlich.; Bedanke dich bei deinen Zuhörern.; Erkundige dich, ob deine Zuhörer Fragen haben.

SF 10, Merkaufgabe:

b) *For me that isn't true. I like to spend my time with other things like sports or meeting real people.*

SF 11, Merkaufgabe:

a) *sport*

b) *places*

SF 1

Vokabeln lernen

Erklär-
film

▶ Unit 1 | p. 17 ▶ Unit 2 | p. 48

Führe dein VOCAB FILE aus Klasse 5 weiter.

Neue Vokabeln lernst du am besten an einem ruhigen und aufgeräumten Platz, an dem du nicht abgelenkt wirst.

Wiederholen kannst du sie überall – beim Warten, im Bus, im Bett, ... Für unterwegs kannst du sie dir aufs Handy sprechen oder per Vokabeltrainer-App üben. Je öfter du die Vokabeln wiederholst, desto besser wirst du sie dir merken können.

Wie merke ich mir neue Wörter besser?

Erstelle Wortfelder

- Ordne die Wörter unter einem Oberbegriff *(umbrella word)*. Du kannst eine Liste machen oder auch eine Mindmap, die du immer weiter ergänzt.
- Oder du arbeitest mit Karteikarten. Schreibe den Oberbegriff in Großbuchstaben auf die Vorderseite einer Karteikarte und die dazu passenden Wörter auf die Rückseite. Später kannst du neue Wörter ergänzen.

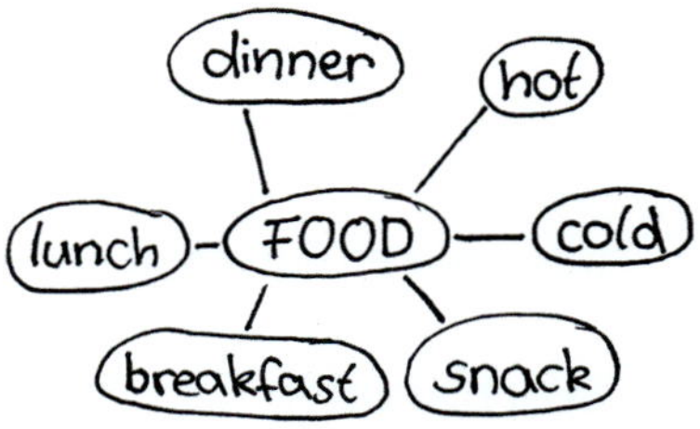

Finde Gegensatzpaare

Sammle Gegensatzpaare und schreibe sie z. B. auf die letzte Seite von deinem VOCAB FILE. Füge Bilder hinzu. Das hilft dir beim Lernen.

Lerne *phrases* statt Einzelwörter

Phrases sind Ausdrücke, die aus mehreren Wörtern bestehen, z. B. *a bottle of water = eine Flasche Wasser.* Lerne also nicht *bottle* und *water* als Einzelwörter, sondern den ganzen Ausdruck: *a bottle of water.*

Weitere Beispiele:
night → at night
listen → listen to music
sad → feel sad

Merkaufgabe 1

Gehe dein VOCAB FILE aus Klasse 5 und 6 durch. Erstelle eine Liste mit Gegensatzpaaren.

Checkliste Vokabeln lernen

- ✓ Lerne nur 5–10 Vokabeln auf einmal.
- ✓ Lerne jeden Tag 10 Minuten.
- ✓ Lerne zusammen mit Freunden. Das macht mehr Spaß.
- ✓ Lerne unterwegs mit einer Vokabellern-App.
- ✓ Schreibe schwierige Wörter auf (mehrmals!).
- ✓ Sprich die Wörter und nimm dich mit dem Handy auf.

SF 2

Unbekannte Wörter erschließen

▶ Unit 2 | p. 56

Du kannst englische Texte verstehen, auch wenn du nicht alle Wörter kennst. So kannst du die Bedeutung herausfinden:

Bilder

Bilder zeigen oft Dinge in einem Text, die du nicht verstehst, Schaue sie deshalb genau an.

He has long, black hair.
He's wearing it in plaits.
He has an earring in his left ear.

Ähnliche Wörter im Deutschen oder in anderen Sprachen

Viele englische Wörter klingen ähnlich wie im Deutschen, werden ähnlich geschrieben, oder du kennst sie vielleicht aus anderen Sprachen und kannst sie deshalb verstehen.

- garage
- die Garage
- le garage
- гараж
- garaj

Wortfamilien und Wortbildungsgesetze

Ein Wort gehört immer zu einer Wortfamilie. Kennst du ein Wort aus der Wortfamilie, z. B. das Verb *act*, verstehst du auch die Nomen *action* und *activity* und das Adjektiv *active*.
Mit Regeln zur Wortbildung kannst du die Bedeutung ableiten:

Vorsilben		
un-	Aus einem positiven Adjektiv wird ein negatives.	friendly → unfriendly happy → unhappy
Nachsilben		
-ful	Aus einem Nomen wird ein Adjektiv.	colour → colourful use → useful
-er	Aus einem Tätigkeitsverb wird eine Person.	listen → listener sing → singer
-ness	Aus einem Adjektiv wird ein Nomen.	happy → happiness kind → kindness

Kontextsätze

Manchmal helfen dir die Sätze vor und nach dem Wort dabei, es zu verstehen.

Please turn up the volume. I can't hear the song.

Was soll ich hochdrehen? Sie kann das Lied nicht hören? Ah! Die Lautstärke.

Merkaufgabe 2

Schaue dir die Wörter an. Mit welcher Strategie kannst du ihre Bedeutung herausfinden?

a) ocean b) speaker c) unsure

(Die Lösung findest du auf Seite 156.)

SF 3

Erklär-film

Im Wörterbuch nachschlagen

▶ Unit 4 | p. 103 ▶ Unit 5 | p. 130

Wie finde ich Wörter und Ausdrücke im *Dictionary*?

Die Wörter im Wörterbuch sind alphabetisch aufgelistet:
g kommt vor h
ga kommt vor ge
gal kommt vor garn

In Online-Wörterbüchern stellst du nur die Suchrichtung (E–D oder D–E) ein und tippst dann das Wort ein.

Der Haupteintrag (z. B. *much*) steht farbig oder **fett** am Anfang. Daneben oder darunter findest du oft zusammengesetzte Wörter oder Redewendungen (z. B. *first name*).

G
°**gallery** [ˈɡæləri] die Galerie
game [ɡeɪm]:
1. das Spiel 5
2. Computerspiele spielen 6: 5 (130)
gamer [ˈɡeɪmə] der Gamer, die Gamerin *(Computerspieler/in)* 6: 5 (130)
gaming [ˈɡeɪmɪŋ] das Gaming *(Spielen am Computer)* 6: 3 (80)
garden [ˈɡɑːdn] der Garten 5
gave [ɡeɪv] *siehe* **give**
°**Gemini** [ˈdʒemɪnaɪ] die Zwillinge

much [mʌtʃ] viel; sehr 5 **How much is/are ...?** Was (Wie viel) kostet/kosten ...? 6: 5 (138) **Thank you very much.** Vielen Dank. / Danke vielmals. 5

Was erfahre ich aus dem Dictionary?

Aussprache

Du erfährst, wie das Wort ausgesprochen wird. Schaue dir dafür die Lautschrift hinter dem Wort an.

Wenn du ein Online-Wörterbuch verwendest, kannst du dir das Wort anhören.

Unregelmäßigkeiten

Hat ein Wort einen unregelmäßigen Plural oder eine unregelmäßige Zeitform, findest du diese Form vor oder hinter der Lautschrift.

child [tʃaɪld], *pl* **children** das Kind 6: 2 (47)

Unterschiedliche Bedeutungen und unterschiedliche Wortarten

Die Ziffern 1, 2 usw. zeigen, dass ein Wort mehrere Bedeutungen hat oder sogar als unterschiedliche Wortarten vorkommt. Lies also immer den ganzen Eintrag und entscheide dann, welche Bedeutung die richtige ist.

floor [flɔː]:
1. der Fußboden 5
2. die Etage, der Stock, das Stockwerk 5
top floor die oberste Etage, der oberste Stock, das oberste Stockwerk 5

Merkaufgabe 3

Was heißt *floor* in diesen Sätzen?

a) The bathroom is on the first floor.

b) My glasses fell to the floor – but I was lucky, they didn't break.

(Die Lösung findest du auf Seite 156.)

SF 4

Im Internet recherchieren

Erklär-film

▶ Unit 2 | p. 57

Im Internet kannst du dir schnell Informationen aus aller Welt besorgen. Mit ein paar Tricks behältst du den Überblick.

Suchen

- Überlege dir Suchbegriffe, die zu deinem Thema passen.
- Gib nicht nur einen Suchbegriff ein, sondern zwei oder mehrere. Du suchst z. B. Informationen zum englischen König. Wenn du nur *king* eingibst, wirst du zunächst wenig Passendes finden. Wenn du aber eingibst *king + England* oder *king + UK*, hast du schon bessere Ergebnisse.

Nicht alle Informationen, die du findest, sind richtig und wichtig. Prüfe sie also sorgfältig, und verlasse dich nicht nur auf eine einzige Internetseite als Quelle.

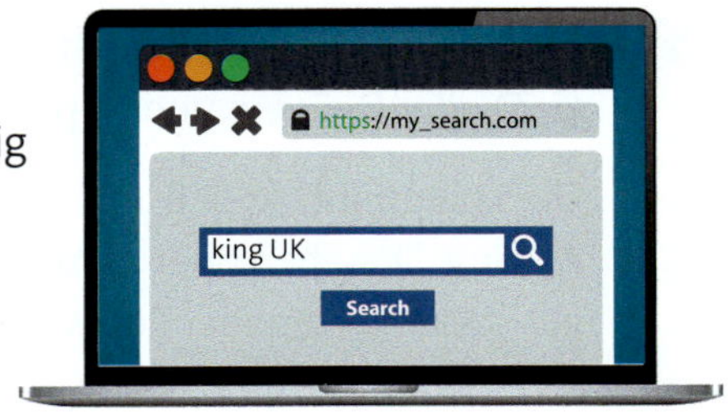

Auswählen

Beschäftige dich nur mit den Seiten und Links, die wirklich zu deinem Thema / deiner Aufgabe passen. Prüfe:

- Von wem stammt die Seite? Wie verlässlich ist die Information? Ist es z. B. ein Online-Lexikon oder ein Chat-Forum? Achte auf die Endung der Internetadresse oder URL, sie kann dir wichtige Hinweise geben:
  - .com bedeutet, es ist eine kommerzielle Webseite, die auch Werbung enthalten kann.
  - .gov weist auf eine offizielle Webseite der Regierung hin.
  - .uk bedeutet, es ist eine britische Seite.
- Passen die Informationen zu deinem Thema? Überfliege die Seite und achte auf Überschriften und Bilder.

Vorsicht bei Wikipedia.
Das Onlinelexikon ist von freiwilligen Helfern geschrieben und kann Fehler enthalten.

Sichern

- Setze *bookmarks* (digitale Lesezeichen), um die ausgewählten Seiten später schnell wieder aufzurufen. Mache dir Notizen und markiere wichtige Textstellen.
- Schreibe die Texte nicht wörtlich ab, sondern gib die Inhalte in deinen eigenen Worten wieder.

Wenn du Inhalte einer Webseite verwendest, nenne immer den Autor oder Urheber der Seite und die dazugehörige URL, die du direkt in dein Dokument hineinkopieren kannst. Schreibe auch das Datum dazu, wann du die Website zuletzt aufgerufen hast.

Merkaufgabe 4

Hannes möchte einen Kurzvortrag zum Thema „A school day in the UK“ vorbereiten. Was sind die besten Suchbegriffe?

a) school + day **b)** school + routine + UK **c)** school + UK

(Die Lösung findest du auf Seite 156.)

SF 5

Notizen erstellen

▸ Unit 1 | p. 29 ▸ Unit 2 | p. 49, 51 ▸ Unit 4 | p. 109 ▸ Unit 5 | p. 140

In vielen Situationen ist es hilfreich, wenn du deine Gedanken sammelst und Notizen machst, z. B. wenn du eine Geschichte planst oder wenn du den Inhalt eines Textes zusammenfassen oder eine Geschichte nacherzählen möchtest.

Wie erstelle ich Notizen?

- Verwende für deine Notizen kleine Zettel oder Karteikarten.
- Schreibe Stichpunkte auf, keine ganzen Sätze.
- Schreibe nicht alles auf. Sammle nur die Punkte, die besonders wichtig sind.
- Strukturiere deine Notizen optisch, z. B. durch Überschriften und Absätze. Du kannst beispielsweise *wh*-Fragewörter *(what, where, when, who, why)* als Zwischenüberschriften verwenden.
- Schreibe deine Notizen gleich in der Reihenfolge auf, in der du deine Gedanken vortragen möchtest. Verwendest du kleine Zettel oder Karteikarten kannst du diese am Ende leicht sortieren und nummerieren.

1

favourite family party →
Grandma's 70th birthday

when: Aug 15
where: Grandma's garden

2

favourite family party →
Grandma's 70th birthday

what: all my family
barbecue
play with cousins ☺
pool 👍

Worauf muss ich achten?

Halte dich kurz:

- Schreibe Ziffern anstelle von Zahlen, z. B. „15“ statt „fifteen“
- Verwende Abkürzungen, z. B. „Aug“ statt „August“, „&“ statt „and“, „/“ statt „or“
- Verwende Symbole und Zeichnungen anstelle von Stichwörtern, z. B. Smileys für Gefühle, Flaggen für Länder, Strichzeichnungen für Personen usw.

Merkaufgabe 5

Probiere es gleich aus. Stelle dir vor, du möchtest jemandem über deine letzte Geburtstagsparty berichten. Mache dir Notizen dazu.

Es gibt auch Apps, mit denen du deine Notizen anfertigen kannst.
Denke aber daran, dass du mit deinen Eltern sprichst, bevor du eine kostenpflichtige App herunterlädst.

SF 6

Hörtexte verstehen

▶ Unit 1 | p. 18 ▶ Unit 2 | p. 48 ▶ Unit 3 | p. 76 ▶ Unit 4 | p. 108 ▶ Unit 5 | p. 131

Nicht nur im Englischunterricht, sondern auch im Alltag oder im Urlaub kommt es darauf an, einen englischen Hörtext zu verstehen, z. B. in Gesprächen, Filmen, im Hotel oder am Flughafen. Mit ein paar Tipps lassen sich Hörtexte gut bewältigen:

Nutze unterschiedliche Möglichkeiten, um englische Texte zu hören. Wähle etwas aus, was dir gefällt, z. B. dein Lieblingslied oder dein Lieblingsbuch als Hörbuch auf Englisch. Schaue Filme und Serien auf Englisch. Blende Untertitel ein, falls du Probleme beim Verstehen hast. Blende sie aus, wenn du dich sicherer fühlst oder eine Episode schon mehrfach gesehen hast.

Vor dem Hören

Lies dir die Aufgabenstellung genau durch und überlege, was du tun sollst. Wenn du etwas nicht verstehst, frage nach. Finde die Schlüsselwörter in der Aufgabenstellung. Diese zeigen dir, worauf du beim Hören achten musst.

Im Alltag gibt es viele Hinweise, die sich aus der Situation ergeben, in der du dich gerade befindest, z. B. bei einer Durchsage an einem Bahnhof.

Beim Hören

Versuche, zunächst grob zu verstehen, worum es in dem Text geht. Konzentriere dich auf die Schlüsselwörter aus der Aufgabenstellung.

Die Aufgaben stehen in der Regel in der gleichen Reihenfolge, in der die entsprechenden Stellen im Text vorkommen.

Achte auf den Kontext. Manchmal gibt der Text weitere Informationen, die klar machen, was gemeint ist. So kannst du Wörter erschließen, die du nicht kennst.

Mache dir kurze Notizen auf einem Notizzettel oder mit Bleistift auf deinem Aufgabenblatt. Bleibe ruhig, wenn du beim ersten Mal nicht alles verstehst. Du hörst den Text meist zweimal.

▶ Skills file 4, p. 160

Nach dem Hören

Vervollständige deine Notizen sofort.

Auch wenn du es nicht geschafft hast, alles aufzuschreiben, sind die Informationen wahrscheinlich noch in deinem Gedächtnis.

Lies noch einmal genau durch, was du geschrieben hast. Passen deine Antworten zu den Fragen?

Konzentriere dich beim zweiten Hören auf das, was du beim ersten Mal nicht verstanden hast.

Merkaufgabe 6

Höre dir ein englisches Lied an. Versuche zuerst, den Refrain zu verstehen, um das Thema herauszufinden. Höre das Lied dann noch einmal und versuche, Details zu verstehen.

SF 7

Lesetexte verstehen

▶ Unit 1 | p. 25 ▶ Unit 2 | p. 53 ▶ Unit 3 | p. 83
▶ Unit 4 | p. 111 ▶ Unit 5 | p. 141

In diesem Buch findest du viele verschiedene Texte, z. B. Dialoge, Bildergeschichten, Tagebucheinträge.
Diese Strategien helfen dir beim Verstehen:

Je mehr englische Texte du liest, desto größer wird dein Wortschatz und desto schneller und besser verstehst du Texte.

Vor dem Lesen

Schaue dir die Überschrift und die Bilder an, die zum Text gehören, mit ihrer Bildunterschrift. Sie geben dir bereits Hinweise über den Inhalt des Textes.

Lies dir auch die Aufgaben zum Text gut durch und achte auf Schlüsselwörter. So weißt du, worauf du beim Lesen achten musst.

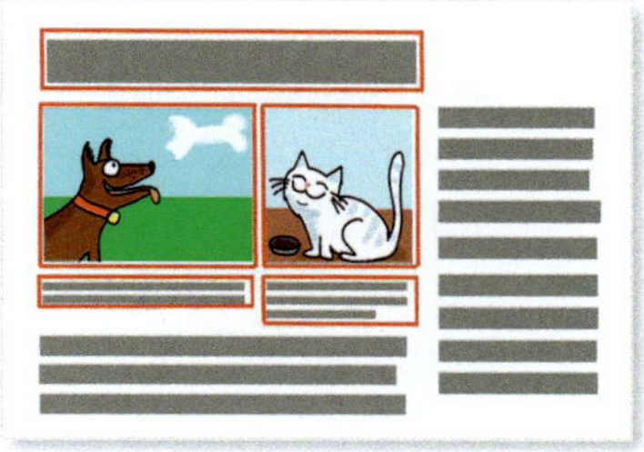

Beim Lesen

Lies den Text einmal ganz durch und versuche, ihn insgesamt zu verstehen. Lass unbekannte Wörter erst einmal beiseite.

Versuche, die fünf W-Fragen zum Text zu beantworten: *Who? Where? When? What? Why?* (Wer macht etwas? Wo? Wann? Was? Warum?) So siehst du, ob du den Text verstanden hast.

Du musst nicht jedes Wort in einem Text verstehen, um den Inhalt zu verstehen. Erst wenn du merkst, dass du ein Wort wirklich brauchst, um eine Aufgabe zu beantworten, solltest du es nachschlagen oder erfragen.

Zerteile längere Texte in Abschnitte und gib den Abschnitten Überschriften. Das hilft dir beim Verstehen, und du kannst so den gesamten Text später einfacher zusammenfassen.

Überlege, ob du die Aufgaben schon beantworten kannst. Falls nicht, lies den Text noch einmal mit den Aufgaben im Hinterkopf. Wenn nötig, mache dir Notizen. Triffst du auf ein unbekanntes Wort, versuche, die Bedeutung zu erschließen.

▶ Skills file 5, p. 161
▶ Skills file 2, p. 158

Nach dem Lesen

Beantworte nun die Fragen zum Text. Wenn möglich, vergleiche deine Ergebnisse mit einem Partner oder einer Partnerin.

Merkaufgabe 7

Schaue dir die Broschüre auf Seite 72 an. Lies die Überschriften und sieh dir die Bilder an. Was weißt du nun schon über den Inhalt der Broschüre?

(Die Lösung findest du auf S. 156.)

SF 8

Mediation

▸ Unit 1 | p. 22 ▸ Unit 2 | p. 45 ▸ Unit 4 | p. 101 ▸ Unit 5 | p. 139

In manchen Situationen musst du zwischen zwei Sprachen vermitteln. Dies nennt man Mediation. Du überträgst die wichtigsten Informationen von der einen Sprache in die andere.

Wann vermitteln?

Deutsch → Englisch

- Du möchtest jemandem z. B. englische Spielregeln oder einen englischen Artikel auf Deutsch erläutern.
- Du bist mit deiner Familie in England. Dein kleiner Bruder will z. B. Süßigkeiten kaufen oder wissen, was in einer Broschüre oder auf einem Schild steht.

Englisch → Deutsch

- Jemand spricht dich an der Bushaltestelle auf Englisch an, weil er oder sie den Anzeigetext nicht versteht.
- Ein Austauschschüler / eine Austauschschülerin besucht dich und spricht nicht sehr gut Deutsch.

Worauf muss ich achten?

Keine Panik vor unbekannten Wörtern

Du musst nicht 1:1 übersetzen. Deshalb ist es auch in Ordnung, wenn du nicht jedes Wort verstehst. Es reicht aus, dass du die zentrale Aussage verstehst.

Gib nur die wichtigsten Informationen weiter

Lasse unwichtige Wörter und Satzteile weg. In der Broschüre deines Urlaubshotels z. B. heißt es: *Play football on our great football field behind our hotel with the wonderful view.*
Du erklärst deinem kleinen Bruder: *Es gibt einen Fußballplatz hinter dem Hotel.*

Checkliste Mediation
- ✓ nur die wichtigen Infos weitergeben
- ✓ unbekannte Wörter umschreiben
- ✓ kurze und einfache Sätze verwenden
- ✓ auf Pronomen achten

Sage es anders

Wenn du ein Wort nicht kennst, versuche es mit anderen Wörtern zu umschreiben. Beispiele:

außer dienstags	*but not on Tuesdays*
Mindestalter 14 Jahre	*you must be 14 or older*
ermäßigte Eintrittskarten	*cheaper tickets*

▸ Skills file 11, p. 167

Sage es kurz

Bilde kurze und einfache Sätze, um Fehler zu vermeiden.

Achte in Gesprächen auf die Pronomen

Überlege immer, an wen du dich gerade wendest: Pronomen ändern sich.

Achte auf kulturelle Unterschiede

Versetze dich in dein Gegenüber hinein und überlege, was für diese Person wichtig ist, um die Situation oder die Inhalte verstehen zu können.

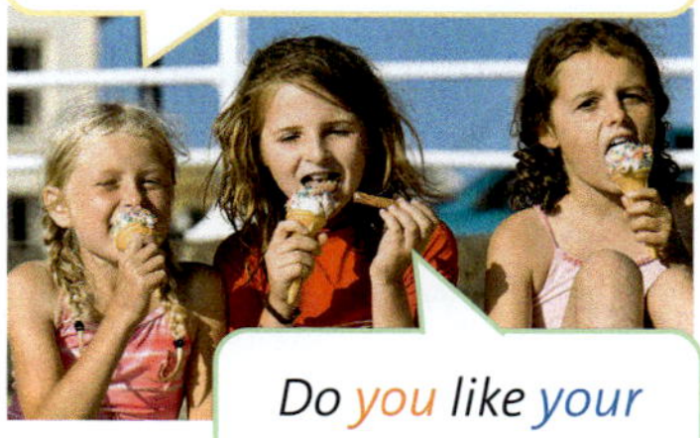

Eis essen war eine super Idee, oder? Frag Jane doch mal, wie ihr ihr Eis schmeckt.
Do you like your ice cream?

Merkaufgabe 8

Du bist mit deiner Familie in Brighton und deine kleine Schwester möchte wissen, was auf dem Bildschirm des Fahrkartenautomaten von S. 19 steht. Was sagst du ihr?

a) Hier kann man für unterschiedliche Tage Hin- und Rückfahrkarten in verschiedene Städte kaufen.

b) Oben wählst du „London" aus, in der Mitte eine Fahrkarte für die Hinfahrt und unten einen Tag.

c) Wenn du eine Fahrkarte kaufen möchtest, musst du das hier am Automaten tun.

(Die Lösung findest du auf Seite 156.)

SF 9

Einen Kurzvortrag halten

► Unit 4 | p. 114

Um einen guten Kurzvortrag halten zu können, musst du ihn gut vorbereiten und üben.

Erklär-film

Einen Kurzvortrag vorbereiten

Schritt 1: Informationen sammeln

Nutze verschiedene Medien, um Informationen zu sammeln.

Nutze das Internet, Bücher, Zeitschriften und Zeitungen.

► Skills file 4, p. 160

Schritt 2: Strukturieren und Ordnen

Ein Kurzvortrag sollte folgendermaßen aufgebaut sein:

- **Einleitung:** Nenne das Thema.
- **Hauptteil:** Nenne deine Hauptpunkte. Erzähle dann mehr zu jedem Punkt.
- **Schluss:** Bedanke dich fürs Zuhören und erkundige dich, ob deine Mitschüler/innen Fragen haben.

I'd like to talk about ...

First I'd like to tell you about ...
This picture shows ...

Thank you for listening.
Do you have any questions?

Schritt 3: Veranschaulichen

Veranschauliche deinen Vortrag mit Bildern oder Gegenständen. Achte darauf, dass die Verwendung der Bilder erlaubt ist, nutze daher z. B. *creative commons*-Bilder.

Suchst du Bilder im Internet, kannst du im Suchfeld nach creative commons filtern.

My favourite animal is a seagull
© jobikoe.example.com

Bei einer Präsentation am Computer:

- Wähle ein einfaches Folienlayout.
- Verwende eine Schriftgröße von mindestens 16 pt.
- Beschränke dich auf wenig Text.
- Wähle nur ein Bild pro Folie. Schreibe dazu, woher du dein Bild hast, z. B. die genaue URL und das Datum des Abrufes.

Schritt 4: Informationen aufschreiben

Mache dir kurze Notizen auf Karteikarten. Strukturiere deine Notizen genauso wie deine Präsentation. Hebe die wichtigsten Begriffe mit verschiedenen Farben hervor. Du kannst auch kleine Erinnerungen zum Ablauf deines Vortrags notieren, z. B. wann du welches Bild zeigst.

▸ Skills file 5, p. 167

Schritt 5: Den Kurzvortrag üben

Übe deinen Vortrag mehrmals vor dem Spiegel oder mit einem Partner / einer Partnerin. Gebt euch gegenseitig Tipps, wie ihr euch verbessern könnt. Du kannst dich auch selbst mit dem Smartphone aufnehmen. Achte auf die Zeit.

Den Kurzvortrag halten

Überprüfe zu Beginn, ob alles vorbereitet ist: Ist das Poster aufgehängt? Ist der Computer bereit? Liegen die Vortragskarten richtig sortiert? Dann beginne deinen Vortrag:

- Schaue dein Publikum an und warte, bis es ruhig ist.
- Sprich langsam, laut und deutlich.
- Zeige während deines Vortrags auf Bilder oder dein Poster.

Merkaufgabe 9

Schaue dir Video 1 von Kats Vortrag an. Gib ihr zwei Tipps, wie sie es beim nächsten Mal besser machen kann.

(Die Lösung findest du auf Seite 156 und in Video 2 von Kats Vortrag.)

SF 10

Die eigene Meinung äußern

▸ Unit 3 | p. 86

Wie drücke ich aus, was ich denke?

Zu Beginn einer Diskussion sagst du, was du über ein Thema denkst.

In my opinion ...
I think ...
I'm sure that ...

Wie frage ich nach der Meinung?

In Diskussionen geht es nicht nur um die eigene Meinung. Daher fragst du die anderen auch nach ihrer Meinung.

What do you think?

Wie reagiere ich angemessen?

Gehe auf die Beiträge anderer ein und respektiere sie. Sei auch bei Meinungsverschiedenheiten sachlich und höflich.

I agree.
You're right.
For me that's true.
I think so too.

I'm not sure here.
Well, I don't agree.
I don't think so.
I don't think that's true.

Merkaufgabe 10

Welche Aussage ist in einer Diskussion angemessen?

a) I don't agree. It's stupid to spend hours on your phone.

b) Well, for me that isn't true. I like to spend my time with other things.

(Die Lösung findest du auf Seite 156.)

SF 11

Wörter umschreiben

▸ Unit 1 | p. 36 ▸ Unit 4 | p. 112

Fehlt dir beim Sprechen ein Wort oder fällt es dir nicht ein, kannst du es umschreiben.

Finde zunächst einen passenden **Oberbegriff** (*umbrella word*). **Umschreibe**, indem du weitere Details nennst.

It's a kind of ...
It's a person ...
It's a place ...
It's an activity ...

	Beispiele für *umbrella words*	Beispiele für Umschreibungen
waitress	It's a person.	She works in a restaurant.
kitchen	It's a room in the house.	You make food there.

	umbrella words
Personen	person • man • woman • boy • girl • child • ...
Orte	place • building • room • country • ...
Dinge	food • drink • game • musical instrument • sport • thing • ...

Merkaufgabe 11

Finde das richtige *umbrella word*.

a) rugby • tennis • football • cricket

b) school • park • town hall • supermarket

(Die Lösung findest du auf Seite 156.)

SF 12

Eine Geschichte planen

▸ Unit 1 | p. 28

Schritt 1: Ideen sammeln

Sammle zuerst wichtige Ideen und Wörter, z. B. in einer Mindmap. Beantworte dafür die *wh*-Fragen: *Who? When? Where? What? Why?*

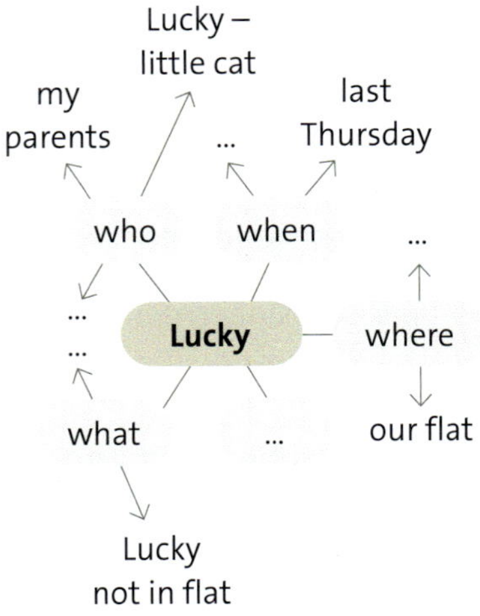

Schritt 2: Die Geschichte strukturieren

Deine Geschichte ist viel besser zu verstehen, wenn du sie gliederst. Unterteile sie deshalb in:

- **Anfang** *(beginning)*: In einem einleitenden Satz beschreibst du, worum es in deiner Geschichte geht.
- **Mittelteil** *(middle)*: Im Mittelteil beschreibst du die Umstände und Ereignisse deiner Geschichte.
- **Schluss** *(end)*: Schließe deine Geschichte mit einer kleinen Zusammenfassung ab.

beginning → Last week something bad happened.

middle → When I came home from school last Thursday, I wanted to play with my cute little cat, Lucky. I looked for her everywhere in the flat, but she wasn't there. Then I saw the open window. I was scared because I thought Lucky fell out of the window. When my parents came home from work, I was very sad. Then we had an idea. We wrote a note with a nice picture of Lucky and my dad's phone number. We put up the note in our neighbourhood. Two days later a man called my dad. There was a little cat in his small garden, so my dad and I went to his house. When the man opened his door, there she was: Lucky! She was back!

end → In the end my parents and I were very happy that Lucky was home again.

Schritt 3: Einen Textentwurf erstellen

Möchtest du die Geschichte mündlich vortragen, mache dir nun Stichpunkte. Schreibe dafür wichtige Wörter auf Karteikarten und übe, sie frei sprechend vorzutragen.

Möchtest du die Geschichte aufschreiben, erstelle einen Textentwurf – auf einem Blatt Papier oder am Computer.

Überlege dir eine sinnvolle Reihenfolge und beginne bei neuen Punkten mit einer neuen Zeile, z. B. nach deiner Einleitung und vor deinem Schluss.

Schritt 4: Deine Geschichte interessant klingen lassen

Deine Geschichte klingt viel interessanter, wenn du Adjektive und Bindewörter verwendest: Beschreibe Personen, Orte oder Dinge mit Adjektiven. So können sich deine Zuhörer oder Leser deine Geschichte besser vorstellen. Verbinde deine Sätze mithilfe von *Bindewörtern*, z. B. *and, or, but, because, so, then*.

Merkaufgabe 12

Beantworte zum Thema „My last weekend“ die *wh*-Fragen. Sammle die Antworten in einer kleinen Mindmap wie oben im Beispiel.

SF 13

Texte überprüfen und verbessern

▸ Unit 5 | p. 144

Ein Text ist noch nicht fertig, wenn du ihn zu Ende geschrieben hast. Du solltest ihn noch mehrmals durchlesen bzw. in Partnerkorrektur durchlesen lassen und auf folgende Punkte achten:

Erstes Lesen: Ist der Text vollständig und verständlich?

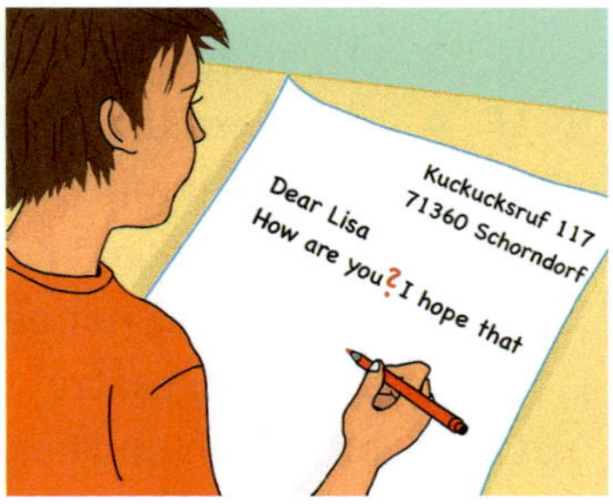

Lies den Text und prüfe:

- Hast du irgendwo ein Wort oder Satzzeichen vergessen?
- Sind die Sätze gut verständlich?
- Ist die Reihenfolge der Sätze sinnvoll?
- Hast du Absätze gemacht?
- Hast du *linking words* benutzt?
- Hast du Personen, Orte oder Dinge mithilfe von Adjektiven beschrieben?

Zweites Lesen: Findest du noch Fehler?

1 Groß- und Kleinschreibung

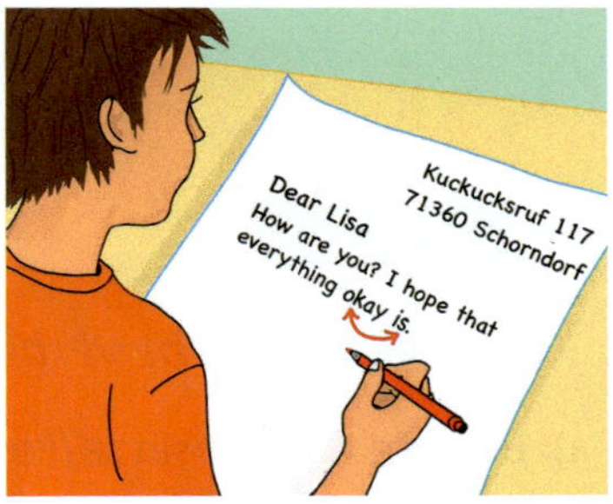

- Im Englischen schreibt man fast alles klein. Prüfe also: Hast du Wörter wie *football, cinema, train*, ... kleingeschrieben?
- In manchen Fällen schreibt man aber groß – prüfe also: Hast du alle Satzanfänge großgeschrieben?
  Our school starts at 8 o'clock.
  Hast du das Wort *I* (= ich) immer großgeschrieben?
  Maybe I'll play football.

2 Die richtige Zeitform

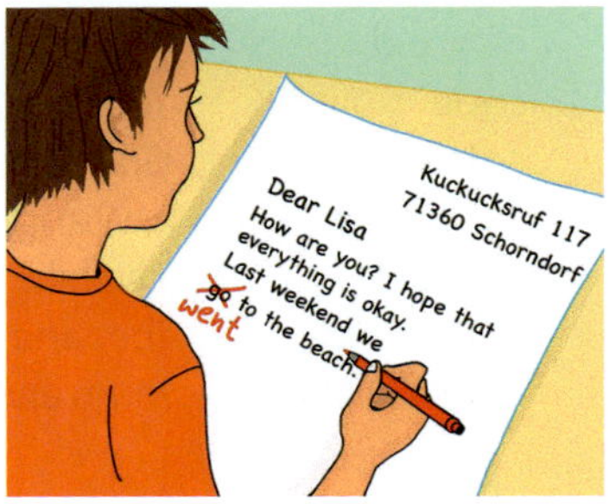

- Schreibst du über die Gegenwart? Oder über Dinge, die du regelmäßig machst? (Signalwörter: *today, often, always*)
  – Dann brauchst du das *simple present*:
    I often go to the swimming pool.
- Oder schreibst du über Sachen, die schon passiert sind? (Signalwörter: *yesterday, last Friday*)
  – Dann brauchst du das *simple past*:
    Yesterday I went to the swimming pool.

Merkaufgabe 13

Probiere es gleich aus. Nimm dir einen englischen Text, den du in letzter Zeit geschrieben hast. Lies ihn dir zweimal durch und wende dabei die Punkte von oben an.

Inhalt

Erklärfilm: Dieses Symbol zeigt dir, dass du einen Erklärfilm zu diesem Thema in der App findest.

Revision 1

Das Verb *be* *(The verb be)*

Erklärfilm

a) Bejahte Aussagesätze *(Positive statements)*

Kurzformen	Langformen
I'm old.	I am old.
You're old.	You are old.
He's old.	Grandpa is old.
She's old.	Ms Lang is old.
It's old.	The bike is old.
We're old.	Tom and I are old.
They're old.	Mum and Dad are old.

Yes

Es gibt Kurz- und Langformen. Bei den Kurzformen ist ein Buchstabe weggefallen. Dafür steht ein Apostroph (').

Kurzformen werden eher beim Sprechen und in persönlichen E-Mails oder Chats verwendet. Sie stehen nach Pronomen (*I, you, ...*).

Langformen benutzt du nach Eigennamen (*Zane, Sunita*) oder Nomen (*bike, teachers*). Man verwendet sie auch bei offiziellen Schreiben.

Revision 1

Das Verb *be* *(The verb be)*

Erklärfilm

b) Verneinte Aussagesätze *(Negative statements)*

Kurzformen	Langformen (No)
I'm not old.	(I am not old.)
You aren't old.	(You are not old.)
He isn't old.	(Grandpa is not old.)
She isn't old.	(Ms Lang is not old.)
It isn't old.	(The bike is not old.)
We aren't old.	(Tom and I are not old.)
They aren't old.	(Mum and Dad are not old.)

Bei der Verneinung benutzt du fast immer die Kurzformen.

I'm not messy, I'm smart!

Erklärfilm

c) Fragen und Kurzantworten *(Questions and short answers)*

Fragen (?)		Kurzantworten
		Yes, I am.
		Yes, he / she / it is.
Am I		Yes, you / we / they are.
Are you		
Is he / she / it	late?	No, I'm not.
Are we		No, he / she / it isn't.
Are they		No, you / we / they aren't.

Antworte auf eine Frage im Englischen nicht einfach mit *yes* oder *no*. Das klingt meist unhöflich. Verwende Kurzantworten.

Are you a parrot?
No, I'm not.

Revision 2

Die einfache Gegenwart *(The simple present)*

Erklärfilm

a) Bejahte Aussagesätze *(Positive statements)*

bejahte Sätze (Yes)	
I You We They	start.
He David She Anna It	starts.

He, she, it – ein -s muss mit!

Mit dem *simple present* sagst du, was oft oder täglich oder auch selten oder nie geschieht. Diese Signalwörter findest du oft in Sätzen im *simple present: always, never, often, rarely, sometimes, usually.*

Bei *he, she* und *it* musst du immer ein -s ans Verb anhängen.

! Manchmal gibt es Besonderheiten, z. B.:
do – does *have – has* *tidy – tidies*

Revision 2

Die einfache Gegenwart *(The simple present)*

Erklärfilm

b) Verneinte Aussagesätze *(Negative statements)*

verneinte Sätze	No
I / You / We / They	don't start.
He / She / It	doesn't start.

Aussagen im *simple present* musst du mit *don't* oder *doesn't* verneinen.
Das Verb steht dann immer im Infinitiv (der Grundform): *He doesn't start.*

Erklärfilm

c) Fragen mit *Do / Does (Do / Does-questions)*

Fragen		?
Do	I / you / we they / your parents	like music?
Does	he / your dad she / Lily it	like music?

Fragen, auf die man mit „Ja" oder „Nein" antworten kann, heißen Entscheidungsfragen. Sie beginnen mit *Do* oder *Does*.

Mit *I, you, we, they* verwendest du *Do*.

Mit *he, she, it* verwendest du *Does*.

d) Kurzantworten *(Short answers)*

Kurzantworten	
Yes, I do.	No, I don't.
Yes, you do.	No, you don't.
Yes, he / she / it does.	No, he / she / it doesn't.
Yes, we do.	No, we don't.
Yes, they do.	No, they don't.

Es ist unhöflich, auf Entscheidungsfragen nur mit *yes* oder *no* zu antworten.
Besser ist eine Kurzantwort.

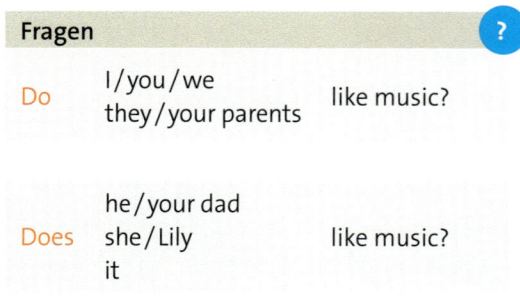

Yes, I do.
Do you live in Brighton too?

Erklärfilm

e) Fragen mit Fragewörtern *(Questions with question words)*

How do you get home?
Wie kommst du nach Hause?

Who does Luca love?
Wen liebt Luca?

Who loves Luca?
Wer liebt Luca?

Auch Fragen mit Fragewörtern stellst du mit *do* oder *does*. Das Fragewort steht wie im Deutschen am Anfang.

Wenn mit *Who* oder *What* nach dem Subjekt des Satzes gefragt wird, bildest du die Frage ohne *do* oder *does*.

Erklär-
film

Die Verlaufsform der Gegenwart *(The present progressive)*

I'm reading a comic.
Ich lese gerade einen Comic.

Dad is cooking dinner.
Papa macht gerade das Abendessen.

What are you doing at the moment?
Was machst du jetzt gerade?

Mit dem *present progressive* sagst du, was jemand jetzt gerade tut. Damit beschreibst du auch, was auf Bildern passiert.
Diese Zeitangaben findest du oft in Sätzen im *present progressive*:
now, at the moment, today.

Im Deutschen sagst du meist „Ich bin gerade am / beim ..."

bejahte Sätze Yes

I'm	
You're	
He's	
She's	working.
It's	
We're	
They're	

Das *present progressive* besteht aus zwei Teilen:

am ('m)		
are ('re)	+	Verb + *-ing*
is ('s)		

verneinte Sätze No

I'm not	
You aren't	
He isn't	
She isn't	working.
It isn't	
We aren't	
They aren't	

Bei Verben, die auf *-e* enden, fällt das *-e* bei der *ing*-Form weg:
have – having
make – making
give – giving

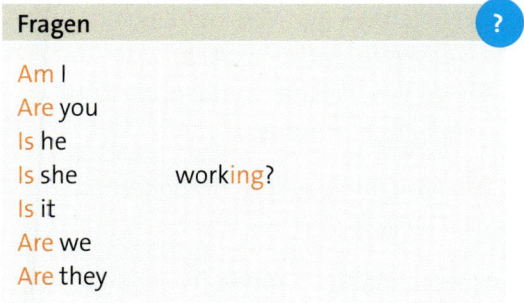

Scout is giving a talk.

Fragen ?

Am I	
Are you	
Is he	
Is she	working?
Is it	
Are we	
Are they	

Bei einigen Verben wird der letzte Buchstabe verdoppelt, z. B.:
plan — planning
stop — stopping
sit — sitting

LF 1

Die einfache Vergangenheit *(The simple past)*

I was in Berlin last weekend.
Letztes Wochenende war ich in Berlin.

Yesterday dad and I visited grandma.
Gestern haben Papa und ich Oma besucht.

Mit dem *simple past* sprichst du über Dinge, die in der Vergangenheit geschehen sind. Du verwendest es oft mit Zeitangaben wie *yesterday, last week / year / summer, in 2020.*

Erklär-film

a) Das Verb *be (The verb be)*

▶ Unit 1 | p. 13

bejahte und verneinte Aussagesätze

I / He / She / It Noah / Mum	was wasn't	at home.
You / We / They	were weren't	at home.

Fragen ?

Was	he / she	at home?
Were	you / they	at home?

Das Verb *be* (sein) hat besondere Vergangenheitsformen: *was* und *were*.

Yesterday Scout was at the beach.

LF 2

Erklär-film

b) Bejahte Aussagesätze *(Positive statements)*

▶ Unit 1 | p. 14,16

Yesterday evening I watched TV.
Gestern Abend habe ich ferngesehen / sah ich fern.

I arrived in London last week.
Ich bin letzte Woche in London angekommen. / Ich kam letzte Woche in London an.

bejahte Aussagesätze Yes

I / You He / She / It We / They	watched TV yesterday.

Die Vergangenheitsform der Verben ist für alle Personen gleich.

Bei regelmäßigen Verben hängst du *-ed* an das Verb: *walk – walked*
Bei Verben, die auf *-e* enden, wird nur *-d* angehängt: *arrive – arrived*.

! Manchmal gibt es Besonderheiten, z. B.:
plan – planned *try – tried*

Unregelmäßige Formen musst du lernen, z. B.:
do – did *go – went* *see – saw*
Du kannst sie auf S. 271 nachschlagen.

LF 3

Die einfache Vergangenheit *(The simple past)*

Erklärfilm

c) Verneinte Aussagesätze *(Negative statements)*

▶ Unit 1 | p. 20

I didn't watch TV yesterday.
Gestern habe ich nicht ferngesehen.

verneinte Sätze	No
I / You He / She / It We / They	didn't help.

Wenn du sagen willst, dass etwas nicht geschah, setzt du *didn't* vor das Verb.

Das Verb steht dann immer im Infinitiv (der Grundform): *He didn't help.*

Wenn Didi kommt, muss Ede gehen!

LF 4

Erklärfilm

d) Fragen und Kurzantworten *(Questions and short answers)*

▶ Unit 2 | p. 46

Did you watch the parade last weekend?
Hast du letztes Wochenende den Umzug gesehen?

Fragen		?
Did	I / you he / she / it we / they	help?

Yes, I / you did.	No, I / you didn't.
Yes, he / she / it did.	No, he / she / it didn't.
Yes, we / they did.	No, we / they didn't.

Fragen im *simple past* bildest du mit *did* und dem Infinitiv des Verbs: *Did he help?*

Did you eat my fish?
No, I didn't.

Kurzantworten bildest du mit *did* oder *didn't*.

LF 5

Erklärfilm

e) Fragen mit Fragewörtern *(Questions with question words)*

▶ Unit 2 | p. 47

Fragen			?
What	did	she	watch?
When	did	it	finish?
Where	did	they	go?

How did it go? – It went well.

Auch bei Fragen mit Fragewörtern verwendest du *did* bei allen Personen und das Verb im Infinitiv: *How did it go?*

Bei den Antworten musst du das Verb in die Vergangenheitsform setzen.

LF 6

Nebensätze mit Konjunktionen
(Subordinate clauses with conjunctions)

▸ Unit 2 | p. 68

I listen to music when I do my exercises.
Ich höre Musik, wenn ich meine Aufgaben mache.

She went to bed because she was tired.
Sie ging ins Bett, weil sie müde war.

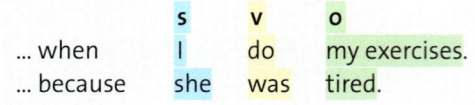

	s	v	o
... when	I	do	my exercises.
... because	she	was	tired.

Mit Konjunktionen wie *because*, *so* oder *when* kannst du Sätze miteinander verknüpfen.

Dabei ist die Wortstellung im Nebensatz nach der Konjunktion genauso wie im Hauptsatz: subject – verb – object.

Im Deutschen ist das im Nebensatz anders:

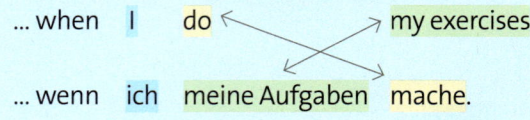

... when	I	do	my exercises.
... wenn	ich	meine Aufgaben	mache.

LF 7

Die Zukunft mit *going to* *(The going to-future)* rezeptiv*

Erklärfilm

a) Aussagesätze *(Statements)*

▸ Unit 3 | p. 73

We're going to have a picnic on Sunday.
Wir haben vor, am Sonntag zu picknicken.

It isn't going to rain.
Es wird nicht regnen.

bejahte Aussagesätze Yes

I'm You're He's / She's / It's We're They're	going to	fall.

verneinte Aussagesätze No

I'm not You aren't He / She / It isn't We aren't They aren't	going to	fall.

Mit *going to ...* sagst du,
– was du vorhast oder planst und
– was wahrscheinlich bald passieren wird.

Going to hat hier nichts mit dem deutschen „gehen" zu tun, sondern bedeutet „werden".

Das *going to*-future besteht aus drei Teilen:

am ('m) *are ('re)* *is ('s)*	+	going to	+	Verb

Das Verb bleibt immer im Infinitiv:
I'm going to watch a video.

* Das *going to-future* soll in Jgst. 6 nur rezeptiv angewandt werden. Die produktive Einführung erfolgt in Jgst. 7.

LF 8

Die Zukunft mit *going to* (*The going to-future*) rezeptiv*

Erklär-film

b) Fragen und Kurzantworten *(Questions and short answers)*

▶ Unit 3 | p. 75

Are you going to leave soon?
Wirst du bald gehen?

Is the rain going to stop?
Wird der Regen aufhören?

Bei Fragen stehen *am*, *are* oder *is* am Beginn des Fragesatzes, vor dem Subjekt.

Are you going to swim?
No, I'm not.

Entscheidungsfragen		
Am I		
Are you		
Is he / she / it	going to	fall?
Are we		
Are they		

?

Kurzantworten	
Yes, I am.	No, I'm not.
Yes, you are.	No, you aren't.
Yes, he / she / it is.	No, he / she / it isn't.
Yes, we are.	No, we aren't.
Yes, they are.	No, they aren't.

LF 9

c) Fragen mit Fragewörtern *(Questions with question words)*

▶ Unit 3 | p. 75

Who am I going to meet?
Wen werde ich treffen?

Why are you going to leave so early?
Warum wirst du so früh gehen?

Fragewörter stehen wie im Deutschen am Satzanfang.

When is the rain going to stop?

Entscheidungsfragen			
	am I		
Where	are you		
How	is he / she / it	going to	play?
When	are we		
What	are they		

?

LF 10

Steigerung und Vergleich *(Comparison)*

a) Der Komparativ *(The comparative)*

Erklärfilm

▶ Unit 3 | p. 77

Mum is taller than dad.
Mama ist größer als Papa.

This shop is more expensive than the market.
Dieses Geschäft ist teurer als der Markt.

fast	faster
loud	louder
big	bigger
hot	hotter
noisy	noisier
happy	happier
famous	more famous
expensive	more expensive

Leon is as old as Malik.
The red bike is as expensive as the blue one.

Personen und Sachen kann man vergleichen, indem man Adjektive steigert.

Bei einsilbigen Adjektiven und zweisilbigen, die auf *-y* enden, hängst du *-er* an das Adjektiv.

! Bei einigen Adjektiven musst du bei der Schreibung aufpassen (z. B. *hot* oder *noisy*).

! Diese Ausnahmen musst du lernen:
good – better *bad – worse* *little – less*

Bei dreisilbigen Adjektiven und zweisilbigen Adjektiven, die nicht auf *-y* enden, setzt du *more* vor das Adjektiv.

Wenn du sagen willst, dass zwei Personen oder Dinge genau gleich groß, alt, teuer usw. sind, verwendest du *as ... as*.
Im Deutschen sagst du *so ... wie*:
Leon ist so alt wie Malik.

LF 11

b) Der Superlativ *(The superlative)*

Erklärfilm

▶ Unit 3 | p. 78

Leon is the oldest student in our class.
Leon ist der älteste Schüler in unserer Klasse.

This game is the most expensive.
Dieses Spiel ist am teuersten.

fast	the fastest
loud	the loudest
big	the biggest
happy	the happiest
famous	the most famous
expensive	the most expensive

Mit dem Superlativ sagst du, dass etwas am größten, ältesten, teuersten, besten usw. ist. Dazu hängst du bei einsilbigen Adjektiven und bei zweisilbigen, die auf *-y* enden, *-est* an das Adjektiv.

! Bei einigen Adjektiven musst du bei der Schreibung aufpassen (z. B. *big* oder *happy*).

! Diese Ausnahmen musst du lernen:
good – best *bad – worst* *little – least*

Bei dreisilbigen Adjektiven und zweisilbigen Adjektiven, die nicht auf *-y* enden, setzt du *most* vor das Adjektiv.

LF 12

some / any

Erklär-
film

▶ Unit 4 | p. 101

some

I can make some sandwiches.
Can I have some sugar, please?

Would you like some pizza?

any

There isn't any tea.
We don't have any cake today.

Anders als im Deutschen muss man im Englischen *some* oder *any* einsetzen, wenn man über eine Menge oder Anzahl spricht und keine genaue Zahl nennen kann.

Some bedeutet *einige* oder *etwas*.
Du verwendest *some*
- in bejahten Aussagen,
- wenn du um etwas bittest,
- wenn du jemandem etwas anbietest.

In verneinten Sätzen verwendest du *not ... any*. Auf Deutsch: *kein, keine, keinen*.

LF 13

a little / a few

Erklär-
film

▶ Unit 4 | p. 102

zählbar

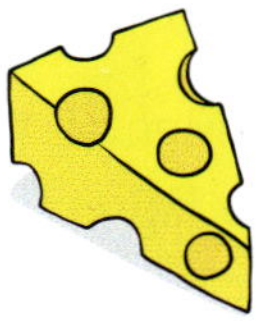

nicht zählbar

a few

There are only a few sausages left.
There are a few pencils on the table.

a little

Can I have a little milk in my tea, please?
I take my coffee with a little sugar.

Wenn du über Mengen sprichst, ist es wichtig, ob es sich um zählbare oder nicht zählbare Nomen handelt.

Zählbare Nomen haben eine Pluralform: *one apple – two apples*.

Nicht zählbare Nomen kannst du nicht in die Mehrzahl setzen: *cheese, fruit, music, love*.

Für größere Mengen kennst du schon *much* (für nicht zählbare Nomen) und *many* (für zählbare Nomen).

Mit *a little* oder *a few* kannst du über kleine Mengen sprechen.

Bei zählbaren Nomen verwendest du *a few* (einige).

Bei nicht zählbaren Nomen sagst du *a little* (ein wenig).

LF 14

Das *present perfect* rezeptiv*

Erklär-film

a) Aussagesätze *(Statements)*

▶ Unit 4 | p. 105

Ben is happy. He has done his homework.
Ben ist froh. Er hat seine Hausaufgaben gemacht.

My little sister has never been on a plane.
Meine kleine Schwester ist noch nie geflogen.

bejahte Aussagesätze Yes

I You We They	have started early. 've started early.
He She It	has started early. 's started early.

verneinte Aussagesätze No

I You We They	haven't started early.
He She It	hasn't started early.

Mit dem *present perfect* sagst du,
– dass du etwas schon oder gerade eben gemacht hast. Oft hat die Handlung Auswirkungen auf die Gegenwart. Signalwörter: *already, just, yet*.
– dass du etwas schon einmal, öfter oder noch nie gemacht hast. Signalwörter: *ever, never, once, twice, lots of times*.

Das *present perfect* besteht aus zwei Teilen:

have ('ve) *has ('s)*	+	*past participle* (eine besondere Verbform)

Wie bildest du das *past participle*?
Bei regelmäßigen Verben hängst du *-ed* an das Verb: *walk – walked*.
Bei Verben, die auf *-e* enden, wird nur *-d* angehängt: *arrive – arrived*.

Unregelmäßige *past participle*-Formen musst du lernen, z. B.:

be – been
do – done
eat – eaten
give – given
go – gone
have – had
see – seen
sing – sung

Du kannst sie in der dritten Spalte der *List of irregular verbs* auf S. 271 nachschlagen.

* Das *present perfect* soll in Jgst. 6 nur rezeptiv angewandt werden. Die produktive Einführung erfolgt in Jgst. 7.

LF 15

Das *present perfect* rezeptiv*

Erklärfilm

b) Fragen und Kurzantworten *(Questions and short answers)*

▶ Unit 4 | p. 105

Have you ever been to France?
Bist du schon einmal in Frankreich gewesen? / Warst du schon einmal in Frankreich?

Fragen und Kurzantworten	?
Have you started?	Yes, I have. No, I haven't.
Has she started?	Yes, she has. No, she hasn't.

Entscheidungsfragen im *present perfect* beginnen mit *have* oder *has*.

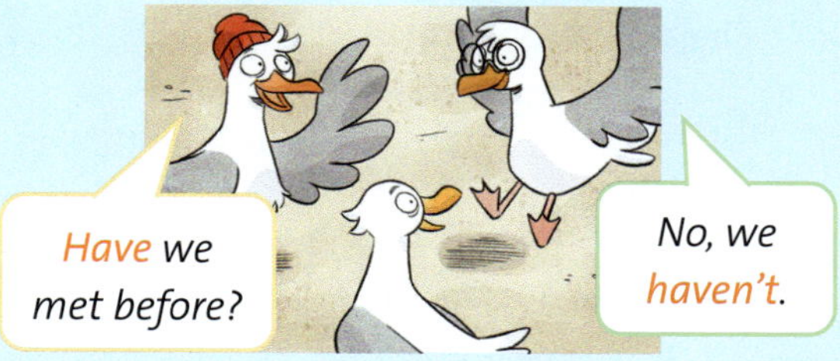

Have we met before?
No, we haven't.

LF 16

Erklärfilm

Zusammensetzungen mit *some / any*
(Compounds with some / any)

▶ Unit 4 | p. 109

some

Some of my friends live in America.
Einige meiner Freunde leben in Amerika.

There's somebody in the kitchen.
Da ist jemand in der Küche.

It must be somewhere in my room.
Es muss irgendwo in meinem Zimmer sein.

any

There isn't any tea. Is there any juice?
Es ist kein Tee da. Gibt es Saft?

I don't have anything to wear.
Ich habe nichts anzuziehen.

Can you see Mum anywhere?
Kannst du Mama irgendwo sehen?

Some bedeutet *einige* oder *etwas*.
Es gibt das Wort auch in Zusammmensetzungen:
somebody / someone – jemand
something – etwas
somewhere – irgendwo

Du benutzt *some* und seine Zusammensetzungen **in bejahten Aussagen**.

In verneinten Aussagen und Fragen verwendest du *any* und seine Zusammensetzungen:
not ... anybody / anyone – niemand
not ... anything – nichts
not ... anywhere – nirgendwo
anybody / anyone – jemand
anything – etwas
anywhere – irgendwo

Auch *every* und *no* gibt es in Zusammensetzungen, z. B. *everyone, nowhere*.

* Das *present perfect* soll in Jgst. 6 nur rezeptiv angewandt werden. Die produktive Einführung erfolgt in Jgst. 7.

LF 17

Die Zukunft mit *will* (*The will-future*)

Erklär-film

▶ Unit 5 | p. 132

I think you'll have a great party.
Ich glaube, du wirst eine tolle Party haben.

Maybe we'll go swimming tomorrow.
Vielleicht gehen wir morgen schwimmen.

bejahte Aussagesätze Yes

It	will 'll	be sunny tomorrow.

verneinte Aussagesätze No

It	will not won't	be sunny tomorrow.

Fragen und Kurzantworten ?

Will it be sunny?	Yes, it will. No, it won't.

Wenn du sagst, was in der Zukunft wahrscheinlich geschehen wird, verwendest du das *will-future*.

Die Sätze beginnen oft mit *I think, maybe, I'm sure*.

Du bildest das *will-future* mit *will* und dem Infinitiv des Verbs.

Die Kurzform von *will* ist *'ll*.

I think we'll be good friends.

Die Kurzform von *will not* ist *won't*.

LF 18

Die Wortstellung (*Word order*)

▶ Unit 5 | p. 137

Hauptsätze

s	v	o
Deniz	loves	old cars.

Ortsangaben

s	v	o	*(Where?)*
I	have	lunch	at school

Zeitangaben

(When?)	s	v	o	*(When?)*
At 12.30	he / she	has	lunch	at 12.30.

Orts- und Zeitangaben

s	v	o	*(Where?)*	*(When?)*
She	met	him	in Dublin	yesterday.
He	has	lunch	at home	at 12.30.

In einfachen Aussagesätzen ist die Wortstellung wie im Deutschen:

subject – verb – object.

subject
verb
object

Ortsangaben (*in town, at home, at school* usw.) stehen meist nach Verb und Objekt.

Zeitangaben (*at 2 o'clock, in the morning, yesterday* usw.) stehen ganz am Anfang oder ganz am Ende des Satzes.

Bei Orts- und Zeitangaben in einem Satz gilt im Englischen die Regel:

Ort vor Zeit.

Häufigkeitsadverbien			
s	a	v	o
Yusuf	always	tidies	his room.
Mila	sometimes	cleans	her bike.

Mit Häufigkeitsadverbien (*always, often, sometimes, rarely, never*) sagst du, wie oft etwas geschieht.

Anders als im Deutschen stehen sie im Englischen meist direkt vor dem Hauptverb.

Dad	often	makes	breakfast.
Papa	macht	oft	das Frühstück.

Grammatical terms *(Grammatische Fachbegriffe in diesem Buch)*

adjective	das Adjektiv: *good, old, nice*
adverb (of frequency)	das (Häufigkeits-)Adverb: *often, always, sometimes, never*
article	der Artikel: *a, an, the*
comparative	der Komparativ: *younger, more difficult*
comparison	der Vergleich: *He's older than me.*
compound	die Zusammensetzung
conjunction	die Konjunktion: *because, when, so*
form	die Form
future	die Zukunft
irregular	unregelmäßig
linking word	das Bindewort: *and, so, because*
long form	die Langform: *I am, do not, you are*
negative	die negative Form: *don't go, can't*
noun	das Nomen / Substantiv: *friend, car*
object	das Objekt: *I like cats.*
past participle	das Partizip Perfekt, 3. Form des Verbs: *gone, seen, said*
personal pronoun	das Personalpronomen: *I, you, he, she, it, we, they*
plural	der Plural: *books, stories*
positive	die positive Form: *do, can, …*
possessive determiner	der Possessivbegleiter: *my, your, his, her, its, our, their*
preposition	die Präposition: *in, at, on*
present perfect	das *present perfect*: *I have never been to Rome.*
present progressive	die Verlaufsform der Gegenwart: *I'm speaking*
regular	regelmäßig
short answer	die Kurzantwort: *Yes, I do. / No, I'm not. / Yes, she does.*
sentence starter	der Satzanfang
short form	die Kurzform: *I'm, don't*
simple past	die einfache Vergangenheit: *We saw a lot of sights.*
simple present	die einfache Gegenwart: *I speak English. / He likes it.*
statement	die Aussage, der Aussagesatz
subject	das Subjekt: *They eat dinner.*
subordinate clause	der Nebensatz: *I like comics because they're fun.*
tense	die Zeitform
superlative	der Superlativ: *the youngest, the most difficult*
verb	das Verb: *(to) go, (to) do*
wh-question	die Frage mit Fragewort: *What's this? Who are you?*
word order	die Wortstellung
yes/no-question	die Entscheidungsfrage: *Are you 12? Do I look OK?*

Wichtige Schreibregeln im Englischen

Groß- und Kleinschreibung

Im Englischen wird fast alles klein geschrieben. Merke dir nur diese Ausnahmen:

– das Wort *I* (*ich*);
– Monatsnamen (*January, February, ...*);
– Wochentage (*Monday, Tuesday, ...*);
– Eigennamen und geografische Namen (*Tom, Lisa, Brighton, ...*);
– Länder, deren Bewohner/innen und Adjektive (*Germany, the Germans, German*);
– das erste Wort am Satzanfang und in Überschriften.

Stumme Buchstaben

Manche Wörter enthalten Buchstaben, die du zwar schreibst, aber nicht sprichst:

b lamb
c science
d sandwich
g design
h technology
i fruit
k (to) know, knife
l (to) walk, (to) talk
u guitar, building
t (to) listen
w (to) answer, two, wrong, (to) write

Verdoppelung der Endkonsonanten

(to) stop – stopping, stopped
(to) win – winning, winner

-y wird zu -ie

– im Plural: *story – stories, a pony – three ponies*

– in der 3. Person Singular: *(to) tidy – he tidies;*
– bei der Steigerung von Adjektiven: *busy – busier, easy – easier.*

Buchstabenverbindungen

Manche Buchstabenverbindungen kommen häufiger vor. Wenn du sie dir merkst, können sie dir beim Schreiben helfen:

-ee- see, deep, meet, street
-ea- beach, meat, pea
-igh- sight, fight, right, night
-oo- book, good
-ous- dangerous, nervous, famous
-tion station, competition

Kleine Unterschiede Englisch – Deutsch

Manche Wörter sind im Englischen und Deutschen fast gleich – aber achte auf diese Unterschiede:

– k wird zu c: perfekt – *perfect*, Musik – *music*;
– f wird zu ph: Foto – *photo*;
– isch wird zu ic: elektrisch – *electric*, hektisch – *hectic*;
– el wird zu le: Titel – *title*, Artikel – *article*;
– sch wird zu sh: britisch – *British*, stylisch – *stylish*;
– deutsches -e am Wortende entfällt: Melone – *melon*, Lampe – *lamp*, Ende – *end*.

Wordbank 1: Holiday activities

▶ Unit 1 | p. 17

holiday activities

water activities

(to) go rafting

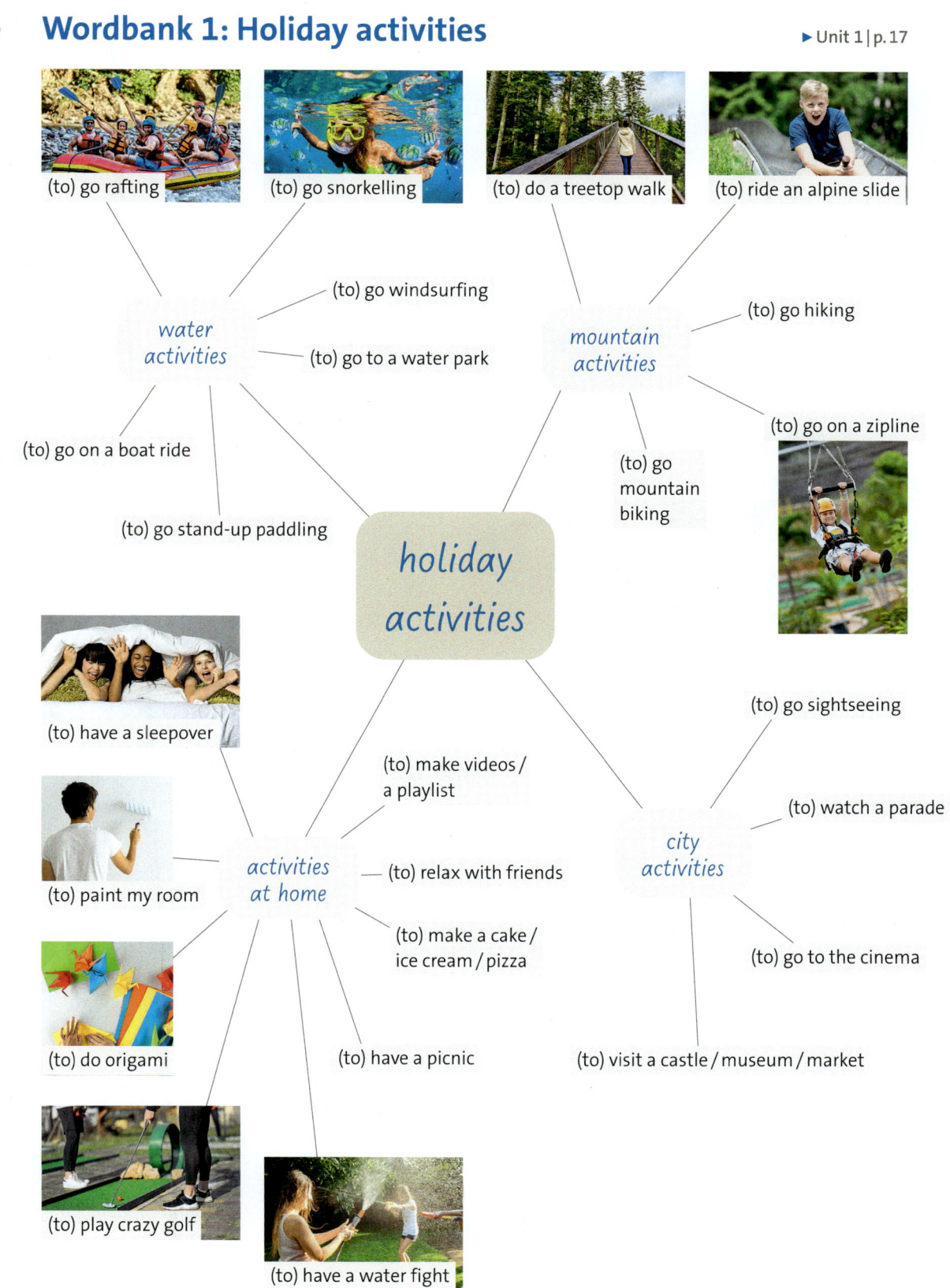

(to) go snorkelling

- (to) go windsurfing
- (to) go to a water park
- (to) go on a boat ride
- (to) go stand-up paddling

mountain activities

(to) do a treetop walk

(to) ride an alpine slide

- (to) go hiking
- (to) go mountain biking

(to) go on a zipline

activities at home

(to) have a sleepover

(to) paint my room

(to) do origami

(to) play crazy golf

(to) have a water fight

- (to) make videos / a playlist
- (to) relax with friends
- (to) make a cake / ice cream / pizza
- (to) have a picnic

city activities

- (to) go sightseeing
- (to) watch a parade
- (to) go to the cinema
- (to) visit a castle / museum / market

Wordbank 2: Describing a person

▸ Unit 2 | p. 41, 42

He/She has ...
blond / brown / red / short / long / straight / curly hair, braces, ...

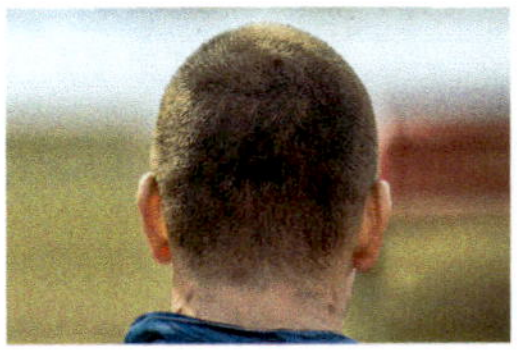
a crew cut

gelled hair

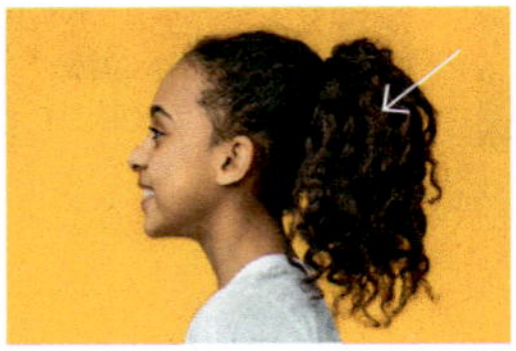
a ponytail

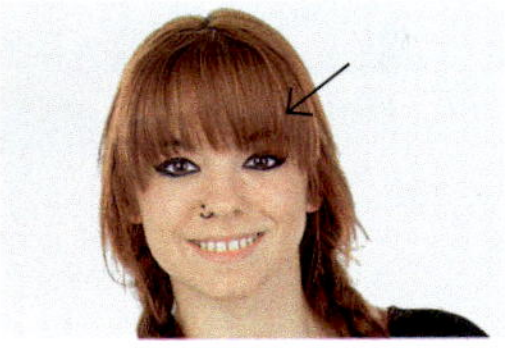
a fringe

braided hair

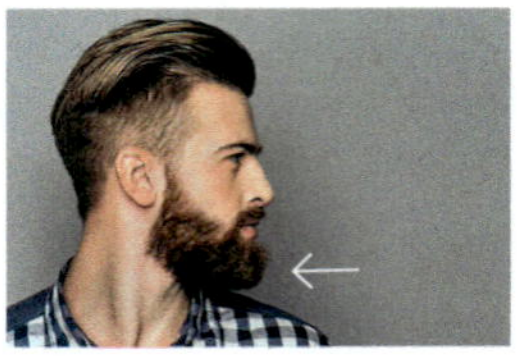
a beard

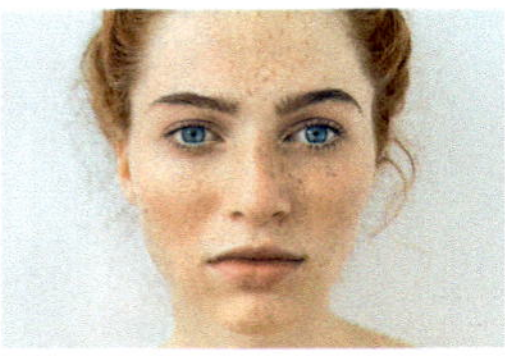
freckles

nail varnish

airbrushed nails

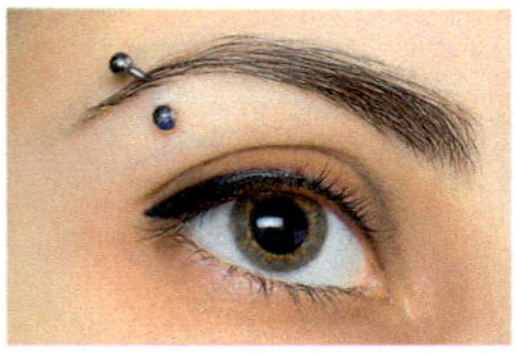
a piercing

a tattoo

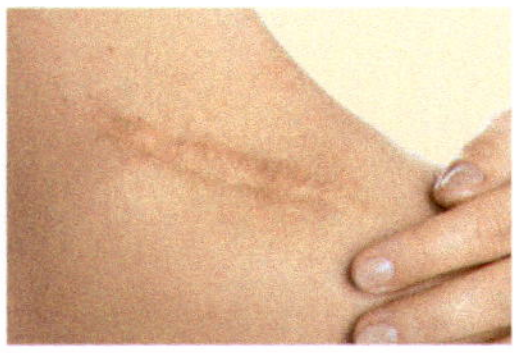
a scar

Skills and activities
He or she is good at maths, sports, listening, drawing, organizing things, solving problems, ...
He or she is good with children, animals, computers, ...

Personality

ambitious	*ehrgeizig*	honest	*ehrlich*
artistic	*künstlerisch*	imaginative	*fantasievoll*
brave	*mutig*	independent	*unabhängig*
calm	*ruhig*	motivated	*motiviert*
caring	*mitfühlend*	open-minded	*aufgeschlossen*
cheerful	*fröhlich*	organized	*organisiert*
clever, smart	*klug*	patient	*geduldig*
confident	*selbstbewusst*	practical	*praktisch*
creative	*kreativ*	punctual	*pünktlich*
curious	*neugierig*	reliable	*verlässlich*
dramatic	*dramatisch*	romantic	*romantisch*
easy-going	*gelassen, locker*	sensitive	*sensibel, empfindsam*
energetic	*aktiv*	shy	*schüchtern*
flexible	*flexibel*	sociable	*kontaktfreudig, gesellig*
generous	*großzügig*	strong	*stark*
hard-working	*fleißig*	tidy	*ordentlich*
helpful	*hilfsbereit*	tolerant	*tolerant*

Wordbank 3: Clothes and accessories

▶ Unit 2 | p. 50, 51

Wordbank 4: Parts of the body

▸ Unit 2 | p. 54

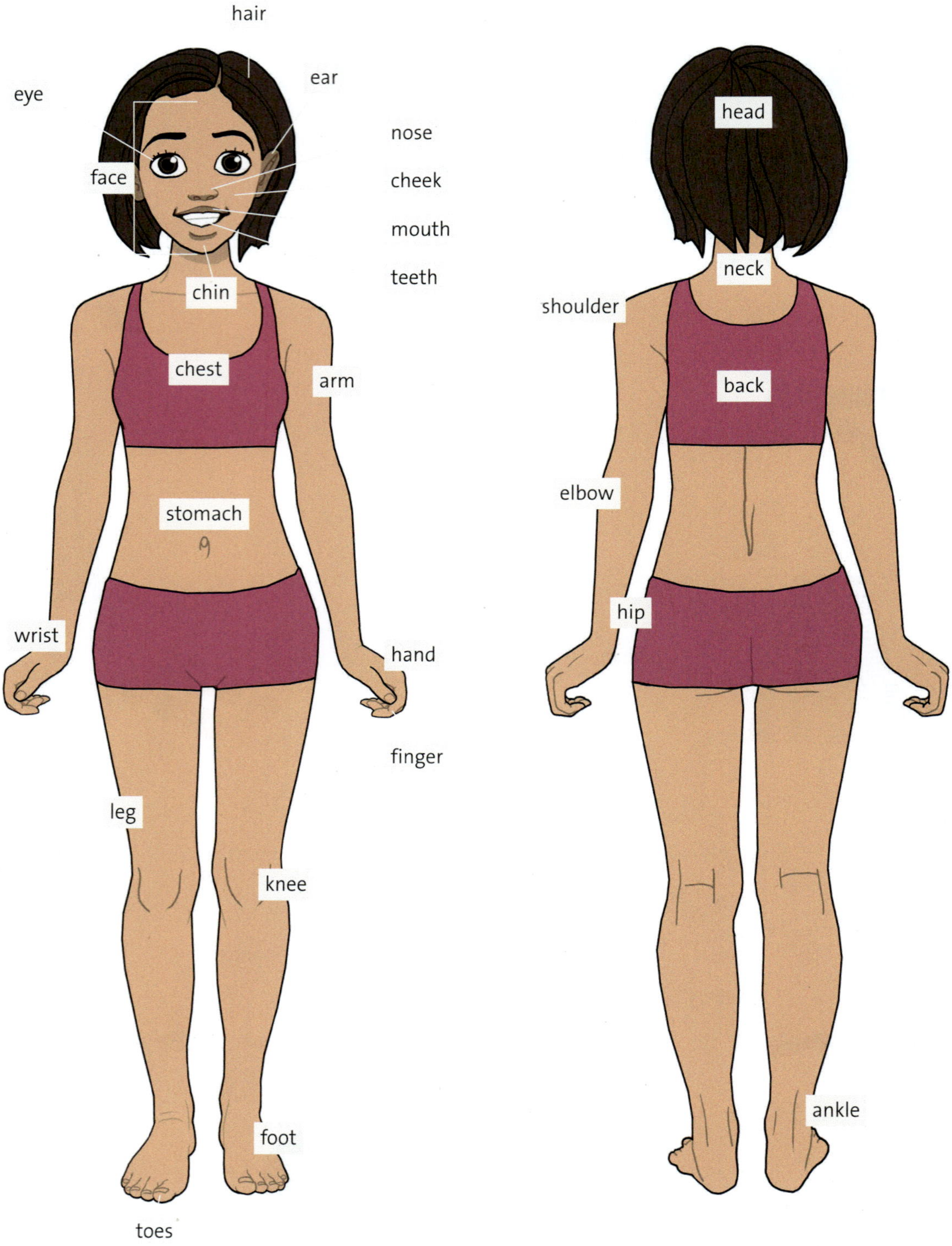

Wordbank 5: Films and shows

▶ Unit 3 | p. 79

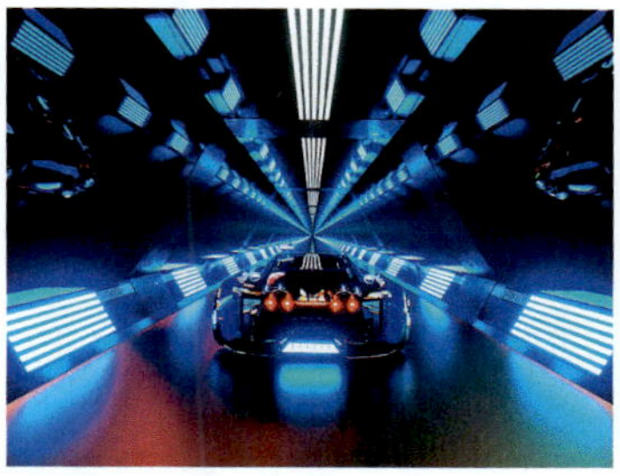
action film

cartoon

comedy

cooking show

disaster film

documentary

fantasy film

game show

horror film

reality show

romance

science fiction (sci-fi) film

soap

sports show

thriller

Wordbank 6: Online activities

► Unit 3 | p. 82

Social media	**Soziale Medien**
(to) like photos / posts	Fotos / Posts liken
(to) post comments	Kommentare posten
(to) post photos	Fotos posten
(to) write on my wall	an meine Pinnwand schreiben

Video sharing sites	**Webseiten zum Austausch von Videos**
(to) watch videos for fun	Videos zum Spaß anschauen
(to) watch fitness videos and (to) do workouts	Fitness-Videos anschauen und trainieren
(to) upload videos	Videos hochladen

Messaging services	**Messaging-Dienste**
(to) chat	chatten
(to) make new friends	neue Freunde gewinnen
(to) send / read messages	Nachrichten senden / lesen

Gaming and puzzle sites	**Spiel- und Rätselwebseiten**
(to) play multiplayer games	Multiplayer-Spiele spielen
(to) play e-sports	E-Sportarten spielen
(to) do interactive puzzles	interaktive Spiele spielen

Music sites	**Musik-Webseiten**
(to) listen to music	Musik hören
(to) make playlists	Playlisten erstellen

Sites for information and help	**Informations- und Hilfewebseiten**
(to) find the way	den Weg finden
(to) plan routes	Routen planen
(to) look up new words	neue Wörter nachschlagen
(to) check facts	Fakten überprüfen
(to) find photos	Fotos finden
(to) watch online tutorials	Online-Anleitungen anschauen

Other websites	**Andere Webseiten**
(to) take a virtual tour	eine virtuelle Tour machen
(to) listen to podcasts and audio stories	Podcasts und andere Audios anhören
(to) create stories	Geschichten schreiben
(to) do slide shows	Slideshows erstellen
(to) make short films	Kurzfilme drehen
(to) create animations	Animationen erstellen

Wordbank 7: Food

▶ Unit 4 | p. 102, 103

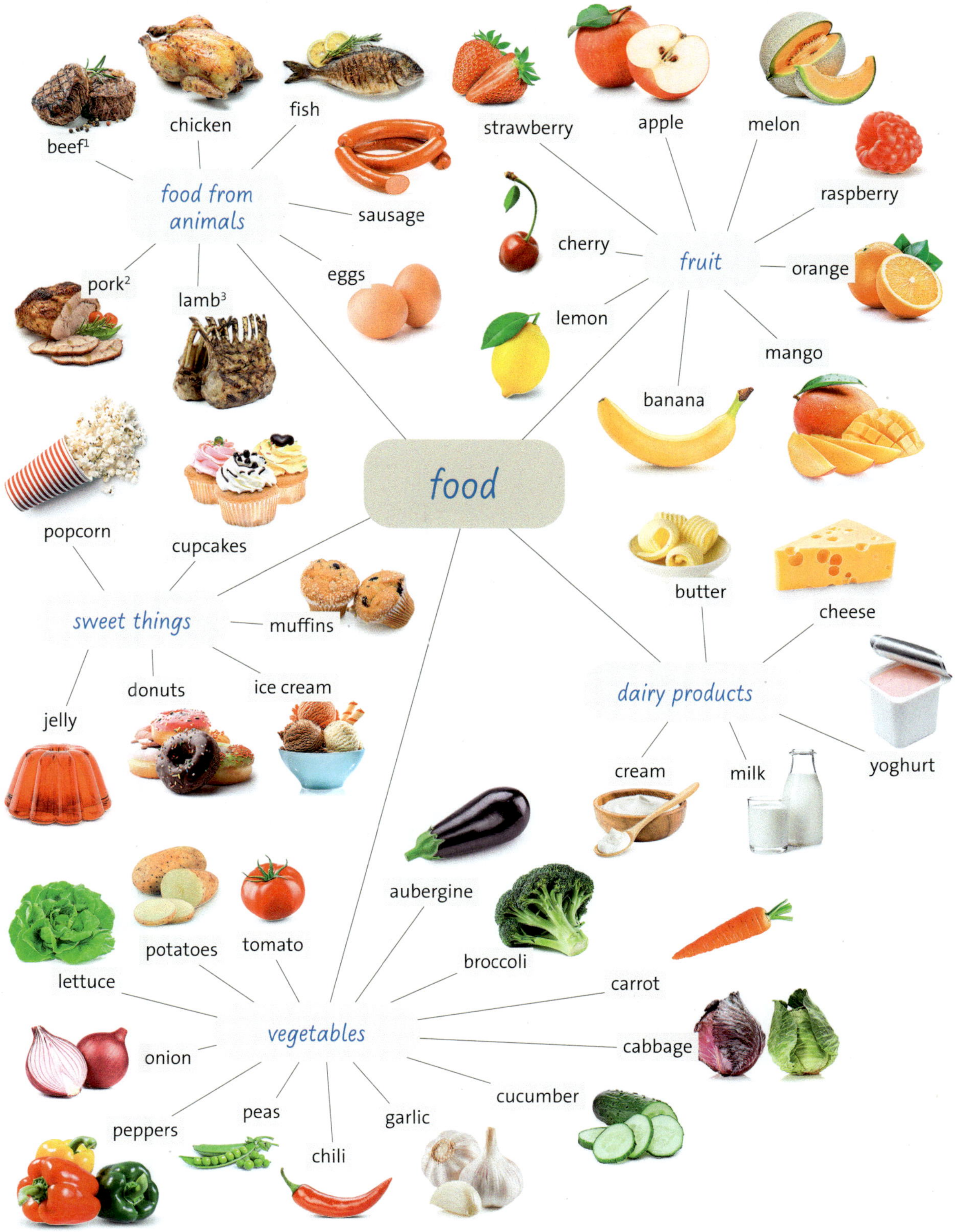

[1] **beef** *das Rindfleisch* [2] **pork** *das Schweinefleisch* [3] **lamb** *das Lamm; Lammfleisch*

Wordbank 8: Presentations

▸ Unit 4 | p. 114, 115

Continue the presentation

First ... / Let me start with ...

Next ...

Finally ...

Start the presentation

Hello, everyone!

Can everyone hear me?

I'm going to talk about ...

Talk about pictures and videos

Let's look at this picture of ...

In this picture you can see ...

This photo shows ...

End the presentation

That's the end of my presentation.

Thank you for listening.

Do you have any questions?

Explain and correct yourself

This word means ...

Sorry, that's the wrong word. I mean ...

Sorry, I've forgotten the word. It's when ...

Wordbank 9: Jobs and workplaces

▶ Unit 5 | p. 130, 132

My mum / dad / ... is a/an ...

architect, artist, bus driver, business owner, cook, dancer, firefighter, gamer, footballer, hairdresser, mechanic, nurse, police officer, plumber, programmer, teacher, train driver, vet, writer

beautician

builder

call centre agent

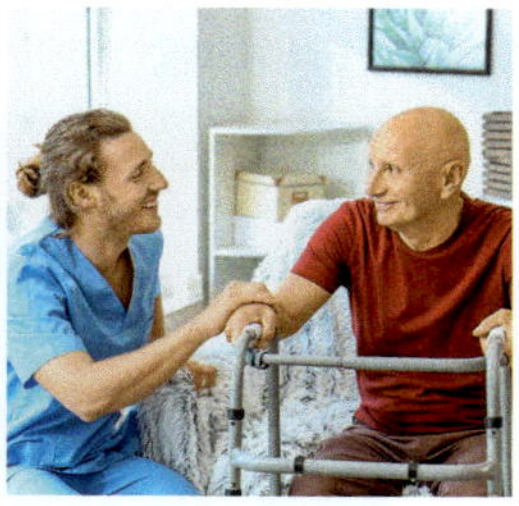
care worker

cashier

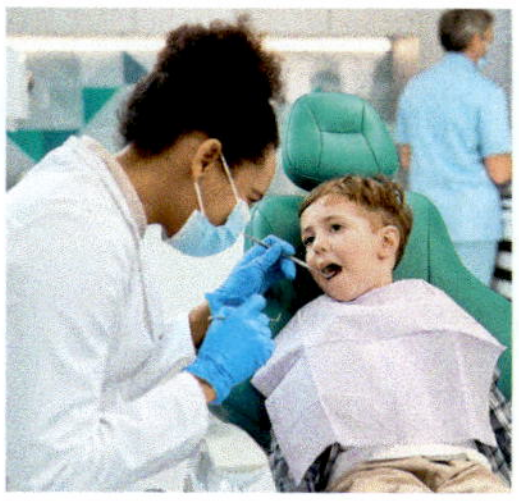
dentist

electrician

engineer

lawyer

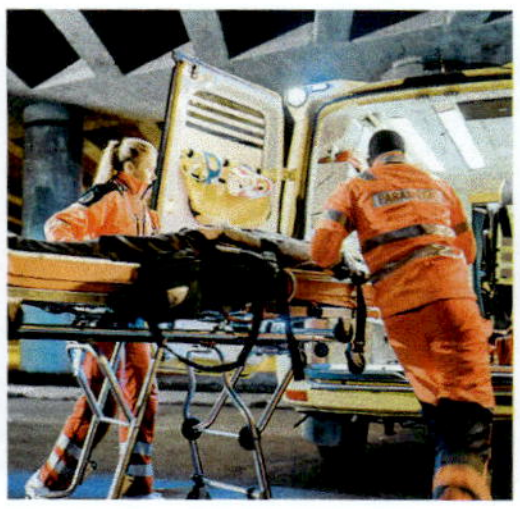
paramedic

salesperson

secretary

My mum / dad / ... works at / on / in a/an ...

cafe, cinema, hospital, library, museum, office, restaurant, school, shop, shopping centre, sports centre, supermarket, train station

factory

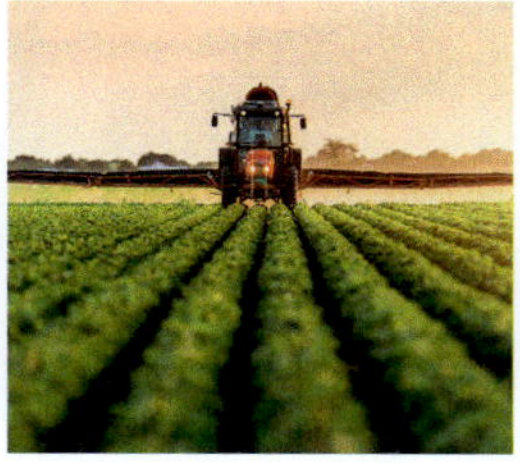
farm

garage

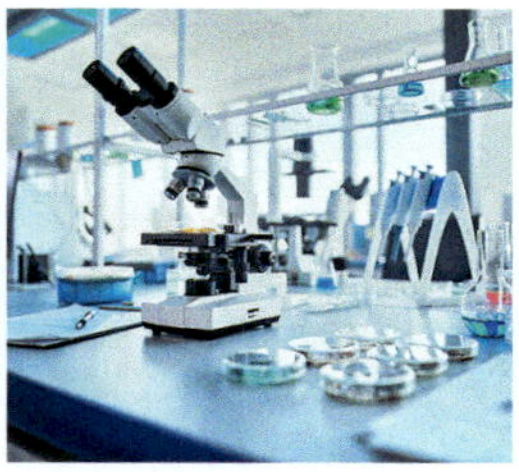
laboratory

My mum / dad / ... is unemployed. (She / He doesn't have a job.)
My mum / dad is a full-time parent.

Wordbank 10: Chores

▸ Unit 5 | p. 135

(to) babysit, (to) clean the bathroom, (to) do the washing, (to) empty the dishwasher, (to) fold the clean clothes, (to) look after the family's pet, (to) make my bed, (to) set the table, (to) take out the rubbish, (to) tidy my room, (to) vacuum the floors

Cleaning

(to) clean out my pet's cage
den Käfig meines Haustiers saubermachen

(to) do the dusting
Staub wischen

(to) take bottles to the bottle bank
Flaschen zum Container bringen

(to) clean my bike
mein Fahrrad putzen

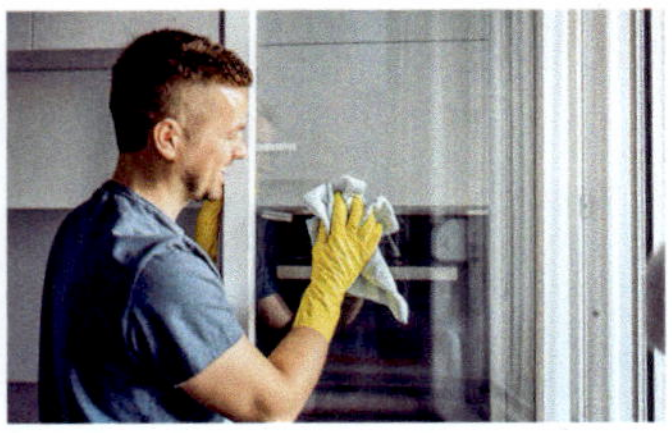

(to) wash the windows
die Fenster putzen

(to) take cans / paper / plastic to the recycling containers
Dosen / Papier / Plastik zu den Recyclingcontainern bringen

Meals

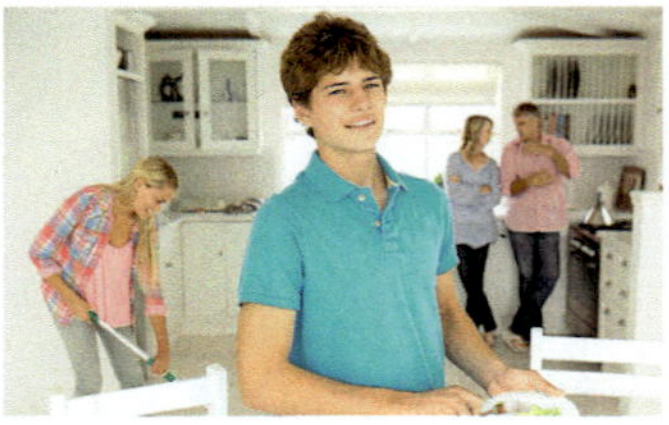

(to) clear the table
den Tisch abräumen

(to) dry the dishes
abtrocknen

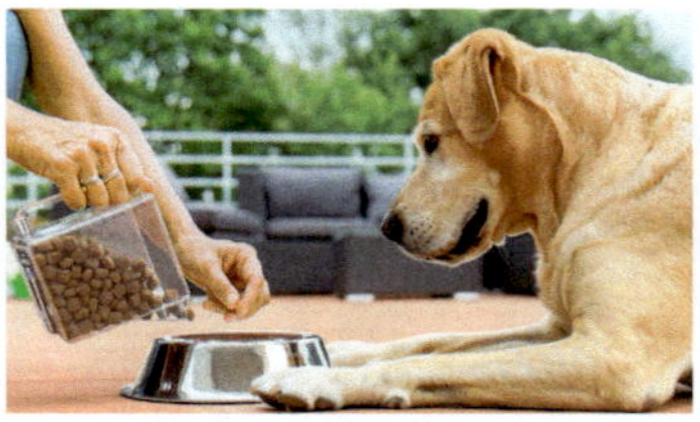

(to) feed the pets
die Haustiere füttern

(to) wash up
abwaschen

(to) load the dishwasher
die Spülmaschine einräumen

Clothes

(to) clean my shoes
meine Schuhe putzen

(to) do the ironing
bügeln

(to) tidy up the wardrobe
den Kleiderschrank aufräumen

(to) hang up the washing
die Wäsche aufhängen

Hier findest du englische Sätze mit ihrer deutschen Übersetzung. Höre sie dir in der App an. Da jede Sprache anders funktioniert, ist eine wortwörtliche Übersetzung oft nicht möglich: Achte daher auf die kleinen Unterschiede.

1 Sich und andere vorstellen

Sich kennenlernen

(Band 1)	Hello, I'm … / Hi! I'm …	Hallo, ich bin …
	What's your name?	Wie heißt du?
	How old are you?	Wie alt bist du?
	I'm … years old. What about you?	Ich bin … Jahre alt. Und du?
	Nice to meet you. – Nice to meet you too.	Freut mich, dich / euch / Sie kennenzulernen. – Freut mich auch.
Unit 1	I'm from Dresden.	Ich komme aus Dresden.

Über Hobbys, Vorlieben und Abneigungen sprechen

(Band 1)	My favourite animal is a fish.	Meine Lieblingstiere sind Fische.
	What's your favourite animal / hobby / …?	Was ist dein Lieblingstier / -hobby / …?
	My favourite sport is … What about you?	Mein Lieblingssport ist … Und deiner?
	Which places / things / … do you like?	Welche Orte / Dinge / … magst du?
	I don't like …	Ich mag … nicht.
Unit 1	What do you like to do in your free time?	Was machst du gerne in deiner Freizeit?
	Do you have any pets? – We have a cat.	Hast du Haustiere? – Wir haben eine Katze.
	I love cake, but I don't like chocolate.	Ich liebe Kuchen, aber Schokolade mag ich nicht.
Unit 3	What kind of music do you like?	Welche Art von Musik magst du?
	I love photography!	Ich liebe Fotografie!
	I'm not really a fan of history.	Ich bin nicht wirklich ein Geschichts-Fan.
	I think Scout's World is the best show ever.	Ich finde, dass Scout's World die beste Show überhaupt ist.
	I'm sorry, I think it's boring.	Es tut mir leid, ich finde es langweilig.

Sich und andere beschreiben

▸ Wordbank 2, p. 186

Unit 2	She has brown eyes and blond hair.	Sie hat braune Augen und blondes Haar.
	I have curly / straight hair.	Ich habe lockiges / glattes Haar.
	My mum is tall and my dad is short.	Meine Mutter ist groß und mein Vater ist klein.
	My uncle is funny and kind.	Mein Onkel ist witzig und nett.
	I am very creative and calm.	Ich bin sehr kreativ und gelassen.
	Finn is good with computers.	Finn kann gut mit Computern umgehen.
	Lily is good at drawing.	Lily kann gut zeichnen.
	He always helps others.	Er hilft immer anderen.

2 Sich verabreden und etwas planen

Eine Einladung schreiben und auf eine Einladung reagieren

(Band 1)	Send me a message if you can come or not.	Sende mir eine Nachricht, ob du kommen kannst oder nicht.
	Where's the party?	Wo ist die Party?
Unit 4	I'd like to invite you to my birthday.	Ich möchte dich / euch zu meinen Geburtstag einladen.
	I hope you can come!	Ich hoffe du kannst / ihr könnt kommen!
	Thanks for the invitation to your party.	Danke für die Einladung zu deiner / eurer Party.
	Should I / we bring something?	Soll ich / Sollen wir etwas mitbringen?

Sich verabreden: Vorschläge machen und darauf reagieren

(Band 1)	Let's meet in the afternoon.	Lass uns nachmittags / am Nachmittag treffen.
	Let's meet at the weekend.	Lass uns am Wochenende treffen.
	Are you free on Sunday?	Hast du am Sonntag Zeit?
	What do you do in your free time?	Was machst du in deiner Freizeit?
Unit 3	What are we doing this weekend?	Was machen wir am Wochenende?
	What are you going to do on Sunday morning / afternoon / evening?	Was machst du am Sonntagmorgen / -nachmittag / -abend?
	Are you doing anything today?	Machst du heute irgendetwas?
	Do you want to come round and have dinner with us?	Möchtest du vorbeikommen und mit uns zu Abend essen?
	I'm sorry, I'm really busy.	Es tut mir leid, ich bin sehr beschäftigt.
	I'm not going to do anything special then.	Ich mache dann / zu dem Zeitpunkt nichts Besonderes.
	Sorry, I can't. I'm going to ...	Tut mir leid, da kann ich nicht. Ich werde ...
	What time is it now?	Wie viel Uhr ist es?
	What time is your dance class?	Um wie viel Uhr / Wann ist dein Tanzunterricht?
	Can we meet?	Können wir uns treffen?
	Saturday would be best.	Samstag wäre am besten.
	Let's meet at the station / in the park at 7.30 pm.	Lass uns um 19.30 Uhr am Bahnhof / im Park treffen.

3 Beim Essen und bei Tisch

▶ Wordbank 7, p. 191

(Band 1)	Are you hungry?	Hast du Hunger?
	I'm really hungry.	Ich habe großen Hunger. / Ich bin sehr hungrig.
	No, I'm not hungry.	Nein, ich habe keinen Hunger. / Nein, ich bin nicht hungrig.
	My favourite dish is pizza.	Mein Lieblingsgericht ist Pizza.
Unit 2	Would you like some more cake?	Möchtest du noch mehr Kuchen?
	No, thanks.	Nein, danke.

Unit 4	Would you like some potato curry?	Möchtest du etwas Kartoffelcurry?
	Yes, please! / No, thanks.	Ja, bitte! / Nein, danke.
	Can I have some salad, please?	Kann ich bitte etwas Salat haben?
	Can I have a little fruit, please?	Kann ich bitte ein bisschen Obst haben?
	Enjoy your meal!	Guten Appetit!
	Would you like some more juice?	Möchtest du noch etwas mehr Saft?
	No, thanks, I still have a little juice.	Nein danke, ich habe noch etwas Saft.

4 Über die Ferien und das Wetter sprechen

Über Ferienaktivitäten sprechen

▶ Wordbank 1, p. 185

Unit 1	What did you do on your holiday?	Was hast du im Urlaub gemacht?
	How were your holidays?	Wie waren deine Ferien?
	I was in Spain with my family.	Ich war mit meiner Familie in Spanien.
	We were in in a holiday apartment / in a hotel.	Wir waren in einer Ferienwohnung / in einem Hotel.
	I was at home in Brighton.	Ich bin zuhause in Brighton geblieben.
	I went to the cinema with my sister.	Ich war mit meiner Schwester im Kino.
	I went to my grandparents' house.	Ich war bei meinen Großeltern.
Unit 3	Where are you going on your holiday?	Wohin fährst du in den Urlaub?

Über das Wetter sprechen

Unit 1	How is / was the weather?	Wie ist / war das Wetter?
	What was the weather like in Spain?	Wie war das Wetter in Spanien?
	The weather is / was hot and sunny.	Das Wetter ist / war heiß und sonnig.
	It is / was rainy, windy and cold.	Es ist / war regnerisch, windig und kalt.

Einen Brief schreiben

Unit 5	Dear Finn ...	Lieber Finn ...
	Hello, everyone!	Hallo an alle!
	How are you?	Wie geht es dir / euch?
	I hope everything is OK.	Ich hoffe, dass alles OK ist.
	I'm sending you German chocolate.	Ich schicke dir deutsche Schokolade.
	I'm happy because ...	Ich bin glücklich, weil ...
	What are your summer plans?	Was sind deine Pläne für den Sommer?
	I hope you have a great holiday!	Ich hoffe, dass du einen großartigen Urlaub hast!
	I miss you. / I'll miss you.	Ich vermisse dich. / Ich werde dich vermissen.
	Please write soon.	Bitte schreibe mir bald.
	Best wishes from Sunita	Herzliche / Liebe Grüße von Sunita

5 Über Berufe und die Zukunft sprechen

▸ Wordbank 9, p. 193

Unit 5	My dad is a firefighter / an artist.	Mein Vater ist Feuerwehrmann / Künstler.
	I want to be a police officer / an architect.	Ich möchte Polizist / Polizistin / Architekt / Architektin werden.
	I want to be a / an ...	Ich möchte ... werden.
	In the future maybe I'll be a / an ...	In der Zukunft werde ich vielleicht ... sein.
	I'll live in a big house.	Ich werde in einem großen Haus leben.

6 Seine Meinung äußern und diskutieren

(Band 1)	I don't think ... because ...	Ich denke / glaube nicht ..., weil ...
	Let me think.	Lass mich nachdenken.
	I don't know.	Das weiß ich nicht.
	Please be polite.	Bitte sei höflich.
	Yes, that's right. / No, that's wrong.	Ja, das stimmt. / Nein, das ist falsch.
	I think you're right / wrong.	Ich glaube, da hast du recht / unrecht.
	I think that's true / false.	Ich glaube, das ist richtig / falsch.
	Do you think it's interesting?	Denkst du, es ist interessant?
	Why do you think it's interesting?	Warum denkst du, es ist interessant?
	Sorry, can you say that again?	Entschuldigung, kannst du das noch einmal sagen?
Unit 1	I'm sorry, I don't understand.	Es tut mir leid, ich verstehe es nicht.
	What do you mean?	Was meinst du?
Unit 3	That looks really interesting.	Das sieht sehr interessant aus.
	I'd like to do that too.	Ich möchte das / dies auch gerne tun.
	I don't agree with Lily.	Ich stimme Lily nicht zu.
	In my opinion, ...	Meiner Meinung nach ...
	I'm sorry, I don't agree.	Es tut mir leid, ich bin anderer Meinung.
	That's not a good idea.	Das ist keine gute Idee.
	Sorry, but I don't like ...	Es tut mir leid, aber ich mag ... nicht.
	I'm not really a fan of ...	Ich bin nicht wirklich Fan von ...
	For me that isn't true.	Für mich ist das nicht so.
	What do you think?	Was meinst du?
Unit 5	That's a great idea!	Das ist eine sehr gute Idee!

7 Feedback geben

(Band 1)	I like the photos on your poster.	Ich mag die Bilder auf deinem Poster.
	You can use more words or pictures.	Du kannst mehr Wörter oder Bilder verwenden.
	Your presentation was too long / short.	Deine Präsentation war zu lang / kurz.
	Please speak more loudly and clearly.	Sprich bitte ein bisschen lauter und deutlicher.
	Don't speak so fast, please.	Sprich bitte nicht so schnell.
	Please look at me / us more.	Schau mich / uns bitte öfter an.
	That was useful information.	Das waren nützliche Informationen.
	Your notes are really helpful.	Deine Notizen sind wirklich nützlich.
	Check your spelling.	Prüfe deine Rechtschreibung.
Unit 1	Your presentation needs a better structure.	Deine Präsentation sollte besser strukturiert werden.
Unit 4	Great job!	Sehr gut gemacht!
	I liked your slides.	Ich fand deine Folien gut.
	Your pictures were good / too small.	Deine Bilder waren gut / zu klein.
	Try to speak loudly and clearly.	Versuche, laut und deutlich zu sprechen.
	Don't just read your text. Talk freely.	Lies deinen Text nicht nur vor. Sprich frei.
	I understood most of / some of what you said.	Ich habe ein das meiste / ein bisschen von dem, was du gesagt hast, verstanden.
	You looked at me / at the class.	Du hast mich / die Klasse angesehen.
	You looked at your cards.	Du hast auf deine Karten geschaut.
	You smiled / didn't smile.	Du hast gelächelt / nicht gelächelt.

8 Einkaufen und über Preise sprechen

(Band 1)	How much does a bus ticket cost?	Wie viel kostet eine Busfahrkarte?
	How much is / are the ...?	Wie viel kostet / kosten der / die / das ...?
	The ... costs / is 50p / pounds.	Der / Die / Das ... kostet 50 Pence / Pfund.
Unit 3	That's too expensive.	Das ist zu teuer.
Unit 5	Can I help you? – I'm just looking.	Kann ich dir / Ihnen helfen? – Ich schaue nur.
	Could you help me, please?	Könnten Sie mir bitte helfen?
	Do you have this / these in size ...?	Haben Sie das / die in Größe ...?
	Do you have this / these in black / in size M?	Haben Sie das / diese in Schwarz / in M?
	Can I try this / these on?	Kann ich das / diese anprobieren?
	I'll take it / them.	Ich nehme es / sie.
	I'd like to pay cash / by card.	Ich würde gerne bar / mit Karte bezahlen.
	I'd like a bag, please.	Ich hätte gerne eine Tüte, bitte.

Let's talk!

Classroom English

You and your teacher	Du und deine Lehrerin / dein Lehrer
Good morning, Mr / Mrs / Ms ... bis 12 Uhr	Guten Morgen, Herr / Frau ...
Good afternoon, Mr / Mrs / Ms ... ab 12 Uhr	Guten Tag, Herr / Frau ...
Sorry, I'm late.	Entschuldigung, dass ich zu spät komme.
Can I open / close the window, please?	Kann ich bitte das Fenster öffnen / zumachen?
Can I go to the toilet, please?	Kann ich bitte zur Toilette gehen?

Homework and exercises	Hausaufgaben und Übungen
Sorry, I have no exercise book.	Es tut mir leid, ich habe mein Heft nicht dabei.
I don't understand this exercise.	Ich verstehe die Übung nicht.
I can't do number 3.	Ich kann Nummer 3 nicht lösen.
Sorry, I haven't finished.	Entschuldigung, ich bin noch nicht fertig.
I have ... Is that right too?	Ich habe ... Ist das auch richtig?
Sorry, I don't know.	Es tut mir leid, das weiß ich nicht.
What's for homework?	Was haben wir als Hausaufgabe auf?

You need help	Du brauchst Hilfe
Can you help me, please?	Können Sie / Kannst du mir bitte helfen?
What page is it, please?	Auf welcher Seite sind wir / steht das?
What's ... in English / German?	Was heißt ... auf Englisch / Deutsch?
Can you write it on the board, please?	Können Sie das bitte an die Tafel schreiben?
Can I say it in German?	Kann ich das auf Deutsch sagen?
Can you speak louder, please?	Können Sie / Kannst du bitte lauter sprechen?
Can you say / play that again, please?	Können Sie das bitte noch einmal sagen / abspielen?

Work with a partner	Partnerarbeit
Can I work with Julian?	Kann ich mit Julian arbeiten?
Can I use your pen, please?	Kann ich bitte deinen Stift benutzen?
Yes, here you are.	Hier, bitte.
It's my / your turn.	Ich bin dran. / Du bist dran.
Let's make / draw a / an ...	Lass uns ein / eine / einen ... machen / zeichnen.
Let's act the story / the dialogue.	Lass uns die Geschichte / den Dialog spielen.

What your teacher says	Was deine Lehrerin / dein Lehrer sagt
Let's go.	Lasst uns anfangen. / Los geht's.
Listen, please. / Quiet, please.	Hört bitte zu. / Ruhe bitte.
Open your books at page 24, please.	Schlagt bitte Seite 24 auf.
Do exercise 5 for homework, please.	Macht bitte Übung 5 als Hausaufgabe.
Write the correct words.	Schreibt die richtigen Wörter hin.
Correct the false sentences.	Korrigiert die falschen Sätze.
Where's your book, Dana?	Wo ist dein Buch, Dana?
Try again!	Versuche es noch einmal.
That's all for today. You can go now.	Das ist alles für heute. Ihr könnt jetzt gehen.

Im ***Vocabulary*** findest du alle neuen Wörter und Wendungen, die du lernen musst. Sie stehen in der Reihenfolge, in der sie im Buch zum ersten Mal vorkommen. Höre dir in der App jedes Wort beim Lernen genau an und sprich es nach.

Symbole und Abkürzungen

► p. 14 ► pp. 40/41	Die Seitenzahl in der linken Spalte zeigt dir, wo das Wort zum ersten Mal in diesem Buch vorkommt (*p.* = *page,* Seite; *pp.* = *pages,* Seiten).
►► **small**	Die doppelten Pfeile weisen auf ein Wort mit gleicher Bedeutung hin, das du bereits kennst.
first ◄ ► **last**	Das „Gegenteil"-Zeichen bedeutet: *first* ist das Gegenteil von *last*.
! *German:* **auf der Straße** *English:* **in the street**	Das **!** bedeutet: Vorsicht, hier keinen Fehler machen!
when **1. wann** **When** are you ready? **2. wenn** You can start **when** you're ready. **3. als** I started **when** I was ready.	In den Merkboxen findest du wichtige Hinweise zu den neuen Wörtern und Wendungen.

sb. = *somebody* (jemand)	*adj* = *adjective* (Adjektiv)
sth. = *something* (etwas)	*adv* = *adverb* (Adverb)
infml. = *informal* (informell, umgangssprachlich)	*AE* = *American English*
pl. = *plural* (Plural, Mehrzahlform)	*BE* = *British English*

Hinweise

Tipps zum Vokabellernen findest du im **Skills file** auf S. 157.
Die **Wordbanks** (S. 185–194) bieten dir nach wichtigen Themen gesammelte Stichwörter.
Let's talk (S. 195–200) enthält Wendungen für wichtige Situationen, z. B.: seine Meinung äußern und diskutieren.
Im **Dictionary** (S. 234–249) kannst du englische Wörter nachschlagen.

Hello again!

► pp. 10/11	**last**	letzte(r, s); als letztes	**first ◄► last** **last week/month/year** = die letzte/vorige Woche, der letzte/vorige Monat, das letzte/vorige Jahr
	back	zurück	Mum is **back** at home. (wieder zu Hause) ! **back** = **1.** zurück; **2.** der Rücken; die Rückseite, der hintere Teil • at **the back** (of the bus/cinema) = hinten (im Bus/im Kino) • at **the back** of your book = hinten in deinem Buch • at **the back** of the card = auf der Rückseite der Karte
	boring	langweilig	Maths isn't **boring**! I find it very interesting. ! **boring**: The film was **boring**. (langweilig) **bored**: I was really **bored**. (gelangweilt) (to) **be bored**/**get bored** = sich langweilen

Unit 1: Travel and holidays

► pp. 12/13	**I was ...**	Ich war ...	• **I am** – **I was** ich bin – ich war • **he/she/it is** – **he/she/it was** er/sie/es ist – er/sie/es war
	We were ...	Wir waren ...	• **we are** – **we were** wir sind – wir waren • **you are** – **you were** du bist; ihr seid – du warst; ihr wart • **they are** – **they were** sie sind – sie waren
	I wasn't (= was not) ... / We weren't (= were not) ...	Ich war nicht ... / Wir waren nicht ...	YES – NO **I was** – **I wasn't** **you were** – **you weren't** **he/she/it was** – **he/she/it wasn't** **we were** – **we weren't** **you were** – **you weren't** **they were** – **they weren't**
	campsite	der Campingplatz	Time for a holiday, but no money? Go camping! **Campsites** aren't very expensive.
	apartment *(AE)*	die Wohnung	►► *BE* flat
	little	klein	►► small We have a cute **little** rabbit.

Topic 1

▸ p. 14	(to) **move**	(sich) bewegen	! (to) **move** = **1.** bewegen – I can't **move** my arm. **2.** sich bewegen – Don't **move**. There's a snake behind you.
	foot, *pl* **feet**	der Fuß	! **foot** = **1.** der Fuß *(Körperteil)* **2.** der Fuß *(Längenmaß; ca. 30 cm)*
	street	die Straße *(in Ortschaften)*	! *German:* **auf der Straße** *English:* **in the street**
	plan	der Plan	• noun: **plan** – • verb: (to) **plan** (planen) I'm **planning** dinner with my friends. – Oh, nice! What do you **plan to cook?** (Was planst du zu kochen?)
	(to) **look (for)**	suchen; Ausschau halten nach	I'm **looking for** my red T-shirt. Do you know where it is?
▸ p. 15	**every**	jede(r, s)	I go to my yoga class **every** Tuesday. **every 30 minutes** = alle 30 Minuten
	into town / **into** the room	in die Stadt / ins Zimmer (hinein)	Don't walk **into** the studio! They're making a video.
	when	als *(zeitlich)*	**when** **1. wann** **When** do you get up? **2. wenn** You can start **when** you're ready. **3. als** I started **when** I was ready.
▸ p. 16	(to) **go**: we **went**	gehen: wir gingen; wir sind gegangen	Our holiday was great. We **went** to Spain.
	plane	das Flugzeug	When we go to Peru, we travel by **plane**. 
	(to) **do**: we **did**	machen, tun: wir machten/taten; wir haben gemacht/getan	I don't know what you **did**, but now my computer works again!
	(to) **see**: we **saw**	sehen: wir sahen; wir haben gesehen	I **saw** Dave in town last week.
	sight	die Sehenswürdigkeit	! **sight** = **1.** der Anblick, das Bild – Scout and the tourists ... what a **sight**! **2.** die Sehenswürdigkeit – Let's take a red London bus and look at the **sights**.
	scary	unheimlich, beängstigend, gruselig	• adj: **scary** (ängstlich); **scared** (verängstigt) (to) **be scared (of)** = Angst haben (vor) • verb: (to) **scare sb.** (jn. erschrecken, jm. Angst machen)
	like	wie; wie zum Beispiel	• At Halloween I looked **like** a vampire. (wie ein Vampir) • I like team sports **like** cricket or football. (wie zum Beispiel) • What's your new school **like**? (Wie ist ...?)
	vampire	der Vampir	! Betonung auf der 1. Silbe: **vam**pire

(to) **tell**: he **told**	erzählen, sagen: er erzählte / er sagte; er hat erzählt / er hat gesagt	I don't know what Joe **told** you. Maybe he was wrong ...
a bit	ein bisschen, ein wenig	Would you like sugar in your tea? – Yes, please, but only **a bit**. (= not much)
(to) **have to do** sth., *simple past:* **had**	etwas tun müssen	Look, it's late. We **have to** go now. **I have to go.** = Ich muss Schluss machen. *(am Telefon/Briefschluss)* ! German "müssen" = **1.** (to) have to; **2.** must (**have to** wird häufiger verwendet als **must**)
(to) **say**: I **said**	sagen: ich sagte; ich habe gesagt	She looked at my idea and **said** "Yes, OK!"
(to) **jump**	springen; *(vor Schreck)* zusammenzucken	They're **jumping** into the water.  When I saw the snake, I **jumped**. I was so scared!
(to) **laugh (at)**	lachen (über)	He's a bit slow sometimes, but it's not fair to **laugh at** him. (to) **laugh at sb.** = jn. auslachen
river	der Fluss	
restaurant	das Restaurant	Let's eat **at a restaurant** this evening. (= **in** einem Restaurant)
trip	der Ausflug; die Reise	(to) **go on a trip** / (to) **take a trip** = eine Reise machen **boat trip** = der Bootsausflug, die Bootsfahrt
castle	die Burg	a Scottish **castle** 
► p. 17 **advert** (*infml auch:* **ad**)	die Anzeige, das Inserat; der Werbespot	You find job **ads/adverts** in newspapers and on the internet.
(to) **arrive**	ankommen	The bus **arrived** in Berlin at 8 o'clock. verb: (to) **arrive** – noun: **arrival** (die Ankunft)
modern	modern	! Betonung auf der 1. Silbe: <u>mo</u>dern
everything	alles	Do you have all your school things? – Yes, **everything** is in my bag.
transport *(no pl)*	das Fortbewegungsmittel; die Beförderung	Which **transport** do you use to go to school? Do you walk or go by bus or by bike?

Topic 2

▶ p. 18	**pride**	der Stolz	

pride – proud (of)
- *noun:* **pride** – She looked at her work with **pride**.
- *adj:* **proud (of)** (stolz (auf)) – She was **proud** of her work.

Pride (oder **Pride parade**) ist ein jährlich stattfindender Fest-, Gedenk- und Demonstrationstag von Lesben, Schwulen, Bisexuellen und Transgender-Personen.
In Deutschland wird er meist Christopher Street Day (CSD) genannt.
parade = die Parade, der Umzug

	(to) **get up**: he **got up**	aufstehen: er stand auf; er ist aufgestanden	On Sundays I always get up late, but this Sunday I **got up** at 8 a.m.
	early	früh	5.30 a.m.? That's very **early** in the morning! **early ◀ ▶ late**
	(to) **wait (for)**	warten (auf)	• **Wait a minute.** = Warte mal. / Einen Moment. • **I can't wait!** = Ich kann es kaum erwarten! **I can't wait** to go to France and see my French friends again!
	platform	der Bahnsteig	! *German:* Der Zug kommt **auf Gleis 4** an. *English:* The train arrives **at platform 4**.
▶ p. 19	**single**	Einzel-, einzelne(r, s)	**single ticket ▶▶ one-way ticket** (einfache Fahrkarte) A **single ticket** is a ticket for only **one way**.
	return (*kurz für:* **return ticket**)	die (Hin- und) Rückfahrkarte	**return ticket ◀ ▶ one-way ticket / single ticket** (to) **return** = zurückkehren, -kommen
	the United Kingdom (= the UK)	das Vereinigte Königreich *(England, Schottland, Wales und Nordirland)*	▶▶ England, Scotland, Wales and Northern Ireland
	penny (= p), *pl* **pence**	der Penny, Pence *(Plural)*	

Pounds and euros

In **England** you have **pounds** and **pence.**

You say:	*You write:*
fifty p / fifty pence	**50 p**
one pound / a pound	**£ 1**
two pounds fifty	**£ 2.50**

In **Germany** you have **euros** and **cents.**

You say:	*You write:*
fifty cents	**€ 0.50**
one euro / a euro	**€ 1**
two euros fifty	**€ 2.50**

	(to) **fly,** *simple past:* **flew**	fliegen	Seagulls and parrots can **fly**.
	for free	kostenlos, umsonst	You can go to our yoga classes **for free**! (= You don't need to pay.)
▶ p. 20	(to) **wear**: he **wore** ...	tragen, anhaben *(Kleidung)*: er trug ... / er hatte ... an; er hat ... getragen, er hat ... angehabt	School started on Monday, and I **wore** my new school uniform.
	(to) **eat**: she **ate**	essen: sie aß; sie hat gegessen	She was very hungry. She **ate** four sandwiches.
	(to) **buy**: she **bought**	kaufen: sie kaufte; sie hat gekauft	We **bought** fish and chips and ate them on the beach.

	flag	die Fahne, die Flagge	 the British **flag**
	I **didn't buy** ... (**= did not**)	ich kaufte nicht; ich habe nicht gekauft	**I bought ◄ ► I didn't buy**
	(to) **make**: I **made**	machen, herstellen: ich machte / ich habe gemacht; ich stellte her / ich habe hergestellt	I **made** muffins this morning. Everyone loved them.
	decoration	die Dekoration, der Schmuck, die Verzierung	noun: **decoration** – verb: (to) **decorate** (dekorieren, schmücken) ! Achte auf die unterschiedliche Betonung: (to) <u>de</u>corate / deco<u>ra</u>tion
	rainbow	der Regenbogen	
	girlfriend	die (feste) Freundin	**girlfriend ◄ ► boyfriend** (der (feste) Freund)
	concert	das Konzert	! Betonung auf der 1. Silbe: <u>**con**</u>cert
	musician	der Musiker, die Musikerin	I'm a **musician**. I play the guitar in a band. **street musician** = der Straßenmusiker, die Straßenmusikerin
► p. 21	**not ... anything**	nichts	It's so quiet here. You ca**n't** do **anything**.

Topic 3

► p. 22	**plastic**	das Plastik, der Kunststoff	No **plastic** bags for me, please. I always bring my own shopping bag.
	bottle	die Flasche	! *German:* eine **Flasche** Wasser *English:* a **bottle of** water
	glove	der Handschuh	 a **pair of gloves** = ein Paar Handschuhe **pair** = das Paar
► p. 23	(to) **find**: they **found**	finden: sie fanden / sie haben gefunden	We had a beach clean-up and **found** lots of rubbish.
	time	das Mal	Today I travelled alone for the first **time**.

time
1. die Zeit We had a great **time**. / Do you have **time**? / It's **time** for lunch.
2. das Mal **for the first time** (zum ersten Mal) / **this time** (dieses Mal) / **three times** (dreimal) / **lots of times** (viele Male, oft) / **the last time** (letztes Mal) / **(the) next time** (nächstes Mal)

	yesterday	gestern	**Yesterday** was Monday, so today is Tuesday.
	night	die Nacht	

- **in the morning** morgens, am Morgen
  in the afternoon nachmittags, am Nachmittag
  in the evening abend, am Abend
- **at night** nachts, in der Nacht
- **on Monday** am Montag
- **on Mondays** montags

	exciting	aufregend	**exciting ◄ ► boring**

Story

► p. 24	(to) **happen** (**to** sb.)	(jm.) geschehen, passieren	Tell us what **happens** in the story.
	(to) **swim**: he **swam**	schwimmen: er schwamm; er ist geschwommen	Zoe is a very good swimmer. Last June she **swam** 10 km!
	(to) **get (to)**	gelangen, (hin)kommen (nach)	**Get down!** = Komm (da) runter!

(to) **get, *simple past:*** **got**

1. bekommen	She **got** a job in London.	Sie bekam eine Stelle in London.
2. holen, besorgen	Can you go and **get** some fruit?	Kannst du etwas Obst holen gehen.
3. gelangen, (hin)kommen	How do we **get** to the museum?	Wie kommen wir zum Museum?

	(to) **get on (a train/bus)** (to) **get off (a train/bus)**	einsteigen (in einen Zug/Bus) aussteigen (aus einem Zug/Bus)	
	(to) **think**: I **thought**	denken: ich dachte; ich habe gedacht	When I saw Sam, I **thought** he looked sad. (to) **think about** = nachdenken über
	(to) **try**	versuchen, (aus)probieren	**Try** to answer my question. (versuchen) I'd like to **try** parkour. (ausprobieren) verb: (to) **try** – noun: **try** (der Versuch) – **Have a try! / Give it a try!** (Versuch's/Probier's doch mal!)
	wonderful	wunderbar	►► very good, great
► p. 25	(to) **put**: I **put**	legen, stellen: ich stellte/legte, ich habe gestellt/gelegt	I can't find my phone. I don't know where I **put** it ...
	calm	ruhig, besonnen	Please stay **calm**. It's only a little mouse!
► p. 26	(to) **worry (about)**	sich Sorgen machen (wegen, um)	

(to) **worry**

• verb:	(to) **worry (about)**	Don't **worry**! Everything is OK. Mum **worries about** me when I'm late.	sich Sorgen machen (wegen, um)
	(to) **worry sb.**	It **worries** me that Dave looks so sad.	jn. beunruhigen
• adj:	**worried (about)**	I'm **worried about** Dave. Why is he so sad?	beunruhigt / besorgt (wegen)
• noun:	**worry**	What is your biggest **worry**?	die Sorge

(to) **pick** sth. **up**	etwas aufheben *(vom Boden)*, etwas hochheben; etwas abholen	• (to) **pick** = (aus)wählen, aussuchen – **Pick** the right word from the box. • (to) **pick sth. up** = etwas aufheben, etwas hochheben – Can you **pick up** all that rubbish? • (to) **pick sb./sth. up** = jn./etwas abholen – Can you **pick up** the kids from school today?
thunderstorm	das Gewitter	

	(to) **ride a horse,** *simple past:* **rode**	(ein Pferd / auf einem Pferd) reiten	• (to) **ride a bike** = Fahrrad fahren • (to) **ride a horse** = (ein Pferd / auf einem Pferd) reiten

Study skills

► p. 28	**crazy**	verrückt	You want to walk home in this weather? You must be **crazy**. (to) **be crazy about sth.** = wild auf etwas sein, versessen auf etwas sein
	bird	der Vogel	
	surprise	die Überraschung	noun: **surprise** – verb: (to) **surprise sb.** (jn. überraschen)

Unit task

► p. 29	(to) **meet:** I **met**	treffen: ich traf; ich habe getroffen	I **met** your brother in town yesterday.

Irregular verbs

Infinitive	Simple past		Infinitive	Simple past	
(to) **be**	**was/were**	sein	(to) **make**	**made**	machen, herstellen
(to) **buy**	**bought**	kaufen	(to) **meet**	**met**	(sich) treffen
(to) **do**	**did**	machen, tun	(to) **put**	**put**	legen, stellen
(to) **eat**	**ate**	essen	(to) **ride**	**rode**	(Rad) fahren; reiten
(to) **find**	**found**	finden	(to) **say**	**said**	sagen
(to) **fly**	**flew**	fliegen	(to) **see**	**saw**	sehen
(to) **get**	**got**	bekommen; holen; gelangen	(to) **swim**	**swam**	schwimmen
(to) **go**	**went**	gehen, fahren	(to) **tell**	**told**	erzählen
(to) **have**	**had**	haben	(to) **think**	**thought**	denken
(to) **make**	**made**	machen, herstellen	(to) **wear**	**wore**	tragen, anhaben

► List of irregular verbs, p. 271

Unit 2: Friends and heroes

► pp. 40/41	**hero,** *pl* **heroes**	der Held, die Heldin	Sometimes it's hard for her, but she always helps others. She's a **hero**!
	curly	lockig	He has **curly** hair. = He has **curls**. **curl** = die Locke
	dark	dunkel	It's so **dark** in here! I can't see anything.
	straight	gerade; *(Haare)* glatt	

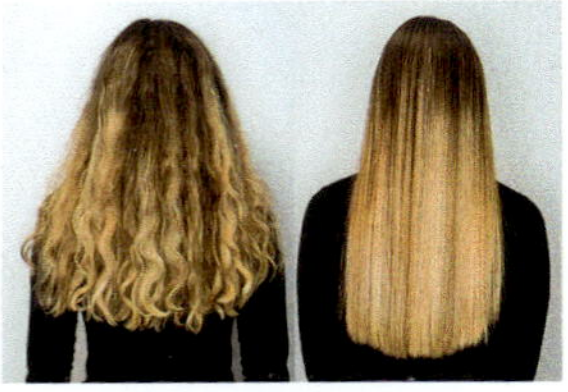

curly **straight**

They have **blond** hair.

	hair	das Haar, die Haare	! *German:* Deine **Haare sind** schwarz. *English:* Your **hair is** black.
	braces *(pl)*	die Zahnspange, die Zahnklammer	
	glasses *(pl)*	die Brille	! Die Wörter **glasses, sunglasses** (die Sonnenbrille) u. **braces** sind Pluralwörter: I need my **glasses**. Where **are they**? (... Wo **ist sie**?) A lot of kids wear **braces**. (... tragen **eine Zahnspange**.)
	(to) **think of** sb./sth.	an jn./etwas denken	! (to) **think of sb./sth.** = an jn./etwas denken; (to) **think of sth.** = sich etwas überlegen, sich etwas ausdenken

Topic 1

▸ p. 42	**profile**	das Profil; die Beschreibung, das Portrait	! Betonung auf der 1. Silbe: **pro**file
	confident	(selbst)sicher; zuversichtlich	• You're a great person. Why aren't you more **confident**? ((selbst)sicher) • I have a good feeling – I'm **confident** that my test went well. (zuversichtlich)
	honest	ehrlich	Scout, be **honest**: did you eat all the muffins? To be **honest**, I don't know the answer. (Um ehrlich zu sein, ...)
	brave	mutig	! **brave** = mutig – Sunita is **brave**. **good** = brav – **Good** dog!
	(to) **describe**	beschreiben	verb: (to) **describe** – noun: **description** (die Beschreibung) ! *English:* **Describe** the picture **to him/her**. *German:* **Beschreibe ihm/ihr** das Bild.
▸ p. 43	**important (for/to** sb.**)**	wichtig (für jn.)	Listen, please. This is very **important**.
	(to) **agree (with** sb./sth.**)**	jm. zustimmen; mit etwas einverstanden sein	(to) **agree on** sth. = sich auf etwas einigen ! *German:* Ich **stimme dir zu**. *English:* I **agree with you**.
▸ p. 44	**right**	rechts; nach rechts	! **right** = **1.** (nach) rechts; **2.** richtig
	left	links; nach links	

left – right
Do you write with your **left** hand or your **right** hand?
I looked **left** and **right** but there was no one there.
on the left = links, auf der linken Seite
to the left of sb./sth. = links von jm./etwas
on the right = rechts, auf der rechten Seite
to the right of sb./sth. = rechts von jm./etwas

Topic 2

▶ p. 46	(to) **save**	retten; sparen; sichern *(Daten)*	• There's a cat in the water! Can we **save** it? (retten) • I need to **save** money. (sparen) • When you write your presentation, remember to **save** your files. (sichern)
	(to) **fall,** *simple past:* **fell**	fallen; hinfallen	Be careful! Don't **fall** into the water! I wasn't careful, so I **fell** into the water.
	(to) **call**	nennen; rufen; anrufen	• This is Fiona, but we **call** her Fi. (nennen) • It's time for a snack – **call** the kids! (rufen) • **Call** me tomorrow. Here's my number. (anrufen) verb: (to) **call** – noun: **(phone) call** (der Ruf; der (Telefon-)Anruf)
	(to) **hurt,** *simple past:* **hurt**	verletzen; wehtun	• I **hurt** my hand. (Ich habe mir die Hand verletzt.) • And now my hand **hurts**. (tut weh) (to) **be hurt** = verletzt sein (to) **get hurt** = sich verletzen; verletzt werden
▶ p. 47	(to) **marry**	heiraten	Jack **married** Alex in May. = They **married** in May. = They **got married** in May. They**'re married** now. (to) **get married (to sb.)** = (jn.) heiraten (to) **be married (to)** = verheiratet sein (mit)
	child, *pl* **children**	das Kind	! one **child** – two **children** Das i in **chi**l**d** klingt wie **my**. Das i in **chi**l**dren** klingt wie **skill**.
	he was **born**	er wurde geboren	! *German:* Wann **bist** du **geboren**? – Ich **bin** 2012 **geboren**. *English:* When **were** you **born**? – I **was born** in 2012.
	(to) **become,** *simple past:* **became**	werden	My cousin **became** a superhero, and now she's always tired. Too much work! 
	(to) **leave** (sth.), *simple past:* **left**	lassen; verlassen; zurücklassen	

(to) **leave,** ***simple past:*** **left**
1. lassen Don't **leave** the windows open when you go. / Please **leave** your pets at home.
2. verlassen I don't want to **leave** my country. / Many people **left** the village.
3. zurücklassen Don't **leave** your bag on the bus. / Where did you **leave** your bike?
! (to) **leave sb. alone** =
1. jn. allein lassen – We can't **leave** our dog **alone** at home.
2. jn. in Ruhe lassen – Just go away and **leave** me **alone**!

	(to) **come**: he **came**	(mit)kommen: er kam (mit); er ist (mit)gekommen	Joe was very late. He **came** to school at 9:30!
▶ p. 48	**activist**	der Aktivist, die Aktivistin	! Betonung auf der 1. Silbe: **ac**tivist

	planet	der Planet	 our **planet** ! Betonung auf der 1. Silbe: <u>**pla**</u>net
	charity	die wohltätige Organisation	**animal charity** = die wohltätige Organisation, die Tiere unterstützt **charity shop** = das Geschäft, das gespendete Waren für wohltätige Zwecke verkauft
▶ p. 49	**kilometre (km)**	der Kilometer	1,000 **metres** = 1 **kilometre**
	(to) **give**: they **gave**	geben: sie gaben, sie haben gegeben	Jill **gave** me a very interesting book for my birthday.
	ill	krank	adj: **ill** – noun: **illness** (die Krankheit)
	magic	magisch, Zauber-; die Zauberei	I can do a **magic trick**. (Zaubertrick) I'd like to see a **magic show**. (Zaubershow) Can you **do magic**? (zaubern)

Topic 3

▶ p. 50	**power**	die Kraft, die Macht, die Energie; der (elektrische) Strom	Do we have the **power** to change all the things that are bad on earth? **super** = super – **superpower** = die Superkraft
	thousand	tausend	ten **thousand** (10,000) = zehntausend (10.000)

Im Englischen steht oft ein **Komma** in Zahlen, die größer als 1 000 sind.
Im Deutschen steht dort manchmal ein **Punkt.**

English: **10,400** (ten thousand four hundred)
German: **10.400** (zehntausendvierhundert)

▶ p. 51	**any**	jede(r/s) (beliebige), jegliche(r/s)	

any
- in **Fragen** u. **verneinten Sätzen**: Did you learn **any** new tricks? ... (irgendwelche) neuen Fertigkeiten ...?
  I do**n't** have **any** money. ... kein Geld
- in **bejahten Sätzen**: You can use this ticket on **any** train. ... in jedem (beliebigen) Zug
  You can call me **(at) any time**. ... zu jeder Zeit, jederzeit

	boot	der Stiefel	**walking boots** = die Wanderstiefel 
	silver	das Silber; silberfarben	**silver** 
	helmet	der Helm	**helmets** 

dolphin	der Delfin	
man, *pl* **men**	der Mann, die Männer	one **man** – two **men** one **woman** – two **women** (eine Frau – zwei Frauen)
chemical	die Chemikalie; chemisch	Be careful when you work with this **chemical**. (die Chemikalie) Please draw the **chemical** structure of water. (chemisch)
swimsuit	der Badeanzug	**Swimsuits** or bikinis are clothes that you wear for swimming.
earth	die Erde	Superman wasn't born **on earth**. (**auf der Erde**) ! *German* "Erde": **1.** *(der Planet)* **earth** **2.** *(der Erdboden)* **ground**
strong	stark	
nose	die Nase	
trousers *(pl)*	die Hose	! **trousers** ist ein Pluralwort: **Are** your **trousers** new? **They're** cool. (**Ist** deine **Hose** neu? **Sie ist** cool.)
eye	das Auge	
mask	die Maske	At carnival people wear **masks**. 
(to) **climb**	klettern (auf)	verb: (to) **climb** – nouns: **climb** (der Aufstieg, die Klettertour; der Anstieg); **climber** (der Kletterer, die Kletterin) ! *German:* **auf einen Baum klettern** *English:* (to) **climb a tree**
(to) **kill**	töten	verb: (to) **kill** – noun: *(person)* **killer** (der Mörder, die Mörderin)
handy	praktisch, nützlich; handlich; griffbereit, zur Hand	• Having eight arms would be very **handy**. (praktisch, nützlich) • This small e-book reader is very **handy**. (handlich) • Do you have a pen **handy**? (griffbereit, zur Hand) ! Vorsicht: Das englische Wort für Handy ist **phone**.

dress	das Kleid	a nice red **dress**  noun: **dress** – verb: (to) **dress** (sich kleiden, sich anziehen)

Story

▶ p. 52	**accident**	der Unfall; der Zufall	! **accident** = **1.** Unfall – Finn had an **accident**. He was hurt. **2.** Zufall – It's no **accident** that her test went well. I saw her **by accident** at the station. (zufällig, versehentlich, unabsichtlich)
	wall	die Wand, die Mauer	! *German:* **an der Wand; an die Wand** *English:* **on the wall**
	down	hinunter, herunter	**down** ◄► **up** (hinauf, hoch)
	(to) **land**	landen	verb: (to) **land** – noun: **land** (das Land *(Grund und Boden)*) ! *German* "Land": **1.** *(Staat)* **country** **2.** *(Grund und Boden)* **land**
	dangerous	gefährlich	 a **dangerous** fish adj: **dangerous** – noun: **danger** (die Gefahr)
▶ p. 53	**face**	das Gesicht	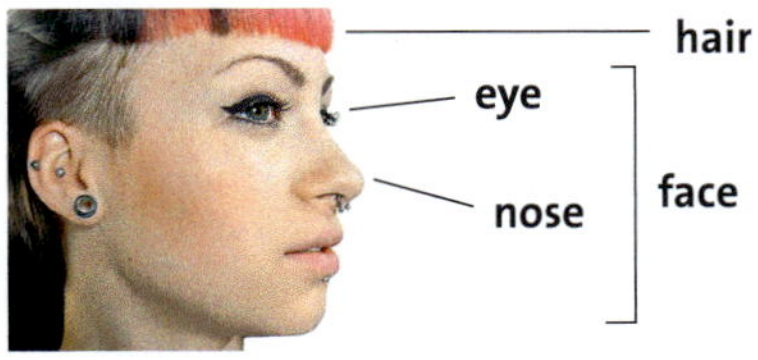
	ankle	der Knöchel, das Fußgelenk	My **ankle** hurts. 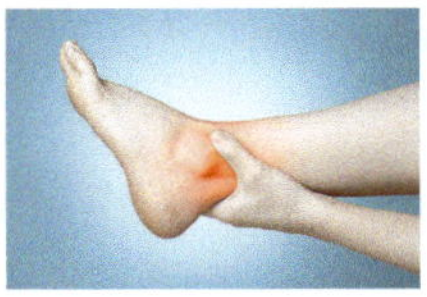
	ambulance	der Krankenwagen	an **ambulance**  ! Betonung auf der 1. Silbe: **am**bulance
	leg	das Bein	We have two arms and two **legs**.

	(to) **show**	zeigen	**Show** your teacher your story. = **Show** your story **to** your teacher. verb: (to) **show** – noun: **show** (die Show, die Aufführung; die Ausstellung)
	(to) **breathe (in/out)**	(ein-/aus-)atmen	You can't **breathe** under water.
	blanket	die Decke *(zum Zudecken u.Ä.)*	a **blanket** 
	so (that)	sodass	! **so** = **1.** (*auch* **so that**) = sodass; **2. so** big/cold/... = so groß/kalt/... **3.** also, daher
	(to) **fall asleep** / (to) **be asleep**	einschlafen/ schlafen	I was so tired that I **fell asleep** on the sofa. 
	joke	der Witz, der Scherz	At night I become a vampire. – Good **joke**!
► p. 54	(to) **feel**: he **felt**	(sich) fühlen: er fühlte (sich); er hat (sich) gefühlt	I made him very sad, and I **felt** horrible.
	body	der Körper	You already know the English words for some parts of the **body**: head, hand, arm, foot ...
	fine	gut, in Ordnung; schön	He feels **fine**. = Er fühlt sich gut. / Es geht ihm gut.
	broken	kaputt; zerbrochen	 **broken** windows

Study skills

► p. 56	(to) **work** sth. **out**	etwas herausfinden, etwas erarbeiten, etwas verstehen	Try and **work out** the answers to the questions.
	language	die Sprache	She speaks three **languages:** English, German and French.
	false friend	der „falsche Freund" *(die Übersetzungsfalle)*	**false** = falsch, unrichtig The English word "become" is a **false friend**: it looks like the German word "bekommen", but it means "werden".

Unit task

► p. 57	**famous (for)**	berühmt (für, wegen)	This town is **famous for** its old castle. adj: **famous** – noun: **fame** (der Ruhm)

(to) **die (of)**	sterben (an)	! *simple past*: **died** – She **died** last year. *ing*-Form: **dying** – This tree is **dying**. 
(to) **win:** he **won**	gewinnen: er gewann; er hat gewonnen	My sister **won** a singing competition last month.
(to) **discover**	entdecken	Did you know that a woman **discovered** this chemical?
mother **father**	die Mutter der Vater	your **mother** (**mum**) and your **father** (**dad**) = your **parents**
(to) **fight (for),** *simple past:* **fought**	kämpfen (für); bekämpfen	verb: (to) **fight** – nouns: **fight** (der Kampf); *(person)* **fighter** (der Kämpfer, die Kämpferin)

Verbs and nouns with the same form

(to) **call**	nennen; rufen; anrufen	**call**	der Ruf; der (Telefon-)Anruf
(to) **climb**	klettern (auf)	**climb**	der Aufstieg, die Klettertour; der Anstieg
(to) **dress**	sich kleiden, sich anziehen	**dress**	das Kleid
(to) **fight**	kämpfen; bekämpfen	**fight**	der Kampf
(to) **land**	landen	**land**	das Land *(Grund und Boden)*
(to) **laugh**	lachen	**laugh**	das Lachen
(to) **plan**	planen	**plan**	der Plan
(to) **show**	zeigen	**show**	die Show, die Aufführung; die Ausstellung
(to) **surprise**	überraschen	**surprise**	die Überraschung
(to) **try**	versuchen, (aus)probieren	**try**	der Versuch
(to) **worry**	sich Sorgen machen	**worry**	die Sorge

against	gegen	I love tennis and often play **against** my friend Pete. Are you for or **against** these plans?

Irregular verbs

Infinitive	Simple past	
(to) **become**	**became**	werden
(to) **come**	**came**	(mit)kommen
(to) **fall**	**fell**	(hin)fallen
(to) **feel**	**felt**	fühlen; sich fühlen
(to) **fight**	**fought**	kämpfen; bekämpfen

Infinitive	Simple past	
(to) **give**	**gave**	geben
(to) **hurt**	**hurt**	verletzen; wehtun
(to) **leave**	**left**	(ver)lassen, zurücklassen
(to) **win**	**won**	gewinnen

▶ List of irregular verbs, p. 271

Unit 3: Activities and games

► pp. 70/71	**theatre**	das Theater	! Betonung auf der 1. Silbe: **the**atre
	full (of ...)	voll; voller ...	Help! Our house is **full of** mice! More sandwiches? – No thanks, I'm **full**. (... ich bin satt.)
	delicious	köstlich, lecker	Strawberries with cream – **delicious**! Can I have some more, please?
	creative	kreativ	! Betonung auf der 2. Silbe: cre**a**tive adj: **creative** – verb: (to) **create** ((er)schaffen, erstellen)
	insect	das Insekt	**Insects** are small. They have six legs and their bodies have three parts. ! Betonung auf der 1. Silbe: **in**sect
	actor	der Schauspieler, die Schauspielerin	Which **actor** played the killer in this film? noun: **actor** – verbs: (to) **act** (Theater spielen, schauspielern); (to) **act sth. out** (etwas aufführen, vorspielen)
	(to) **be on**	gezeigt werden, „laufen" *(Kino, Fernsehen)*, stattfinden; an sein *(eingeschaltet sein)*	What**'s on** at the theatre this evening? All the lights **are on**. They must be at home. (to) **be on** ◄► (to) **be off** (aus sein *(ausgeschaltet sein)*)
	course	der Kurs	! **course** = **1.** der Kurs; **2.** das Gericht *(Gang beim Essen)*, z. B. **main course**

Topic 1

► p. 72	(to) **role-play** sth.	etwas in einem Rollenspiel darstellen	**role** = die Rolle *(Film, Theater)*
	(to) **practise**	üben	I **practise** the guitar every day. verb: (to) **practise** – noun: **practice** (die Übung(en))
	real	echt, wirklich	• adj: **real** – That's a plastic tree, not a **real** tree. • adv: **really** – Our maths teacher is **really** nice.
	goat	die Ziege	 a **goat**
	We**'re going to** visit	Wir werden ... besuchen.	What **are** you **going to** do on Saturday? – I**'m going to** go to the cinema.
	(to) **knit**	stricken	! Wie bei **know** wird der erste Buchstabe von **knit** nicht gesprochen – die Aussprache beginnt mit dem Laut „n".
	photography	die Fotografie *(Hobby)*, das Fotografieren	! Betonung auf der 2. Silbe: pho**to**graphy

	skill	die Fähigkeit, die Fertigkeit	
	(to) **prepare (for)**	vorbereiten, zubereiten; sich vorbereiten (auf)	• Let's **prepare** food for the party. (vorbereiten, zubereiten) • I must **prepare for** the maths test tomorrow. (mich vorbereiten auf) verb: (to) **prepare** – noun: **preparation** (die Vorbereitung; die Zubereitung)
► p. 73	(to) **choose**, *simple past:* **chose**	(aus)wählen	Red or blue? You **choose**.
	camera	die Kamera	a **camera** 
► p. 74	**quarter to 7**	viertel vor 7	 **quarter to 7**
	quarter past 7	viertel nach 7	**quarter past 7** 
	half past 6	halb 7	 **half past 6** ! *German:* **halb sieben** *English:* **half past six**

Topic 2

► p. 76	**classical**	klassisch	**classical music** = die klassische Musik
	acoustic	akustisch	I like **acoustic** music because it's not so loud.
	popular with	beliebt bei	! *German:* Die Beatles sind immer noch sehr **beliebt bei** vielen Leuten. *English:* The Beatles are still very **popular with** lots of people. ! The word **pop music** (or **pop**) is short for **popular music**.
	louder/older **than** ...	lauter/älter als ...	! *German:* älter **als ich**/**er**/**wir**/... *English:* older **than me**/**him**/**us**/...
► p. 77	**as** bad **as** ...	so schlecht/schlimm wie ...	My new bike is better than Joe's, but still not **as good as** my mum's. **as ... as** = genauso ... wie **not as ... as** = nicht so ... wie
	worse	schlechter, schlimmer	! good – **better** ◄ ► bad – **worse** Your text isn't **better** or **worse** than Sam's, it's just different!
	better	besser	(to) **like sth. better**/**best** = etwas lieber / am liebsten mögen

	relaxing	entspannend	(to) **relax** = sich entspannen **relaxed** = entspannt ! *German:* Ich **entspanne mich**. *English:* I'm **relaxing**.
	energetic	aktiv, tatkräftig, energiegeladen	adj: **energetic** – noun: **energy** (die Energie) ! Betonung auf der 1. Silbe: energy
► p. 78	**worst**	der/die/das schlechteste, schlimmste; am schlechtesten, am schlimmsten	! good – **better** – **best** ◄ ► bad – **worse** – **worst**
	doctor (Dr)	der Arzt, die Ärztin	! *German:* **beim Arzt / zum Arzt** *English:* **at the doctor's / to the doctor's**
	agent	der Agent, die Agentin	! Betonung auf der 1. Silbe: agent
	space	der Weltraum; der Raum, die Fläche; der Platz	• My flat is too small. I need more **space**. (der Platz) • Would you like to fly into **space**? (der Weltraum)
► p. 79	**character**	der Charakter; die Figur *(aus einer Geschichte)*	• It's a nice old town. It has **character**. (der Charakter) • Two **characters** in this story are very mean. (die Figur in einer Geschichte) ! Betonung auf der 1. Silbe: character
	(to) **take place**, *simple past:* **took**	stattfinden	The festival **takes place** every year.

Topic 3

► p. 80	**adventure**	das Abenteuer	A bike trip to Italy? What an **adventure**!
	bridge	die Brücke	a **bridge** over a river in a **forest** 
	forest	der Wald	
	mountain	der Berg	 a **campsite** in the **mountains**
	stairs *(pl)*	die Treppe; die (Treppen-)Stufen	
	key	der Schlüssel; Schlüssel-	an old **key** 
	through	durch	Let's walk **through** the forest. ! Beachte Aussprache und Schreibung! Du schreibst **through** – du sprichst ein langes **u**.

	(to) **turn right/left**	(nach) rechts/links abbiegen	 **Turn left.** **Turn right.** **Go straight on.**
	straight on	geradeaus (weiter)	
	past	vorbei an, vorüber an	The way to the library? Walk **past** the station, then turn left.
	across a bridge/a street/...	über eine Brücke/Straße/...	 Birds can fly **across** the sea.
► p. 81	**trophy**	die Trophäe; der Pokal	**trophies** 
	above	über, oberhalb (von); oben	

above ◄► below
1. über ◄► unter The title of the story is **above** the text. Write your name **below** all the other names.
2. oben ◄► unten Find the new words in the text **above**. Look at the pictures **below**.

between	zwischen	What's the difference **between** your bike and Joe's?
round	rund	• A ball is **round**. (rund) • They travelled **round** the world. (*or:* ... **around** the world) (um ... (herum))
the round **one**	der/die/das Runde	

one / ones

Wenn du ein schon einmal genanntes **Nomen** nicht wiederholen willst, musst du **one** (Singular) bzw. **ones** (Plural) verwenden:

I have three **cats**, two black **ones** and a white **one**.	Ich habe drei Katzen, zwei schwarze und eine weiße.
Can you give me a **pen**? – Which **one**? This **one**? – No, the blue **one**, please.	Kannst du mir einen Stift geben? – Welchen? Diesen? – Nein, den blauen, bitte.

bottom	das untere Ende	**(at the) top ◄► (at the) bottom**
level	der Grad, die Stufe; das Niveau, die Ebene	It's often not easy to get to the next **level** in a computer game. **sea level** = der Meeresspiegel

Story

► p. 82	(to) **spend time/money (on)**, *simple past:* **spent**	Zeit verbringen (mit) / Geld ausgeben (für)	I **spend** a lot of **time** with my friends. My brother **spends** a lot of **money on** sweets.
	usually	normalerweise, meistens	Do you often go to work by car? – No, never. I **usually** cycle. When it rains, I take the bus.

	about	ungefähr	We get up at **about** 8.30 on Sundays. ! **about** = **1.** ungefähr; **2.** über *(Präposition)*
	cough	der Husten	Zane has a bad **cough**. ! Beachte Aussprache und Schreibung! Du schreibst **cough** – aber du sprichst es wie **coffee**.
	(to) **have a headache**	Kopfschmerzen haben	! Mit Artikel: I **have a headache**. (Ich habe Kopfschmerzen.) I **have a cough**. (Ich habe Husten.)
	(to) **go out**	rausgehen, weggehen; ausgehen	Let's **go out** and play football. • **out** = heraus, hinaus, nach draußen • **out of ...** = aus ... (heraus/hinaus) **into the house** ◄► **out of the house**
	(to) **click (on)**	klicken (auf), anklicken	Don't **click on** the link in this email!
	screen	der Bildschirm; die Leinwand *(Kino)*	a computer **screen** 
	rule	die Regel	This game is fun because its **rules** are so easy.
	one hour **a** day	eine Stunde pro Tag	I go shopping two or three times **a** week.
	until / **till**	bis *(zeitlich)*	We can play **until**/**till** 2 o'clock. ! **not until** / **not till** = erst, wenn *German:* Wir können **erst essen**, **wenn** Mama heimkommt. *English:* We ca**n't eat until** / **till** mum comes home.
► p. 83	(to) **smile**	lächeln	She told me the news and **smiled** (**at** me). (to) **smile at sb.** = jn. anlächeln
	calendar	der Kalender	! Betonung auf der 1. Silbe: calendar
	(to) **study**	studieren; lernen *(z. B. für Prüfungen)*	When I leave school, I want to **study** languages and become a teacher. I must stay at home this afternoon and **study** for the French test.
	(to) **know**: she **knew**	wissen: sie wusste; sie hat gewusst	When I saw her, I **knew** that something was wrong.
► p. 84	**not (...) any more**	nicht mehr	This bag is very old. I do**n't** use it **any more**.
	tip	der Tipp	Thanks for those **tips!** They're very helpful.

Study skills

► p. 84	**opinion**	die Meinung	**in my opinion** = meiner Meinung nach
	world	die Welt	! *German:* der beste Ort **der Welt** / **auf der Welt** *English:* the best place **in the world**

true	wahr, richtig	Is it **true** that you're the winner of the competition? Wow! Well done! **true ◄ ► false**
not ... at all	überhaupt nicht(s), gar nicht(s); überhaupt kein/e, gar kein/e	He did**n't** say anything **at all**. I do**n't** have any money **at all**.

not ... at all

We did**n't** see anything **at all**.	Wir haben überhaupt nichts gesehen.
I do**n't** like meat **at all**.	Ich mag Fleisch überhaupt nicht. / Ich mag überhaupt kein Fleisch.
It was dark, but I was**n't** scared **at all**.	Es war dunkel, aber ich hatte überhaupt keine Angst.
The vampire film was**n't** scary **at all**.	Der Vampirfilm war überhaupt nicht gruselig.

(to) **stand**, *simple past:* **stood**	stehen; sich (hin)stellen	• I often **stand** at the bus stop and wait for the bus. (stehen) Last week I **stood** in the rain for two hours. • **Stand** here, please. (sich hinstellen)

Irregular verbs

Infinitive	Simple past		Infinitive	Simple past	
(to) **choose**	**chose**	(aus)wählen	(to) **stand**	**stood**	stehen; sich (hin)stellen
(to) **know**	**knew**	wissen; kennen	(to) **take**	**took**	(mit)nehmen
(to) **spend**	**spent**	*(Zeit)* verbringen; *(Geld)* ausgeben			

► List of irregular verbs, p. 271

Unit 4: Celebrate!

► pp. 98/99

(to) **celebrate**	feiern	My grandma **celebrated** her 70th birthday last week. verb: (to) **celebrate** – noun: **celebration** (die Feier, das Fest)
fireworks *(pl)*	das Feuerwerk	**fireworks** *(pl)* (das Feuerwerk) **fire** = das Feuer

(to) **throw**, *simple past:* **threw**	werfen	I often **throw** a ball for my dog. He loves to run after it. Don't **throw away** this hat! It still looks good. (wegwerfen)
carnival	der Karneval	
(to) **break the fast**, *simple past:* **broke**	das Fasten brechen	(to) **break sth.**, *simple past:* **broke** = etwas (zer)brechen
Easter	(das) Ostern	
Christmas	(das) Weihnachten	**Christmas Day** = der 1. Weihnachtstag (25. 12.)
biscuit	der Keks, das Plätzchen	**!** *German* **Keks** – *English* **biscuit** *German* **Kuchen** – *English* **cake**

	candle	die Kerze	a **candle** 

Topic 1

► p. 100	**during**	während	I fell asleep **during** the film. It was so boring!
	(to) **pray**	beten	verb: (to) **pray** – noun: **prayer** (das Gebet)
	(to) **thank** sb.	jm. danken, sich bei jm. bedanken	I'd like to **thank** everybody for their help. (= say thank you to everybody)
	god	der Gott	He had an accident this morning, but he's OK, **thank God**! (gottlob, Gott sei Dank)
► p. 101	**mosque**	die Moschee	 a **mosque**
	(to) **hope**	hoffen	I **hope** you like my school uniform.
► p. 102	(to) **sell**: I **sold**	verkaufen: ich verkaufte; ich habe verkauft	We **sold** lots of cake last weekend. (to) **buy, bought** ◄ ► (to) **sell, sold**
	a little	ein wenig, ein bisschen	Can I have **a little** milk in my tea, please? ►► **a bit** ! **little** = klein **a little** = ein wenig, ein bisschen
	a few	ein paar, einige	You're hungry? There are **a few** sandwiches in the kitchen. **in the last few weeks** = in den letzten paar Wochen

a little – a few

- **a little** bedeutet **ein wenig, ein bisschen, etwas.** — We need **a little** time/money/milk/music/... Wir brauchen **etwas** Zeit/Geld/Milch/Musik/...
- **a few** bedeutet **ein paar, einige.** Du verwendest **a few** mit dem Plural von Nomen. — We need **a few** minutes/dollars/bottles/songs/... Wir brauchen **einige** Minuten/Dollar/Flaschen/Songs/...

	almost	fast, beinahe	It's **almost** 8 o'clock! We're late!
	yoghurt	der Joghurt	 **yoghurt**
	lamb	das Lamm(fleisch)	! Das **b** wird nicht gesprochen – die Aussprache endet mit dem Laut „m“.
	May I ...?	Darf ich ...?	**May I** use your pen? – Sure! Here you are.
► p. 103	**onion**	die Zwiebel	an **onion** 
	dictionary	das Wörterbuch, das (alphabetische) Wörterverzeichnis	Can I use your **dictionary**?

Topic 2

► p. 104	**wedding**	die Hochzeit	They got married in May. Their **wedding** was wonderful. **wedding ring** = der Ehering
	nervous	nervös, aufgeregt	Are you **nervous** before you give a presentation? ! Betonung auf der 1. Silbe: <u>ner</u>vous
	I have practised … . **I haven't practised … .**	Ich habe … geübt. Ich habe … nicht geübt.	
► p. 105	(to) **do**: I **have done**	tun: ich habe getan	What a mess! And where is my chocolate? Scout, what **have** you **done**?
	not … yet	noch nicht …	**yet** **1.** *in verneinten Sätzen:* **noch nicht** – I'm hungry. I have**n't** had dinner **yet**. **2.** *in Fragen:* **schon** – Have you had dinner **yet**?
	… yet?	… schon …?	
	(to) **finish**	enden; beenden, zu Ende machen	School **finishes** at 15.05. = We **finish** school at 15.05. (Wir haben um 15.05 Schulschluss.) ►► (to) end
	ever	jemals	**ever** ◄► **never** Have you **ever** …? = Bist/Hast du schon einmal … ! **ever** = **1.** jemals, schon einmal; **2.** **the best son ever** = der beste Sohn überhaupt / der beste Sohn, den man sich wünschen kann
	(to) **be**: I **have been**	sein: ich bin gewesen	! *German:* **Bist** du schon mal **in London gewesen**? *English:* **Have** you ever **been to London**?
	(to) **eat**: I **have eaten**	essen: ich habe gegessen	What, you**'ve** never **eaten** jollof rice? It's delicious!
	(to) **see**: I **have seen**	sehen: ich habe gesehen	**Have** you **seen** my bag? – No, sorry, I don't know where it is.
	(to) **meet**: I **have met**	treffen: ich habe getroffen	I**'ve** never **met** your sister. How old is she?
	(to) **give**: I **have given**	geben: ich habe gegeben	Give Ms Hill your text this week, please. Or **have** you **given** it to her already?
	(to) **swim**: I **have swum**	schwimmen: ich bin geschwommen	I love swimming, but I **have** never **swum** more than 3 km.
	(to) **win**: I **have won**	gewinnen: ich habe gewonnen	**Have** you ever **won** a competition?
► p. 106	**just**	gerade (eben)	I've **just** made biscuits. Want to try one? ! **just** = **1.** gerade (eben); **2.** nur, bloß; einfach
	(to) **come**: they **have come**	kommen: sie sind gekommen	He **hasn't come** to any of our shows yet.
	chore	die (Haus-)Arbeit, die *(lästige)* Pflicht	(to) **do chores** = (Haus-)Arbeiten erledigen
	soon	bald	Don't eat in class. It's time for break **soon**!

	you **mustn't** do it	du darfst es nicht tun	! **you mustn't** = du darfst nicht **you don't have to** = du musst nicht, du brauchst nicht
	(to) **vacuum**	Staub saugen	verb: (to) **vacuum** – noun: **vacuum cleaner** (der Staubsauger)
	(to) **take out** the rubbish	den Müll rausbringen	Can you **take out the rubbish**, please? 
	(to) **set,** *simple past:* **set**	stellen, legen, setzen	(to) **set the table** = den Tisch decken
► p. 107	**lonely**	einsam	I have my own flat and I'm often alone, but I never feel **lonely**.
	at least	wenigstens, zumindest	A good bike costs **at least** £600. (= £600 or more) You can **at least** tell them that you're sorry.
	stepson **stepdaughter**	der Stiefsohn die Stieftochter	**step-** ("Stief-") **stepmother**, **stepfather**, **stepmum**, **stepdad** **stepsister**, **stepbrother**, **stepdaughter**, **stepson** **daughter** = die Tochter

Topic 3

► p. 108	**member**	das Mitglied	I'm a **member** of a very nice yoga group.
	(to) **rhyme**	(sich) reimen	Careful! The two words 'cough' and 'through' look almost the same, but they don't **rhyme**!
► p. 109	**tradition**	die Tradition	noun: **tradition** – adjective: **traditional** (traditionell) ! Betonung auf der 2. Silbe: tradition / traditional
	poem	das Gedicht	
	onto the table	auf den Tisch	He's jumping **onto** a box. 
	(to) **knock**	stoßen, klopfen	(to) **knock sth. over** = etwas umstoßen (to) **knock (at)** = (an)klopfen (an) *(z. B. Tür)* ! Wie bei **know** und **knit** wird das „k" von **knock** nicht gesprochen – die Aussprache beginnt mit dem Laut „n".
	(to) **sing**: we **sang**	singen: wir sangen; wir haben gesungen	During the concert the band **sang** many of their old songs.
	(to) **sound**	klingen *(sich ... anhören)*	This old recording **sounds** really weird. That karaoke party **sounds** fun. Let's go there!

Verbs and nouns with the same form

(to) **click**	klicken, anklicken	**click**	der Klick, das Klicken
(to) **fast**	fasten	**fast**	das Fasten, die Fastenzeit
(to) **finish**	enden; beenden, zu Ende machen	**finish**	das Ende, das Ziel *(beim Sport)*
(to) **hope**	hoffen	**hope**	die Hoffnung
(to) **rhyme**	(sich) reimen	**rhyme**	der Reim
(to) **role-play** sth.	etwas in einem Rollenspiel darstellen	**role-play**	das Rollenspiel
(to) **score**	erzielen *(Punkt / Tor / Treffer)*	**score**	der Spiel- / Punktestand; *(im Spiel / Sport erzielter)* Punkt
(to) **smile**	lächeln	**smile**	das Lächeln
(to) **sound**	klingen	**sound**	das Geräusch; der Klang, der Laut

Story

► p. 110	**on time**	pünktlich	Our train arrived **on time**.
	excited	aufgeregt, gespannt	**excit<u>ed</u>** = aufgeregt, gespannt **excit<u>ing</u>** = aufregend ! Beachte die Schreibweise: **ex<u>c</u>ited**
	(to) **put** sth. **on**	etwas anziehen *(Kleidung)*, aufsetzen *(Hut, Brille)*	
	(to) **take** sth. **off**	etwas ausziehen *(Kleidung)*, ablegen *(Hut, Brille)*	(to) **take sth. off** ◄► (to) **put sth. on** He **took off** his glasses and **put on** a pullover.
	beautiful	wunderschön	adj: **beautiful** – Your horse is very **beautiful**! noun: **beauty** – Your horse is a **beauty**! (die Schönheit)
	(to) **wear**: I **have worn**	tragen, anhaben *(Kleidung)*: ich habe getragen/angehabt	I bought this dress last year, but I **have** never **worn** it.
	suit	der (Herren-)Anzug; das (Damen-)Kostüm	**suits** 
► p. 111	(to) **take**: they **have taken**	(mit)nehmen: sie haben (mit)genommen	Oh! **Have** you **taken** out the rubbish? Thanks!
	just then / **just** there	genau dann / genau dort	We started to eat, and **just** then our parrot flew onto the table. The accident happened **just** here – **just** in front of our eyes!
	slippers *(pl)*	die Hausschuhe	a pair of **slippers** 
	as	als, während	! **as** = **1.** wie – **As** I was saying, it's not easy. **2.** als, während – She watched me **as** I ate my sandwich. **3. as good as** ... – My bike is **as good as** new. (so gut wie neu)
	terrible	schrecklich, fürchterlich	►► horrible

	still	trotzdem	! **still** = **1.** trotzdem – It was cold, but we **still** went out. **2.** noch – It's **still** raining, but I need to walk the dog.
	he **could**	er könnte	! **I could** = **1.** ich **konnte** – I looked everywhere, but I **couldn't** find my keys. **2.** ich **könnte** – **Could** you say that again, please?
▸ p. 112	**jacket**	die Jacke; das Jackett	 a **jacket**  a **rain jacket**
	multicultural	multikulturell	
	scarf, *pl* **scarves**	der Schal	two **scarves** 
	shirt	das Shirt, das Hemd	Ben wore a suit with a nice **shirt** and a tie for his wedding.

Study skills

▸ p. 114	**along** the river	den Fluss entlang, am Fluss entlang	Walk across the bridge and then **along** the river till you get to the old village.
	church	die Kirche	 a **church**
	all over the world	überall auf der Welt, auf der ganzen Welt, weltweit	**all over** the world = (a)round the world = everywhere in the world
	mirror	der Spiegel	a wardrobe with **mirrors** 

Irregular verbs

Infinitive	Simple past		Infinitive	Simple past	
(to) **break**	**broke**	(zer)brechen	(to) **sing**	**sang**	singen
(to) **sell**	**sold**	verkaufen	(to) **throw**	**threw**	werfen
(to) **set**	**set**	stellen, legen, setzen			

▸ List of irregular verbs, p. 271

Unit 5: Getting ready for the future

▸ pp. 128/129

future	die Zukunft; zukünftige(r, s)	! Betonung auf der 1. Silbe: **fu**ture noun: **future** – Please be more careful in the **future**. adj: **future** – What are your **future** plans?
(to) **fix** sth. *(infml)*	etwas in Ordnung bringen; etwas reparieren	**Fix** your hair! It looks terrible. Problems with your bike? I can **fix** it.
sick	krank	adj: **sick** – noun: **sickness** (die Krankheit) **sickness** ►► **illness** Malaria is a dangerous **sickness/illness**.
artist	der Künstler, die Künstlerin	! Betonung auf der 1. Silbe: **ar**tist
firefighter	der Feuerwehrmann, die Feuerwehrfrau	a **firefighter** trying to stop a **fire** 
hairdresser	der Friseur, die Friseurin	

! Wenn man das Geschäft oder den Laden meint, wird **'s** an die Berufsbezeichnung angehängt.
Vergleiche: **hairdresser** = der Friseur/die Friseurin *(die Person)*
hairdresser's = der Friseursalon – Jake is **at the hairdresser's**.

mechanic	der Mechaniker, die Mechanikerin	Our car has a problem. A car **mechanic** needs to check it.
nurse	der Krankenpfleger, die Krankenpflegerin	**nurses** 
plumber	der (Sanitär-)Installateur, die (Sanitär-)Installateurin	Call a **plumber**! Our kitchen is full of water! ! Das **b** wird nicht gesprochen – **plumber** klingt nicht wie „number".
programmer	der Programmierer, die Programmiererin	nouns: **program** (das (Computer-)Programm); *(person)* **programmer** – verb: (to) **program** (programmieren) ! **program** = das (Computer-)Programm **programme** = das (Fernseh-)Programm, die Sendung
anybody **anyone**	(irgend)jemand; jede/r (beliebige)	! **anybody/anyone** = **1.** (irgend)jemand – Do you know **anybody/anyone** from Spain? **2.** jede/r (beliebige) – You can ask **anybody/anyone**. **3. not ... anybody/anyone** = niemand – I did**n't** see **anybody/anyone**.
as a teacher	als Lehrer/in	! *German:* **als Lehrer/in; als Gewinner/in** *English:* **as a teacher; as the winner**

Topic 1

▸ p. 130	**mind**	der Geist, der Verstand; die Gedanken; der Kopf *(im übertragenen Sinn)*	(to) **make up your mind** / (to) **make your mind up** = sich entscheiden, sich entschließen I can never **make up my mind** / **make my mind up** about what I want to do.
	I want to be a firefighter.	Ich möchte Feuerwehrmann/ Feuerwehrfrau werden.	! Wenn es um Berufswünsche geht („was man einmal werden möchte"), wird meist **be** benutzt, nicht **become**.
	especially	insbesondere	I love team sports, **especially** football.
	perhaps	vielleicht	►► maybe
	business owner	der Geschäftsinhaber, die Geschäftsinhaberin	• **business** = das Geschäft, der Betrieb (to) **start a business** = ein Geschäft aufmachen, einen Betrieb gründen/ eröffnen • **business card** = die Visitenkarte, die Geschäftskarte
	(to) **own** sth.	etwas besitzen	She's the boss here – the **business owner**. She **owns** this business. verb: (to) **own** – noun *(person)*: **owner** – adj: your **own** house/business/...
▸ p. 131	**architect**	der Architekt, die Architektin	! Betonung auf der 1. Silbe: <u>ar</u>chitect
	(to) **teach**, *simple past:* **taught**	lehren, unterrichten	Mr Schwarz is a teacher. He **teaches** English. My sister is **teaching** me to play the guitar. (... bringt mir das Gitarrespielen bei.) Her aunt **taught** her how to play the game, and now she's a famous gamer.
▸ p. 132	**I'll (= I will)** be ... I **won't (= I will not)** be ...	Ich werde ... sein. Ich werde nicht ... sein.	! Nicht verwechseln: I **will** have fun. = Ich **werde** Spaß haben. I **want to** have fun. = Ich **möchte** Spaß haben.
	anything	(irgend)etwas; alles; egal, was	! **anything** = **1.** (irgend)etwas – **Can** you see **anything**? **2.** alles; egal, was – You can ask her **anything**. **3. not ... anything** = nichts – I **can't** see **anything**.
	respect (for)	der Respekt (vor)	I have a lot of **respect for** my teachers.
	(to) **believe (in** sth.**)**	(an etwas) glauben	! *German:* **Glaubst** du **an** Vampire? *English:* Do you **believe in** vampires?
	prediction	die Vorhersage, die Voraussage	Can you make a **prediction** about how much this will cost?
	(to) **earn**	verdienen *(Geld)*	! *German* "Geld verdienen": **1.** *(Gehalt bekommen)* (to) **earn money** **2.** *(Profit machen)* (to) **make money**
▸ p. 133	**hard-working**	fleißig	working a lot and trying to do your job well
	rich	reich	Would you like to be **rich** and famous?

	successful	erfolgreich	adj: **successful** – Mo had a good business idea – it was very **successful**. noun: **success** – His business was a big **success**.

Topic 2

► p. 134	(to) **notice**	(be)merken	I didn't **notice** him because I was playing a video game.
	washing	die Wäsche	(to) **wash** = waschen; sich waschen (to) **do the washing** = die Wäsche erledigen, Wäsche waschen
	(to) **fold**	falten	You can save space if you **fold** your clothes when you put them into your wardrobe.
	(to) **look after** sb./sth.	sich um jn./etwas kümmern; auf jn./etwas aufpassen	I sometimes **look after** my baby sister.

(to) look

• (to) **look at**	Oh, **look at** the seagulls!	anschauen
• (to) **look after**	Can you **look after** your brother, please?	sich kümmern um; aufpassen auf
• (to) **look for**	Let's **look for** Scout.	suchen
• (to) **look sth. up**	**Look up** this word in a dictionary.	etwas nachschlagen

	(to) **babysit**, *simple past:* **babysat**	babysitten	(to) **babysit a baby / a child** verb: (to) **babysit** – nouns: *(what you do)* **babysitting**; *(person)* **babysitter**
	(to) **empty**	leeren	adj: **empty** – verb: (to) **empty** (leeren)
	dishwasher	die Geschirrspülmaschine	The **dishwasher** is finished! Can you **empty** it, please? 
► p. 135	(to) **hate**	hassen	• verbs: (to) **love (to do** sth.**)** ◄► (to) **hate (to do** sth.**)** • nouns: **love** ◄► **hate** (der Hass)
	least	am wenigsten	! **least** = am wenigsten – the **least** favourite chores = die Arbeiten, die man am wenigsten gerne macht; the **least** popular school club **at least** = wenigstens – **at least** £600

Topic 3

► p. 136	**treat**	der Hochgenuss, das besondere Vergnügen; die (besondere) Leckerei	Let's go to our favourite restaurant. I'll pay! – Oh, thanks! What a nice **treat**.
	pocket money	das Taschengeld	**pocket** = die Tasche *(an Kleidungsstücken)* This hoodie has big **pockets** for my phone, my keys and my money.

	magazine (*infml auch:* **mag**)	die Zeitschrift	**magazines** 
	(to) **shop (for** sth.**)**	(ein)kaufen, „shoppen"; etwas kaufen (gehen)	I need to **shop for** (= go and buy) new shoes. verb: (to) **shop** – nouns: **shop**; *(person)* **shopper** (der Kunde, die Kundin; der Einkäufer, die Einkäuferin)
	stuff *(infml)*	das Zeug, der Kram	I have so much **stuff**! I need to take some of the things to a charity shop.
	cash	das Cash, das Bargeld	You can only **pay (in) cash** in this shop. (bar bezahlen) (to) **pay cash** / (to) **pay in cash** ◄► (to) **pay by card** (mit Karte bezahlen)
	cash machine	der Geldautomat	I need some cash. Is there a **cash machine** near here? **machine** = der Automat, die Maschine **ticket machine** = der Fahrkartenautomat
	gift	das Geschenk, die Gabe; das Talent	►► present **gift shop** = der Geschenk(artikel)laden, der Souvenirladen
	savings account	das Sparkonto	**savings** *(pl)* = die Ersparnisse **account** = das (Bank-)Konto; der Account
	bank	die Bank *(Geldinstitut)*	I have a weekend job in a cafe. They pay the money into my **bank** account. **banker** = der Banker, die Bankerin
	coin	die Münze	You only have some **coins** – that's not a lot of cash!
	piggy bank	das Sparschwein	I need some cash … I can empty my **piggy bank**.  **coins** →
► p. 137	**bakery**	die Bäckerei	nouns: **bakery**; *(person)* **baker** (der Bäcker, die Bäckerin) – verb: (to) **bake** (backen)

People's jobs: verb + *-er*

(to) **bake** – **baker**	(to) **play** – **player**	(to) **teach** – **teacher**
(to) **clean** – **cleaner**	(to) **program** – **programmer**	(to) **train** – **trainer**
(to) **dance** – **dancer**	(to) **sing** – **singer**	(to) **write** – **writer**
(to) **design** – **designer**	(to) **swim** – **swimmer**	

electronics *(pl)*	die Elektronik; die elektronischen Geräte	 noun: **electronics** – adj: **electronic** (elektronisch)

Pluralwörter
Einige englische Wörter sind immer **Plural** – sie haben keine Singularform.

braces	die Zahnspange, die Zahnklammer	! Zugehörige Begleiter *(these, those)*, Pronomen *(they, them)* und Verben stehen im Plural: Look at **those clothes**! I'd love to buy **them**, but **they are** so expensive. Be careful, **these stairs are** dangerous. **Vegetables are** good for me. I love **them**.
clothes	die Kleidung(sstücke)	
electronics	die Elektronik	
fireworks	das Feuerwerk	
stairs	die Treppe; die Stufen	
vegetables	das Gemüse	
trousers / jeans / shorts	die Hose / die Jeans / die kurze Hose, die Shorts	! Mit **a pair of**, **two pairs of** usw. kannst du eine genaue Anzahl von Hosen, Brillen usw. nennen: I need **a new pair of trousers/jeans/shorts**. Why do you have **two pairs of glasses**?
glasses, sunglasses	die Brille, die Sonnenbrille	
headphones	der Kopfhörer	

newsagent	der Zeitungshändler, die Zeitungshändlerin	! **newsagent** = der Zeitungshändler, die Zeitungshändlerin *(die Person)* **newsagent's** = der Zeitschriftenladen, der Zeitungskiosk: I work **at a newsagent's**.
▸ p. 138 **size**	die Größe	! *German:* Welche **Größe hast** du? *English:* What **size** do you **take**?
large	groß	

large – tall – big – great
! You don't use **large** to describe people.
People can be **tall** (groß), **big** (dick, schwer) or **great** (bedeutend, angesehen).

price	der (Kauf-)Preis	! German "Preis" = **1. price** – £150 is a good **price** for this bike. *(der Kaufpreis)* **2. prize** – She's the winner of a special **prize** in the show for clever kids. *(der Gewinn)*
How much is ...? **How much are ...?**	Was (Wie viel) kostet ...? Was (Wie viel) kosten ...?	Excuse me, please, **how much is** the football? And **how much are** the books? – The football **is** £3. / The books **are** £2.
change	das Wechselgeld	

change – (to) change
- **change** *(noun)*
  1. die Veränderung, der Wechsel, die Verwandlung
  2. das Wechselgeld
  3. change of clothes = die Kleidung zum Wechseln
- **(to) change** *(verb)*
  1. (sich) (ver)ändern; wechseln; (sich) verwandeln
  2. umsteigen
  3. sich umziehen

those	die dort, jene (dort)	

this, that – these, those
- Wenn etwas näher beim Sprecher / bei der Sprecherin ist, sagt man eher **this** und **these.** — I think **this** book here is great, and I love **these** films.
- Wenn etwas weiter entfernt ist, verwendet man eher **that** und **those.** — Oh look, **that** dog and **those** seagulls over there ... they're fighting.

(to) **try** sth. **on**	etwas anprobieren *(Kleidung)*	Excuse me, where can I **try on** these trousers?

► p. 139	**(shop) assistant**	der Verkäufer, die Verkäuferin	! **assistant** = **1.** der Verkäufer, die Verkäuferin; **2.** der Assistent, die Assistentin
	each	jede(r, s) (einzelne), jeweils	**Each** student can ask one question. = You can ask one question **each.** (... jeweils eine Frage)
	customer	der Kunde, die Kundin	"Do you need any help?" the shop assistant asked the **customer**.
	Would you like **anything else**?	Möchten Sie sonst noch etwas?	

... else

Why can't I have a pet? **Everybody else** has a pet.	alle anderen; jede/r andere; sonst jede/r
I'm so tired. **Somebody else** must make dinner today.	jemand anders
Thank you. I don't need **anything else**.	nichts anderes; sonst nichts
What else do you want to know?	was (sonst) noch

Story

► p. 140	(to) **sell**: she **has sold**	verkaufen: sie hat verkauft	(to) **buy, bought, bought** ◄ ► (to) **sell, sold, sold**
► p. 141	(to) **move (to)**	(um)ziehen (nach)	They **moved to** York, to a nice flat in town.
	(to) **miss**	vermissen	I enjoyed my trip to France, but I **missed** my friends.
	hug	die Umarmung	noun: **hug** – verbs: (to) **hug** (einander umarmen); (to) **hug sb.** (jn. umarmen) Beth is **hugging** Jill. = They're **hugging**. 
	each other	einander, sich (gegenseitig)	They like **each other**. Work together – you can learn a lot **from each other**! (voneinander) They talked **to each other**. (miteinander)
	work experience	die Arbeitserfahrung(en), die Praxiserfahrung(en); das Praktikum	• She knows a lot about computers and coding and has a lot of **work experience**. (Arbeits-/Praxiserfahrung(en)) • Last year I did some **work experience** at our local supermarket. (Praktikum))
► p. 142	(to) **repeat**	wiederholen	Could you **repeat** that, please? (= Could you say/do that again, please?)
	contact	der Kontakt	! Betonung auf der 1. Silbe: contact

Verbs and nouns with the same form

(to) **contact** sb.	Kontakt aufnehmen mit jm., sich in Verbindung setzen mit jm.	**contact**	der Kontakt
(to) **email** sb.	jm. mailen, jm. eine E-Mail schicken	**email**	die E-Mail
(to) **experience**	erfahren; erleben	**experience**	die Erfahrung; das Erlebnis
(to) **hate**	hassen	**hate**	der Hass
(to) **hug**	umarmen	**hug**	die Umarmung
(to) **notice**	merken, bemerken	**notice**	der Anschlag, die Bekanntmachung *(an einem Schwarzen Brett)*
(to) **respect**	respektieren, achten	**respect**	der Respekt

	strength	die Stärke, die Kraft	One of my **strengths** is that I speak three languages. noun: **strength** – adj: **strong**
	(to) **solve**	lösen *(Rätsel, Problem)*, lüften *(Geheimnis)*	Who can help me to **solve** this problem?

Study skills

▶ p. 144	**Dear ...**	Liebe/r ...	
	How are you?	Wie geht's? / Wie geht es dir/euch/Ihnen?	**How are you** today? – I'm fine, thanks.
	(to) **look forward to** sth. (to) **look forward to doing** sth.	sich auf etwas freuen sich darauf freuen, etwas zu tun	**!** *German:* Wir **freuen uns darauf**, von Ihnen **zu hören**. *English:* We **look forward to hearing** from you.
	Take care.	Pass auf dich auf. / Mach's gut!	Bye Lily! **Take care**, and see you soon. (to) **take care** = vorsichtig sein, aufpassen **care** = die Sorgfalt, die Vorsicht
	(to) **understand,** *simple past:* **understood**	verstehen	In English, please. I don't **understand** German.

Unit task

▶ p. 145	**horoscope**	das Horoskop	**!** Betonung auf der 1. Silbe: **horoscope**
	star sign	das Sternzeichen	**!** **star** = **1.** der Stern; **2.** der (Film-/Pop-)Star **sign** = das Zeichen; das Schild
	useful	nützlich, hilfreich	These exercises are too hard? Here are some **useful** tips. (= these tips can help you)
	realistic	**realistisch**	I want to see all the sights in London. – Oh, be **realistic**. We only have two days.

Irregular verbs

Infinitive	Simple past		Infinitive	Simple past	
(to) **babysit**	**babysat**	babysitten	(to) **understand**	**understood**	verstehen
(to) **teach**	**taught**	lehren, unterrichten			

▶ List of irregular verbs, p. 271

Im *English-German Dictionary* kannst du nachschlagen, was ein Wort bedeutet oder wie es ausgesprochen wird.

Es werden folgende **Abkürzungen und Symbole** verwendet:

infml = *informal* (umgangssprachlich)
sb. = *somebody* (jemand)
jd. = jemand
jm. = jemandem
pl = *plural* (Mehrzahl)
sth. = *something* (etwas)
jn. = jemanden

° Mit diesem Kringel sind Wörter markiert, die nicht zum Lernwortschatz gehören.

Die **Fundstellenangaben** zeigen, wo ein Wort zum ersten Mal vorkommt. Die Ziffern in Klammern bezeichnen Seitenzahlen.

1 = Lighthouse 1
2: 1 (26) = Lighthouse 2, Unit 1, Seite 26

A

a [ə] ein, eine 1 **one hour a day** eine Stunde pro Tag 2: 3 (82)
about [əˈbaʊt]:
1. ungefähr 2: 3 (82)
2. **about me/you/...** über mich/dich/... 1
What about ...? Wie wäre es mit ...? 1 **What about you?** Und du? / Was ist mit dir? 1
above [əˈbʌv] über, oberhalb (von); oben 2: 3 (81)
accident [ˈæksɪdənt]:
1. der Unfall 2: 2 (12)
2. der Zufall 2: 2 (12)
by accident zufällig 2: 2 (12)
account [əˈkaʊnt] das (Bank-)Konto; der Account 2: 1 (132)
acoustic [əˈkuːstɪk] akustisch 2: 3 (72)
across [əˈkrɒs] über *(quer über)* 2: 3 (80)
act [ækt]:
1. Theater spielen, schauspielern; aufführen 2: 3 (70/71)
2. **act out** aufführen, vorspielen 2: 3 (70/71)
action [ˈækʃn] die Aktion, die (spannende) Handlung 1
activist [ˈæktɪvɪst] der Aktivist, die Aktivistin 2: 2 (48)
activity [ækˈtɪvəti] die Aktivität, die Tätigkeit 1
actor [ˈæktə] der Schauspieler, die Schauspielerin 2: 3 (70/71)
ad [æd] *(infml) siehe* **advert**
add [æd] hinzufügen; addieren 1
address [əˈdres] die Adresse 1
adventure [ədˈventʃə] das Abenteuer 2: 3 (80)
advert [ˈædvɜːt] *infml auch* **ad** die Anzeige, das Inserat; der Werbespot 2: 1 (17)
after [ˈɑːftə]:
1. **after (school)** nach (der Schule) 1
2. **after (you read)** nachdem (du liest) 1
afternoon [ɑːftəˈnuːn] der Nachmittag 1 **in the afternoon** nachmittags, am Nachmittag 1
again [əˈgen] wieder, noch einmal 1
against [əˈgenst] gegen 2: 2 (17)
agent [ˈeɪdʒənt] der Agent, die Agentin 2: 3 (78)
°**ago** [əˈgəʊ]: **some years ago** vor einigen Jahren
agree [əˈgriː]: **agree (with sb./sth.)** jm. zustimmen; mit etwas einverstanden sein 2: 2 (43) **agree on** sich einigen auf 2: 2 (43)
°**air** [eə] die Luft
album [ˈælbəm] das Album 2: 3 (72)
all [ɔːl] alle(s) 1 **all day** der ganze Tag, den ganzen Tag (lang) 2: 3 (70/71) **all over the world** überall auf der Welt, auf der ganzen Welt, weltweit 2: 4 (114) **all the family** die ganze Familie 2: 3 (70/71) **all the time** die ganze Zeit, ständig 2: 3 (70/71) **not ... at all** überhaupt nicht(s), gar nicht(s); überhaupt kein/e, gar kein/e 2: 3 (82)
allergic (to) [əˈlɜːdʒɪk] allergisch (gegen) 1
almost [ˈɔːlməʊst] fast, beinahe 2: 4 (102)
alone [əˈləʊn] allein 1
along the river [əˈlɒŋ] den Fluss entlang, am Fluss entlang 2: 4 (114)
alphabet [ˈælfəbet] das Alphabet 1
already [ɔːlˈredi] schon 1
also [ˈɔːlsəʊ] auch 1
always [ˈɔːlweɪz] immer 1
am [æm]: **I'm (= I am)** ich bin 1
a.m. [eɪˈem]: **4 a.m.** 4 Uhr (früh-)morgens 1 **9 a.m.** 9 Uhr vormittags 1
°**amazement** [əˈmeɪzmənt] das Erstaunen, die Verwunderung
amazing [əˈmeɪzɪŋ] erstaunlich; großartig 1
ambulance [ˈæmbjələns] der Krankenwagen 2: 2 (13)
an [ən] ein/e *(vor Vokalen)* 1
and [ænd], [ənd] und 1
angry [ˈæŋgri] wütend 1
animal [ˈænɪml] das Tier 1
animal charity [ˈænɪml tʃærəti] die wohltätige Organisation, die Tiere unterstützt 2: 2 (48)
ankle [ˈæŋkl] der Knöchel, das Fußgelenk 2: 2 (13)
°**announcement** [əˈnaʊnsmənt] die Durchsage, die Ansage, die Ankündigung
°**another** [əˈnʌðə] ein/e andere/r/s; noch ein/e
answer [ˈɑːnsə]:
1. die Antwort 1
2. (be)antworten 1
any [ˈeni] jede(r/s) (beliebige), jegliche(r/s) 2: 2 (11) **(at) any time** zu jeder Zeit, jederzeit 2: 2 (11) **Do you have any questions?** Habt ihr / Hast du (irgendwelche) Fragen? 1 **not (...) any more** nicht mehr 2: 3 (84) **there aren't any ...** es gibt keine ... 1
anybody [ˈenibɒdi] irgendjemand; jede/r (beliebige) 2: 1 (128/129) **not (...) anybody** niemand 2: 1 (128/129)
anyone [ˈeniwʌn] irgendjemand; jede/r (beliebige) 2: 1 (128/129) **not (...) anyone** niemand 2: 1 (128/129)
anything [ˈeniθɪŋ] (irgend)etwas; alles; egal, was 2: 1 (132) **not ... anything** nichts 2: 1 (21)
apartment [əˈpɑːtmənt] die Wohnung 2: 1 (12/13)
app [æp] die App 1
apple [ˈæpl] der Apfel 1
April [ˈeɪprəl] der April 1
°**Aquarius** [əˈkweəriəs] der Wassermann *(Sternzeichen)*
architect [ˈɑːkɪtekt] der Architekt, die Architektin 2: 1 (131)
are [ɑː]: **The books are £2.** Die Bücher kosten 2 Pfund. 2: 1 (138) **they are** sie sind 1 **they aren't** sie sind nicht 1 **you are** du bist / ihr seid 1
area [ˈeəriə] der Bereich, die Gegend, die Fläche 1
°**Aries** [ˈeəriːz] der Widder *(Sternzeichen)*
arm [ɑːm] der Arm 2: 2 (11)
around ... [əˈraʊnd] um (... herum), in ... umher 2: 3 (81)
arrival [əˈraɪvl] die Ankunft 2: 1 (17)
arrive [əˈraɪv] ankommen 2: 1 (17)
art [ɑːt] die Kunst 1
°**article** [ˈɑːtɪkl] der Artikel
artist [ˈɑːtɪst] der Künstler, die Künstlerin 2: 1 (128/129)
as [æz], [əz]:
1. als, während *(Konjunktion)* 2: 4 (111)
as they walk während sie gehen 2: 4 (111)
2. als *(Präposition)* 2: 1 (128/129)
as a teacher als als Lehrer/in 2: 1 (128/129)

3. wie *(Präposition)* 2: 3 (77)
(not) as bad as (nicht) so schlecht/ schlimm wie 2: 3 (77)
ask [ɑːsk]:
1. fragen 1
ask a question eine Frage stellen 1
2. **ask sb. for sth.** jn. um etwas bitten 1
ask sb. to do sth. jn. bitten, etwas zu tun 1
asleep [əˈsliːp]: **be asleep** schlafen 2: 2 (13) **fall asleep** einschlafen 2: 2 (13)
assembly [əˈsembli] die Schulversammlung 1
assistant [əˈsɪstənt] der Assistent, die Assistentin 2: 1 (139) *(= shop assistant)* der Verkäufer, die Verkäuferin 2: 1 (139)
at [æt], [ət] an; in; bei; auf 1 **at 8 o'clock** um 8 Uhr 1 **at least** wenigstens, zumindest 2: 4 (107) **at night** nachts, in der Nacht 2: 1 (23) **at the cinema** im Kino 1 **at the top (of)** oben, am oberen Ende (von); an der Spitze (von) 1 **at work** bei der Arbeit, am Arbeitsplatz 1 **be good at sth. / at doing sth.** etwas gut können; gut in etwas sein 1 **Open your books at page 10.** Schlagt eure Bücher auf Seite 10 auf. 1
ate [eɪt], [et] *siehe* eat
August [ˈɔːgəst] der August 1
aunt [ɑːnt] die Tante 1
away [əˈweɪ] weg, fort 1
°awesome [ˈɔːsəm] *(infml)* klasse, stark, großartig

B

baby [ˈbeɪbi] das Baby 2: 1 (134)
babysat [ˈbeɪbisæt] *siehe* babysit
babysit [ˈbeɪbisɪt], **babysat** babysitten 2: 1 (134)
babysitter [ˈbeɪbisɪtə] der Babysitter, die Babysitterin 2: 1 (134)
babysitting [ˈbeɪbisɪtɪŋ] das Babysitten 2: 1 (134)
back [bæk]:
1. zurück 2: (10/11)
back at home wieder zu Hause 2: (10/11)
2. **at the back (of the bus)** hinten (im Bus) 2: (10/11) **at the back of the book** hinten im Buch 2: (10/11) **on the back of the card** auf der Rückseite der Karte 2: (10/11)
bad [bæd] schlecht; schlimm 1
bag [bæg] die Tasche 1
bake [beɪk] backen 2: 1 (137)
baker [ˈbeɪkə] der Bäcker, die Bäckerin 2: 1 (137)
bakery [ˈbeɪkəri] die Bäckerei 2: 1 (137)
ball [bɔːl] der Ball 1
balloon [bəˈluːn] der Ballon 1
banana [bəˈnɑːnə] die Banane 1
band [bænd] die Band, die Musikgruppe 1
°bandstand [ˈbændstænd] der Musikpavillon
bank [bæŋk] die Bank *(Geldinstitut)* 2: 1 (132)
bank account [ˈbæŋk əkaʊnt] das Bankkonto 2: 1 (132)
barbecue [ˈbɑːbɪkjuː] das Grillfest, das Grillen 2: 1 (23)
bark (at sb.) [bɑːk] (jn. an)bellen 1
basketball [ˈbɑːskɪtbɔːl] der Basketball 1
bathroom [ˈbɑːθruːm] das Bad(ezimmer) 1
be [biː], **was/were, been** sein 1
I want to be a firefighter. Ich möchte Feuerwehrmann/-frau werden. 2: 1 (130)
beach [biːtʃ] der Strand 1 **on the beach** am Strand 1 **to the beach** zum Strand, an den Strand 1
°beast [biːst] das Tier; die Bestie; das Biest
beautiful [ˈbjuːtɪfl] wunderschön 2: 4 (110)
beauty [ˈbjuːti] die Schönheit 2: 4 (110)
became [bɪˈkeɪm] *siehe* become
because [bɪˈkɒz] weil 1
become [bɪˈkʌm], **became** werden 2: 2 (47)
bed [bed] das Bett 1 **go to bed** ins Bett gehen 1
bedroom [ˈbedruːm] das Schlafzimmer 1
been [biːn] *siehe* be
before [bɪˈfɔː]:
1. **before (school / the lesson)** vor (der Schule / der Unterrichtsstunde) 1
2. **before (you read)** bevor (du liest) 1
°beginning [bɪˈgɪnɪŋ] der Anfang
behind [bɪˈhaɪnd] hinter 1
believe (in) [bɪˈliːv] glauben (an) 2: 1 (132)
below [bɪˈləʊ] unter(halb von); unten 2: 3 (81)
best [best] beste(r, s); am besten 1
like sth. best etwas lieber / am liebsten mögen 2: 3 (77)
better [ˈbetə] besser 2: 3 (77) **like sth. better** etwas lieber mögen 2: 3 (77)
between [bɪˈtwiːn] zwischen 2: 3 (81)
big [bɪg]:
1. groß 1
2. schwer, dick *(Person)* 2: 1 (138)
bike [baɪk] das Fahrrad 1
°bin [bɪn] der (Müll-)Eimer
bird [bɜːd] der Vogel 2: 1 (28)
birthday [ˈbɜːθdeɪ] der Geburtstag 1
Happy birthday! Herzlichen Glückwunsch zum Geburtstag! 1 **My birthday is in April.** Ich habe im April Geburtstag. 1 **on my birthday** an meinem Geburtstag 1 **When's your birthday?** Wann hast du Geburtstag? 1
biscuit [ˈbɪskɪt] der Keks, das Plätzchen 2: 4 (98/99)
black [blæk] schwarz 1
blanket [ˈblæŋkɪt] die Decke *(zum Zudecken u. Ä.)* 2: 2 (13)
blond [blɒnd] blond 2: 2 (40/41)
blue [bluː] blau 1
board [bɔːd] die Tafel 1
boat [bəʊt] das Boot; das Schiff 1
body [ˈbɒdi] der Körper 2: 2 (14)
book [bʊk] das Buch 1
boot [buːt] der Stiefel 2: 2 (11)
bored [bɔːd] gelangweilt 2: (10/11)
be bored / get bored sich langweilen 2: (10/11) **I'm bored** mir ist langweilig 2: (10/11)
boring [ˈbɔːrɪŋ] langweilig 2: (10/11)
born [bɔːn]: **he was born** er wurde geboren 2: 2 (47)
boss [bɒs] der Boss, der Chef, die Chefin 2: 1 (132)
°both [bəʊθ] beide
bottom [ˈbɒtəm] das untere Ende 2: 3 (81)
bought [bɔːt] *siehe* buy
bowling [ˈbəʊlɪŋ] das Bowling, das Kegeln 1
box [bɒks] die Box, der Kasten 2: 3 (70/71)
boy [bɔɪ] der Junge 1
boyfriend [ˈbɔɪfrend] der (feste) Freund 2: 1 (20)
braces *(pl)* [ˈbreɪsɪz] die Zahnspange, die Zahnklammer 2: 2 (40/41)
°bracket [ˈbrækɪt] die *(runde)* Klammer *(in Texten)*
°brainstorm [ˈbreɪnstɔːm] Ideen (ungeordnet) sammeln
brave [breɪv] mutig 2: 2 (42)
bread [bred] das Brot 1
break [breɪk] die Pause 1
break [breɪk], **broke** (zer)brechen 2: 4 (98/99) **break the fast** das Fasten brechen 2: 4 (98/99)
breakfast [ˈbrekfəst] das Frühstück 1
breathe (in/out) [briːð] (ein-/aus-) atmen 2: 2 (13)
bridge [brɪdʒ] die Brücke 2: 3 (80)
bring [brɪŋ] bringen, mitbringen 1
Britain [ˈbrɪtn] Großbritannien 1
British [ˈbrɪtɪʃ] britisch 1
°brochure [ˈbrəʊʃə] die Broschüre, der Prospekt
broke [brəʊk] *siehe* break
broken [ˈbrəʊkən]: **be broken** zerbrochen, kaputt, sein 2: 2 (14)
brother [ˈbrʌðə] der Bruder 1
brown [braʊn] braun 1
brunch [brʌntʃ] das Brunch 2: 3 (83)
brush [brʌʃ]:
1. die Bürste 1
2. bürsten 1
brush your teeth (sich) die Zähne putzen 1
°buddy [ˈbʌdi] *(infml)* der Freund, die Freundin; der Kumpel
building [ˈbɪldɪŋ] das Gebäude 1
bully [ˈbʊli]:
1. der Mobber, die Mobberin; der Tyrann, die Tyrannin 1
2. tyrannisieren, mobben 1
bus [bʌs] der Bus 1 **by bus** mit dem Bus 1 **on the bus** im Bus 1
business [ˈbɪznəs] das Geschäft, der Betrieb 2: 1 (130) **start a business** ein

Geschäft aufmachen, einen Betrieb gründen/eröffnen 2: 1 (130)
business card [ˈbɪznəs kɑːd] die Visitenkarte, die Geschäftskarte 2: 1 (130)
business owner [ˈbɪznəs əʊnə] der Geschäftsinhaber, die Geschäftsinhaberin 2: 1 (130)
busy [ˈbɪzi] (viel)beschäftigt 1 **be busy** beschäftigt sein, (viel) zu tun haben 1
but [bʌt], [bət] aber 1
butter [ˈbʌtə] die Butter 1
°button [ˈbʌtn] der Button; die Schaltfläche; der Knopf
buy [baɪ], **bought, bought** kaufen 1
by [baɪ]: **by bus** mit dem Bus 1 **by the sea** am Meer, an der See 1 **pay by card** mit Karte (be)zahlen *(z. B. Bankkarte)* 2: 1 (132) **°one by one** der Reihe nach, nacheinander
Bye. [baɪ] Tschüs. 1

C

cafe [ˈkæfeɪ] das Café 1
cake [keɪk] der Kuchen, die Torte 1 **°piece of cake** das Stück Kuchen
calendar [ˈkælɪndə] der Kalender 2: 3 (83)
call [kɔːl]:
1. nennen; rufen; anrufen 2: 2 (42)
2. der Ruf 2: 2 (42)
3. *(kurz für:* **phone call***)* der (Telefon-)Anruf 2: 2 (42)

called [kɔːld]: **be called** heißen 1
calm [kɑːm] ruhig, besonnen 2: 1 (21)
came [keɪm] *siehe* **come**
camera [ˈkæmərə] die Kamera 2: 3 (73)
campsite [ˈkæmpsaɪt] der Campingplatz 2: 1 (12/13)
can [kæn], [kən] können 1
°Cancer [ˈkænsə] der Krebs *(Sternzeichen)*
candle [ˈkændl] die Kerze 2: 4 (98/99)
can't [kɑːnt]: **I can't (= cannot)** ich kann nicht 1
canteen [kænˈtiːn] die Kantine, die (Schul-)Mensa 1
cap [kæp] die (Schirm-)Mütze, die Kappe 1
cape [keɪp] das Cape *(Umhang)* 2: 2 (11)
°Capricorn [ˈkæprɪkɔːn] der Steinbock *(Sternzeichen)*
°caption [ˈkæpʃn] die Bildunterschrift
car [kɑː] das Auto 1
card [kɑːd] die Karte 1 **business card** die Visitenkarte, die Geschäftskarte 2: 1 (130) **pay by card** mit Karte (be)zahlen *(z. B. Bankkarte)* 2: 1 (132) **playing card** die Spielkarte 1
care [keə] die Sorgfalt, die Vorsicht 2: 1 (144) **take care** vorsichtig sein, aufpassen 2: 1 (144)
careful [ˈkeəfl] vorsichtig 1
carnival [ˈkɑːnɪvl] der Karneval 2: 4 (98/99)
carrot [ˈkærət] die Möhre, die Karotte 1
cartoon [kɑːˈtuːn] der Zeichentrickfilm; der Comic, der Cartoon 2: 3 (78)
case [keɪs] das Etui, der Behälter, der Kasten 1
cash [kæʃ] das Cash, das Bargeld 2: 1 (132) **pay (in) cash** bar bezahlen 2: 1 (132)
cash machine [ˈkæʃ məʃiːn] der Geldautomat 2: 1 (132)
castle [ˈkɑːsl] die Burg 2: 1 (12)
cat [kæt] die Katze 1
°'cause [kɔːz] *(infml)* weil (= because)
celebrate [ˈselɪbreɪt] feiern 2: 4 (98/99)
celebration [selɪˈbreɪʃn] die Feier, das Fest 2: 4 (98/99)
cent [sent] der Cent 2: 1 (19)
centre [ˈsentə] das Zentrum; die Mitte 1
chair [tʃeə] der Stuhl 1
change [tʃeɪndʒ]:
1. **change (into)** (sich) (ver)ändern (zu/in); wechseln; (sich) verwandeln (in), werden (zu) 2: 1 (138)
change (clothes) sich umziehen *(frische Kleidung anziehen)* 2: 1 (138)
change (trains) umsteigen 2: 1 (138)
2. die Veränderung, der Wechsel, die Verwandlung 2: 1 (138)
a change of clothes die (frische) Kleidung zum Wechseln 2: 1 (138)
3. das Wechselgeld 2: 1 (138)

character [ˈkærəktə] der Charakter; die Figur *(aus einer Geschichte)* 2: 3 (79)
charity [ˈtʃærəti] die wohltätige Organisation 2: 2 (48) **animal charity** die wohltätige Organisation, die Tiere unterstützt 2: 2 (48)
charity shop [ˈtʃærəti ʃɒp] *das Geschäft, das gespendete Waren für wohltätige Zwecke verkauft* 2: 2 (48)
°chart [tʃɑːt] das Diagramm; die Tabelle
chat [tʃæt]:
1. **chat (with)** chatten (mit); sich unterhalten (mit) 2: 3 (82)
2. die Unterhaltung; der Chat 2: 3 (82)
have a chat eine Unterhaltung führen, sich unterhalten 2: 3 (82)

°cheap [tʃiːp] billig, preiswert
check [tʃek]:
1. die (Über-)Prüfung, die Kontrolle 1
2. (über)prüfen, kontrollieren 1
check sb./sth. out *(infml)* sich jn./etwas anschauen, anhören; etwas ausprobieren 2: 2 (13)

checklist [ˈtʃeklɪst] die Checkliste 2: 1 (144)
°checkpoint [ˈtʃekpɔɪnt] der Kontrollpunkt
cheese [tʃiːz] der Käse 1
°cheesy [ˈtʃiːzɪ] kitschig
chemical [ˈkemɪkl]:
1. Chemikalie 2: 2 (11)
2. chemisch 2: 2 (11)

chicken [ˈtʃɪkɪn] das Huhn; das (Brat-)Hähnchen 1
child [tʃaɪld], *pl* **children** das Kind 2: 2 (47)
children [tʃɪldrən] *Plural von* **child**
chips *(pl)* [tʃɪps] die Pommes frites 1 **fish and chips** der Fisch mit Pommes Frites 1
chocolate [ˈtʃɒklət] die Schokolade 1 **hot chocolate** der Kakao, die heiße (Trink-)Schokolade 1
choose [tʃuːz], **chose** (aus)wählen 2: 3 (73)
chore [tʃɔː] die (Haus-)Arbeit, die *(lästige)* Pflicht 2: 4 (102) **do chores** (Haus-)Arbeiten erledigen 2: 4 (102)
chose [tʃəuz] *siehe* **choose**
Christmas [ˈkrɪsməs] (das) Weihnachten 2: 4 (98/99)
Christmas Day [krɪsməs ˈdeɪ] der 1. Weihnachtstag (25. 12.) 2: 4 (98/99)
church [tʃɜːtʃ] die Kirche 2: 4 (114)
cinema [ˈsɪnəmə] das Kino 1 **at the cinema** im Kino 1
circle [ˈsɜːkl] der Kreis 1
circus [ˈsɜːkəs] der Zirkus 1
city [ˈsɪti] die (Groß-)Stadt 1
class [klɑːs] die Klasse; der Unterricht; der Kurs 1 **in class** im Unterricht 1
class teacher [ˈklɑːs tiːtʃə] der Klassenlehrer, die Klassenlehrerin 1
classical [ˈklæsɪkl] klassisch 2: 3 (72)
classical music [klæsɪkl ˈmjuːzɪk] klassische Musik 2: 3 (72)
classroom [ˈklɑːsruːm] das Klassenzimmer 1
clean [kliːn]:
1. sauber 1
2. sauber machen, putzen 1
clean sth. up etwas aufräumen, sauber machen 1

clean-up [ˈkliːn ʌp] das Säubern, das Saubermachen 1
clean-up day [ˈkliːn ʌp deɪ] der Dreckweg-Tag *(Aktionstag zum Müllsammeln)* 1
cleaner [ˈkliːnə] die Reinigungskraft 1
clear [klɪə] klar, deutlich 2: 4 (103)
clearly [ˈklɪəli]: **speak clearly** deutlich sprechen 1
clever [ˈklevə] schlau, klug 1
click [klɪk]:
1. der Klick, das Klicken 2: 3 (82)
2. **click (on)** klicken (auf), anklicken 2: 3 (82)

climb [klaɪm]:
1. der Aufstieg, die Klettertour; der Anstieg 2: 2 (11)
2. klettern (auf) 2: 2 (11)

climber [ˈklaɪmə] der Kletterer, die Kletterin 2: 2 (11)
clock [klɒk] die (Wand-, Stand-, Turm-)Uhr 1
close [kləʊz] schließen, zumachen 1
closed [kləʊzd] geschlossen 1
clothes *(pl)* [kləʊðz] die Kleidung, die Kleidungsstücke 1 **a change of clothes** (frische) Kleidung zum Wechseln 2: 1 (138)
clothes swap [ˈkləʊðz swɒp] der Kleidertausch, die Kleidertauschparty 1
cloud [klaʊd] die Wolke 1
cloudy [ˈklaʊdi] wolkig, bewölkt 1
clown [klaʊn] der Clown 1

club [klʌb] der Klub, der Verein 1
school club die AG *(in der Schule)* 1
°**join a club** in einen Klub eintreten
cocoa ['kəʊkəʊ] der Kakao 1
code [kəʊd] programmieren *(Computer)*; kodieren 1
coding ['kəʊdɪŋ] das Programmieren *(Computer)* 1
coffee ['kɒfi] der Kaffee 1
coin [kɔɪn] die Münze 2: 1 (132)
cola ['kəʊlə] die Cola 1
cold [kəʊld]:
1. kalt 1
be cold frieren 1
2. die Kälte 1
3. die Erkältung 1
have a cold erkältet sein 1
collect [kə'lekt] (ein)sammeln 1
colour ['kʌlə] die Farbe 1 **What colour is ...?** Welche Farbe hat ...? 1
°**colourful** ['kʌləfl] farbig, bunt
come [kʌm], **came, come** (mit)kommen 1
comic ['kɒmɪk] der Comic 1
°**comment (about/on sth.)** ['kɒment] der Kommentar (über/zu etwas)
°**compare** [kəm'peə] vergleichen
competition [kɒmpə'tɪʃn] der Wettbewerb 1
°**complete** [kəm'pli:t] vervollständigen
computer [kəm'pju:tə] der Computer 1
computing [kəm'pju:tɪŋ] die Informatik 1
concert ['kɒnsət] das Konzert 2: 1 (20)
confident ['kɒnfɪdənt] (selbst)sicher; zuversichtlich 2: 2 (42)
console [kən'səʊl] die Konsole 1
contact ['kɒntækt]:
1. der Kontakt 2: 1 (142)
2. **contact sb.** Kontakt aufnehmen mit jm., sich in Verbindung setzen mit jm. 2: 1 (142)
°**conversation** [kɒnvə'seɪʃn] das Gespräch
cook [kʊk]:
1. der Koch, die Köchin 1
2. kochen 1
cooking ['kʊkɪŋ] das Kochen 1
cool [ku:l] cool 1
°**copy** ['kɒpi] kopieren, abschreiben
°**correct** [kə'rekt]:
1. korrekt
2. korrigieren
°**correctly** [kə'rektli] korrekt *(Adv.)*
cost [kɒst]:
1. die Kosten; der Preis 1
2. kosten 1
cough [kɒf]:
1. husten 2: 3 (82)
2. der Husten 2: 3 (82)
could [kʊd]:
1. **I could** ich konnte 2: 4 (111)
2. **he could** er könnte 2: 4 (111)
°**count** [kaʊnt] zählen
country ['kʌntri] das Land, *(auch:)* die ländliche Gegend 1
course [kɔ:s]:
1. der Kurs 2: 3 (70/71)
2. **main course** das Hauptgericht 1
cousin ['kʌzn] der Cousin, die Cousine 1
crafts *(pl)* [krɑ:fts] das Kunsthandwerk, das Basteln 1
crazy ['kreɪzi] verrückt 2: 1 (28) **be crazy about sth.** wild auf etwas sein, versessen auf etwas sein 2: 1 (28)
cream [kri:m] die Sahne 1
create [kri'eɪt] (er)schaffen, erstellen 2: 3 (70/71)
creative [kri'eɪtɪv] kreativ 2: 3 (70/71)
cricket ['krɪkɪt] das Kricket *(Mannschaftssportart)* 1
°**cross** [krɒs] mit einem Kreuz versehen
°**culture** ['kʌltʃə] die Kultur
cupcake ['kʌpkeɪk] der Cupcake *(kleiner Muffin-ähnlicher Kuchen)* 2: 1 (140)
curl [kɜ:l] die Locke 2: 2 (40/41)
curly ['kɜ:li] lockig 2: 2 (40/41)
curry ['kʌri] das Curry *(Gewürz und auch Gericht)* 2: 4 (102)
cushion ['kʊʃn] das Kissen 1
custard ['kʌstəd] der Custard *(Vanillesoße)* 1
customer ['kʌstəmə] der Kunde, die Kundin 2: 1 (139)
cut [kʌt]:
1. der Schnitt 1
2. schneiden 1
cute [kju:t] niedlich, süß 1
cycle ['saɪkl] Rad fahren 1
cycling ['saɪklɪŋ] das Radfahren 1

D

dad [dæd] der Papa, der Vati 1
dance [dɑ:ns]:
1. tanzen 1
2. der Tanz 1
dancer ['dɑ:nsə] der Tänzer, die Tänzerin 1
dancing ['dɑ:nsɪŋ] das Tanzen 1
danger ['deɪndʒə] die Gefahr 2: 2 (12)
dangerous ['deɪndʒərəs] gefährlich 2: 2 (12)
dark [dɑ:k] dunkel 2: 2 (40/41)
date [deɪt]:
1. das Datum 1
birthday date das Datum des Geburtstags 1
°2. die Verabredung, das Date *(auch die Person, mit der man ausgeht)*
daughter ['dɔ:tə] die Tochter 2: 4 (107)
day [deɪ] der Tag 1 **the days of the week** *(pl)* die Wochentage 1 **work long days** lange arbeiten, lange Arbeitstage haben 1
dead [ded] tot 1
Dear ... [dɪə] Liebe/r ... 2: 1 (144)
December [dɪ'sembə] der Dezember 1
°**decide** [dɪ'saɪd] beschließen, sich entscheiden
decorate ['dekəreɪt] dekorieren, schmücken 2: 1 (20)
decoration [dekə'reɪʃn] der Dekoration, der Schmuck, die Verzierung 2: 1 (20)
°**definition** [defɪ'nɪʃn] die Definition
delicious [dɪ'lɪʃəs] köstlich, lecker 2: 3 (70/71)
describe [dɪ'skraɪb] beschreiben 2: 2 (42)
description [dɪ'skrɪpʃn] die Beschreibung 2: 2 (42)
design [dɪ'zaɪn]:
1. die Gestaltung, das Design 1
2. entwerfen, gestalten 2: 3 (81)
design and technology [dɪzaɪn ən tek'nɒlədʒi] das Werken, der Werkunterricht 1
designer [dɪ'zaɪnə] der Designer, die Designerin 2: 3 (81)
desk [desk] der Schreibtisch 1
dessert [dɪ'zɜ:t] die Nachspeise, das Dessert 1 **for dessert** zum/als Nachtisch 1
°**destination** [destɪ'neɪʃn] das Ziel, der Bestimmungsort
°**diary** ['daɪəri] das Tagebuch; der Kalender
dictionary ['dɪkʃənri] das Wörterbuch, das *(alphabetische)* Wörterverzeichnis
did [dɪd] *siehe* **do** **they didn't go ... (= did not)** sie gingen nicht; sie sind nicht gegangen 2: 1 (20)
die (of) [daɪ] sterben (an) 2: 2 (17)
difference ['dɪfrəns] der Unterschied 1
different (to) ['dɪfrənt] verschieden; anders (als) 1
dig [dɪg] graben 1
°**digital** ['dɪdʒɪtl] digital
dining area ['daɪnɪŋ eəriə] der Essbereich, die Essecke 1
dining room ['daɪnɪŋ ru:m] das Esszimmer 1
dinner ['dɪnə] das Abendessen 1 **for dinner** zum Abendessen 1
°**direct** [də'rekt] direkt, unmittelbar
°**direct train** [dərekt 'treɪn] die Direktverbindung, der durchgehende Zug *(ohne Umsteigen)*
°**directions** *(pl)* [də'rekʃnz] die Wegbeschreibung(en)
dirty ['dɜ:ti] schmutzig 1
disco ['dɪskəʊ] die Disco 2: 3 (87)
discover [dɪ'skʌvə] entdecken 2: 2 (17)
°**discuss** [dɪ'skʌs] diskutieren
dish [dɪʃ]:
1. die Schüssel, die Schale 1
2. das Gericht *(Mahlzeit)* 1
main dish das Hauptgericht 1
dishwasher ['dɪʃwɒʃə] die Geschirrspülmaschine 2: 1 (134)
do [du:], **did, done** machen, tun 1 **do your homework** Hausaufgaben machen 1
doctor (Dr) ['dɒktə] der Arzt, die Ärztin / der Doktor, die Doktorin (Dr.) 2: 3 (78)
dog [dɒg] der Hund 1
dolphin ['dɒlfɪn] der Delfin 2: 2 (11)

done [dʌn] *siehe* **do** **Well done.** Gut gemacht! 1
donut [ˈdəʊnʌt] der Donut *(ringförmiges Gebäck aus Hefeteig)* 2: 1 (138)
door [dɔː] die Tür 1
down [daʊn] hinunter, herunter 2: 2 (12)
°dragon [ˈdræɡən] der Drache
draw [drɔː], **drew** zeichnen 1
drawing [ˈdrɔːɪŋ]:
1. die Zeichnung 1
2. das Zeichnen 1
dream [driːm]:
1. der Traum 1
2. **dream (of/about sth.)** träumen (von etwas) 1
dress [dres]:
1. das Kleid 2: 2 (11)
2. sich kleiden, sich anziehen 2: 2 (11)
dressed [drest]: **get dressed** sich anziehen 1
°drew [druː] *siehe* **draw**
drink [drɪŋk]:
1. das Getränk 1
2. trinken 1
drone [drəʊn] die Drohne 1
°dungeon [ˈdʌndʒən] der Kerker, das Verlies *(in einer Burg)*
during [ˈdjʊərɪŋ] während 2: 4 (100)

E

each [iːtʃ] jede(r, s) (einzelne), jeweils 2: 1 (139)
each other [iːtʃ ˈʌðə] einander, sich (gegenseitig) 2: 1 (141)
early [ˈɜːli] früh 2: 1 (18)
earn [ɜːn] verdienen *(Geld)* 2: 1 (132)
earth [ɜːθ] die Erde 2: 2 (11)
Easter [ˈiːstə] (das) Ostern 2: 4 (98/99)
easy [ˈiːzi] einfach, leicht 1
eat [iːt], **ate, eaten** essen; fressen 1
eaten [ˈiːtn] *siehe* **eat**
egg [eɡ] das Ei 1
°Eid al-Fitr [iːd ɔːl ˈfɪtrə] das Zuckerfest *(im Islam)*
°Eid Mubarak! [iːd mʊˈbɑːrək] Eid Mubarak! *(Frohes (Zucker-)Fest!)*
eight [eɪt] acht 1
eighteen [eɪˈtiːn] achtzehn 1
eighty [ˈeɪti] achtzig 1
electro [ɪˈlektrəʊ] der Electro, die Elektromusik 2: 3 (72)
electronic [ɪlekˈtrɒnɪk] elektronisch 2: 1 (137)
electronics *(pl)* [ɪlekˈtrɒnɪks] die Elektronik; die elektronischen Geräte 2: 1 (137)
elephant [ˈelɪfənt] der Elefant 1
eleven [ɪˈlevən] elf 1
else [els]: **What else?** Was sonst noch? 2: 1 (139) **Would you like anything else?** Möchten Sie sonst noch etwas? 2: 1 (139)
email [ˈiːmeɪl] die E-Mail 2: 1 (142) **email sb.** jm. mailen, eine E-Mail schicken 2: 1 (142)
empty [ˈempti]:
1. leer 2: 1 (134)
2. leeren 2: 1 (134)
end [end]:
1. enden; beenden 1
2. das Ende, der Schluss 1
at the end (of) am Ende (von) 1 **in the end** schließlich; zum Schluss 1
°ending [ˈendɪŋ] die Endung; das Ende *(Text, Geschichte)*
energetic [enəˈdʒetɪk] aktiv, tatkräftig, energiegeladen 2: 3 (77)
energy [ˈenədʒi] Energie 2: 3 (77)
England [ˈɪŋɡlənd] England 1
English [ˈɪŋɡlɪʃ] Englisch; englisch 1
enjoy [ɪnˈdʒɔɪ] genießen 1 **enjoy doing sth.** es genießen, etwas zu tun 1 **Enjoy your meal.** Guten Appetit! 2: 4 (102) **Enjoy!** Viel Vergnügen! / Guten Appetit! 1
°enough [ɪˈnʌf] genug
°envelope [ˈenvələʊp] der (Brief-)Umschlag
°equipment *(no pl)* [ɪˈkwɪpmənt] die Ausrüstung
especially [ɪˈspeʃəli] insbesondere 2: 1 (130)
estate [ɪˈsteɪt] die Wohnsiedlung; das Gewerbegebiet 1
euro [ˈjʊərəʊ], *pl* **euros** Euro 1
°event [ɪˈvent] das Ereignis
ever [ˈevə] jemals, schon einmal 2: 4 (101) **the best party ever** die beste Party überhaupt / die beste Party, die man sich wünschen kann 1
every [ˈevri] jede(r, s) 2: 1 (11) **every 30 minutes** alle 30 Minuten 2: 1 (11)
everybody [ˈevribɒdi] jeder; alle 1 **Hello everybody!** Hallo allerseits! 1
everyone [ˈevriwʌn] jeder, alle 1
everything [ˈevriθɪŋ] alles 2: 1 (17)
everywhere [ˈevriweə] überall 1
°example [ɪɡˈzɑːmpl] das Beispiel **for example** zum Beispiel
°exchange student [ɪksˈtʃeɪndʒ stjuːdnt] der Austauschschüler, die Austauschschülerin
excited [ɪkˈsaɪtɪd] aufgeregt, gespannt 2: 4 (110)
exciting [ɪkˈsaɪtɪŋ] aufregend 2: 1 (23)
Excuse me, … [ɪksˈkjuːz miː] Entschuldigung, … / Entschuldigen Sie, … 1
exercise [ˈeksəsaɪz] die Übung, die Aufgabe 1
exercise book [ˈeksəsaɪz bʊk] das Schulheft, das Übungsheft 1
expensive [ɪkˈspensɪv] teuer 1
experience [ɪkˈspɪəriəns]:
1. die Erfahrung; das Erlebnis 2: 1 (141)
2. **experience sth.** etwas erfahren; erleben 2: 1 (141)
explain sth. to sb. [ɪkˈspleɪn] jm. etwas erklären 1
explanation [ekspləˈneɪʃn] die Erklärung 1
extra [ˈekstrə] Extra-, zusätzliche(r, s) 2: 1 (132)
eye [aɪ] das Auge 2: 2 (11)

F

face [feɪs] das Gesicht 2: 2 (13)
fair [feə] fair 2: 2 (42)
fall [fɔːl], **fell** fallen; hinfallen 2: 2 (42)
false [fɔːls] falsch, unrichtig 2: 2 (12)
false friend [fɔːls ˈfrend] der „falsche Freund" *(Übersetzungsfalle)* 2: 2 (12)
fame [feɪm] Ruhm 2: 2 (17)
family [ˈfæməli] die Familie 1 **°join a family** Mitglied einer Familie werden
famous (for) [ˈfeɪməs] berühmt (für, wegen) 2: 2 (17)
fan [fæn] der Fan 1
°far [fɑː] weit (entfernt) **go far** es weit bringen
farm [fɑːm] der Bauernhof, die Farm 2: 3 (72)
fast [fɑːst] schnell 1
fast [fɑːst]:
1. fasten 2: 4 (98/99)
2. das Fasten, die Fastenzeit 2: 4 (98/99)
break the fast das Fasten brechen 2: 4 (98/99)
father [ˈfɑːðə] der Vater 2: 2 (17)
favourite [ˈfeɪvərɪt]:
1. der Liebling, der Favorit, die Favoritin 1
2. Lieblings- 1
February [ˈfebruəri] der Februar 1
°feedback (on sth.) *(no pl)* [ˈfiːdbæk] das Feedback (zu etwas) *(Rückmeldung)*
feel [fiːl], **felt** fühlen; sich fühlen 1 **feel sorry for sb.** Mitleid haben mit jm. 1
feeling [ˈfiːlɪŋ] das Gefühl 1
feet [fiːt] *Plural von* **foot**
fell [fel] *siehe* **fall**
felt [felt] *siehe* **feel**
festival [ˈfestɪvl] das Fest(ival) 2: 1 (21)
few [fjuː]: **a few** ein paar, einige 2: 4 (102)
fifteen [fɪfˈtiːn] fünfzehn 1
fifty [ˈfɪfti] fünfzig 1
fight [faɪt]:
1. der Kampf 2: 2 (17)
2. **fight, fought** kämpfen, bekämpfen 2: 2 (17)
fighter [ˈfaɪtə] der Kämpfer die Kämpferin 2: 2 (17)
file [faɪl] die Datei; der Ordner, die Liste 1
°fill in [fɪl ˈɪn] einsetzen; ausfüllen
film [fɪlm] der Film 1
finally [ˈfaɪnəli] schließlich, endlich 1
find [faɪnd], **found, found** finden 1 **find out (about)** herausfinden; sich informieren (über) 1
fine [faɪn] gut, in Ordnung; schön 2: 2 (14) **He feels fine.** Er fühlt sich gut. / Es geht ihm gut. 2: 2 (14)
finish [ˈfɪnɪʃ]:
1. das Ende, das Ziel *(z. B. beim Sport)* 2: 4 (101)
2. enden; beenden, zu Ende machen 2: 4 (101)
fire [ˈfaɪə] das Feuer 2: 4 (98/99) **stop a fire** ein Feuer löschen 2: 1 (128/129)

firefighter ['faɪəfaɪtə] der Feuerwehrmann, die Feuerwehrfrau 2: 1 (128/129)
fireworks *(pl)* ['faɪəwɜːks] das Feuerwerk 2: 4 (98/99)
first [fɜːst]:
1. erste(r, s) 1
2. zuerst, als Erstes 1
at first zuerst, am Anfang 1
fish [fɪʃ] der Fisch 1
fish and chips [fɪʃ ən 'tʃɪps] der Fisch mit Pommes Frites 1
five [faɪv] fünf 1
fix sth. [fɪks] *(infml)* etwas in Ordnung bringen; etwas reparieren 2: 1 (128/129)
flag [flæg] die Fahne, die Flagge 2: 1 (20)
flat [flæt] die Wohnung 1
flew [fluː] *siehe* **fly**
floor [flɔː]:
1. der Fußboden 1
2. die Etage, der Stock, das Stockwerk 1
top floor die oberste Etage, der oberste Stock, das oberste Stockwerk 1
flour ['flaʊə] das Mehl 1
fly [flaɪ], **flew** fliegen 2: 1 (19)
fold [fəʊld] falten 2: 1 (134)
°**follow** ['fɒləʊ] (be)folgen; verfolgen
food [fuːd] das Essen, das Lebensmittel; das Futter 1
foot [fʊt], *pl* **feet**:
1. der Fuß *(Körperteil)* 2: 1 (14)
2. der Fuß *(Längenmaß; ca. 30 cm)* 2: 1 (14)
football ['fʊtbɔːl] der Fußball 1
footballer ['fʊtbɔːlə] der Fußballspieler, die Fußballspielerin 2: 3 (79)
for [fɔː] für 1 **What's for homework?** Was haben wir als Hausaufgabe(n) auf? 1
forest ['fɒrɪst] der Wald 2: 3 (80)
forty ['fɔːti] vierzig 1
forward ['fɔːwəd]: **look forward to doing sth.** sich darauf freuen, etwas zu tun 2: 1 (144) **look forward to sth.** sich auf etwas freuen 2: 1 (144)
fought [fɔːt] *siehe* **fight**
found [faʊnd] *siehe* **find**
four [fɔː] vier 1
fourteen [fɔː'tiːn] vierzehn 1
free [friː]:
1. frei 1
free time die Freizeit, die freie Zeit 1 **Are you free after school?** Hast du nach der Schule Zeit? 1 **for free** kostenlos, umsonst 2: 1 (19)
2. kostenlos 1
Friday ['fraɪdeɪ], ['fraɪdi] der Freitag 1
fried [fraɪd] frittiert, gebraten 1
friend [frend] der Freund, die Freundin 1
friendly ['frendli] freundlich, nett 1
from [frɒm] von, aus 1
front [frʌnt]: **a house with trees in front** ein Haus mit Bäumen davor 1 **in front of** vor 1
front door [frʌnt 'dɔː] die Haustür, die Eingangstür 2: 4 (111)
fruit [fruːt] das Obst 1
fry [fraɪ] braten; frittieren 1
frying pan ['fraɪɪŋ pæn] die Bratpfanne 1
full [fʊl]:
1. voll 2: 3 (70/71)
2. satt 2: 3 (70/71)
full of ... [fʊl] voller ... 2: 3 (70/71)
fun [fʌn]: **be fun** Spaß machen; lustig sein 1 **have fun** Spaß haben 1
funny ['fʌni] witzig, komisch 1
future ['fjuːtʃə]:
1. die Zukunft 2: 1 (128/129)
2. zukünftige(r, s) 2: 1 (128/129)

G

°**gallery** ['gæləri] die Galerie
game [geɪm]:
1. das Spiel 1
2. Computerspiele spielen 2: 1 (130)
gamer ['geɪmə] der Gamer, die Gamerin *(Computerspieler/in)* 2: 1 (130)
gaming ['geɪmɪŋ] das Gaming *(Spielen am Computer)* 2: 3 (80)
garden ['gɑːdn] der Garten 1
gave [geɪv] *siehe* **give**
°**Gemini** ['dʒemɪnaɪ] die Zwillinge *(Sternzeichen)*
geography [dʒi'ɒgrəfi] die Geografie, die Erdkunde 1
German ['dʒɜːmən] deutsch; Deutsch; der/die Deutsche 1
Germany ['dʒɜːməni] Deutschland 1
get [get], **got, got**:
1. bekommen 1
get sth. sich etwas holen/besorgen 1
2. werden 1
get ready (for) sich fertig machen (für), sich vorbereiten (auf) 2: 1 (18)
get wet nass werden 1
3. **get (to)** gelangen, (hin)kommen (nach) 2: 1 (24)
Get down! Komm (da) runter! 2: 1 (24) **get on a train/bus** in einen Zug/Bus einsteigen 2: 1 (24) **get off a train/bus** aus einem Zug/Bus aussteigen 2: 1 (24) **get up** aufstehen 1
gift [gɪft] das Geschenk, die Gabe; das Talent 2: 1 (132)
gift shop ['gɪft ʃɒp] der Geschenk(artikel)laden, der Souvenirladen 2: 1 (132)
girl [gɜːl] das Mädchen 1 **a girls' group** eine Mädchengruppe, eine Gruppe für Mädchen 1
girlfriend ['gɜːlfrend] die (feste) Freundin 2: 1 (20)
give [gɪv], **gave, given** geben 1
given ['gɪvn] *siehe* **give**
°**glad** [glæd]: **I'm glad** ich bin froh
glasses *(pl)* ['glɑːsɪz] die Brille 2: 2 (40/41)
glove [glʌv] der Handschuh 2: 1 (22)
glue [gluː] der Kleber, der Klebstoff 1
glue stick ['gluː stɪk] der Klebestift 1
go [gəʊ], **went**:
1. gehen; fahren 1
go out rausgehen, weggehen; ausgehen 2: 3 (82) **How's it going?** *(infml)* Wie geht's? / Wie läuft's? 2: 1 (130) °**go on** weitermachen, weiterreden; (sich) fortsetzen
2. werden 1
go green grün/umweltbewusst werden 1 **go red** erröten, rot werden 1 °**go wrong** schiefgehen
3. **I'm going to ...** ich werde ... *(Plan, Vorhaben)* 2: 3 (72)
goat [gəʊt] die Ziege 2: 3 (72)
god [gɒd] der Gott 2: 4 (100) **thank God** gottlob, Gott sei Dank 2: 4 (100)
gold [gəʊld]:
1. das Gold 1
2. goldfarben 1
°**gonna** ['gɒnə] *infml für* **going to**
good [gʊd]:
1. gut 1
be good at sth. etwas gut können; gut in etwas sein 1 **be good with ...** gut umgehen können mit ... 1
2. brav 2: 2 (42)
Goodbye. [gʊd'baɪ] Auf Wiedersehen! 1
got [gɒt] *siehe* **get**
grandma ['grænmɑː] die Oma 1
grandpa ['grænpɑː] der Opa 1
grandparents *(pl)* ['grænpeərənts] die Großeltern 2: 1 (11)
great [greɪt]:
1. großartig, toll 1
2. groß *(bedeutend, angesehen)* 2: 1 (138)
Great Britain [greɪt 'brɪtn] Großbritannien 1
green [griːn]:
1. grün 1
2. umweltbewusst 1
go green grün/umweltbewusst werden 1
grey [greɪ] grau 1
°**grid** [grɪd] das Gitter; das Raster; das Rechteckschema
ground [graʊnd] der (Erd-)Boden 1
ground floor [graʊnd 'flɔː] das Erdgeschoss 1
group [gruːp] die Gruppe 1
guess [ges]:
1. die Vermutung 1
2. (er)raten 1
guessing game das Ratespiel 1
3. glauben, annehmen 1
I guess ich glaube, ich nehme an 1
°**guest** [gest] der Gast
guide [gaɪd]:
1. führen, leiten 1
2. *(= tour guide)* der Reiseleiter, die Reiseleiterin / der Fremdenführer, die Fremdenführerin 1
guide dog ['gaɪd dɒg] der Blindenhund 1
guitar [gɪ'tɑː] die Gitarre 1
°**guys** *(pl)* [gaɪz] Leute *(Anrede)*

H

had [hæd] *siehe* **have**
hair [heə] das Haar, die Haare 2: 2 (40/41)
hairdresser [ˈheədresə] der Friseur, die Friseurin 2: 1 (128/129)
hairdresser's [ˈheədresəz] der Friseursalon 2: 1 (128/129)
half [hɑːf]:
1. **half past 6** halb 7 2: 3 (74)
°2. **half,** *pl* **halves** die Hälfte
hall [hɔːl]:
1. der Flur, die Diele 1
2. die Halle, der Saal 1
sports hall die Sporthalle 1
Halloween [hæləʊˈiːn] das Halloween *(Abend des 31. Oktober)* 2: 4 (98/99)
°**halves** [hɑːvz] *Plural von* **half**
ham [hæm] der Schinken 1
hamster [ˈhæmstə] der Hamster 1
hand [hænd] die Hand 1 **put your hand up** sich melden, aufzeigen 1
handball [ˈhændbɔːl] der Handball 2: 1 (23)
handy [ˈhændi] praktisch, nützlich; handlich; griffbereit, zur Hand 2: 2 (11)
°**hang sth. up** [hæŋ ˈʌp] etwas aufhängen
°**Hanukkah** [ˈhænʊkə] die Chanukka *(jüdisches Lichterfest)*
happen (to sb.) [ˈhæpən] (jm.) geschehen, passieren 2: 1 (24)
happy [ˈhæpi] glücklich, froh 1 **Happy birthday!** Herzlichen Glückwunsch zum Geburtstag! 1
hard [hɑːd] schwer, schwierig; hart 1
hard-working [hɑːd ˈwɜːkɪŋ] fleißig 2: 1 (133)
has [hæz], [həz]: **he/she/it has** er/sie/es hat 1
hat [hæt] der Hut, die Mütze 1
hate [heɪt]:
1. hassen 2: 1 (131)
2. der Hass 2: 1 (131)
have [hæv], **had, had** haben 1 **have to do sth.** etwas tun müssen 2: 1 (12) **I have to go.** Ich muss Schluss machen. *(am Telefon/Briefschluss)* 2: 1 (12)
he [hiː] er 1 **he's (= he is)** er ist 1
head [hed] der Kopf 1
°**head student** [hed ˈstjuːdnt] der Mentor, die Mentorin; der Vertrauensschüler, die Vertrauensschülerin
headache [ˈhedeɪk] die Kopfschmerzen 2: 3 (82) **have a headache** Kopfschmerzen haben 2: 3 (82)
°**heading** [ˈhedɪŋ] die Überschrift
headphones *(pl)* [ˈhedfəʊnz] der Kopfhörer 1
hear [hɪə] hören 1
Hello. [həˈləʊ] Hallo. 1 **Hello everybody!** Hallo allerseits! 1
helmet [ˈhelmɪt] der Helm 2: 2 (11)
help [help]:
1. helfen 1
2. die Hilfe 1
helpful [ˈhelpfl] hilfsbereit; hilfreich, nützlich 1
her [hɜː], [hə]:
1. sie; ihr 1
2. **her friends** ihre Freunde/Freundinnen 1
here [hɪə] hier; hierher 1 **Here you are.** Bitte schön. / Hier, bitte. 1
hero [ˈhɪərəʊ], *pl* **heroes** der Held, die Heldin 2: 2 (40/41)
Hi. [haɪ] Hallo. 1
°**high five sb.** [haɪ ˈfaɪv] jn. abklatschen
highlight [ˈhaɪlaɪt]:
1. der Höhepunkt, das Schlaglicht 1
2. hervorheben, markieren, unterstreichen 1
him [hɪm] ihm, ihn 1
his room [hɪz] sein Zimmer *(zu „he")* 1
history [ˈhɪstri] die Geschichte *(vergangene Zeiten)* 1
hobby [ˈhɒbi] das Hobby 1
hockey [ˈhɒki] das Hockey 1
°**Holi** [ˈhəʊli] das Holi-Fest *(hinduistisches Frühlingsfest)*
holiday [ˈhɒlədeɪ] der Urlaub 1 **holidays** die Ferien 1 **on holiday** im/in den Urlaub 1
home [həʊm]:
1. das Heim, das Zuhause 1
at home zu Hause 1
2. nach Hause 1
go home nach Hause gehen 1
homework [ˈhəʊmwɜːk] die Hausaufgabe(n) 1 **do your homework** Hausaufgaben machen 1 **What's for homework?** Was haben wir als Hausaufgabe(n) auf? 1
honest [ˈɒnɪst] ehrlich 2: 2 (42)
hope [həʊp]:
1. die Hoffnung 2: 4 (101)
2. hoffen 2: 4 (101)
horoscope [ˈhɒrəskəʊp] das Horoskop 2: 1 (141)
horrible [ˈhɒrəbl] schrecklich 1
horse [hɔːs] das Pferd 1
hospital [ˈhɒspɪtl] das Krankenhaus 1
hot [hɒt] heiß, warm 1
hot chocolate [hɒt ˈtʃɒklət] der Kakao, die heiße (Trink-)Schokolade 1
hot dog [ˈhɒt dɒg] das Hot Dog *(heißes Würstchen in einem Brötchen)* 2: 1 (21)
hot meal [hɒt ˈmiːl] die warme Mahlzeit 1
hotel [həʊˈtel] das Hotel 2: 1 (12/13)
hour [ˈaʊə] die Stunde 1
house [haʊs] das Haus 1
how [haʊ] wie 1 **How are you?** Wie geht's? / Wie geht es dir/euch/Ihnen? 2: 1 (144) **How much is/are ...?** Was (Wie viel) kostet/kosten ...? 2: 1 (138) **how to do sth.** wie man etwas tut / tun kann / tun soll 1
hug [hʌg]:
1. die Umarmung 2: 1 (141)
2. **hug (sb.)** (jn.) umarmen; einander umarmen 2: 1 (141)
hundred [ˈhʌndrəd]: **a/one hundred** (ein)hundert 1
hungry [ˈhʌŋgri] hungrig 1 **I'm hungry.** Ich habe Hunger. 1
hurt [hɜːt], **hurt** verletzen; wehtun 2: 2 (42) **be hurt** verletzt sein 2: 2 (42) **get hurt** sich verletzen 2: 2 (42)
husband [ˈhʌzbənd] der Ehemann 1

I

I [aɪ] ich 1 **I'm (= I am)** ich bin 1
ice cream [aɪs ˈkriːm] das (Speise-)Eis 1
ice rink [ˈaɪs rɪŋk] die Schlittschuhbahn 1
icing [ˈaɪsɪŋ] die Glasur, der Zuckerguss 1
icing sugar [ˈaɪsɪŋ ʃʊgə] der Puderzucker 1
idea [aɪˈdɪə] die Idee 1
if [ɪf]:
1. wenn, falls 1
What if? Was wäre, wenn? 1
2. ob 1
ill [ɪl] krank 2: 2 (49)
illness [ˈɪlnəs] die Krankheit 2: 2 (49)
°**imagine sth.** [ɪˈmædʒɪn] sich etwas vorstellen
important (for/to sb.) [ɪmˈpɔːtnt] wichtig (für jn.) 2: 2 (43)
in [ɪn] in; auf 1 **in English** auf Englisch 1 **in the afternoon** nachmittags, am Nachmittag 1 **in the country** auf dem Land 1 **in the morning** morgens, am Morgen 1 **in the photo** auf dem Foto 1 **in the picture** auf dem Bild 1 **in town** in der Stadt 1
°**incomplete** [ɪnkəmˈpliːt] unvollständig
influencer [ˈɪnfluənsə] der Influencer, die Influencerin 2: 2 (48)
information [ɪnfəˈmeɪʃn] die Information(en) 1 **visitor information centre** die Touristeninformation, das Fremdenverkehrsbüro 1
insect [ˈɪnsekt] Insekt 2: 3 (70/71)
inside [ɪnˈsaɪd] innerhalb (von) 1 **inside the house** im Haus 1
interesting [ˈɪntrəstɪŋ] interessant 1
internet [ˈɪntənet] das Internet 1
interview [ˈɪntəvjuː] das Interview 2: 2 (49)
into [ˈɪntu], [ˈɪntə] in (... hinein) 2: 1 (11) **cut sth. into pieces** etwas in Stücke schneiden 2: 1 (11)
invitation (to) [ɪnvɪˈteɪʃn] die Einladung (zu, nach) 1
invite (to) [ɪnˈvaɪt] einladen (zu, nach) 1
is [ɪz] *(er/sie/es)* ist 1 **he isn't (= is not)** er ist nicht 1 **The football is £3.** Der Fußball kostet 3 Pfund. 2: 1 (138)
it [ɪt] es *(bei Sachen und Tieren auch: er; sie)* 1
its [ɪts] sein/seine, ihr/ihre *(besitzanzeigend: Dinge und Tiere)* 1

J

jacket [ˈdʒækɪt] die Jacke, das Jackett 2: 4 (112) **rain jacket** die Regenjacke 2: 4 (112)
January [ˈdʒænjuəri] der Januar 1
jazz [dʒæz] der Jazz 2: 4 (114)
jeans *(pl)* [dʒiːnz] die Jeans(hose) 2: 1 (137)
jigsaw (puzzle) [ˈdʒɪgsɔː] das Puzzle 1
job [dʒɒb] der Job, die (Arbeits-)Stelle; die Aufgabe 2: 2 (47)
°join [dʒɔɪn]**: join a family / a club** Mitglied (einer Familie / in einem Klub) werden **join sb./sth.** sich jm. anschließen; bei etwas mitmachen
joke [dʒəʊk] der Witz, der Scherz 2: 2 (13)
journey [ˈdʒɜːni] die Reise, die Fahrt; der Weg 1
judo [ˈdʒuːdəʊ] das Judo 2: 1 (23) **do judo** Judo machen 2: 1 (23)
juggle [ˈdʒʌgl] jonglieren 1
°juice [dʒuːs] der Saft
July [dʒuˈlaɪ] der Juli 1
jump [dʒʌmp] springen; *(vor Schreck)* zusammenzucken 2: 1 (12)
June [dʒuːn] der Juni 1
just [dʒʌst]**:**
1. nur, bloß; einfach 1
It's just us. Es sind nur wir. 1
2. gerade (eben) 2: 4 (102)
3. **just then / just there** genau dann / genau dort 2: 4 (111)

K

karaoke [kæriˈəʊki] das Karaoke 2: 1 (23)
karate [kəˈrɑːti] Karate 2: 3 (72)
kebab [kɪˈbæb] der Kebab 2: 4 (102)
°keep [kiːp] halten; behalten; aufbewahren; *(z. B. eine Liste)* führen **keep a file** eine Datei / einen Ordner / eine Liste führen
key [kiː] der Schlüssel; Schlüssel- 2: 3 (80)
°keyword [ˈkiːwɜːd] das Stichwort, das Schlagwort
kid [kɪd] das Kind, der/die Jugendliche 1
kill [kɪl] töten 2: 2 (11)
killer [ˈkɪlə] der Mörder, die Mörderin 2: 2 (11)
kilometre (km) [ˈkɪləmiːtə] der Kilometer 2: 2 (49)
kind [kaɪnd] nett, freundlich 1
kind (of) [kaɪnd] die Art (von), die Sorte (von) 1
°kindness [ˈkaɪndnəs] die Güte, die Freundlichkeit
Kingdom [ˈkɪŋdəm]**: the United Kingdom (= the UK)** das Vereinigte Königreich 2: 1 (19)
kitchen [ˈkɪtʃɪn] die Küche 1
knew [njuː] *siehe* **know**
knit [nɪt] stricken 2: 3 (72)
knock [nɒk] stoßen, klopfen 2: 4 (109) **knock at (sth.)** (an)klopfen an (etwas, z. B. Tür) 2: 4 (109) **knock sth. over** etwas umstoßen 2: 4 (109)
know [nəʊ], **knew** wissen; kennen 1

L

°lady [ˈleɪdi] die Dame
lamb [læm] das Lamm(fleisch) 2: 4 (102)
lamp [læmp] die Lampe 1
land [lænd]**:**
1. das Land *(Grund und Boden)* 2: 2 (12)
2. landen 2: 2 (12)
large [lɑːdʒ] groß 2: 1 (138)
last [lɑːst] letzte(r, s); als letztes 2: (10/11) **last week/month/year** die letzte/vorige Woche, der letzte/vorige Monat, das letzte/vorige Jahr 2: (10/11)
late [leɪt] (zu) spät 1 **I'm late.** Ich habe mich verspätet. 1
later [ˈleɪtə] später 1 **Speak later.** Tschüs. / Bis später. 1
laugh [lɑːf]**:**
1. das Lachen 2: 1 (12)
2. **laugh (at)** lachen (über) 2: 1 (12) **laugh out loud** laut auf-/loslachen 2: 3 (82)
learn [lɜːn] lernen 1
least [liːst] am wenigsten 2: 1 (131) **at least** wenigstens, zumindest 2: 4 (107) **the least favourite chores** die Arbeiten (im Haus), die man am wenigsten gerne macht 2: 1 (131)
leave [liːv], **left** lassen; verlassen; zurücklassen 2: 2 (47) **leave sb. alone** jn. allein lassen; jn. in Ruhe lassen 2: 2 (47)
left [left] *siehe* **leave**
left [left] links; nach links 2: 2 (44) **on the left** links, auf der linken Seite 2: 2 (44) **to the left of ...** links von ... 2: 2 (44)
leg [leg] das Bein 2: 2 (13)
lemon [ˈlemən] die Zitrone 1
lemonade [leməˈneɪd] die Limonade 1
°Leo [ˈliːəʊ] der Löwe *(Sternzeichen)*
lesson [ˈlesn] die (Unterrichts-) Stunde 1
let's (= let us) [lets] lass(t) uns 1
°letter [ˈletə]**:**
1. der Brief
2. der Buchstabe
level [ˈlevl] der Grad, die Stufe; das Niveau, die Ebene 2: 3 (81)
°Libra [ˈliːbrə] die Waage *(Sternzeichen)*
library [ˈlaɪbrəri] die Bücherei, die Bibliothek 1
°life [laɪf], *pl* **lives** das Leben
°life skills *(pl)* [ˈlaɪf skɪlz] die Alltagskompetenzen, die lebenswichtigen Fertigkeiten
light [laɪt] das Licht; die Lampe 1
like [laɪk] mögen 1 **I like singing.** Ich singe gerne. 1 **I'd (= I would) like ...** Ich hätte gern ... / Ich möchte ... 1 **I'd (= I would) like to meet ....** Ich würde mich gerne mit ... treffen. 1
like [laɪk] wie; wie zum Beispiel 2: 1 (12) **like a vampire** wie ein Vampir 2: 1 (12) **like this** so, auf diese Art 1 **a story like this** so/solch eine Geschichte 1 **What's ... like?** Wie ist ...? / Wie sieht ... aus? 1
line [laɪn]**:**
1. die Reihe 1
2. die Zeile 1
°link (to/with) [lɪŋk] verbinden (mit)
lion [ˈlaɪən] der Löwe 1
list [lɪst]**:**
1. die Liste 1
2. (auf)listen 1
listen (to) [ˈlɪsn] (sich etwas) anhören; zuhören 1 **listening to music** Musik (an)hören 1
little [ˈlɪtl]**:**
1. klein 2: 1 (12/13)
2. **a little** ein wenig, ein bisschen 2: 4 (102)
live [lɪv] leben, wohnen 1
°lives [laɪvz] *Plural von* **life**
living room [ˈlɪvɪŋ ruːm] das Wohnzimmer 1
lizard [ˈlɪzəd] die Eidechse 1
lonely [ˈləʊnli] einsam 2: 4 (107)
long [lɒŋ] lang 1 **work long days** lange arbeiten, lange Arbeitstage haben 1
°long-legged [lɒŋ ˈlegɪd] langbeinig, mit langen Beinen
look [lʊk]**:**
1. aussehen 1
2. sehen, schauen 1
look after sb./sth. sich um jn./etwas kümmern; auf jn./etwas aufpassen 2: 1 (134) **look at sth.** sich etwas anschauen 1 **look for** suchen; Ausschau halten nach 2: 1 (14) **look forward to doing sth.** sich darauf freuen, etwas zu tun 2: 1 (144) **look forward to sth.** sich auf etwas freuen 2: 1 (144) **look sth. up** etwas nachschlagen 1 **°look out for** Ausschau halten nach, achten auf
lot [lɒt]**: a lot (of) / lots (of)** viel/e 1 **a lot** sehr 1
loud [laʊd] laut 1 **laugh out loud** laut auf-/loslachen 2: 3 (82)
loudly [laʊdli]**: speak more loudly** lauter sprechen 1
love [lʌv]**:**
1. die Liebe 1
2. lieben, sehr mögen 1
I'd (= I would) love ... Ich hätte liebend gern ... / Ich möchte liebend gern ... 1 **I'd (= I would) love to meet ...** Ich würde mich liebend gerne mit ... treffen. 1
°luck [lʌk] das Glück *(gutes Gelingen, glücklicher Zufall)*
lucky [ˈlʌki]**: be lucky** Glück haben 1
lunch [lʌntʃ] das Mittagessen 1 **What's for lunch?** Was gibt es zum Mittagessen? 1

lunchtime ['lʌntʃtaɪm] die Mittagszeit 2: 1 (23) **at lunchtime** zur Mittagszeit 2: 1 (23)
°lyrics *(pl)* ['lɪrɪks] der Liedtext

M

machine [mə'ʃi:n] der Automat, die Maschine 2: 1 (132) **ticket machine** der Fahrkartenautomat 2: 1 (132)
made [meɪd] *siehe* **make**
mag [mæg] *siehe* **magazine**
magazine [mægə'zi:n], *infml auch* **mag** die Zeitschrift 2: 1 (132)
magic ['mædʒɪk]:
1. magisch 2: 2 (49)
2. die Zauberei 2: 2 (49)
do magic zaubern 2: 2 (49)
magic show [mædʒɪk 'ʃəʊ] die Zaubershow 2: 2 (49)
magic trick [mædʒɪk 'trɪk] der Zaubertrick 2: 2 (49)
main [meɪn] Haupt-, wichtigste(r, s) 1
main course [meɪn 'kɔ:s] das Hauptgericht 1
main dish [meɪn 'dɪʃ] das Hauptgericht 1
make [meɪk], **made, made** machen, herstellen 1 **make (money)** (Geld) verdienen 2: 1 (132) **°I'll make a great ...** Ich werde ein/e großartige/r ...
make-up ['meɪk ʌp] das Make-up 2: 1 (18)
man [mæn], *pl* **men** der Mann 2: 2 (11)
mango ['mæŋgəʊ], *pl* **mangoes** die Mango 2: 2 (12)
many ['meni] viele 1 **how many?** wie viele? 1
map [mæp] die Landkarte, der Stadtplan 1
March [mɑ:tʃ] der März 1
marina [mə'ri:nə] der Jachthafen 1
market ['mɑ:kɪt] der Markt 1
married (to) ['mærid] verheiratet (mit) 1
marry ['mæri] heiraten 2: 2 (47)
mask [mɑ:sk] die Maske 2: 2 (11)
°match [mætʃ] (passend) zusammenfügen **match to** zuordnen
match [mætʃ] das Spiel, der Wettkampf 1
maths [mæθs] die Mathe(matik) 1
May [meɪ] der Mai 1
may [meɪ] dürfen 2: 4 (102) **May I ...?** Darf ich ...? 2: 4 (102)
maybe ['meɪbi] vielleicht 1
me [mi:]:
1. mich; mir 1
2. *(in bestimmten Wendungen)* ich 1 **It's me.** Ich bin's. 1 **Not me!** Ich nicht! *(= Ich bin/war/habe/... es/das nicht!)* 1
meal [mi:l] die Mahlzeit, das Essen 1 **Enjoy your meal.** Guten Appetit! 2: 4 (102) **hot meal** die warme Mahlzeit 1
mean [mi:n]:
1. bedeuten 1
2. meinen *(sagen wollen)* 1
mean [mi:n] gemein, fies 1
meaning ['mi:nɪŋ] die Bedeutung 1
meat [mi:t] das Fleisch 1
mechanic [mɪ'kænɪk] der Mechaniker, die Mechanikerin 2: 1 (128/129)
°medal ['medl] die Medaille
°mediation [mi:di'eɪʃn] die Vermittlung, die Sprachmittlung
medium ['mi:diəm] medium *(Kleidergröße: mittelgroß/M)* 2: 1 (138)
meet [mi:t], **met, met** kennenlernen; (sich) treffen 1 **Nice to meet you.** Freut mich, dich/euch/Sie kennenzulernen. 1
meeting ['mi:tɪŋ] das Meeting *(Treffen, Zusammenkunft)* 2: 3 (82)
melon ['melən] die Melone 1
member ['membə] das Mitglied 2: 4 (108)
men [men] *Plural von* **man**
°meow [mi'aʊ] miau
mess [mes] das Chaos, die Unordnung 1
message ['mesɪdʒ] die Nachricht, die Mitteilung 1
messy ['mesi] unordentlich 1
met [met] *siehe* **meet**
metre ['mi:tə] der Meter 2: 2 (49)
mice [maɪs] *Plural von* **mouse**
°middle ['mɪdl] die Mitte **in the middle (of)** in der Mitte (von)
milk [mɪlk] die Milch 1
mind [maɪnd] der Geist, der Verstand; die Gedanken; der Kopf *(im übertragenen Sinn)* 2: 1 (130) **make up your mind / make your mind up** sich entscheiden, sich entschließen 2: 1 (130)
mind map ['maɪnd mæp] Gedankenkarte, Wörternetz, Mindmap 1
mini ['mɪni] Mini- 1
mini-drone [mɪnɪ 'drəʊn] die Minidrohne 1
minigolf ['mɪnigɒlf] das Minigolf 2: 1 (17)
minute ['mɪnɪt] die Minute 1
mirror ['mɪrə] der Spiegel 2: 4 (114)
miss [mɪs] vermissen 2: 1 (141)
°missing ['mɪsɪŋ]: **the missing words** die Wörter, die fehlen
°mistake [mɪ'steɪk] der Fehler
mix [mɪks] (ver)mischen 1
mixture ['mɪkstʃə] die Mischung 1
modern ['mɒdn] modern 2: 1 (17)
moment ['məʊmənt] der Moment 1 **at the moment** im Moment, zurzeit 1
Monday ['mʌndeɪ], ['mʌndi] der Montag 1
money ['mʌni] das Geld 1 **pocket money** das Taschengeld 2: 1 (132)
monkey ['mʌŋki] der Affe 1
month [mʌnθ] der Monat 1
°moon [mu:n] der Mond **be over the moon** ganz aus dem Häuschen sein (= hocherfreut sein)
more [mɔ:] mehr, weitere 1 **speak more loudly** lauter sprechen 1 **three more** noch drei, drei weitere 1
morning ['mɔ:nɪŋ] der Morgen 1 **in the morning** morgens, am Morgen 1
mosque [mɒsk] die Moschee 2: 4 (101)
most schools [məʊst] die meisten Schulen 1
mother ['mʌðə] die Mutter 2: 2 (17)
mountain ['maʊntən] der Berg 2: 3 (80)
mountain biking ['maʊntən baɪkɪŋ] das Mountainbiking 2: 1 (133)
mouse [maʊs], *pl* **mice** die Maus 1
move [mu:v]:
1. (sich) bewegen 2: 1 (14)
2. **move (to)** (um)ziehen (nach) 2: 1 (141)
Mr Lee ['mɪstə] Herr Lee 1
Mrs Lee ['mɪsɪz] Frau Lee *(Anrede für verheiratete Frauen)* 1
Ms Lee [mɪz] Frau Lee *(allgemeine Anrede f. Frauen)* 1
much [mʌtʃ] viel; sehr 1 **How much is/are ...?** Was (Wie viel) kostet/kosten ...? 2: 1 (138) **Thank you very much.** Vielen Dank. / Danke vielmals. 1
multicultural [mʌlti'kʌltʃərəl] multikulturell 2: 4 (112)
mum [mʌm] die Mama, die Mutti 1
°Munich ['mju:nɪk] München
museum [mju'zi:əm] das Museum 1
music ['mju:zɪk] die Musik 1 **classical music** klassische Musik 2: 3 (72)
musical ['mju:zɪkl] das Musical 2: 3 (87)
musician [mju'zɪʃn] der Musiker, die Musikerin 2: 1 (20)
must [mʌst] müssen 1
mustn't do ['mʌsnt] nicht tun dürfen 2: 4 (102)
my [maɪ] mein/e 1

N

name [neɪm] der Name 1 **What's your name?** Wie heißt du? 1
near [nɪə] nahe (bei), in der Nähe von 1
need [ni:d] brauchen 1 **need to do sth.** etwas tun müssen 1
neighbour ['neɪbə] der Nachbar, die Nachbarin 1
neighbourhood ['neɪbəhʊd] die Nachbarschaft, die Gegend, das Viertel 1
nervous ['nɜ:vəs] nervös, aufgeregt 2: 4 (104)
nest [nest] das Nest 2: 1 (28)
never ['nevə] nie, niemals 1
new [nju:] neu 1
news [nju:z] die Nachrichten 1
newsagent ['nju:zeɪdʒənt] der Zeitungshändler, die Zeitungshändlerin 2: 1 (137)
newsagent's ['nju:zeɪdʒənts] der Zeitschriftenladen, der Zeitungskiosk 2: 1 (137)
newspaper ['nju:speɪpə] die (Tages-)Zeitung 1
next [nekst]:
1. nächste(r, s) 1
the next day am nächsten Tag 1
2. **Next ...** Als Nächstes ... 1
next to ['nekst tə] neben 1
nice [naɪs] nett, schön 1

night [naɪt] die Nacht 2: 1 (23) **at night** nachts, in der Nacht 2: 1 (23)
nine [naɪn] neun 1
nineteen [naɪnˈtiːn] neunzehn 1
ninety [ˈnaɪnti] neunzig 1
no [nəʊ]:
1. nein 1
2. kein/e; verboten 1
No dogs! Hunde verboten! 1
noise [nɔɪz] das Geräusch; der Lärm 1
noisy [ˈnɔɪzi] laut, voller Lärm; lärmend 1
nose [nəʊz] die Nase 2: 2 (11)
not [nɒt] nicht 1 **I'm not a boy.** Ich bin kein Junge. 1
note [nəʊt]:
1. die Notiz; der kurze Brief 1
make notes (sich) Notizen machen *(zur Vorbereitung)* 1 °**sticky note** die Haftnotiz, der Klebezettel
°2. **note sth. down** sich etwas aufschreiben, notieren
notice [ˈnəʊtɪs]:
1. (be)merken 2: 1 (134)
2. der Anschlag, die Bekanntmachung *(an einem Schwarzen Brett)* 2: 1 (134)
November [nəʊˈvembə] der November 1
now [naʊ] nun, jetzt 1
°**nowhere** [ˈnəʊweə] nirgendwo(hin)
number [ˈnʌmbə] die Zahl, die Ziffer, die Nummer 1
nurse [nɜːs] der Krankenpfleger, die Krankenpflegerin 2: 1 (128/129)

O

o'clock [əˈklɒk]: **at 8 o'clock** um 8 Uhr 1
October [ɒkˈtəʊbə] der Oktober 1
of [ɒv], [əv] von 1 **bags of rubbish** Tüten/Säcke mit/voller Müll 1 **the days of the week** *(pl)* die Wochentage 1
of course [əv ˈkɔːs] natürlich, selbstverständlich 1
off [ɒf]: **be off** aus sein *(ausgeschaltet sein)* 2: 3 (70/71)
office [ˈɒfɪs] das Büro 1
often [ˈɒfn], [ˈɒftən] oft 1
oh [əʊ] Null *(im gesprochenen Englisch)* 1
OK [əʊˈkeɪ] okay, in Ordnung 1 **Are you OK?** Geht es dir gut? / Bist du okay? 1 **I'm OK.** Es geht mir gut. 1
old [əʊld] alt 1
°**Olympic** [əˈlɪmpɪk] olympisch
on [ɒn]:
1. auf 1
on holiday im/in den Urlaub 1 **on Monday** am Montag 1 **on Mondays** an jedem Montag, montags 1 **on my birthday** an meinem Geburtstag 1 **on the beach** am Strand 1 **on the bus** im Bus 1
2. **be on** gezeigt werden *(Kino, Fernsehen)*, stattfinden, „laufen"; an sein *(eingeschaltet sein)* 2: 3 (70/71)
one [wʌn]:
1. eins 1
one way eine Strecke *(= ohne Rückfahrt/Rückflug)* 2: 1 (19) **one-way ticket** die einfache Fahrkarte *(= ohne Rückfahrt)* 2: 1 (19)
2. **the round one** der/die/das Runde 2: 3 (81)
onion [ˈʌnjən] die Zwiebel 2: 4 (103)
online [ɒnˈlaɪn] online, Online- 1
only [ˈəʊnli] nur, bloß; erst 1
onto the table [ˈɒntu], [ˈɒntə] auf den Tisch 2: 4 (109)
open [ˈəʊpən]:
1. öffnen; aufschlagen *(Buch)* 1
2. offen, geöffnet 1
opinion [əˈpɪnjən] die Meinung 2: 3 (82) **in my opinion** meiner Meinung nach 2: 3 (82)
opposite [ˈɒpəzɪt] das Gegenteil 1
or [ɔː] oder; sonst 1
orange [ˈɒrɪndʒ]:
1. orange(farben) 1
2. die Orange, die Apfelsine 1
°**order** [ˈɔːdə] Reihenfolge **in order** in eine(r) Reihenfolge **in the right order** in die richtige Reihenfolge; in der richtigen Reihenfolge
°**organize** [ˈɔːɡənaɪz] organisieren
other [ˈʌðə] andere(r, s) 1 **each other** einander, sich (gegenseitig) 2: 1 (141) **the others** die anderen 1
our [ˈaʊə] unser/e 1
out (of ...) [aʊt]:
1. **out** heraus, hinaus, nach draußen 2: 3 (82)
go out rausgehen, weggehen; ausgehen 2: 3 (82)
2. **out of ...** aus ... (heraus/hinaus) 2: 3 (82)
outside [aʊtˈsaɪd] außerhalb (von) 1 **outside the house** außerhalb des Hauses 1
oven [ˈʌvn] der Backofen 1
over [ˈəʊvə]:
1. **over 50** über / mehr als 50 1 **over here** hier herüber; hier drüben 1 **over there** da drüben, dort drüben 1 **all over the world** überall auf der Welt, auf der ganzen Welt, weltweit 2: 4 (114)
2. hinüber, herüber 2: 4 (110) **come / walk over** hinüberkommen/-gehen, rüberkommen/-gehen 2: 4 (110)
own [əʊn]:
1. **my/your own room** mein/dein/ein eigenes Zimmer 1
2. **own sth.** etwas besitzen 2: 1 (130)
owner [ˈəʊnə] der Besitzer, die Besitzerin 2: 1 (130)

P

packet [ˈpækɪt] die Packung, das Päckchen 1
page (= p.) [peɪdʒ] die (Buch-/Heft-) Seite 1 **Open your books at page 10.** Schlagt eure Bücher auf Seite 10 auf. 1
pair [peə] das Paar 2: 1 (22)
pan [pæn] die Pfanne 1
°**panic** [ˈpænɪk] in Panik geraten **Don't panic.** Keine Panik. / Immer mit der Ruhe.
°**panto** [ˈpæntəʊ] *kurz für* **pantomime** [ˈpæntəmaɪm] *das lustige, traditionelle, meist zu Weihnachten aufgeführte Theaterstück, besonders für Kinder*
paper [ˈpeɪpə]:
1. die (Tages-)Zeitung 1
2. das Papier 1
°**piece of paper** das Stück Papier, der Zettel
parade [pəˈreɪd] die Parade, der Umzug 2: 1 (18)
°**paragraph** [ˈpærəɡrɑːf] der (Text-) Abschnitt
°**parallel** [ˈpærəlel] parallel, Parallel-
parents *(pl)* [ˈpeərənts] die Eltern 1
park [pɑːk] der Park 1
parkour [pɑːˈkʊə] der Parkour *(akrobatischer Hindernislauf in der Stadt)* 1
parrot [ˈpærət] der Papagei 1
part (of) [pɑːt] der Teil (von) 1
partner [ˈpɑːtnə] der Partner, die Partnerin 1
party [ˈpɑːti] die Party 1
°**passport** [ˈpɑːspɔːt] der (Reise-)Pass
°**past** [pɑːst] die Vergangenheit
past [pɑːst]:
1. nach *(bei Uhrzeitangaben)* 2: 3 (74) **half past 6** halb 7 2: 3 (74) **quarter past 7** viertel nach 7 2: 3 (74)
2. vorbei an, vorüber an 2: 3 (80)
pasta [ˈpæstə] die Pasta *(italienische Bezeichnung für Teigwaren)* 1
pay (for sth.) [peɪ] zahlen; (etwas) bezahlen 1 **pay by card** mit Karte (be)zahlen *(z. B. Bankkarte)* 2: 1 (132)
PE (= physical education) [piː ˈiː] der (Schul-)Sport 1
pea [piː] die Erbse 1
pen [pen] der Kugelschreiber, der Stift; der Füller 1
pence [pens] *Plural von* **penny**
pencil [ˈpensl] der Bleistift 1
pencil case [ˈpensl keɪs] das Federmäppchen 1
pencil sharpener [ˈpensl ʃɑːpnə] der Bleistift(an)spitzer 1
penny (= p) [ˈpeni] Penny *(kleinste britische Münze)* 2: 1 (19)
people *(pl)* [ˈpiːpl] die Leute, die Menschen 1
perfect [ˈpɜːfɪkt] perfekt 1
perfectly (still) [ˈpɜːfɪktli] ganz/völlig (still) 1
perhaps [pəˈhæps] vielleicht 2: 1 (130)
person [ˈpɜːsn] die Person 1
°**personality** [pɜːsəˈnæləti] die Persönlichkeit; der Charakter
pet [pet] das (Haus-)Tier 1
phone [fəʊn]:
1. anrufen; telefonieren 1
2. das Telefon 1
on the phone am Telefon 1

phone call [ˈfəʊn kɔːl] der (Telefon-)Anruf 2: 2 (42)
phone number [ˈfəʊn nʌmbə] die Telefonnummer 1
photo [ˈfəʊtəʊ] das Foto 1 **in the photo** auf dem Foto 1 **take photos** Fotos machen 1 **taking photos** das Fotografieren *(Hobby)* 1
photography [fəˈtɒgrəfi] die Fotografie *(Hobby)*, das Fotografieren 2: 3 (72)
°**phrase** [freɪz] der Ausdruck, die (Rede-)Wendung
physical education (PE) [fɪzɪkl edʒuˈkeɪʃn] der (Schul-)Sport 1
pick [pɪk] (aus)wählen, aussuchen 2: 1 (22) **pick sb./sth. up** jn./etwas abholen 2: 1 (22) **pick sth. up** etwas aufheben *(vom Boden)*, etwas hochheben 2: 1 (22)
picnic [ˈpɪknɪk] das Picknick 1 **have a picnic** ein Picknick machen 1
picture [ˈpɪktʃə] das Bild 1
°**piece** [piːs] das Stück, das Teil **piece of cake** das Stück Kuchen **piece of paper** das Stück Papier, der Zettel
pier [pɪə] der Pier, die Seebrücke 1
pig [pɪg] das Schwein 1
piggy bank [ˈpɪgi bæŋk] das Sparschwein 2: 1 (132)
pink [pɪŋk] rosa 1
°**Pisces** [ˈpaɪsiːz] die Fische *(Sternzeichen)*
pizza [ˈpiːtsə] die Pizza 2: 1 (23)
place [pleɪs] der Ort, der Platz 1 **take place** stattfinden 2: 3 (79)
plan [plæn]:
1. der Plan 2: 1 (14)
2. planen 2: 1 (14)
plan to do sth. planen, etwas zu tun 2: 1 (14)
plane [pleɪn] das Flugzeug 2: 1 (12)
planet [ˈplænɪt] der Planet 2: 2 (48)
plastic [ˈplæstɪk] das Plastik, der Kunststoff 2: 1 (22)
platform [ˈplætfɔːm] der Bahnsteig 2: 1 (18) **at platform 4** auf Gleis 4 2: 1 (18)
play [pleɪ] spielen 1
player [ˈpleɪə] der Spieler, die Spielerin 1
playing card [ˈpleɪɪŋ kɑːd] die Spielkarte 1
playlist [ˈpleɪlɪst] die Playlist 1
please [pliːz] bitte 1
plumber [ˈplʌmə] der (Sanitär-)Installateur, die (Sanitär-)Installateurin 2: 1 (128/129)
p.m. [piːˈem]: **4 p.m.** 4 Uhr nachmittags, 16 Uhr 1 **9 p.m.** 9 Uhr abends, 21 Uhr 1
pocket [ˈpɒkɪt] die Tasche *(an Kleidungsstücken)* 2: 1 (132)
pocket money [ˈpɒkɪt mʌni] das Taschengeld 2: 1 (132)
poem [ˈpəʊɪm] das Gedicht 2: 4 (109)
point [pɔɪnt] der Punkt 1
polite [pəˈlaɪt] höflich 1
pool [puːl] *(kurz für swimming pool)* das Schwimmbad 1
pop (music) [ˈpɒp mjuːzɪk] der Pop, die Popmusik 2: 3 (72)
popular [ˈpɒpjələ] beliebt, populär 1
popular with [ˈpɒpjələ] beliebt bei 2: 3 (72)
pork [pɔːk] das Schweinefleisch 1
°**positive** [ˈpɒzətɪv] positiv
post [pəʊst]:
1. der Post *(Teil eines Blogs)* 1
2. posten *(im Internet veröffentlichen)* 1
poster [ˈpəʊstə] das Poster 1
potato [pəˈteɪtəʊ], *pl* **potatoes** die Kartoffel 1
pound (£) [paʊnd] das Pfund *(britische Währung)* 1
powder [ˈpaʊdə] das Pulver 1
power [ˈpaʊə] die Kraft, die Macht, die Energie; der (elektrische) Strom 2: 2 (10)
practice [ˈpræktɪs] die Übung(en) 2: 3 (72)
practise [ˈpræktɪs] üben 2: 3 (72)
pray [preɪ] beten 2: 4 (100)
prayer [preə] das Gebet 2: 4 (100)
prediction [prɪˈdɪkʃn] die Vorhersage, die Voraussage 2: 1 (132)
preparation [prepəˈreɪʃn] die Vorbereitung; die Zubereitung 2: 3 (72)
prepare (for) [prɪˈpeə] vorbereiten, zubereiten; sich vorbereiten (auf) 2: 3 (72)
present [ˈpreznt] das Geschenk 1
°**present** [ˈpreznt] die Gegenwart
present sth. (to sb.) [prɪˈzent] (jm.) etwas präsentieren, vorstellen 1
presentation [preznˈteɪʃn] das Referat, die Präsentation 1
price [praɪs] der (Kauf-)Preis 2: 1 (138)
pride [praɪd] der Stolz 2: 1 (18)
prize [praɪz] der Preis, der Gewinn 1
prize show [ˈpraɪz ʃəʊ] die Preisverleihung *(Zeremonie)* 1
problem [ˈprɒbləm] das Problem 1
profile [ˈprəʊfaɪl] das Profil; die Beschreibung, das Portrait 2: 2 (42)
program [ˈprəʊgræm]:
1. das (Computer-)Programm 2: 1 (128/129)
2. programmieren 2: 1 (128/129)
programme [ˈprəʊgræm] das (Fernseh-)Programm, die Sendung 2: 1 (128/129)
programmer [ˈprəʊgræmə] der Programmierer, die Programmiererin 2: 1 (128/129)
project [ˈprɒdʒekt] das Projekt 1
°**prop** [prɒp] die Requisite
proud (of) [praʊd] stolz (auf) 2: 1 (18)
punk [pʌŋk] der Punk 2: 4 (114)
purple [ˈpɜːpl] violett, lila 1
put [pʊt], **put** *(etwas wohin)* tun, legen, stellen, stecken 1 **put sth. on** etwas anziehen *(Kleidung)*, aufsetzen *(z. B. Hut, Brille)* 2: 4 (110) **put your hand up** sich melden, aufzeigen 1
puzzle [ˈpʌzl] das Rätsel 1

Q

quarter [ˈkwɔːtə]: **quarter past 7** viertel nach 7 2: 3 (74) **quarter to 7** viertel vor 7 2: 3 (74)
question [ˈkwestʃən] die Frage 1 **ask a question** eine Frage stellen 1
quiet [ˈkwaɪət] ruhig, still, leise 1
°**quite** [kwaɪt] ziemlich, ganz
quiz [kwɪz], *pl* **quizzes** das Quiz, das Ratespiel; der Test 1 **do a quiz** ein Quiz / ein Ratespiel / einen Test machen 1
quizzes [ˈkwɪzɪz] *Plural von quiz*

R

rabbit [ˈræbɪt] das Kaninchen 1
rain [reɪn]:
1. der Regen 1
2. regnen 1
rain jacket [ˈreɪn dʒækɪt] die Regenjacke 2: 4 (112)
rainbow [ˈreɪnbəʊ] der Regenbogen 2: 1 (20)
rainy [ˈreɪni] regnerisch 1
rap [ræp]:
1. der Rap 2: 3 (72)
2. rappen 2: 3 (72)
read [riːd] lesen 1
reader [ˈriːdə] der Leser, die Leserin 1
ready [ˈredi] fertig, bereit 1 **get ready (for)** sich fertig machen (für), sich vorbereiten (auf) 2: 1 (18)
real [rɪəl] echt, wirklich 2: 3 (72)
realistic [riːəˈlɪstɪk] realistisch 2: 1 (141)
really [ˈriːəli], [ˈrɪəli] wirklich 1
°**reason** [ˈriːzn] der Grund, die Begründung **for many reasons / for this reason** aus vielen Gründen / aus diesem Grund
recipe [ˈresəpi] das (Koch-)Rezept 1
recipe book [ˈresəpi bʊk] das Kochbuch 1
record [rɪˈkɔːd] aufnehmen, aufzeichnen 1
recording [rɪˈkɔːdɪŋ] die Aufnahme 1
red [red] rot 1 **go red** erröten, rot werden 1
relax [rɪˈlæks] sich entspannen 2: 3 (77)
relaxed [rɪˈlækst] entspannt 2: 3 (77)
relaxing [rɪˈlæksɪŋ] entspannend 2: 3 (77)
°**remain seated** [rɪmeɪn ˈsiːtɪd] sitzen bleiben, auf seinem Platz bleiben
remember [rɪˈmembə]:
1. daran denken, nicht vergessen 1
remember to do sth. daran denken, etwas zu tun 1
2. sich erinnern an 1
remember doing sth. sich daran erinnern, etwas getan zu haben 1
repeat [rɪˈpiːt] wiederholen 2: 1 (142)
°**research** [rɪˈsɜːtʃ] erforschen, untersuchen, recherchieren
respect [rɪˈspekt]:
1. respektieren, achten 2: 1 (132)

2. **respect (for)** der Respekt (vor) 2: 1 (132)
restaurant ['restrɒnt] das Restaurant 2: 1 (12)
°**result** [rɪ'zʌlt] das Ergebnis
return [rɪ'tɜ:n]:
1. zurückkehren, zurückkommen 2: 1 (19)
2. *(kurz für:* **return ticket***)* (Hin- und) Rückfahrkarte 2: 1 (19)
return ticket [rɪ'tɜ:n tɪkɪt] (Hin- und) Rückfahrkarte 2: 1 (19)
°**rewrite** [ri:'raɪt] neu schreiben, umschreiben
rhyme [raɪm]:
1. (sich) reimen 2: 4 (108)
2. der Reim 2: 4 (108)
rice [raɪs] der Reis 1
rich [rɪtʃ] reich 2: 1 (133)
ride [raɪd], **rode**: **ride a bike** mit dem Fahrrad fahren 2: 1 (22) **ride a horse** reiten 2: 1 (22)
right [raɪt]:
1. richtig 1
be right Recht haben 1
°2. **right here** genau hier
right [raɪt] rechts; nach rechts 2: 2 (44) **on the right** rechts, auf der rechten Seite 2: 2 (44) **to the right of ...** rechts von ... 2: 2 (44)
ring [rɪŋ] der Ring 1 **wedding ring** der Ehering 2: 4 (104)
river ['rɪvə] der Fluss 2: 1 (12)
road [rəʊd] die Straße *(in oder zwischen Orten)* 1
robot ['rəʊbɒt] der Roboter 1
rock [rɒk] der Rock *(Rockmusik)* 2: 3 (72)
rode [rəʊd] *siehe* **ride**
role [rəʊl] die Rolle *(Film, Theater)* 2: 3 (72)
role-play ['rəʊlpleɪ]:
1. das Rollenspiel 2: 3 (72)
2. **role-play sth.** etwas in einem Rollenspiel darstellen 2: 3 (72)
room [ru:m] der Raum, das Zimmer 1
round [raʊnd]:
1. rund 2: 3 (81)
2. **round ...** um (... herum), in ... umher 2: 3 (81)
rubber ['rʌbə] das Radiergummi 1
rubbish ['rʌbɪʃ] der (Haus-)Müll, der Abfall 1
rucksack ['rʌksæk] der Rucksack 1
rule [ru:l]:
1. die Regel 2: 3 (82)
°2. herrschen (über)
ruler ['ru:lə] das Lineal 1
run [rʌn] rennen, laufen 1
running ['rʌnɪŋ] das Laufen *(Sport)* 1

S

sad [sæd] traurig 1
°**Sagittarius** [sædʒɪ'teəriəs] der Schütze *(Sternzeichen)*
said [sed] *siehe* **say**
°**sailor** ['seɪlə] der Seemann, die Seemännin / der Matrose, die Matrosin
salad ['sæləd] der Salat *(als Gericht oder Beilage)* 1
same [seɪm]: **the same** gleich; derselbe/dieselbe/dasselbe; dieselben 1
sandwich ['sænwɪtʃ], ['sænwɪdʒ] das Sandwich 1
sang [sæŋ] *siehe* **sing**
°**sangeet** [sʌn'gi:t] das Sangeet *(eine traditionelle vorhochzeitliche Zeremonie in Indien)*
sari ['sɑ:ri] der Sari *(Kleid/Gewand indischer Frauen)* 2: 4 (112)
Saturday ['sætədeɪ], ['sætədi] der Samstag 1
sauce [sɔ:s] die Soße 1
sausage ['sɒsɪdʒ] das (Brat-, Bock-) Würstchen, die Wurst 1
save [seɪv]:
1. retten 2: 2 (42)
2. sparen 2: 2 (42)
savings *(pl)* ['seɪvɪŋz] die Ersparnisse 2: 1 (132)
savings account ['seɪvɪŋz əkaʊnt] das Sparkonto 2: 1 (132)
saw [sɔ:] *siehe* **see**
say [seɪ], **said** sagen 1
scare sb. [skeə] jn. erschrecken, jm. Angst machen 2: 1 (12)
scared [skeəd]: **be scared (of)** Angst haben (vor) 1
scarf [skɑ:f], *pl* **scarves** Schal 2: 4 (112)
scarves [skɑ:vz] *Plural von* **scarf**
scary ['skeəri] unheimlich, beängstigend, gruselig 2: 1 (12)
scene [si:n] die Szene 1
school [sku:l] die Schule 1 **at school** in der Schule 1
school club ['sku:l klʌb] die AG *(in der Schule)* 1
school uniform [sku:l 'ju:nɪfɔ:m] die Schuluniform 1
sci-fi ['saɪ faɪ] *siehe* **science fiction**
science ['saɪəns] die Naturwissenschaft 1
science fiction [saɪəns 'fɪkʃn] *infml auch* **sci-fi** die Sciencefiction 2: 3 (79)
score [skɔ:]:
1. der Score *(Spielstand, Spielergebnis)* 2: 3 (81)
2. scoren *(einen Punkt / ein Tor / einen Treffer erzielen)* 2: 3 (81)
°**Scorpio** ['skɔ:piəʊ] der Skorpion *(Sternzeichen)*
screen [skri:n] der Bildschirm; die Leinwand *(Kino)* 2: 3 (82)
sea [si:] das Meer, die See 1 **by the sea** am Meer, an der See 1
sea level ['si: levl] der Meeresspiegel 2: 3 (81)
seagull ['si:gʌl] die Möwe 1
°**seated** ['si:tɪd]: **remain seated** sitzen bleiben, auf seinem Platz bleiben
second (2nd) ['sekənd] zweite(r, s) 1
secret ['si:krət]:
1. geheim 1
2. das Geheimnis 1
see [si:], **saw, seen** sehen 1 **See you soon.** Bis bald! 1 **See you.** Bis dann. / Tschüs. 1
seen [si:n] *siehe* **see**
sell [sel], **sold, sold** verkaufen 1
send [send] senden, schicken 1
°**sentence** ['sentəns] der Satz
September [sep'tembə] der September 1
set [set], **set** stellen, legen, setzen 2: 4 (102) **set the table** den Tisch decken 2: 4 (102)
seven ['sevn] sieben 1
seventeen [sevn'ti:n] siebzehn 1
seventy ['sevnti] siebzig 1
°**shake your head** [ʃeɪk] den Kopf schütteln
shame [ʃeɪm]: **a shame** schade; eine Schande 1 **That's / It's a shame!** Das/Es ist schade! 1 **What a shame!** Wie schade! 1
share [ʃeə] teilen 1
sharpener ['ʃɑ:pnə] der Anspitzer 1
she [ʃi:] sie *(weibliche Person)* 1 **she's (= she is)** sie ist 1
shelf [ʃelf], *pl* **shelves** das Regal(brett) 1
shelves [ʃelvz] *Plural von* **shelf**
shirt [ʃɜ:t] das Shirt, das Hemd 2: 4 (112)
°**shocked** [ʃɒkt] schockiert
shoe [ʃu:] der Schuh 1
shop [ʃɒp]:
1. das Geschäft, der Laden 1
be at the shops Einkäufe erledigen 1
2. (ein)kaufen, „shoppen" 2: 1 (132)
shop for sth. etwas kaufen (gehen) 2: 1 (132)
shop assistant ['ʃɒp əsɪstənt] der Verkäufer, die Verkäuferin 2: 1 (139)
shopper ['ʃɒpə] der Kunde, die Kundin; der Einkäufer, die Einkäuferin 2: 1 (132)
shopping ['ʃɒpɪŋ] das Einkaufen; die Einkäufe 1 **do the shopping** die Einkäufe erledigen, einkaufen gehen 1 **go shopping** einkaufen gehen 1
shopping list ['ʃɒpɪŋ lɪst] die Einkaufsliste 1
short [ʃɔ:t]:
1. klein *(Person; Körpergröße)* 1
2. kurz 1
shorts *(pl)* [ʃɔ:ts] die kurze Hose, die Shorts 2: 1 (137)
°**should** [ʃʊd]: **you should ...** du solltest ...
show [ʃəʊ]:
1. zeigen 2: 2 (13)
2. die Show, die Aufführung; die Ausstellung 1
prize show die Preisverleihung *(Zeremonie)* 1
shower ['ʃaʊə] die Dusche 1 **have a shower** (sich) duschen 1
sick [sɪk] krank 2: 1 (128/129)
sickness ['sɪknəs] die Krankheit 2: 1 (128/129)
°**side** [saɪd] die Seite
sight [saɪt]:
1. die Sehenswürdigkeit 2: 1 (12)
2. der Anblick, das Bild 2: 1 (12)

sign [saɪn] das Zeichen; das Schild 2: 1 (141)
silver ['sɪlvə]:
1. Silber 2: 2 (11)
2. silberfarben 2: 2 (11)
simple ['sɪmpl] einfach 1
sing [sɪŋ], **sang** singen 1
singer ['sɪŋə] der Sänger, die Sängerin 1
singing ['sɪŋɪŋ] das Singen 1
single ['sɪŋgl] Einzel-, einzelne(r, s) 2: 1 (19)
single ticket [sɪŋgl 'tɪkɪt] die einfache Fahrkarte *(= ohne Rückfahrt)* 2: 1 (19)
sister ['sɪstə] die Schwester 1
sit [sɪt] sitzen; sich setzen 1 **sit down** sich hinsetzen 1
°**situation** [sɪtʃu'eɪʃn] die Situation
six [sɪks] sechs 1
sixteen [sɪks'tiːn] sechzehn 1
sixty ['sɪksti] sechzig 1
size [saɪz] die Größe 2: 1 (138) **What size do you take?** Welche Größe hast du? 2: 1 (138)
skateboard ['skeɪtbɔːd]:
1. das Skateboard 1
2. Skateboard fahren 1
skateboarding ['skeɪtbɔːdɪŋ] das Skateboardfahren 1
skatepark ['skeɪt pɑːk] der Skatepark 1
ski [skiː]:
1. der Ski 1
2. Ski laufen, Ski fahren 1
go skiing (zum) Skilaufen gehen 1
skill [skɪl]:
1. die Fähigkeit, die Fertigkeit 2: 3 (72)
°2. die Lern- und Arbeitstechnik
sleep [sliːp]:
1. der Schlaf 1
2. schlafen 1
°**sleep in** ausschlafen
slide [slaɪd] das Dia; die Folie *(Präsentationssoftware)* 1
slippers *(pl)* [slɪpə] die Hausschuhe 2: 4 (111)
slow [sləʊ] langsam 1
small [smɔːl] klein 1
smart [smɑːt]:
1. schick 1
2. intelligent, clever 1
smile [smaɪl]:
1. das Lächeln 2: 3 (83)
2. lächeln 2: 3 (83)
smile at sb. jn. anlächeln 2: 3 (83)
smiley ['smaɪli] das Smiley 2: 3 (81)
snake [sneɪk] die Schlange 1
snow [snəʊ]:
1. der Schnee 1
2. schneien 1
snowboarding ['snəʊbɔːdɪŋ] das Snowboarding 2: 1 (133)
snowy ['snəʊi] schneebedeckt; verschneit 1
so [səʊ]:
1. so 1
so weird so seltsam, so komisch 1
2. also, daher 1
3. **so (that)** sodass 2: 2 (13)

°**sock** [sɒk] die Socke
sofa ['səʊfə] das Sofa 1
sold [səʊld] *siehe* **sell**
solve [sɒlv] lösen *(Rätsel, Problem)*, lüften *(Geheimnis)* 2: 1 (142)
some [sʌm], [səm] einige, ein paar; etwas, ein wenig 1
somebody ['sʌmbədi] jemand 1
someone ['sʌmwʌn] jemand 1
something ['sʌmθɪŋ] etwas 1
sometimes ['sʌmtaɪmz] manchmal 1
°**somewhere** ['sʌmweə] irgendwo(hin)
son [sʌn] der Sohn 1
song [sɒŋ] das Lied 1
soon [suːn] bald 2: 4 (102)
sorry ['sɒri]: **Sorry. / I'm sorry.** Tut mir leid. / Entschuldigung. 1 **be/feel sorry for sb.** Mitleid haben mit jm. 1 **I'm / I feel sorry for him.** Ich habe Mitleid mit ihm. / Er tut mir leid. 1
sound [saʊnd]:
1. der Laut; das Geräusch; der Klang 2: 4 (109)
2. klingen *(sich ... anhören)* 2: 4 (109)
°**source** [sɔːs] die Quelle *(z. B. Website, Text)*
space [speɪs] der Weltraum; der Raum, die Fläche; der Platz 2: 3 (78)
spaghetti [spə'geti] die Spaghetti 2: 1 (23)
speak (to) [spiːk], **spoke** sprechen (mit) 1 **Speak later.** Tschüs. / Bis später. 1
speaking ['spiːkɪŋ] das Sprechen 1
special ['speʃl] besondere(r, s) 1 **... is special** ... ist etwas Besonderes 1 **What's special about this place?** Was ist das Besondere an diesem Ort? 1
special effects *(pl)* [speʃl ɪ'fekts] die Special Effects *(in Filmen)* 2: 3 (79)
°**speech bubble** ['spiːtʃ bʌbl] die Sprechblase
spell [spel] buchstabieren 1
spelling ['spelɪŋ] die Schreibweise, die Rechtschreibung 1
spend [spend], **spent: spend money (on ...)** Geld ausgeben (für ...) 2: 3 (82) **spend time** Zeit verbringen 2: 3 (82)
spent [spent] *siehe* **spend**
spice [spaɪs] das Gewürz 1
spicy ['spaɪsi] würzig 1
°**spoke** [spəʊk] *siehe* **speak**
sport [spɔːt] der Sport; die Sportart 1
sports hall ['spɔːts hɔːl] die Sporthalle 1
°**sportsperson** ['spɔːtspɜːsn], *pl* **sportspeople** der Sportler, die Sportlerin
°**spring** [sprɪŋ] der Frühling
stadium ['steɪdiəm] das Stadion 1
stairs *(pl)* [steəz] die Treppe; die (Treppen-)Stufen 2: 3 (80)
stand [stænd], **stood** stehen; sich (hin)stellen 2: 3 (82) **stand up** aufstehen 1
star [stɑː]:
1. der Stern 2: 1 (141)
2. der (Film-/Pop-)Star 2: 1 (132)
star sign ['stɑː saɪn] das Sternzeichen 2: 1 (141)

start [stɑːt]:
1. der Anfang, der Start 1
2. beginnen, anfangen (mit) 1
start a business ein Geschäft aufmachen, einen Betrieb gründen/eröffnen 2: 1 (130)
station ['steɪʃn] der Bahnhof 1
stay [steɪ]:
1. der Aufenthalt 1
2. bleiben; übernachten 1
stay up aufbleiben *(nicht ins Bett gehen)* 2: 1 (132)
step [step] die Stufe; der Schritt 1
stepbrother ['stepbrʌðə] der Stiefbruder 2: 4 (107)
stepdad ['stepdæd] der Stiefvater 2: 4 (107)
stepdaughter ['stepdɔːtə] die Stieftochter 2: 4 (107)
stepfather ['stepfɑːθə] der Stiefvater 2: 4 (107)
stepmother ['stepmʌθə] die Stiefmutter 2: 4 (107)
stepmum ['stepmʌm] die Stiefmutter 2: 4 (107)
stepsister ['stepsɪstə] die Stiefschwester 2: 4 (107)
stepson ['stepsʌn] der Stiefsohn 2: 4 (107)
°**sticky note** [stɪki 'nəʊt] die Haftnotiz, der Klebezettel
still [stɪl]:
1. (immer) noch 1
2. trotzdem 2: 4 (111)
stood [stʊd] *siehe* **stand**
stop [stɒp]:
1. der Halt, der Haltepunkt; die Unterbrechung 1
2. (an)halten; stoppen; aufhören (mit) 1
stop a fire ein Feuer löschen 2: 1 (128/129)
story ['stɔːri] die Geschichte *(Erzählung)* 1
straight [streɪt]:
1. gerade; *(Haare)* glatt 2: 2 (40/41)
2. **straight on** geradeaus (weiter) 2: 3 (80)
strawberry ['strɔːbəri] die Erdbeere 1
street [striːt] die Straße *(in Ortschaften)* 2: 1 (14)
street musician ['striːt mjuzɪʃn] der Straßenmusiker, die Straßenmusikerin 2: 1 (20)
strength [streŋθ] die Stärke, die Kraft 2: 1 (142)
strong [strɒŋ] stark 2: 2 (11)
structure ['strʌktʃə]:
1. die Struktur 1
2. strukturieren, aufbauen 1
student ['stjuːdnt] der Schüler, die Schülerin / der Student, die Studentin 1
study ['stʌdi] studieren; lernen *(z. B. für Prüfungen)* 2: 3 (83)
°**study skills** *(pl)* ['stʌdi skɪlz] die Lerntechniken
stuff [stʌf] *(infml)* das Zeug, der Kram 2: 1 (132)

subject ['sʌbdʒɪkt] das (Schul-)Fach 1
success [sək'ses] der Erfolg 2: 1 (133)
successful [sək'sesfl] erfolgreich 2: 1 (133)
sugar ['ʃʊgə] der Zucker 1
suit [su:t] der (Herren-)Anzug; das (Damen-)Kostüm 2: 4 (110)
°**summary** ['sʌməri] die Zusammenfassung
summer ['sʌmə] der Sommer 1
sun [sʌn] die Sonne 1
°**sunbathe** ['sʌnbeɪð] sonnenbaden
Sunday ['sʌndeɪ], ['sʌndi] der Sonntag 1
sunglasses *(pl)* ['sʌnglɑ:sɪz] die Sonnenbrille 1
sunny ['sʌni] sonnig 1 **It's sunny.** Die Sonne scheint. 1
super ['su:pə] super 2: 2 (10)
superhero ['su:pəhɪərəʊ], *pl* **superheroes** der Superheld, die Superheldin 2: 2 (10)
supermarket ['su:pəmɑ:kɪt] der Supermarkt 1
superpower ['su:pəpaʊə] die Superkraft 2: 2 (10)
sure [ʃʊə], [ʃɔ:] sicher 1
surf [sɜ:f] surfen 2: 1 (133)
surfing ['sɜ:fɪŋ] das Surfing 1
surprise [sə'praɪz]:
1. die Überraschung 2: 1 (28)
2. überraschen 2: 1 (28)
surprised [sə'praɪzd] überrascht 1
swam [swæm] *siehe* **swim**
swap [swɒp]:
1. tauschen 1
2. der Tausch 1
clothes swap der Kleidertausch, die Kleidertauschparty 1
sweatshirt ['swetʃɜ:t] das Sweatshirt 1
sweet [swi:t]:
1. süß 1
2. das Bonbon 1
sweets *(pl)* [swi:ts] die Süßigkeiten 1
swim [swɪm], **swam, swum** schwimmen 1
swimmer ['swɪmə] der Schwimmer, die Schwimmerin 1
swimming ['swɪmɪŋ] das Schwimmen 1
swimming pool ['swɪmɪŋ pu:l] das Schwimmbad 1
swimsuit ['swɪmsu:t] der Badeanzug 2: 2 (11)
swum [swʌm] *siehe* **swim**

T

T-shirt ['ti: ʃɜ:t] das T-Shirt 1
table ['teɪbl]:
1. der Tisch 1
set the table den Tisch decken 2: 4 (102)
°2. die Tabelle
table tennis ['teɪbl tenɪs] das Tischtennis 1
take [teɪk], **took, taken:**
1. dauern, *(Zeit)* brauchen, in Anspruch nehmen 1
2. (mit)nehmen; bringen 1
take out the rubbish den Müll rausbringen 2: 4 (102) **take photos** Fotos machen 1 **take place** stattfinden 2: 3 (79) **take sth. off** etwas ausziehen *(Kleidung)*, ablegen *(z. B. Hut, Brille)* 2: 4 (110) **taking photos** das Fotografieren *(Hobby)* 1
taken ['teɪkn] *siehe* **take**
talk [tɔ:k]:
1. das Gespräch; die Rede, der Vortrag 1
2. **talk (to)** sprechen, reden (mit) 1
talk about sprechen, reden über 1
tall [tɔ:l] groß *(Person)*; hoch *(Gebäude)* 2: 1 (138)
°**task** [tɑ:sk] die Aufgabe **do a task** eine Aufgabe machen
taught [tɔ:t] *siehe* **teach**
°**Taurus** ['tɔ:rəs] der Stier *(Sternzeichen)*
tea [ti:] der Tee 1
teach [ti:tʃ], **taught** lehren, unterrichten 2: 1 (131)
teacher ['ti:tʃə] der Lehrer, die Lehrerin 1
team [ti:m] das Team, die Mannschaft 1
teamwork ['ti:mwɜ:k] das Teamwork, die Zusammenarbeit 2: 2 (14)
tech [tek] *(infml) siehe* **technology**
technology [tek'nɒlədʒi], *infml auch:* **tech** die Technik, der Technikunterricht; die Technologie 1
teeth [ti:θ] *Plural von* **tooth** **brush your teeth** (sich) die Zähne putzen 1
tell [tel], **told** erzählen, sagen 1
ten [ten] zehn 1
ten thousand [ten 'θaʊznd] zehntausend (10000) 2: 2 (10)
tennis ['tenɪs] das Tennis 1
terrarium [te'reəriəm] das Terrarium 1
terrible ['terəbl] schrecklich, fürchterlich 2: 4 (111)
test [test]:
1. der Test; die Klassenarbeit 1
2. testen 1
text [tekst]:
1. der Text 1
2. die SMS 1
3. **text sb.** jm. eine SMS schicken 1
thank sb. [θæŋk] jm. danken, sich bei jm. bedanken 2: 4 (100) **thank God** gottlob, Gott sei Dank 2: 4 (100)
thank you ['θæŋk ju:] danke (schön) 1 **Thank you very much.** Vielen Dank. / Danke vielmals. 1
thanks [θæŋks] danke (schön) 1
that [ðæt]:
1. das (dort) 1
that's (= that is) das (da) ist 1
2. **so that** sodass 2: 2 (13)
3. der, die, das *(Relativpronomen)* 1
things that people can use Dinge, die Menschen gebrauchen/benutzen können 1
the [ðə] der, die, das 1
theatre ['θɪətə] das Theater 2: 3 (70/71)
their [ðeə] ihr/e *(Plural)* 1
them [ðem], [ðəm] sie, ihnen 1
then [ðen] dann, danach 1
there [ðeə] da, dort; dahin, dorthin 1
there are es sind ... / es gibt ... 1
there's (= there is) es ist ... / es gibt ... 1
these [ði:z] diese (hier) 1 **These are my friends.** Das hier sind meine Freunde/Freundinnen. 1
they [ðeɪ] sie *(Plural)* 1 **they're (= they are)** sie sind 1
thing [θɪŋ] das Ding, die Sache 1
think [θɪŋk], **thought, thought** denken, meinen, glauben 1 **think about** nachdenken über 2: 1 (24) **think of sb./sth.** an jn./etwas denken 2: 2 (40/41) **think of sth.** sich etwas überlegen, ausdenken 2: 2 (40/41)
I think ... Ich denke/meine/glaube/finde, ... 1
third (3rd) [θɜ:d] dritte(r, s) 1
thirteen [θɜ:'ti:n] dreizehn 1
thirty ['θɜ:ti] dreißig 1
this [ðɪs] dies; diese(r, s) 1
those [ðəʊz] die dort, jene (dort) 2: 1 (138)
thought [θɔ:t]:
1. *siehe* **think**
°2. der Gedanke
thousand ['θaʊznd] tausend 2: 2 (10)
three [θri:] drei 1
threw [θru:] *siehe* **throw**
through [θru:] durch 2: 3 (80)
throw [θrəʊ], **threw** werfen 2: 4 (98/99) **throw away** wegwerfen 2: 4 (98/99)
thunderstorm ['θʌndəstɔ:m] das Gewitter 2: 1 (22)
Thursday ['θɜ:zdeɪ], ['θɜ:zdi] der Donnerstag 1
°**thx** [θæŋks] *(infml for* thanks, *in writing)* danke (schön)
°**tick** [tɪk] ankreuzen, abhaken
ticket ['tɪkɪt] die Eintrittskarte, die Fahrkarte, das Ticket 1 **one-way ticket** die einfache Fahrkarte *(= ohne Rückfahrt)* 2: 1 (19) **single ticket** die einfache Fahrkarte *(= ohne Rückfahrt)* 2: 1 (19)
ticket machine ['tɪkɪt məʃi:n] der Fahrkartenautomat 2: 1 (132)
tidy ['taɪdi]:
1. ordentlich 1
2. aufräumen 1
tie [taɪ] die Krawatte 1
till [tɪl] bis 2: 3 (82) **not ... till** erst, wenn ... 2: 3 (82)
time [taɪm]:
1. die Zeit; die Uhrzeit 1
have a great/good time (viel) Spaß haben, sich vergnügen 2: 1 (20) **on time** pünktlich 2: 4 (110) **What's the time?** Wie spät ist es? 1
2. das Mal 2: 1 (23)
for the first time zum ersten Mal 2: 1 (23) **this time** dieses Mal 2: 1 (23)
°**timeline** ['taɪmlaɪn] der Zeitstrahl, die Zeitachse, die Chronik
timetable ['taɪmteɪbl] der Stundenplan 1

tip [tɪp] der Tipp 2: 3 (84)
tired [ˈtaɪəd] müde 1
title [ˈtaɪtl] der Titel, die Überschrift 1
to [tu], [tə]:
1. zu, nach 1
to sb. an jn. *(z.B. schreiben an jn., eine E-Mail an jn.)* 1 **Have you ever been to London?** Bist du schon mal in London gewesen? 2: 4 (101) **the answer to the question** die Antwort auf die Frage 1
2. bis 1
(from) 2 o'clock to 5 o'clock (von) 2 Uhr / 14 Uhr bis 5 Uhr / 17 Uhr 1
3. (um) zu 1
how to do sth. wie man etwas tut / tun kann / tun soll 1 **things to eat** Dinge zum Essen 1
4. vor *(bei Uhrzeitangaben)* 2: 3 (74)
quarter to 7 viertel vor 7 2: 3 (74)
today [təˈdeɪ] heute 1
together [təˈgeðə] zusammen 1
toilet [ˈtɔɪlət] die Toilette 1
told [təʊld] *siehe* **tell**
tomato [təˈmɑːtəʊ], *pl* **tomatoes** die Tomate 1
tomato sauce [təˈmɑːtəʊ sɔːs] die Tomatensoße 1
°**tomorrow** [təˈmɒrəʊ] morgen
too [tuː]:
1. auch 1
from York too auch aus York 1
2. **too slow** zu langsam 1
took [tʊk] *siehe* **take**
tooth [tuːθ], *pl* **teeth** Zahn 1
top [tɒp] die Spitze, das obere Ende 1 **top floor** die oberste Etage, der oberste Stock, das oberste Stockwerk 1 **at the top (of)** oben, am oberen Ende (von); an der Spitze (von) 1 **the top five hobbies** die fünf besten/beliebtesten Hobbys 1
°**topic** [ˈtɒpɪk] das Thema
°**touch** [tʌtʃ] anfassen, berühren
°**tough** [tʌf] hart, schwer, schwierig
tour (of) [tʊə] die Tour, die Reise, der Rundgang / die Rundfahrt (durch) 1
tour guide [ˈtʊə gaɪd] der Reiseleiter, die Reiseleiterin / der Fremdenführer, die Fremdenführerin 1
tourist [ˈtʊərɪst] der Tourist, die Touristin 1
town [taʊn] die Stadt 1
town centre [taʊn ˈsentə] das Stadtzentrum 1
toy [tɔɪ] das Spielzeug 1
tradition [trəˈdɪʃn] die Tradition 2: 4 (109)
traditional [trəˈdɪʃənl] traditionell 2: 4 (109)
trailer [ˈtreɪlə] der Trailer *(Filmvorschau)* 2: 3 (79)
train [treɪn] der Zug, die Eisenbahn 1
train station [ˈtreɪn steɪʃn] der Bahnhof 1
trainer [ˈtreɪnə] der Trainer, die Trainerin 1
trampoline [ˈtræmpəliːn] das Trampolin 1
trampolining [ˈtræmpəliːnɪŋ] das Trampolinspringen/-turnen 1
transport *(no pl)* [ˈtrænspɔːt] das Fortbewegungsmittel; die Beförderung 2: 1 (17)
travel [ˈtrævl]:
1. das Reisen 1
2. reisen, fahren 1
treat [ˈtriːt] der Hochgenuss, das besondere Vergnügen; die (besondere) Leckerei 2: 1 (132)
tree [triː] der Baum 1
trick [trɪk] der Trick, das Kunststück 1
trip [trɪp] der Ausflug; die Reise 2: 1 (12) **boat trip** der Bootsausflug, die Bootsfahrt 2: 1 (12) **go on a trip** eine Reise machen 2: 1 (12) **take a trip** eine Reise machen 2: 1 (12)
trophy [ˈtrəʊfi] die Trophäe; der Pokal 2: 3 (81)
trouble [ˈtrʌbl] der Ärger, Schwierigkeiten 1 **be in trouble** Ärger haben, in Schwierigkeiten sein 1
trousers *(pl)* [ˈtraʊzəz] die Hose 2: 2 (11)
true [truː] wahr, richtig 2: 3 (82)
try [traɪ]:
1. versuchen, (aus)probieren 2: 1 (24)
try sth. on anprobieren *(Kleidung)* 2: 1 (138) **try to do sth.** versuchen, etwas zu tun 2: 1 (24)
2. der Versuch 2: 1 (24)
Have a try! / Give it a try! Versuch's/ Probier's doch mal! 2: 1 (24)
Tuesday [ˈtjuːzdeɪ], [ˈtjuːzdi] der Dienstag 1
turn [tɜːn] (sich) (um)drehen 1 **Turn it upside down.** Dreh/Stell es auf den Kopf. 1 **turn right/left** (nach) rechts/ links abbiegen 2: 3 (80) **turn sth. (over)** etwas umdrehen 1
turn [tɜːn]: **it is sb.'s turn (to do sth.)** jd. ist dran / an der Reihe (etwas zu tun) 1 **take turns (to do sth.)** sich abwechseln; sich dabei abwechseln, etwas zu tun 1
TV [tiːˈviː] der Fernseher; das Fernsehen 1
twelfth (12th) [twelfθ] zwölfte(r, s) 1
twelve [twelv] zwölf 1
twenty [ˈtwenti] zwanzig 1
°**twice** [twaɪs] zweimal
two [tuː] zwei 1

U

UK [juː ˈkeɪ] das Vereinigte Königreich 2: 1 (19)
°**umbrella** [ʌmˈbrelə] der (Regen-) Schirm
°**umbrella word** [ʌmˈbrelə wɜːd] der Oberbegriff, der Sammelbegriff
uncle [ˈʌŋkl] der Onkel 1
uncool [ʌnˈkuːl] uncool 2: 2 (48)
under [ˈʌndə] unter 1
understand [ʌndəˈstænd], **understood** verstehen 2: 1 (144)
understood [ʌndəˈstʊd] *siehe* **understand**
°**underwater** [ʌndəˈwɔːtə] unter Wasser, Unterwasser-
unfair [ʌnˈfeə] unfair 2: 2 (42)
unfriendly [ʌnˈfrendli] unfreundlich 1
unhappy [ʌnˈhæpi] unglücklich, unzufrieden 2: 2 (48)
unhelpful [ʌnˈhelpfl] nicht hilfreich; nicht hilfsbereit 2: 2 (48)
uniform [ˈjuːnɪfɔːm] die Uniform 1 **school uniform** die Schuluniform 1
unit [ˈjuːnɪt] die Unit *(Lerneinheit)* 1
United Kingdom (= the UK) [junaɪtɪd ˈkɪŋdəm] das Vereinigte Königreich 2: 1 (19)
unkind [ʌnˈkaɪnd] unfreundlich, herzlos 2: 2 (48)
unlucky [ʌnˈlʌki] unglücklich 2: 2 (48)
untidy [ʌnˈtaɪdi] unordentlich, unaufgeräumt 2: 2 (48)
until [ənˈtɪl] bis *(zeitlich)* 2: 3 (82)
not ... until erst, wenn ... 2: 3 (82)
up [ʌp] hinauf, hoch 2: 2 (12)
upside down [ʌpsaɪd ˈdaʊn] verkehrt herum, auf dem Kopf 1
us [ʌs], [əs] uns 1 **It's just us.** Es sind nur wir. 1
use [juːz] benutzen, verwenden 1
useful [ˈjuːsfl] nützlich, hilfreich 2: 1 (141)
user [ˈjuːzə] der (Be-)Nutzer, die (Be-)Nutzerin 1
usually [ˈjuːʒuəli] normalerweise, meistens 2: 3 (82)

V

vacuum [ˈvækjuəm] Staub saugen 2: 4 (102)
vacuum cleaner [ˈvækjuəm kliːnə] der Staubsauger 2: 4 (102)
vampire [ˈvæmpaɪə] der Vampir 2: 1 (12)
vanilla [vəˈnɪlə] die Vanille 1
vegetables *(pl)* [ˈvedʒtəblz] das/die Gemüse 1
vegetarian [vedʒəˈteəriən], *infml auch* **veggie**:
1. der/die Vegetarier/in 1
2. vegetarisch 1
veggie [ˈvedʒi] *siehe* **vegetarian**
very [ˈveri] sehr 1
vet [vet] der Tierarzt, die Tierärztin 1
video [ˈvɪdiəʊ] das Video; Video- 1
video game [ˈvɪdiəʊ geɪm] das Videospiel 1
°**viewing** [ˈvjuːɪŋ] das Fernsehen, das Betrachten *(von DVDs, Filmen usw.)*
village [ˈvɪlɪdʒ] das Dorf 1
°**Virgo** [ˈvɜːgəʊ] die Jungfrau *(Sternzeichen)*
visit [ˈvɪzɪt]:
1. der Besuch 1
2. besuchen 1
visitor [ˈvɪzɪtə] der Besucher, die Besucherin; der Gast 1
visitor information centre [vɪzɪtə ɪnfəˈmeɪʃn sentə] die Touristeninformation, das Fremdenverkehrsbüro 1
vocab [ˈvəʊkæb] *siehe* **vocabulary**

vocabulary [və'kæbjələri], *infml auch* **vocab** der Wortschatz, das Vokabular; das Vokabelverzeichnis 1

W

wait (for) [weɪt] warten (auf) 2: 1 (18) **Wait a minute.** Warte mal. / Einen Moment. 2: 1 (18) **I can't wait!** Ich kann es kaum erwarten! 2: 1 (18)
°waiting room ['weɪtɪŋ ru:m] Wartezimmer
walk [wɔ:k]:
1. der Spaziergang 1
2. (zu Fuß) gehen, wandern 1
walk over hinübergehen, rübergehen 2: 4 (110) **°walk around** umhergehen
walking ['wɔ:kɪŋ] das Wandern 1
walking boot ['wɔ:kɪŋ bu:t] der Wanderstiefel 2: 2 (11)
wall [wɔ:l] die Wand, die Mauer 2: 2 (12) **on the wall** an die Wand; an der Wand 2: 2 (12)
°wanna ['wɒnə] *(infml)* wollen *(= want to)*
want [wɒnt] wollen 1 **want to do sth.** etwas tun wollen 1
wardrobe ['wɔ:drəʊb] der Kleiderschrank 1
warm [wɔ:m] warm 1
was [wɒz], [wəz] *siehe* **be**
wash [wɒʃ] (sich) waschen 2: 1 (134)
washing ['wɒʃɪŋ] die Wäsche 2: 1 (134) **do the washing** die Wäsche erledigen, Wäsche waschen 2: 1 (134)
watch (sth.) [wɒtʃ] (sich etwas) anschauen; (etwas) beobachten 1
water ['wɔ:tə] das Wasser 1
wave (to sb.) [weɪv] (jm. zu)winken 1
way [weɪ] die Strecke, der Weg 2: 1 (19) **one way** eine Strecke *(= ohne Rückfahrt)* 2: 1 (19) **one-way ticket** die einfache Fahrkarte *(= ohne Rückfahrt)* 2: 1 (19)
we [wi:] wir 1 **we're (= we are)** wir sind 1
wear [weə], **wore, worn** tragen, anhaben *(Kleidung)* 1
weather ['weðə] das Wetter, die Witterung 1
website ['websaɪt] die Website 2: 1 (128/129)
wedding ['wedɪŋ] die Hochzeit 2: 4 (104)
wedding ring ['wedɪŋ rɪŋ] der Ehering 2: 4 (104)
Wednesday ['wenzdeɪ], ['wenzdi] der Mittwoch 1
week [wi:k] die Woche 1 **the days of the week** *(pl)* die Wochentage 1
weekday ['wi:kdeɪ] der Werktag, der Wochentag 1
weekend [wi:k'end] das Wochenende 1 **at the weekend** am Wochenende 1
weird [wɪəd] seltsam, komisch 1
welcome ['welkəm]: **Welcome (to ...)!** Willkommen (in/an ...)! 1 **You're welcome.** Bitte, gern geschehen. / Nichts zu danken. 1
well [wel] gut *(Adv.)* 1 **Well done.** Gut gemacht! 1
went [went] *siehe* **go**
were [wɜ:], [wə] *siehe* **be**
°whale [weɪl] der Wal
what [wɒt]:
1. was 1
2. welche(r, s) 1
What about a ... ? Wie wäre es mit einer/einem ... ? 1 **What about you?** Und du? / Was ist mit dir? 1 **What's your name?** Wie heißt du? 1
wheelchair ['wi:ltʃeə] der Rollstuhl 1
when [wen]:
1. wann 1
2. wenn *(zeitlich)* 1
3. als *(zeitlich)* 2: 1 (11)
where [weə] wo; wohin 1
which [wɪtʃ] welche(r, s) 1 **Which part ...?** Welcher Teil ...? 1
white [waɪt] weiß 1
who [hu:]:
1. wer 1
°2. wen; wem
°3. **the girl who ...** das Mädchen, das ...
why [waɪ] warum 1
°wife [waɪf], *pl* **wives** die (Ehe-)Frau
will [wɪl]: **I'll (= I will) be ...** Ich werde ... sein. 2: 1 (132)
win [wɪn], **won, won** gewinnen 1
wind [wɪnd] der Wind 1
window ['wɪndəʊ] das Fenster 1
windsurfing [wɪndsɜ:fɪŋ] das Windsurfing 1
windy ['wɪndi] windig 1
winner ['wɪnə] der Gewinner, die Gewinnerin / der Sieger, die Siegerin 1
winter ['wɪntə] der Winter 1
with [wɪð] mit; bei 1
°without [wɪ'ðaʊt] ohne
°wives [waɪvz] *Plural von* **wife**
woman ['wʊmən], *pl* **women** die Frau 2: 2 (11)
women ['wɪmɪn] *Plural von* **woman**
won [wʌn] *siehe* **win**
wonderful ['wʌndəfl] wunderbar 2: 1 (24)
won't [wəʊnt]: **I won't (= I will not) be ...** Ich werde nicht ... sein. 2: 1 (132)
°woof [wʊf] Wau
word [wɜ:d] das Wort 1 **words (of a song)** *(pl)* der (Song-)Text 2: 4 (108)
°wordbank ['wɜ:dbæŋk] die Wortbank *(Sammlung von Wörtern zu einem Thema)*
wore [wɔ:] *siehe* **wear**
work [wɜ:k]:
1. arbeiten; funktionieren 1
work long days lange arbeiten, lange Arbeitstage haben 1 **work sth. out** etwas herausfinden, etwas erarbeiten, etwas verstehen 2: 2 (12)
2. die Arbeit 1
at work bei der Arbeit, am Arbeitsplatz 1
work experience ['wɜ:k ɪkspɪəriəns] die Arbeitserfahrung(en), die Praxiserfahrung(en); das Praktikum 2: 1 (141)
world [wɜ:ld] die Welt 2: 3 (82) **the best place in the world** der beste Ort der Welt / auf der Welt 2: 3 (82)
°worm [wɜ:m] der Wurm
worn [wɔ:n] *siehe* **wear**
worried (about) ['wʌrid] beunruhigt, besorgt (wegen) 2: 1 (22)
worry (about) ['wʌri] sich Sorgen machen (wegen, um) 2: 1 (22) **Don't worry.** Mach dir keine Sorgen. 2: 1 (22)
worse [wɜ:s] schlechter, schlimmer 2: 3 (77)
worst [wɜ:st] der/die/das schlechteste, schlimmste; am schlechtesten, am schlimmsten 2: 3 (78)
would [wʊd]: **I'd (= I would) like/love ...** Ich hätte (liebend) gern ... / Ich möchte (liebend gern)... 1 **I'd love/like to meet ....** Ich würde mich (liebend) gerne mit ... treffen. 1
write [raɪt], **wrote** schreiben 1
writer ['raɪtə] der Autor, die Autorin 2: 1 (131)
wrong [rɒŋ] falsch 1 **be wrong** Unrecht haben 1 **Something is wrong.** Irgendetwas ist nicht in Ordnung. / Irgendetwas stimmt nicht. 2: 3 (83) **What's wrong?** Was ist los? / Was/ Wo ist das Problem? 2: 3 (83) **°go wrong** schiefgehen
°wrote [rəʊt] *siehe* **write**

Y

year [jɪə] das Jahr; der Jahrgang 1
yellow ['jeləʊ] gelb 1
yes [jes] ja 1
yesterday ['jestədeɪ] gestern 2: 1 (23)
yet [jet]: **... yet?** ... schon ...? 2: 4 (101) **not ... yet** noch nicht ... 2: 4 (101)
yoga ['jəʊgə] das Yoga 1
yoghurt ['jɒgət] der/die/das Joghurt 2: 4 (102)
you [ju:] du; dich; dir; ihr; euch; Sie; Ihnen 1
your [jɔ:], [jə] dein/e; euer/eure; Ihr/e 1
°yourself [jə'self] du/dir/dich (selbst)
youth [ju:θ] die Jugend; der Jugendliche 1
youth centre ['ju:θ sentə] das Jugendzentrum 1

Z

°zip wire ['zɪp waɪə] die Seilrutsche

Das *German-English Dictionary* enthält den **Lernwortschatz** deines Schulbuchs.
Es kann dir eine erste Hilfe sein, wenn du vergessen hast, wie etwas auf Englisch heißt.
Wenn du wissen möchtest, wo das englische Wort zum ersten Mal in deinem Schulbuch vorkommt, dann kannst du im *English-German Dictionary* (Seiten 234–249) nachschlagen.

Im Dictionary werden folgende **Abkürzungen und Symbole** verwendet:

infml = informal (umgangssprachlich) *pl = plural* (Mehrzahl)
sb. = somebody (jemand) *sth. = something* (etwas)
jd. = jemand jm. = jemandem jn. = jemanden

A

abbiegen (rechts/links), nach rechts/links abbiegen turn left/right [tɜːn]
Abend evening [ˈiːvnɪŋ]
am Abend in the evening
Abendessen dinner [ˈdɪnə]
zum Abendessen for dinner
abends in the evening [ˈiːvnɪŋ]
9 Uhr abends *(21 Uhr)* 9 p.m. [piːˈem]
aber but [bʌt], [bət]
Abenteuer adventure [ədˈventʃə]
A bis Z: (von) A bis Z (from) A to Z [eɪ tu zed]
Abfall rubbish [ˈrʌbɪʃ]
abhängen hang out [hæŋ aʊt]
abschließen *(z. B. Tür)* lock [lɒk]
abwechseln: sich abwechseln take turns [tɜːn] **sich dabei abwechseln, etwas zu tun** take it in turns (to do sth.)
acht eight [eɪt]
achtzehn eighteen [eɪˈtiːn]
achtzig eighty [ˈeɪti]
addieren add [æd]
Adresse address [əˈdres]
Affe monkey [ˈmʌŋki]
AG *(in der Schule)* school club [skuːl klʌb]
aktiv active [ˈæktɪv]
akustisch acoustic [əˈkuːstɪk]
Aktivist, Aktivistin activist [ˈæktɪvɪst]
Aktivität activity [ækˈtɪvəti]
albern stupid [ˈstjuːpɪd]
alle(s) all [ɔːl] **alle 30 Minuten** every 30 minutes [ˈevri]
allein alone [əˈləʊn]
allergisch (gegen) allergic (to) [əˈlɜːdʒɪk]
Alphabet alphabet [ˈælfəbet]
als as [æz], [əz] *(zeitlich)* when [wen]
also so [səʊ] **Also, ...** Well, ... [wel]
alt old [əʊld] **Wie alt bist du?** How old are you?
Alternative; alternativ alternative [ɔːlˈtɜːnətɪv]
am: am Anfang at first [æt], [ət]
am Arbeitsplatz at work
am besten best [best]
am Ende (von) at the end (of)
am größten biggest [ˈbɪgɪst]
am Meer by the sea [baɪ]
am Montag on Monday [ɒn]
am Morgen in the morning [ɪn]
am Nachmittag in the afternoon
am nächsten Tag the next day
am oberen Ende (von) at the top (of)
am Strand on the beach
am Telefon on the phone
am Wochenende at the weekend
an at [æt], [ət] **an sein (eingeschaltet sein)** be on [biː ɒn]
andere(r, s) other [ˈʌðə]
die anderen the others
ein/e andere(r, s) another [əˈnʌðə]
anders different [ˈdɪfrənt]
Anfang start [stɑːt]; beginning [bɪˈgɪnɪŋ]
am Anfang at first [æt], [ət]
anfangen (mit) start [stɑːt]
anfassen, berühren touch [tʌtʃ]
Angst: Angst haben be scared (of) [skeəd]
anhaben *(Kleidung)* wear [weə]
anhalten stop [stɒp]
anhören: sich etwas anhören listen to sth. [ˈlɪsn]
Ankunft arrival [əˈraɪvl]
anlächeln: jn. anlächeln smile at sb. [smaɪl]
Anprobe *(im Geschäft)* changing room [ˈtʃeɪndʒɪŋ ruːm]
anprobieren *(Kleidung)*, **(etwas) anprobieren** try sth. on [traɪ]
Anruf (phone) call [ˈfəʊn kɔːl]
anrufen call [kɔːl]; phone [fəʊn]
Ansage announcement [əˈnaʊnsmənt]
anschauen: etwas/jn. anschauen look at sth./sb. [lʊk] **sich etwas anschauen** watch sth. [wɒtʃ]
Anspitzer sharpener [ˈʃɑːpnə]
Anspruch: in Anspruch nehmen take [teɪk]
Anteil share [ʃeə]
Antwort answer [ˈɑːnsə] **Antwort auf die Frage** the answer to the question
antworten answer [ˈɑːnsə]
Anweisung instruction [ɪnˈstrʌkʃn]
Anzug *(Herrenanzug)* suit [suːt]
anziehen: sich anziehen get dressed [drest] **etwas anziehen** *(Kleidung)*, **aufsetzen** *(Hut)* put sth. on [pʊt]
App app [æp]
April April [ˈeɪprəl]
Arbeit work [wɜːk] **bei der Arbeit, am Arbeitsplatz** at work
Hausarbeit, (lästige) Pflicht chore [tʃɔː]
arbeiten work [wɜːk] **lange arbeiten** work long days [lɒŋ]
Architekt, Architektin architect [ˈɑːkɪtekt]
Ärger trouble [ˈtrʌbl] **Ärger kriegen** be in trouble
arm poor [pɔː], [pʊə]
Art way [weɪ] **auf diese Art** (in) this way, like this [laɪk] **auf unterschiedliche Art** in different ways
eine Art (von) ... a kind (of) ... [kaɪnd], sort (of) [sɔːt]
Artikel article [ˈɑːtɪkl]
Arzt, Ärztin doctor [ˈdɒktə]
atmen, ein-/ausatmen breathe (in/out) [briːð]
auch also [ˈɔːlsəʊ]; too [tuː]
auch aus Berlin from Berlin too
auf at [æt], [ət]; in [ɪn]; on [ɒn]
auf dem Bild, auf dem Foto in the picture **auf dem Kopf** upside down [ʌpsaɪd ˈdaʊn] **auf den Tisch** onto the table [ˈɒntu], [ˈɒntə] **auf dem Land** in the country **auf der Weide** in the field **auf einmal** suddenly [ˈsʌdənli] **auf Englisch** in English
Auf Wiedersehen! Goodbye. [gʊdˈbaɪ]
aufbewahren keep [kiːp]
Aufführung show [ʃəʊ]
Aufgabe exercise [ˈeksəsaɪz]
aufgeregt excited [ɪkˈsaɪtɪd]
aufhören (mit) stop [stɒp]
auflisten list [lɪst]
aufnehmen record [rɪˈkɔːd]
Aufmerksamkeit attention [əˈtenʃn]
aufpassen auf look after [lʊk]
aufräumen tidy [ˈtaɪdi] **etwas aufräumen** clean sth. up [kliːn]
aufregend exciting [ɪkˈsaɪtɪŋ]
aufschlagen *(Buch)* open [ˈəʊpən]
Schlagt eure Bücher auf Seite 10 auf. Open your books at page 10.
aufstehen *(aus dem Bett)* get up [get ˈʌp] **sich hinstellen** stand up [stænd ˈʌp]
aufwachsen grow up [grəʊ ʌp]
aufzeichnen record [rɪˈkɔːd]
Auge eye [aɪ]
August August [ɔːˈgʌst]
aus from [frɒm]
aus ... (heraus/hinaus) out of [aʊt]
Ausdruck phrase [freɪz]
Außerirdische/r; außerirdisch alien [ˈeɪliən]
Ausflug, Reise trip [trɪp]
ausruhen: sich ausruhen relax [rɪˈlæks]
Ausrüstung equipment [ɪˈkwɪpmənt]
ausschneiden: etwas ausschneiden cut sth. out [kʌt]

aussehen look [lʊk]
Aussprache pronunciation [prənʌnsiˈeɪʃn]
außerhalb (von) outside [aʊtˈsaɪd]
aussteigen *(aus einem Zug/Bus)* get off (a train/bus) [get ɒf]
Ausstellung show [ʃəʊ]
auswählen choose [tʃuːz]
Auto car [kɑː]
Autoscheinwerfer car light [ˈkɑː laɪt]

B

babysitten babysit [ˈbeɪbisɪt]
backen bake [beɪk]
Bäckerei bakery [ˈbeɪkəri]
Backofen oven [ˈʌvn]
Backpulver baking powder [ˈbeɪkɪŋ paʊdə]
Badeanzug swimsuit [ˈswɪmsuːt]
Bad(ezimmer) bathroom [ˈbɑːθruːm]
Badminton badminton [ˈbædmɪntən]
Bahnhof (train) station [ˈtreɪn steɪʃn]
Bahnsteig platform [ˈplætfɔːm]
bald soon [suːn]
Balkon balcony [ˈbælkəni]
Ball ball [bɔːl]
Ballon balloon [bəˈluːn]
Banane banana [bəˈnɑːnə]
Band band [bænd]
Bank *(Geldinstitut)* bank [bæŋk]
Bargeld cash [kæʃ]
Basketball basketball [ˈbɑːskɪtbɔːl]
Basteln crafts *(pl)* [krɑːfts]
Bauarbeiter/in, Bauunternehmer/in builder [ˈbɪldə]
Baum tree [triː]
beängstigend scary [ˈskeəri]
beantworten answer [ˈɑːnsə]
bedeuten mean [miːn]
Bedeutung meaning [ˈmiːnɪŋ]
beenden end [end]; finish [ˈfɪnɪʃ]
Beförderung transport [ˈtrænspɔːt]
beginnen start [stɑːt]
Behälter case [keɪs]
bei at [æt], [ət]; with [wɪð]
bei der Arbeit at work
bei ihrer Mutter (zu Hause/daheim) at her mum's (house)
beibringen: jm. beibringen, etwas zu tun teach sb. to do sth. [tiːtʃ]
beide both [bəʊθ]
Bein leg [leg]
Beispiel example [ɪgˈzɑːmpl]
zum Beispiel for example
wie zum Beispiel like [laɪk]
bekommen get [get]
belebt busy [ˈbɪzi]
Beleg receipt [rɪˈsiːt]
beliebt (bei) popular (with) [ˈpɒpjələ]
bellen: (jn. an)bellen bark (at sb.) [bɑːk]
benutzen use [juːz]
Benutzer/in user [ˈjuːzə]
beobachten: (etwas) beobachten watch (sth.) [wɒtʃ]
bequem comfortable [ˈkʌmftəbl]
Bereich area [ˈeəriə]
bereit ready [ˈredi]
Berg mountain [ˈmaʊntən]
berühmt (für, wegen) famous [ˈfeɪməs]
beschäftigt: (viel) beschäftigt busy [ˈbɪzi] **du bist beschäftigt** you're busy
beschreiben describe [dɪˈskraɪb]
Beschreibung description [dɪˈskrɪpʃn]
besondere(r, s) special [ˈspeʃl]
besonnen calm [kɑːm]
besorgen: (sich etwas) besorgen get sth. [get]
besorgt (wegen) worried (about) [ˈwʌrid]
besser better [ˈbetə]
beste(r, s) best [best] **der beste Sohn überhaupt / der beste Sohn, den man sich wünschen kann** the best son ever [ˈevə]
Bestie beast [biːst]
Bestimmungsort destination [destɪˈneɪʃn]
bestürzt upset [ʌpˈset]
Besuch visit [ˈvɪzɪt]
besuchen visit [ˈvɪzɪt]
Besucher/in visitor [ˈvɪzɪtə]
beten pray [preɪ]
Betrieb business [ˈbɪznəs]
Bett bed [bed] **ins Bett gehen** go to bed
beunruhigt worried (about) [ˈwʌrid]
beurteilen rate sth. [ˈreɪt]
bevor before [bɪˈfɔː] **bevor (du liest)** before (you read)
bewegen: sich bewegen move [muːv]
bewerten: etwas bewerten rate sth. [ˈreɪt]
bewölkt cloudy [ˈklaʊdi]
Bibliothek library [ˈlaɪbrəri]
Bild picture [ˈpɪktʃə] **auf dem Bild** in the picture [ɪn]
Bildschirm screen [skriːn]
Bildschirmpräsentation slide show [ˈslaɪd ʃəʊ]
Bildunterschrift caption [ˈkæpʃn]
Biologie biology [baɪˈɒlədʒi]
bis to [tu], [tə] **Bis bald!** See you soon. [ˈsiː ju], [ˈsiː jə] **Bis dann.** See you.
bis jetzt, bis hierher so far [səʊ fɑː]
Bis später. Speak later. [ˈleɪtə]
bis *(zeitlich)* until/till [ənˈtɪl]
bisschen: ein bisschen a little [ˈlɪtl]
bitte please [pliːz] **Bitte schön. / Hier, bitte.** Here you are. [hɪə ju ˈɑː]
Bitte, gern geschehen. You're welcome. [ˈwelkəm]
bitten: jn. bitten, etwas zu tun ask sb. to do sth. [ɑːsk] **jn. um etwas bitten** ask sb. for sth.
blasen blow [bləʊ]
blau blue [bluː]
Blazer *(das Jackett, oft Teil der Schuluniform)* blazer [ˈbleɪzə]
bleiben stay [steɪ]
Bleistift pencil [ˈpensl]
Bleistift(an)spitzer pencil sharpener [ˈpensl ʃɑːpnə]
blind blind [blaɪnd]
Blindenhund guide dog [ˈgaɪd dɒg]
blöd stupid [ˈstjuːpɪd]
bloß just [dʒʌst]; only [ˈəʊnli]
Blume flower [ˈflaʊə]
Blüte flower [ˈflaʊə]
Bockwurst sausage [ˈsɒsɪdʒ]
Boden ground [graʊnd]
Bonbon sweet [swiːt]
Bowling bowling [ˈbəʊlɪŋ]
Boxen boxing [ˈbɒksɪŋ]
boxen box [bɒks]
braten fry [fraɪ] **gebraten** fried [fraɪd]
Brathähnchen chicken [ˈtʃɪkɪn]
Bratwurst sausage [ˈsɒsɪdʒ]
brauchen need [niːd]; *(Zeit)* take [teɪk]
braun brown [braʊn]
brav good [gʊd]
Brief letter [ˈletə] **der kurze Brief** note [nəʊt]
Brille glasses *(pl)* [ˈglɑːsɪz]
bringen bring [brɪŋ]; take [teɪk]
britisch British [ˈbrɪtɪʃ]
Brot bread [bred]
Brücke bridge [brɪdʒ]
Bruder brother [ˈbrʌðə]
Buch book [bʊk]
buchen book [bʊk]
Buchseite page (p.) [peɪdʒ]
Bücherei library [ˈlaɪbrəri]
Büchse tin [tɪn]
Buchstabe letter [ˈletə]
buchstabieren spell [spel]
Burg castle [ˈkɑːsl]
Bürger/in citizen [ˈsɪtɪzn]
Büro office [ˈɒfɪs]
Bürste brush [brʌʃ]
bürsten brush [brʌʃ]
Bus bus [bʌs] **im Bus** on the bus
mit dem Bus by bus
Bushaltestelle bus stop [ˈbʌs stɒp]
Butter butter [ˈbʌtə]

C

Café cafe [ˈkæfeɪ]
Campingplatz campsite [ˈkæmpsaɪt]
Cash cash [kæʃ]
Cent cent [sent]
Chaos mess [mes]
Charakter character [ˈkærəktə]
personality [pɜːsəˈnæləti]
chatten (mit) chat [tʃæt]
Chemikalie; chemisch chemical [ˈkemɪkl]
clever smart [smɑːt]
Code code [kəʊd]
codieren code [kəʊd]
Cola cola [ˈkəʊlə]
Comic comic [ˈkɒmɪk]
Computer computer [kəmˈpjuːtə]
cool cool [kuːl]
Cousin/e cousin [ˈkʌzn]
Cricket *(Mannschaftssportart)* cricket [ˈkrɪkɪt]
Curry *(Gewürz/Gericht)* curry [ˈkʌri]
Custard *(Vanillesoße)* custard [ˈkʌstəd]

D

da there [ðeə] **da drüben** over there
Dachgeschoss top floor [tɒp ˈflɔː]
daher so [səʊ]
dahin there [ðeə]
damit so that [səʊ ðæt]
danach then [ðen]
Dank: Vielen Dank. Thank you very much. [ˈθæŋk juː] **Danke (schön).** Thank you. [ˈθæŋk juː]; thanks [θæŋks] **Danke vielmals.** Thank you very much. [mʌtʃ]
danken: Nichts zu danken. You're welcome. [ˈwelkʌm] **sich bei jm. bedanken** thank sb.
dann then [ðen]
das
1. *(Artikel)* the [ðə]
2. *(Relativpronomen)* that [ðæt]
das (dort) that [ðæt] **das (da)** that's (= that is)
dasselbe the same [seɪm]
Datei file [faɪl]
Datum date [deɪt] **Datum des Geburtstags** birthday date [ˈbɜːθdeɪ]
dauern take [teɪk]
Decke (zum Zudecken) blanket [ˈblæŋkɪt]
dein/e your [jɔː], [jə]
Dekoration decoration [dekəˈreɪʃn]
dekorieren decorate [ˈdekəreɪt]
denken think [θɪŋk] **daran denken (etwas zu tun)** remember (to do sth.) [rɪˈmembə] **Ich denke, ...** I think ... **an jn./etwas denken** think of sb./sth. [θɪŋk]
Delfin dolphin [ˈdɒlfɪn]
der
1. *(Artikel)* the [ðə]
2. *(Relativpronomen)* that [ðæt]
derselbe the same [seɪm]
Design design [dɪˈzaɪn]
Dessert dessert [dɪˈzɜːt]
deutlich clear [klɪə] **deutlich sprechen** speak clearly [spiːk ˈklɪəli]
Deutsch; deutsch German [ˈdʒɜːmən]
Deutsche German [ˈdʒɜːmən]
Deutschland Germany [ˈdʒɜːməni]
Dezember December [dɪˈsembə]
Dia slide [slaɪd]
die
1. *(Artikel)* the [ðə]
2. *(Relativpronomen)* that [ðæt]
die dort those [ðəʊz]
Diele hall [hɔːl]
Dienstag Tuesday [ˈtjuːzdeɪ]
diese (hier) these [ðiːz]
diese(r, s) this [ðɪs]
dieselbe(n) the same [seɪm]
Ding thing [θɪŋ] **Dinge, die Menschen gebrauchen/ benutzen können** things that people can use [θɪŋ] **Dinge zum Essen** things to eat
Donnerstag Thursday [ˈθɜːzdeɪ]
Dorf village [ˈvɪlɪdʒ]
dort there [ðeə] **dort drüben** over there [ˈəʊvə]
dorthin there [ðeə]
Dose tin [tɪn]
Drache dragon [ˈdrægən]
dramatisch dramatic [drəˈmætɪk]
dran: jd. ist dran it is sb.'s turn [tɜːn] **Wann bin ich dran (etwas zu tun)?** When is (it) my turn (to do sth.)?
draußen; nach draußen outside [aʊtˈsaɪd]
drehen turn [tɜːn] **Dreh etwas auf den Kopf.** Turn it upside down. [ʌpsaɪd ˈdaʊn] **etwas umdrehen** turn sth. (over)
drei three [θriː]
dreißig thirty [ˈθɜːti]
dreizehn thirteen [θɜːˈtiːn]
drinnen; nach drinnen inside [ɪnˈsaɪd]
dritte(r, s) third (3rd) [θɜːd]
Drohne drone [drəʊn]
du you [juː] **du bist** you're (= you are) [jɔː] **du bist beschäftigt** you're busy [ˈbɪzi]
du/dir/dich (selbst) yourself [jəˈself]
dürfen: ich darf nicht I mustn't [mʌsnt] **Darf ich ...?** May I ...?
dunkel dark [dɑːk]
dumm stupid [ˈstjuːpɪd]
durch through [θruː]
Durchsage announcement [əˈnaʊnsmənt]
durstig sein, Durst haben be thirsty [ˈθɜːsti]
Dusche shower [ˈʃaʊə]
duschen: (sich) duschen have a shower [ˈʃaʊə]

E

echt, wirklich real [rɪəl]
Ehemann husband [ˈhʌzbənd]
Ei egg [eg]
Eidechse lizard [ˈlɪzəd]
eigene(r, s): mein/ein eigenes Zimmer my own room [əʊn]
Eimer *(Mülleimer)* bin [bɪn]
ein(e) *(Artikel)* a [ə]; *(vor Vokalen)* an [ən] **ein paar** some [sʌm], [səm] **ein paar, einige** a few [fjuː] **ein bisschen, ein wenig** some; a little [ˈlɪtl] **noch ein(e)** another [əˈnʌðə]
einander, sich (gegenseitig) each other [iːtʃ ˈʌðə]
einfach just [dʒʌst]
einfach easy [ˈiːzi]
Einfluss (auf) effect (on) [ɪˈfekt]
Einführung introduction [ɪntrəˈdʌkʃn]
einige some [sʌm], [səm]
Einkäufe shopping [ˈʃɒpɪŋ] **Einkäufe erledigen** do the shopping, be at the shops [ʃɒp]
Einkaufen shopping [ˈʃɒpɪŋ]
einkaufen shop (for sth.) [ʃɒp] **einkaufen gehen** do the shopping [ˈʃɒpɪŋ]; go shopping
Einkaufsliste shopping list [ˈʃɒpɪŋ lɪst]
Einkaufszentrum shopping centre [ˈʃɒpɪŋ sentə]
einladen (zu, nach) invite (to) [ɪnˈvaɪt]
Einladung (zu, nach) invitation (to) [ˌɪnvɪˈteɪʃn]
Einleitung introduction [ɪntrəˈdʌkʃn]
einmal: noch einmal again [əˈgen] **einmal** once [wʌns] **einmal pro Monat** once a month [mʌnθ]
eins one [wʌn]
einsammeln collect [kəˈlekt]
einschlafen fall asleep [əˈsliːp]
einsteigen (in einen Zug, Bus) get on (a train/bus) [get ɒn]
Eintrittskarte ticket [ˈtɪkɪt]
Einzel-, einzelne(r,s) single [ˈsɪŋgl]
Einzugsfeier house-warming (party) [ˈhaʊs wɔːmɪŋ]
Eis *(Speiseeis)* ice cream [ˈaɪs kriːm]
Eisenbahn train [treɪn]
Elefant elephant [ˈelɪfənt]
elektrisch, Elektro- electric [ɪˈlektrɪk]
Elektronik; elektronische Geräte electronics [ɪlekˈtrɒnɪks]
elf eleven [ɪˈlevən]
Eltern parents *(pl)* [ˈpeərənts]
Ende end [end] **das obere Ende** top [tɒp] **am oberen Ende** at the top (of) **das untere Ende** bottom [ˈbɒtəm] **Endung** *(Text, Geschichte)* ending [ˈendɪŋ]
enden end [end] finish [ˈfɪnɪʃ]
Energie power [ˈpaʊə]
England England [ˈɪŋglənd]
Englisch; englisch English [ˈɪŋglɪʃ] **auf Englisch** in English [ɪn]
Enkel grandson [ˈgrænsʌn]
Enkelin granddaughter [ˈgrændɔːtə]
entdecken discover [dɪˈskʌvə]
Entschuldigung. Sorry/I'm sorry. [ˈsɒri] **Entschuldigung, .../Entschuldigen Sie, ...** Excuse me, ... [ɪkˈskjuːz miː]
entspannen: sich entspannen relax [rɪˈlæks]
enttäuscht (von) disappointed (in/with) [dɪsəˈpɔɪntɪd]
er he [hiː] **er ist** he's (= he is) **er ist nicht** he isn't (= is not)
Erbse pea [piː]
Erdbeere strawberry [ˈstrɔːbəri]
Erdboden ground [graʊnd]
Erde earth [ɜːθ]
Erdgeschoss ground floor [graʊnd ˈflɔː]
Erdkunde geography [dʒiˈɒgrəfi]
Ereignis event [ɪˈvent]
Erfahrung experience [ɪkˈspɪəriəns]
erforschen research [rɪˈsɜːtʃ]
erfolgreich successful [səkˈsesfl]
Erholung rest [rest]
erinnern: sich erinnern an remember [rɪˈmembə] **sich daran erinnern, etwas getan zu haben** remember doing sth.
erklären: jm. etwas erklären explain sth. to sb. [ɪkˈspleɪn]
Erklärung explanation [ekspləˈneɪʃn]
Erlebnis experience [ɪkˈspɪəriəns]
ernähren feed [fiːd]
erst only [ˈəʊnli]
erstaunlich amazing [əˈmeɪzɪŋ]
erste(r, s) first [fɜːst] **als Erstes** first
erzählen tell [tel]

es it [ɪt] **es ist** *(bei Sachen und Tieren auch: er ist; sie ist)* it's (= it is)
es ist ... / es gibt ... there's [ðeəz]
es sind ... / es gibt ... there are [ˈðeər ɑː] **es sollte ...** it should [ʃʊd]
Es macht mir nichts aus ... I don't mind [maɪnd]
Essen cooking [ˈkʊkɪŋ]; food [fuːd]; meal [miːl]
essen eat [iːt] **Dinge zum Essen** things to eat
Esslöffel tablespoon [ˈteɪblspuːn]
Esszimmer dining room [ˈdaɪnɪŋ ruːm]
Etage floor [flɔː] **die oberste Etage** top floor [tɒp ˈflɔː]
Etui case [keɪs]
etwas some [sʌm], [səm]; something [ˈsʌmθɪŋ]
euer/eure your [jɔː], [jə]
Euro euro, euros *(pl)* [ˈjʊərəʊ]

F

Fach subject [ˈsʌbdʒɪkt]
Fähigkeit skill [skɪl]
Fahne flag [flæg]
Fähre ferry [ˈferi]
fahren go [gəʊ]; travel [ˈtrævl]
mit dem Fahrrad fahren ride a bike [raɪd] **Rad fahren** cycle [ˈsaɪkl]
Skateboard fahren skateboard [ˈskeɪtbɔːd] **mit dem Auto fahren** drive [draɪv]
Fahrkarte ticket [ˈtɪkɪt]
Fahrrad bike [baɪk]
Fahrt journey [ˈdʒɜːni]
Fakt fact [fækt]
fallen, hinfallen fall [fɔːl]
falls if [ɪf]
falsch wrong [rɒŋ]
falscher Freund *(Übersetzungsfalle)* false friend [fɔːls ˈfrend]
falsche Richtung, (in) die falsche Richtung the wrong way [rɒŋ weɪ]
falten fold [fəʊld]
Familie family [ˈfæməli]
Familienname family name [ˈfæməli neɪm]
Fan fan [fæn]
fantasievoll imaginative [ɪˈmædʒɪnətɪv]
Farbe colour [ˈkʌlə] **Welche Farbe hat ...?** What colour is ...?
fast nearly [ˈnɪəli]
fasten fast [fɑːst]
Fasten brechen break the fast [breɪk ðə fɑːst]
faul lazy [ˈleɪzi]
Favorit/in favourite [ˈfeɪvərɪt]
Februar February [ˈfebruəri]
Federball badminton [ˈbædmɪntən]
Federmäppchen pencil case [ˈpensl keɪs]
Feedback *(Rückmeldung)* feedback *(no pl)* [ˈfiːdbæk]
Fehler mistake [mɪˈsteɪk]
Feier ceremony [ˈserəməni]
feiern celebrate [ˈselɪbreɪt]
Feld field [fiːld]
Fenster window [ˈwɪndəʊ]
Ferien holidays *(pl)* [ˈhɒlədeɪz]
Fernsehen, Fernseher TV [tiːˈviː]
fertig ready [ˈredi]
Fertigkeit skill [skɪl]
Feuer fire [ˈfaɪə]
Feuerwehrauto fire engine [ˈfaɪər endʒɪn]
Feuerwehrmann, Feuerwehrfrau firefighter [ˈfaɪəfaɪtə]
Feuerwerkskörper firework [ˈfaɪəwɜːk]
fies mean [miːn]
Figur *(aus einer Geschichte)* character [ˈkærəktə]
Film film [fɪlm] **die sechs besten Filme** the top six films [tɒp]
Filmstar star [stɑː]
finden find [faɪnd] **Ich finde, ...** I think ... [θɪŋk]
Finger finger [ˈfɪŋgə]
Fisch fish, *(pl)* fish [fɪʃ] **Fisch mit Pommes frites** fish and chips [fɪʃ ən ˈtʃɪps] **Imbissstube, die Fisch mit Pommes frites verkauft** fish and chip shop [ʃɒp]
Flagge flag [flæg]
Flasche bottle [ˈbɒtl]
Fleisch meat [miːt]
fleißig hard-working [hɑːd ˈwɜːkɪŋ]
fliegen fly [flaɪ]
Flugzeug plane [pleɪn]
Flur hall [hɔːl]
Fluss river [ˈrɪvə] **am Fluss** by the river [baɪ ðə ˈrɪvə]
Folie slide [slaɪd]
Forschungen research [rɪˈsɜːtʃ]
fort away [əˈweɪ]
Fortbewegungsmittel transport [ˈtrænspɔːt]
fortfahren continue [kənˈtɪnjuː]
mit etwas fortfahren continue to do sth. [duː]
fortsetzen: (sich) fortsetzen continue [kənˈtɪnjuː]
Foto photo [ˈfəʊtəʊ] **auf dem Foto** in the photo **ein Foto machen** take a photo
Fotografie, Fotografieren photography [fəˈtɒgrəfi]
Fotograf/in photographer [fəˈtɒgrəfə]
Frage question [kwestʃən] **Antwort auf die Frage** the answer to the question [ˈɑːnsə] **eine Frage stellen** ask a question **Habt ihr / Hast du (irgendwelche) Fragen?** Do you have any questions?
fragen ask [ɑːsk]
Frau woman, *(pl)* women [ˈwʊmən], [ˈwɪmɪn] **Frau Lee** *(Anrede für verheiratete Frauen)* Mrs Lee [ˈmɪsɪz] *(allgemeine Anrede für Frauen)* Ms Lee [mɪz] **Ehefrau** wife [waɪf]
frech rude [ruːd]
frei free [friː] **freie Zeit** free time [taɪm]
Freitag Friday [ˈfraɪdeɪ], [ˈfraɪdi]
Freizeit free time [ˈfriː taɪm]
Fremdenverkehrsbüro tourist information centre [tʊərɪst ɪnfəˈmeɪʃn sentə]
fressen eat [iːt]
freuen: Freut mich, dich/euch/Sie kennenzulernen. Nice to meet you. [naɪs] **sich auf etwas freuen** look forward to sth.
Freund/in friend [ˈfrend] **Das hier sind meine Freunde/Freundinnen.** These are my friends. [ðiːz] **ihre Freunde/Freundinnen** her friends [hɜː], [hə] **seine Freunde/Freundinnen** his friends [hɪz] **(feste) Freundin** girlfriend [ˈgɜːlfrend] **einen Freund / eine Freundin / Freunde finden** make a friend/friends [meɪk ə frend]
freundlich friendly [ˈfrendli]; kind [kaɪnd]
frieren be cold [kəʊld]
Friseur/in hairdresser [ˈheədresə]
frittieren fry [fraɪ] **frittiert** fried [fraɪd]
froh happy [ˈhæpi]
früh early [ˈɜːli]
Frühling spring [sprɪŋ]
Frühstück breakfast [ˈbrekfəst]
fühlen: sich fühlen feel [fiːl]
Füller pen [pen]
für for [fɔː] **für 30 Sekunden** for 30 seconds
fünf five [faɪv]
fünfzehn fifteen [fɪfˈtiːn]
fünfzig fifty [ˈfɪfti]
fürchterlich terrible [ˈterəbl]
Fuß foot [fʊt]
Fußball football [ˈfʊtbɔːl]
Fußboden floor [flɔː]
Fußgelenk ankle [ˈæŋkl]
Futter food [fuːd]
füttern feed [fiːd]

G

ganz quite [kwaɪt] **ganz (still)** perfectly (still) [ˈpɜːfɪktli]
die ganze Familie all the family
gar nichts not ... at all [nɒt ət ɔːl]
Garage garage [ˈgærɑːʒ]
Garten garden [ˈgɑːdn]
Gast visitor [ˈvɪzɪtə]
Gebäude building [ˈbɪldɪŋ]
geben give [gɪv] **es gibt ...** there's (= there is) ... [ðeəz]; there are ... [ˈðeər ɑː] **es gibt keine ...** there aren't any ... [ˈeni] **Was gibt es zum Mittagessen?** What's for lunch? [lʌntʃ]
geboren: er wurde geboren he was born [ˈbɔːn]
Geburtstag birthday [ˈbɜːθdeɪ] **an meinem Geburtstag** on my birthday
Datum des Geburtstags birthday date [deɪt] **Herzlichen Glückwunsch zum Geburtstag!** Happy birthday! [ˈhæpi] **Ich habe im April Geburtstag.** My birthday is in April. **Wann hast du Geburtstag?** When's your birthday?
Gedankenkarte mind map [ˈmaɪnd mæp]
Gedicht poem [ˈpəʊɪm]
geduldig patient [ˈpeɪʃnt]

gefährlich dangerous [ˈdeɪndʒərəs]
Gefühl feeling [ˈfiːlɪŋ]
Gegend: ländliche Gegend country [ˈkʌntri] **Gegend** area [ˈeəriə]
Gegenteil opposite [ˈɒpəzɪt]
geheim secret [ˈsiːkrət]
Geheimnis secret [ˈsiːkrət]
gehen go [gəʊ] **ins Bett gehen** go to bed [bed] **nach Hause gehen** go home [həʊm] **Wie geht's? / Wie geht es dir/euch/Ihnen?** How are you? [haʊ] **(zu Fuß) gehen** walk [wɔːk]
Geist ghost [gəʊst]
gelangen, (hin)kommen (nach) get to [get tu]
gelangweilt bored [bɔːd]
gelb yellow [ˈjeləʊ]
Geld money [ˈmʌni]
Geldautomat cash machine [ˈkæʃ məʃiːn]
Gelee jelly [ˈdʒeli]
gemein mean [miːn]
Gemüse vegetables *(pl)* [ˈvedʒtəblz]
gemütlich comfortable [ˈkʌmftəbl]
genießen enjoy [ɪnˈdʒɔɪ] **es genießen, etwas zu tun** enjoy doing sth.
genug enough [ɪˈnʌf]
Geografie geography [dʒiˈɒgrəfi]
Geräusch noise [nɔɪz]
gerade (eben) just [dʒʌst]
gerade; (Haare glatt) straight [streɪt]
geradeaus (weiter) straight on [streɪt ɒn]
Gericht *(Mahlzeit)* dish [dɪʃ]
gern: ich hätte gern ... I'd (= I would like ... [laɪk] **Ich hätte liebend gern ... / Ich möchte liebend gern ...** I'd (= I would) love ... [lʌv] **Ich würde mich (liebend) gerne mit ... treffen.** I'd (= I would) like/love to meet ...
Geruch smell [smel]
Geschäft shop [ʃɒp]
Geschäft business [ˈbɪznəs]
Geschäftsfrau business woman [ˈbɪznəs wʊmən]
geschehen: (jm.) geschehen happen (to sb.) [ˈhæpən] **Bitte, gern geschehen.** You're welcome. [ˈwelkʌm]
Geschenk present [ˈpreznt]; gift [gɪft]
Geschichte *(Erzählung)* story [ˈstɔːri]; **vergangene Zeiten** history [ˈhɪstri] **so/solch eine Geschichte** a story like this [laɪk]
Geschirrspülmaschine dishwasher [ˈdɪʃwɒʃə]
Gesicht face [feɪs]
Gespenst ghost [gəʊst]
Gespräch talk [tɔːk]
gesellig sociable [ˈsəʊʃəbl]
Gestaltung design [dɪˈzaɪn]
Gestank smell [smel]
gestern yesterday [ˈjestədeɪ]
gesund healthy [ˈhelθi]
Gesundheit health [helθ]
Getränk drink [drɪŋk]
Gewerbegebiet estate [ɪˈsteɪt]
Gewinn prize [praɪz]
gewinnen win [wɪn]
Gewinner/in winner [ˈwɪnə]
als Gewinner/in as the winner
Gewürz spice [spaɪs]
Gitarre guitar [gɪˈtɑː]
Glas(gefäß) jar [dʒɑː]
Glasur icing [ˈaɪsɪŋ]
glauben think [θɪŋk] **Ich glaube, ...** I think ...
gleich the same [seɪm]
global, weltweit global [ˈgləʊbl]
Glück: Glücks- lucky [ˈlʌki] **Glück haben** be lucky
Glück, Zufriedenheit happiness [ˈhæpinəs]
glücklich happy [ˈhæpi]; lucky [ˈlʌki]
glücklicherweise luckily [ˈlʌkɪli]
Glückszahl lucky number [lʌki ˈnʌmbə]
Gold gold [gəʊld]
goldfarben gold [gəʊld]
Gott god [gɒd]
graben dig [dɪg]
Gramm gram (g) [græm]
Grad degree [dɪˈgriː]
Grad, Stufe, Niveau level [ˈlevl]
grau grey [greɪ]
Grillen barbecue [ˈbɑːbɪkjuː]
Grillfest barbecue [ˈbɑːbɪkjuː]
groß big [bɪg] **der/die/das größte, am größten** biggest **groß** *(Person)*, **hoch** *(Gebäude)* tall [tɔːl]
großartig amazing [əˈmeɪzɪŋ]; great [greɪt]
Größe size [saɪz]
Großbritannien (Great) Britain [ˈbrɪtn]
Großeltern grandparents *(pl)* [ˈgrænpeərənts]
Großstadt city [ˈsɪti]
großzügig generous [ˈdʒenərəs]
grün green [griːn] **grün/umweltfreundlich werden** go green [gəʊ]
Gruppe group [gruːp]
gruselig scary [ˈskeəri]
gut good [gʊd]; *(Adv.)* well [wel] **Es geht mir gut.** I'm OK. [əʊˈkeɪ] **etwas gut können; gut in etwas sein** be good at sth. / at doing sth. **Gut gemacht.** Well done. [dʌn] **gut umgehen können mit ...** be good with ... **Mir geht es gut.** I'm fine. [faɪn] **so gut** so good [səʊ] **Gute Besserung! / Werde bald gesund!** Get better/well soon!

H

Haar, Haare hair [heə]
haben have [hæv] **er/sie/es hat** he/she/it has [hæz], [həz]
Hähnchen chicken [ˈtʃɪkɪn]
halb sieben half past six [hɑːf]
Halle hall [hɔːl]
Hallo. Hello. [həˈləʊ]; Hi. [haɪ] **Hallo allerseits!** Hello everybody! [ˈevribɒdi]
Hals neck [nek]
halten stop [stɒp]
halten: behalten keep [kiːp]
Hamburger *(Frikadelle)* burger [ˈbɜːgə]
Hamster hamster [ˈhæmstə]
Hand hand [hænd] **Hand/Hände hochstrecken** put your hand/hands up [pʊt]
Handschuh glove [glʌv]
Handy phone [fəʊn]
hart hard [hɑːd]
Hass hate [heɪt]
hassen hate [heɪt]
Haupt- main [meɪn]
Hauptgericht main course [ˈkɔːs]; main dish [dɪʃ]
Hauptstadt capital (city) [ˈkæpɪtl]
Haus house [haʊs]
nach Hause gehen go home [həʊm]
im Haus inside the house [ɪnˈsaɪd]
wieder zu Hause back at home [bæk]
zu Hause at home
Hausaufgabe(n) homework [ˈhəʊmwɜːk] **Hausaufgaben machen** do your homework **Was haben wir als Hausaufgabe(n) auf?** What's for homework? [wɒts fɔː]
Hausmüll rubbish [ˈrʌbɪʃ]
Hausschuhe slippers [slɪpə]
Haustier pet [pet]
heben lift [lɪft]
Heftseite page (p.) [peɪdʒ]
Heim home [həʊm]
heiraten marry [ˈmæri]
heiß hot [hɒt] **heiße (Trink-)-Schokolade** hot chocolate [ˈtʃɒklət]
heißen: Wie heißt du? What's your name? [wɒts jɔː ˈneɪm]
hektisch busy [ˈbɪzi]
Held/in hero [ˈhɪərəʊ]
helfen help [help]
Helm helmet [ˈhelmɪt]
heraus, hinaus out [aʊt]
herausfinden find out (about) [ˌfaɪnd ˈaʊt] **etwas herausfinden** work sth. out [wɜːk]
Herausforderung challenge [ˈtʃælɪndʒ]
Herbst autumn [ˈɔːtəm]
Herr Lee Mr Lee [ˈmɪstə]
herrschen (über) rule [ruːl]
herstellen make [meɪk]
herunter down [daʊn]
hervorheben highlight [ˈhaɪlaɪt]
Herzog duke [djuːk]
heute today [təˈdeɪ] **heute Morgen/Abend** this morning/evening [ðɪs] **heute Nacht/Abend** tonight [təˈnaɪt]
hier here [hɪə] **Hier, bitte.** Here you are. **hier herüber; hier drüben** over here [ˈəʊvə]
hierher here [hɪə]
Highlight (Höhepunkt) highlight [ˈhaɪlaɪt]
Hilfe help [help]
hilfreich helpful [ˈhelpfl]; useful [ˈjuːsfl]
hilfsbereit helpful [ˈhelpfl]
hinauf up [ʌp]
hinaus out [aʊt]
hinsetzen: sich hinsetzen sit down [sɪt ˈdaʊn]
hinter behind [bɪˈhaɪnd]

hinunter down [daʊn] **hinunter von** off [ɒf]
hinzufügen add [æd]
Hobby hobby [ˈhɒbi]
hoch up [ʌp]; high [haɪ]
Hochgenuss treat [ˈtriːt]
Hochzeit wedding [ˈwedɪŋ]
Hockey hockey [ˈhɒki]
hoffen hope [həʊp]
höflich polite [pəˈlaɪt]
holen: (sich etwas) holen get sth. [get]
Honig honey [ˈhʌni]
hören hear [hɪə]
Horoskop horoscope [ˈhɒrəskəʊp]
Hose trousers *(pl)* [ˈtraʊzəz]
Hotdog *(heißes Würstchen in einem Brötchen)* hot dog [ˈhɒt dɒg]
Hügel hill [hɪl]
Huhn chicken [ˈtʃɪkɪn]
Hund dog [dɒg]
Hunger: Ich habe Hunger. I'm hungry. [ˈhʌŋgri]
hungrig hungry [ˈhʌŋgri]
Husten cough [kɒf]
Hut hat [hæt]

I

ich I [aɪ] **Ich bin** I'm (= I am) [æm]
Ich bin's. It's me. **Ich nicht!**
(= Ich bin/war/habe/... es/das nicht!) Not me! [nɒt]
Idee idea [aɪˈdɪə]
ihm, ihn him [hɪm]
Ihnen *(höfliche Anrede)* you [juː]
ihnen them [ðem], [ðəm]
ihr *(Plural von „du")* you [juː]
ihr seid you're (= you are) [jɔː]
Ihr/e ... *(besitzanzeigend zur höflichen Anrede „Sie")* your [jɔː], [jə]
ihr/e ... *(vor Nomen; besitzanzeigend)*
1. *(zu „she")* her ... [hɜː], [hə]
2. *(zu „it")* its ... [ɪts]
3. *(zu „they")* their ... [ðeə]
immer always [ˈɔːlweɪz]
immer noch still [stɪl]
in at [æt], [ət]; in [ɪn]
in den Urlaub on holiday [ˈhɒlədeɪ]
in der Nähe von near [nɪə]
in der Schule at school [skuːl]
in der Stadt in town [taʊn]
in die Stadt / ins Zimmer (hinein) into town / into the room [ˈɪntu], [ˈɪntə]
Indien India [ˈɪndiə]
Informatik computing [kəmˈpjuːtɪŋ]
Information information [ɪnfəˈmeɪʃn]
informieren: sich informieren (über) find out (about) [faɪnd ˈaʊt]
innen; nach innen inside [ɪnˈsaɪd]
innerhalb (von) inside [ɪnˈsaɪd]
insbesondere especially [ɪˈspeʃəli]
Insekt insect [ˈɪnsekt]
intelligent smart [smɑːt]
interessant interesting [ˈɪntrəstɪŋ]
Internet internet [ˈɪntənet]
irgendjemand anybody [ˈenibɒdi]; anyone [ˈeniwʌn]
irgendwo(hin) somewhere [ˈsʌmweə]

J

Ja. Yes. [jes] **Na ja, ...** Well, ... [wel]
Jachthafen marina [məˈriːnə]
Jacke, Jackett jacket [ˈdʒækɪt]
Jahr year [jɪə] **Ich bin elf Jahre alt.** I'm eleven years old. [jɪəz]
Jahreszeit season [ˈsiːzn]
Jahrgang year [jɪə]
Januar January [ˈdʒænjuəri]
jede(r, s) every [ˈevri]
jede(r, s) einzelne each [iːtʃ]
jede(r,s) (beliebige), jegliche(r,s) any [ˈeni]
jeder everybody [ˈevribɒdi]
jemals ever [ˈevə]
jemand somebody [ˈsʌmbədi]; someone [ˈsʌmwʌn]
jene (dort) those [ðəʊz]
jetzt now [naʊ]
jeweils each [iːtʃ]
Joghurt yoghurt [ˈjɒgət]
jonglieren juggle [ˈdʒʌgl]
Jugend youth [juːθ]
Jugendliche kid [kɪd]; youth [juːθ]
Jugendzentrum youth centre [ˈjuːθ sentə]
Juli July [dʒuˈlaɪ]
Junge boy [bɔɪ] **Ich bin kein Junge.** I'm not a boy. [nɒt]
Juni June [dʒuːn]

K

Kaffee coffee [ˈkɒfi]
Kakao cocoa [ˈkəʊkəʊ]; hot chocolate [hɒt ˈtʃɒklət]
Kalender calendar [ˈkælɪndə]
kalt cold [kəʊld] **kalt werden** get cold [get]
Kälte cold [kəʊld]
Kamera camera [ˈkæmərə]
kämpfen (für) fight (for) [faɪt]
Kaninchen rabbit [ˈræbɪt]
Kanne *(Tee/Kaffee)* pot [pɒt]
Kantine canteen [kænˈtiːn]
Kappe cap [kæp]
Karaoke karaoke [kæriˈəʊki]
Karneval carnival [ˈkɑːnɪvl]
Karotte carrot [ˈkærət]
Karte card [kɑːd]
Karton carton [ˈkɑːtn]
Kartoffel potato, *(pl)* potatoes [pəˈteɪtəʊ]
Käse cheese [tʃiːz]
Kassenzettel receipt [rɪˈsiːt]
Kasten case [keɪs]
Katze cat [kæt]
kaufen buy [baɪ]; shop (for sth.) [ʃɒp]
Kebab kebab [kɪˈbæb]
Kegeln bowling [ˈbəʊlɪŋ]
kein/e no [nəʊ] **es gibt keine ...** there aren't any ... [ˈeni]
Keks biscuit [ˈbɪskɪt]
kennen know [nəʊ]
kennenlernen meet [miːt] **Freut mich, dich/euch/Sie kennenzulernen.** Nice to meet you. [naɪs]
Kerker dungeon [ˈdʌndʒən]
Kerze candle [ˈkændl]

Kette chain [tʃeɪn]
Kilometer kilometre (km) [ˈkɪləmiːtə]
Kind kid [kɪd]; child [tʃaɪld]
Kino cinema [ˈsɪnəmə] **im Kino** at the cinema
Kiosk kiosk [ˈkiːɒsk]
Kissen cushion [ˈkʊʃn]
kitschig cheesy [ˈtʃiːzɪ]
klar clear [klɪə]
Klasse class [klɑːs]
Klassenarbeit test [test]
Klassenlehrer/in class teacher [ˈklɑːs tiːtʃə]
Klassenzimmer classroom [ˈklɑːsruːm]
klassisch classical [ˈklæsɪkl]
Kleber glue [gluː]
Klebestift glue stick [ˈgluː stɪk]
Klebstoff glue [gluː]
Kleid dress [dres]
Kleiderschrank wardrobe [ˈwɔːdrəʊb]
Kleidertausch(party) clothes swap [ˈkləʊðz swɒp]
Kleidung clothes *(pl)* [kləʊðz]
Kleidungsstücke clothes *(pl)* [kləʊðz]
klein little [ˈlɪtl]; *(Person; Körpergröße)* short [ʃɔːt]; small [smɔːl]
kleine Mahlzeit snack [snæk]
klettern (auf) climb [klaɪm]
klicken (auf) click (on) [klɪk]
klingen *(sich gut / ... anhören)* sound [saʊnd]
klopfen knock [nɒk]
Klub club [klʌb]
klug clever [ˈklevə]
Knöchel ankle [ˈæŋkl]
Koch, Köchin cook [kʊk]
Kochbuch recipe book [ˈresəpi]
kochen cook [kʊk]; *(in Wasser)* boil [bɔɪl]
Kochen cooking [ˈkʊkɪŋ]
Kochrezept recipe [ˈresəpi]
komisch weird [wɪəd]
Komma *(Dezimalzeichen)* point [pɔɪnt]
1,6 (eins Komma sechs) 1.6 (one point six)
kommen come [kʌm] **Wo kommst du her?** Where are you from?
können can [kæn], [kən] **etwas gut können** be good at sth. / at doing sth. [æt], [ət] **gut umgehen können mit ...** be good at ... [gʊd] **Ich kann ... sehen.** I can see ... **Ich kann ... nicht sehen.** I can't (= cannot) see ... [kɑːnt]
Könnte ich ... ? Could I ...? [kəd]
Konsole console [kənˈsəʊl]
Kontakt contact [ˈkɒntækt]
kontaktfreudig sociable [ˈsəʊʃəbl]
Kontrolle check [tʃek]
kontrollieren check [tʃek]
Konzert concert [ˈkɒnsət]
Kopf head [hed] **Dreh/Stell es auf den Kopf.** Turn it upside down. [ʌpsaɪd ˈdaʊn]
Kopfhörer headphones *(pl)* [ˈhedfəʊnz]
Kopfschmerzen haben have a headache [ˈhedeɪk]
Körper body [ˈbɒdi]
korrekt correct [kəˈrekt]
Korridor corridor [ˈkɒrɪdɔː]

Kosten cost [kɒst]
kosten cost [kɒst]
kostenlos free [fri:]
köstlich delicious [dɪˈlɪʃəs]
Kostüm costume [ˈkɒstju:m]; *(Damenkostüm)* suit [su:t]
Kraft power [ˈpaʊə]; strength [streŋθ]
krank ill [ɪl]
Krankenhaus hospital [ˈhɒspɪtl]
Krankenpfleger, Krankenpflegerin nurse [nɜ:s]
Krankenwagen ambulance [ˈæmbjələns]
Krankheit illness [ˈɪlnəs]; sickness [ˈsɪknəs]
Krawatte tie [taɪ]
kreativ creative [kriˈeɪtɪv]
Kreis circle [ˈsɜ:kl]
Krieg war [wɔ:]
Küche kitchen [ˈkɪtʃɪn]
Kuchen cake [keɪk]
Kugelschreiber pen [pen]
Kultur culture [ˈkʌltʃə]
kümmern: sich kümmern um look after [lʊk]
Kunde, Kundin customer [ˈkʌstəmə]
Kunst art [ɑ:t] **darstellende Kunst** drama [ˈdrɑ:mə]
Künstler, Künstlerin artist [ˈɑ:tɪst]
Kunsthandwerk crafts *(pl)* [krɑ:fts]
Kunststoff plastic [ˈplæstɪk]
Kunststück trick [trɪk]
Kurs class [klɑ:s]; course [kɔ:s]
kurz short [ʃɔ:t] **kuze Hose, Shorts** shorts [ʃɔ:ts]

L

Lächeln smile [smaɪl]
lächeln smile [smaɪl] **lachen (über)** laugh (at) [lɑ:f]
Laden shop [ʃɒp]
Lamm(fleisch) lamb [læm]
Lampe lamp [læmp]; light [laɪt]
Land country [ˈkʌntri] **auf dem Land** in the country
Land *(Grund und Boden)* land [lænd]
Landkarte map [mæp]
lang(e) long [lɒŋ] **30 Sekunden lang** for 30 seconds [fɔ:] **(für) eine lange Zeit** (for) a long time [taɪm] **lange arbeiten, lange Arbeitstage haben** work long days [wɜ:k] **lange schlafen** sleep late [sli:p leɪt]
langsam slow [sləʊ] **zu langsam** too slow [tu:]
langweilig boring [ˈbɔ:rɪŋ]
Lärm noise [nɔɪz]
lassen: lass(t) uns let's (= let us) [lets]
lassen, verlassen, zurücklassen leave [li:v]
Laufen *(Sport)* running [ˈrʌnɪŋ]
laut loud [laʊd] **lauter sprechen** speak more loudly [mɔ:]
leben live [lɪv]
Leben life [laɪf]
Lebensmittel food [fu:d]
lecker delicious [dɪˈlɪʃəs]
leeren empty [ˈempti]
legen: (etwas wohin) legen put [pʊt]
lehren teach [ti:tʃ]
Lehrer/in teacher [ˈti:tʃə]
leicht easy [ˈi:zi]
leidtun: Er tut mir leid. I'm / I feel sorry for him. [ˈsɒri]
leihen: (aus)leihen borrow [bɒrəʊ]
Leinwand screen [skri:n]
leise quiet [ˈkwaɪət]
lernen learn [lɜ:n]; study [ˈstʌdi]
lesen read [ri:d]
Leser/in reader [ˈri:də]
letzte(r,s); als letztes last [lɑ:st] **(der/die/das) Letzte** the last one [lɑ:st wʌn]
Leute people *(pl)* [ˈpi:pl]; *(Anrede)* guys *(pl)* [gaɪz]
Licht light [laɪt]
Liebe love [lʌv]
Liebe/r ... Dear ... [dɪə]
lieben love [lʌv] **Ich hätte liebend gern ... / Ich möchte liebend gern ...** I'd (= I would) love ... **Ich würde mich liebend gerne mit ... treffen.** I'd (= I would) love to meet ... [mi:t]
Liebling favourite [ˈfeɪvərɪt]; love [lʌv]
Lieblings- favourite [ˈfeɪvərɪt]
Lied song [sɒŋ]
Liedtext lyrics [ˈlɪrɪks]
liegen lie [laɪ]
lila purple [ˈpɜ:pl]
Limonade lemonade [leməˈneɪd]
Lineal ruler [ˈru:lə]
links, nach links left [left]
Liste file [faɪl]; list [lɪst]
listen list [lɪst]
lockig curly [ˈkɜ:li]
Löffel spoon [spu:n]
lösen *(Rätsel, Problem)* solve [sɒlv]
Löwe lion [ˈlaɪən]
lüften *(Geheimnis)* solve [sɒlv]
lustig (be) funny [ˈfʌni] **Was ist lustig an ...?** What's funny about ...?

M

machen do [du:]; make [meɪk]
Macht power [ˈpaʊə]
Mädchen girl [gɜ:l]
magisch magical [ˈmædʒɪkl]
Mahlzeit meal [mi:l] **kleine Mahlzeit** snack [snæk] **warme Mahlzeit** hot meal [hɒt]
Mai May [meɪ]
Mal time [taɪm]
malen paint [peɪnt]
Mama mum [mʌm]
Manager/in manager [ˈmænɪdʒə]
manchmal sometimes [ˈsʌmtaɪmz]
markieren highlight [ˈhaɪlaɪt]
Markt market [ˈmɑ:kɪt]
März March [mɑ:tʃ]
Maske mask [mɑ:sk]
Mathe(matik) maths [mæθs]
Mauer wall [wɔ:l]
Maus mouse, *(pl)* mice [maʊs], [maɪs]
Mechaniker, Mechanikerin mechanic [mɪˈkænɪk]
Meer sea [si:] **am Meer** by the sea
Mehl flour [ˈflaʊə]
mehr more [mɔ:] **mehr als 50** over 50 [ˈəʊvə]
Meile *(ca. 1,6 km)* mile [maɪl] **mit 30 Meilen pro Stunde** at 30 miles per hour [pər ˈaʊə] **Meilen pro Stunde** miles per hour (mph)
mein/e my [maɪ]
meinen *(sagen wollen)* mean [mi:n]; *(denken, glauben)* think [θɪŋk] **Ich meine, ...** I think ...
meiste(r, s): die meisten Schulen most schools [məʊst]
meistens usually [ˈju:ʒuəli]
Melone melon [ˈmelən]
Mensa canteen [kænˈti:n]
Menschen people *(pl)* [ˈpi:pl]
Messer knife, *(pl)* knives [naɪf], [naɪvz]
Meinung opinion [əˈpɪnjən] **meiner Meinung nach** in my opinion
Metall, aus Metall metal [ˈmetl]
Meter metre [ˈmi:tə]
mich me [mi:]
Milch milk [mɪlk]
Milliliter millilitre (ml) [ˈmɪlili:tə]
Mindmap mind map [ˈmaɪnd mæp]
Mini- mini [ˈmɪni]
Minidrohne mini-drone [mɪnɪ ˈdrəʊn]
Minute minute [ˈmɪnɪt]
mir me [mi:]
mischen mix [mɪks]
Mischung mixture [ˈmɪkstʃə]
mit with [wɪð]
mitbringen bring [brɪŋ]
Mitglied member [ˈmembə]
mitkommen come [kʌm]
Mitleid: Mitleid haben mit jm. be/feel sorry for sb. [ˈsɒri]
mitnehmen take [teɪk]
Mittagessen lunch [lʌntʃ] **Was gibt es zum Mittagessen?** What's for lunch?
Mittagszeit lunchtime [ˈlʌntʃtaɪm] **zur Mittagszeit** at lunchtime
Mitte centre [ˈsentə]; middle [ˈmɪdl]
Mitteilung message [ˈmesɪdʒ]
Mittwoch Wednesday [ˈwenzdeɪ], [ˈwenzdi]
mobben bully [ˈbʊli]
Mobber/in bully [ˈbʊli]
möchten: Ich möchte ... I'd (= I would) like ... [laɪk]
Moderator, Moderatorin presenter [prɪˈzentə]
modern modern [ˈmɒdn]
mögen like [laɪk] **sehr mögen** love [lʌv]
Möhre carrot [ˈkærət]
Moment moment [ˈməʊmənt] **in diesem Moment** at the moment
Monat month [mʌnθ]
Mond moon [mu:n]
Montag Monday [ˈmʌndeɪ], [ˈmʌndi] **an jedem Montag** on Mondays
montags on Mondays [ˈmʌndeɪ], [ˈmʌndi]
Morgen morning [ˈmɔ:nɪŋ] **am Morgen** in the morning
morgen tomorrow [təˈmɒrəʊ]

morgens in the morning [ˈmɔːnɪŋ]
4 Uhr (früh) morgens 4 a.m. [eɪˈem]
Moschee mosque [mɒsk]
Möwe seagull [ˈsiːgʌl]
müde tired [ˈtaɪəd]
multikulturell multicultural [mʌltiˈkʌltʃərəl]
Münze coin [kɔɪn]
Museum museum [mjuˈziːəm]
Musik music [ˈmjuːzɪk]
musikalisch musical [ˈmjuːzɪkl]
Musiker, Musikerin musician [mjuˈzɪʃn]
Musikgruppe band [bænd]
Muslim, Muslima; muslimisch muslim [ˈmʊzlɪm]
müssen must [mʌst] **etwas tun müssen** need to do sth. [niːd] **Ich muss Schluss machen.** *(am Telefon / Briefschluss)* I must go.
Müll rubbish [ˈrʌbɪʃ] **Tüten/Säcke voller Müll** bags of rubbish [bægz]
Mülleimer bin [bɪn]
Mut bravery [ˈbreɪvəri]
mutig brave [breɪv]
Mutprobe dare [deə]
Mutter mother [ˈmʌðə]
Mutti mum [mʌm]
Mütze cap [kæp]; hat [hæt]

N

na: Na ja, ... Well, ... [wel]
nach
1. *(örtlich)* to [tu], [tə] **nach draußen** outside [aʊtˈsaɪd] **nach (dr)innen** inside [ɪnˈsaɪd]
2. *(zeitlich)* after [ˈɑːftə] **nach der Schule** after school
Nachbar/in neighbour [ˈneɪbə]
nachdem: nachdem (du liest) after you read [ˈɑːftə]
Nachmittag afternoon [ɑːftəˈnuːn]
am Nachmittag in the afternoon
nachmittags in the afternoon [ɑːftəˈnuːn] **4 Uhr nachmittags (16 Uhr)** 4 p.m. [piːˈem]
Nachname family name [ˈfæməli neɪm]
Nachricht message [ˈmesɪdʒ]
Nachrichten news [njuːz]
nachschauen look sth. up [lʊk ˈʌp]
nachschlagen: etwas nachschlagen look sth. up [lʊk ˈʌp]
nächste(r, s) next [nekst]
Als nächstes ... Next ...
Nacht night [naɪt]
Nachtisch dessert [dɪˈzɜːt]
zum/als Nachtisch for dessert
Nacken neck [nek]
nahe (bei) near [nɪə]
Nähe: in der Nähe von near [nɪə]
Name name [neɪm]
Nase nose [nəʊz]
natürlich of course [əv ˈkɔːs]
Naturwissenschaft science [ˈsaɪəns]
Naturwissenschaftler/in scientist [ˈsaɪəntɪst]
neben next to [ˈnekst tə]
nehmen, in Anspruch nehmen take [teɪk]
nein no [nəʊ]
nennen call [kɔːl]
nett friendly [ˈfrendli]; kind [kaɪnd]; nice [naɪs]
neu new [njuː]
neugierig (auf) curious (about) [ˈkjʊəriəs]
neun nine [naɪn]
neunzehn nineteen [naɪnˈtiːn]
neunzig ninety [ˈnaɪnti]
nicht not [nɒt]
nicht mehr not (...) anymore [nɒt ˈenimɔː]
nichts nothing [ˈnʌθɪŋ]
nie never [ˈnevə]
niedlich cute [kjuːt]
niemals never [ˈnevə]
niemand no one [ˈnəʊ wʌn]; nobody [ˈnəʊbədi] **niemand anders, niemand sonst** no one else [ˈnəʊ wʌn els]
noch: (immer) noch still [stɪl] **noch drei** three more [mɔː] **noch ein/e** another [əˈnʌðə] **noch einmal** again [əˈgen] **noch nicht** not ... yet [nɒt jet]
Norden north [nɔːθ]
nördlich; Nord- north [nɔːθ]
Nordosten; nordöstlich north-east [nɔːθˈiːst]
Nordwesten; nordwestlich northwest [nɔːθˈwest]
normal normal [ˈnɔːml]
normalerweise usually [ˈjuːʒuəli]
Note: Schulnote mark [mɑːk]
Notiz note [nəʊt]
Notizen: (sich) Notizen machen *(zur Vorbereitung)* make notes
(sich) Notizen machen *(beim Lesen oder Zuhören)* take notes
November November [nəʊˈvembə]
Nudeln noodles *(pl)* [nuːdlz]
Null *(im gesprochenen Englisch)* oh [əʊ]
Nummer number [ˈnʌmbə]
nun now [naʊ] **Nun, ...** Well, ... [wel]
nur just [dʒʌst]; only [ˈəʊnli] **Es sind nur wir.** It's just us.
Nutzer/in user [ˈjuːzə]
nützlich helpful [ˈhelpfl]; useful [ˈjuːsfl]

O

ob if [ɪf]
oben at the top (of) [tɒp]
Obergeschoss top floor [tɒp ˈflɔː]
oberhalb (von) above [əˈbʌv]
Objekt *(Gegenstand)* object [ˈɒbdʒɪkt]
Obst fruit [fruːt]
oder or [ɔː]
öffnen open [ˈəʊpən]
oft often [ˈɒfn], [ˈɒftən]
Ohr ear [ɪə]
Oktober October [ɒkˈtəʊbə]
Öl oil [ɔɪl]
Oma grandma [ˈgrænmɑː]
Onkel uncle [ˈʌŋkl]
online; Online- online [ˌɒnˈlaɪn]
Opa grandpa [ˈgrænpɑː]
optisch visual [ˈvɪʒuəl]
orange orange [ˈɒrɪndʒ]
Orange orange [ˈɒrɪndʒ]
ordentlich tidy [ˈtaɪdi]
Ordner file [faɪl]
organisieren organize [ˈɔːgənaɪz]
Ort place [pleɪs]

P

paar: ein paar some [sʌm], [səm]
Päckchen packet [ˈpækɪt]
Packung carton [ˈkɑːtn]; packet [ˈpækɪt]
Palast palace [ˈpæləs]
Papa dad [dæd]
Papagei parrot [ˈpærət]
Papier paper [ˈpeɪpə] **Stück Papier** piece of paper [piːs]
Paprika pepper [ˈpepə]
Park park [pɑːk]
Parkour *(akrobatischer Hindernislauf in der Stadt)* parkour [pɑːˈkʊə]
Partner/in partner [ˈpɑːtnə]
Party party [ˈpɑːti]
passieren happen (to sb.) [ˈhæpən]
passiv passive [ˈpæsɪv]
Pasta *(italienische Bezeichnung für Teigwaren)* pasta [ˈpæstə]
Pause break [breɪk]; rest [rest]
Pause machen take a rest [teɪk]
peinlich embarrassing [ɪmˈbærəsɪŋ]
Penny *(kleinste britische Münze)* penny (p), *(pl)* pence [ˈpeni], [pens]
Peperoni pepper [ˈpepə]
perfekt perfect [ˈpɜːfɪkt]
Person person [ˈpɜːsn]
Persönlichkeit personality [pɜːsəˈnæləti]
Pfannkuchen pancake [ˈpænkeɪk]
Pfeffer pepper [ˈpepə]
Pferd horse [hɔːs]
pflücken; (aus)wählen pick [pɪk]
Pfund *(britische Währung)* pound (£) [paʊnd]
Picknick picnic [ˈpɪknɪk] **ein Picknick machen** have a picnic [hæv]
Pier pier [pɪə]
Plan plan [plæn]
planen plan [plæn] **planen, etwas zu tun** plan to do sth. [duː]
Planet planet [ˈplænɪt]
Plastik plastic [ˈplæstɪk]
Platz place [pleɪs]; *(Sitzplatz)* seat [siːt]; space [speɪs]
Plätzchen biscuit [ˈbɪskɪt]
Playlist playlist [ˈpleɪlɪst]
plötzlich suddenly [ˈsʌdənli]
Pokal trophy [ˈtrəʊfi]
Polizei police [pəˈliːs]
Polizeibeamter, Polizeibeamtin police officer [pəˈliːs ɒfɪsə]
Pommes frites chips *(pl)* [tʃɪps] **Fisch mit Pommes frites** fish and chips
Pool(billiard) pool [puːl]
Popcorn popcorn [ˈpɒpkɔːn]
Popstar star [stɑː]
positiv positive [ˈpɒzətɪv]

Post *(Teil eines Blogs)* post [pəʊst]
posten *(im Internet veröffentlichen)* post [pəʊst]
Poster poster ['pəʊstə]
Postkarte postcard ['pəʊstkɑːd]
praktisch practical ['præktɪkl]
Praline chocolate ['tʃɒklət]
Präsentation presentation [prezn'teɪʃn]
präsentieren: (jm.) etwas präsentieren present sth. (to sb.) [prɪ'zent]
Preis *(Kosten)* cost [kɒst]; *(Gewinn)* prize [praɪz] **(Kauf-)Preis** price [praɪs]
Preisverleihung prize ceremony ['praɪz serəməni]
pro per [pɜː], [pə] **Meilen pro Stunde** miles per hour (mph) [maɪlz] **pro Stunde** per hour ['aʊə]
probieren taste [teɪst]; *(ausprobieren)* try [traɪ]
Problem problem ['prɒbləm] **Was/Wo ist das Problem?** What's wrong?
professionell, Profi- professional [prə'feʃənl]
Programmieren coding ['kəʊdɪŋ]
programmieren *(Computer)* code [kəʊd]
Programmierer, Programmiererin programmer ['prəʊgræmə]
Projekt project ['prɒdʒekt]
Prozent per cent (%) [pə 'sent]
prüfen check [tʃek]
Prüfung check [tʃek]
Publikum audience ['ɔːdiəns]
Puderzucker icing sugar ['aɪsɪŋ ʃʊgə]
Pulver powder ['paʊdə]
Punkt point [pɔɪnt]
Punktestand score [skɔː]
pünktlich on time [ɒn taɪm]
pusten blow [bləʊ]
putzen clean [kliːn] **(sich) die/deine Zähne putzen** brush your teeth [brʌʃ]
Puzzle jigsaw (puzzle) ['dʒɪgsɔː]

Q

Quiz quiz, *(pl)* quizzes [kwɪz], ['kwɪzɪz] **ein Quiz machen** do a quiz [duː]

R

Rad: Rad fahren cycle ['saɪkl]
Radfahren cycling ['saɪklɪŋ]
Radiergummi rubber ['rʌbə]
Ratespiel quiz, *(pl)* quizzes [kwɪz]
probierentaste [teɪst]; (ausprobieren) try [traɪ], ['kwɪzɪz] **ein Ratespiel machen** do a quiz [duː]
Rätsel puzzle ['pʌzl]
rauben steal [stiːl]
Raum *(Zimmer)* room [ruːm]; space [speɪs]
Recherche(n) research [rɪ'sɜːtʃ]
recherchieren (do) research [rɪ'sɜːtʃ]
Recht: Recht haben be right [raɪt]
rechteckig square [skweə]
rechts; nach rechts right [raɪt]
Rechtschreibung spelling ['spelɪŋ]
Rede talk [tɔːk]
reden (mit) talk (to) [tɔːk] **reden über** talk about [ə'baʊt]
Redewendung phrase [freɪz]
Referat presentation [prezn'teɪʃn] **ein Referat halten** give a presentation [gɪv]
Regal shelf, *(pl)* shelves [ʃelf], [ʃelvz]
Regel rule [ruːl]
Regen rain [reɪn]
Regenbogen rainbow ['reɪnbəʊ]
regnen rain [reɪn]
regnerisch rainy ['reɪni]
Reihe line [laɪn]; turn [tɜːn] **Wann bin ich an der Reihe (etwas zu tun)?** When is (it) my turn (to do sth.)?
Reinigungskraft cleaner ['kliːnə]
Reis rice [raɪs]
Reise journey ['dʒɜːni]; tour [tʊə]
Reisen travel ['trævl]
reisen travel ['trævl]
reiten *(ein Pferd / auf einem Pferd)* ride a horse [raɪd]
reservieren book [bʊk]
Respekt respect [rɪ'spekt]
Restaurant restaurant ['restrɒnt]
retten save [seɪv]
Rezept recipe ['resəpi]
richtig right [raɪt]; true [truː]
riechen smell [smel]
Rindfleisch beef [biːf]
Ring ring [rɪŋ]
Roboter robot ['rəʊbɒt]
Roller scooter ['skuːtə]
Rollstuhl wheelchair ['wiːltʃeə]
romantisch romantic [rəʊ'mæntɪk]
rosa pink [pɪŋk]
Rückfahrkarte, Hin- und Rückfahrkarte return [rɪ'tɜːn]
Rucksack rucksack ['rʌksæk]
Ruf call [kɔːl]
Ruhe rest [rest]
ruhen rest [rest]
ruhig quiet ['kwaɪət]; calm [kɑːm]
rühren stir [stɜː]
rumhängen hang out [hæŋ aʊt]
rund round [raʊnd]
Rundfahrt (durch) tour (of) [tʊə]
Rundgang (durch) tour (of) [tʊə]

S

Saal hall [hɔːl]
Saft juice [dʒuːs]
sagen say [seɪ]; tell [tel]
Saison season ['siːzn]
Salat *(als Gericht oder Beilage)* salad ['sæləd]
Salz salt [sɔːlt]
sammeln collect [kə'lekt]
Sammlung collection [kə'lekʃn]
Samstag Saturday ['sætədeɪ], ['sætədi]
Sandwich sandwich ['sænwɪtʃ], ['sænwɪdʒ]
Sänger/in singer ['sɪŋə]
Satz sentence ['sentəns]
sauber clean [kliːn]
sauber machen clean (sth. up) [kliːn]
Saubermachen clean-up ['kliːn ʌp]
Säubern clean-up ['kliːn ʌp]
schade a shame [ʃeɪm]
Schaf sheep [ʃiːp]
Schal scarf [skɑːf]
Schale bowl [bəʊl]
Schande a shame [ʃeɪm]
scharf nachdenken think hard [θɪŋk hɑːd]
schauen look [lʊk]
Schauspiel drama ['drɑːmə]
Schauspieler/in actor ['æktə]
schauspielern act [ækt]
Scheinwerfer spotlight ['spɒtlaɪt]
Scherz joke [dʒəʊk]
scheu shy [ʃaɪ]
schick smart [smɑːt]
schicken send [send]
Schinken ham [hæm]
Schirmmütze cap [kæp]
Schlaf sleep [sliːp]
schlafen be asleep [ə'sliːp]; sleep [sliːp]
Schlafzimmer bedroom ['bedruːm]
schlagen hit [hɪt]
Schlagwort keyword ['kiːwɜːd]
Schlange snake [sneɪk]
schlau clever ['klevə]
schlecht bad [bæd] **der/die/das schlechteste, schlimmste; am schlechtesten, am schlimmsten** worst [wɜːst] **schlecht riechen** smell [smel]
schlechter worse [wɜːs]
schließen close [kləʊz]
schließlich in the end [end]
schlimm bad [bæd] **schlimmer** worse [wɜːs]
Schlittschuhbahn ice rink ['aɪs rɪŋk]
Schloss palace ['pæləs]
Schluss end [end] **Ich muss Schluss machen.** *(am Telefon / Briefschluss)* I must go. [mʌst gəʊ] **zum Schluss** in the end
Schlüssel; Schlüssel- key [kiː]
schmecken taste [teɪst]
schmücken decorate ['dekəreɪt]
schmutzig dirty ['dɜːti]
Schnee snow [snəʊ]
schneebedeckt snowy ['snəʊi]
schneien snow [snəʊ]
schockiert shocked [ʃɒkt]
Schokolade chocolate ['tʃɒklət] **heiße (Trink-)Schokolade** hot chocolate [hɒt]
schon already [ɔːl'redi] **... schon ...?** ... yet [jet]
schön nice [naɪs]
Schönheit beauty ['bjuːti]
schrecklich horrible ['hɒrəbl] **schrecklich** terrible ['terəbl]
schreiben write [raɪt]
Schreibtisch desk [desk]
Schreibweise spelling ['spelɪŋ]
schreien scream [skriːm]
Schritt step [step]
schüchtern shy [ʃaɪ]

Schuh shoe [ʃuː]
Schule school [skuːl] **Hast du nach der Schule Zeit?** Are you free after school? **in der Schule** at school **nach der Schule** after school **weiterführende Schule** secondary school [ˈsekəndri]
Schüler/in student [ˈstjuːdnt]
Schulfach subject [ˈsʌbdʒɪkt]
Schulheft exercise book [ˈeksəsaɪz bʊk]
Schulmensa canteen [kænˈtiːn]
Schulsport PE (= physical education) [piːˈiː], [fɪzɪkl edʒuˈkeɪʃn]
Schulsprecher/in head student [hed ˈstjuːdnt]
Schuluniform school uniform [skuːl ˈjuːnɪfɔːm]
Schulversammlung assembly [əˈsembli]
Schüssel bowl [bəʊl]
schwarz black [blæk]
Schweinefleisch pork [pɔːk]
schwer difficult [ˈdɪfɪkəlt]; hard [hɑːd]
Schwester sister [ˈsɪstə]
schwierig difficult [ˈdɪfɪkəlt]; hard [hɑːd]
Schwierigkeiten trouble [ˈtrʌbl] **in Schwierigkeiten sein** be in trouble
Schwimmen swimming [ˈswɪmɪŋ]
schwimmen swim [swɪm]
Schwimmer/in swimmer [ˈswɪmə]
Sciencefiction science fiction [saɪəns ˈfɪkʃn]
sechs six [sɪks]
sechzehn sixteen [sɪksˈtiːn]
sechzig sixty [ˈsɪksti]
See *(Meer)* sea [siː] **an der See** by the sea [baɪ]
Seebrücke pier [pɪə]
sehen look [lʊk]; see [siː]
sehr lot [lɒt]; much [mʌtʃ]; very [ˈveri]
Seilrutsche zip wire [ˈzɪp waɪə]
sein be [biː] **bist, sind, seid** are [ɑː] **(er/sie/es) ist** is [ɪz]
sein/e its [ɪts]
Seite page (p.) [peɪdʒ]; *(z. B. Straßenseite)* side [saɪd]
seit Stunden for hours [fɔː ˈaʊəs]
Sekunde second [ˈsekənd] **für 30 Sekunden** for 30 seconds [fɔː]
selbst even [ˈiːvn]
selbstverständlich of course [əv ˈkɔːs]
selten *(Adj.)* rare [reə]; *(Adv.)* rarely [ˈreəli]
seltsam funny [ˈfʌni]; weird [wɪəd]; strange [streɪndʒ]
senden send [send]
September September [sepˈtembə]
shoppen shop (for sth.) [ʃɒp]
Show show [ʃəʊ]
sicher *(gefahrlos)* safe [seɪf]; *(ohne Zweifel)* sure [ʃʊə], [ʃɔː]; *(selbstsicher)* confident [ˈkɒnfɪdənt]
sichern save [seɪv]
Sie *(höfliche Anrede)* you [juː] **Sie sind** you're (= you are)
sie
1. *(weibliche Person)* her [hɜː], [hə]; she [ʃiː] **sie ist** she's (= she is)
2. *(bei Dingen und Tieren)* it [ɪt]
3. *(Plural)* them [ðem], [ðəm]; they [ðeɪ] **sie sind** they're (= they are) **sie sind nicht** they aren't
sieben seven [ˈsevn]
siebzehn seventeen [sevnˈtiːn]
siebzig seventy [ˈsevnti]
sieden boil [bɔɪl]
Sieger/in winner [ˈwɪnə]
Silber silver [ˈsɪlvə]
silberfarben silver [ˈsɪlvə]
Singen singing [ˈsɪŋɪŋ]
singen sing [sɪŋ]
sitzen sit [sɪt]
Sitzplatz seat [siːt]
Skateboard (fahren) skateboard [ˈskeɪtbɔːd]
Skateboardfahren skateboarding [ˈskeɪtbɔːdɪŋ]
Skatepark skatepark [ˈskeɪtpɑːk]
Slideshow slide show [ˈslaɪd ʃəʊ]
SMS text [tekst] **jm. eine SMS schicken** text sb.
Snack snack [snæk]
so like this [laɪk]; so [səʊ]
sodass so that [səʊ ðæt]
Sofa sofa [ˈsəʊfə]
Software software [ˈsɒftweə]
so gut wie as good as [æz gʊd æz]
sogar even [ˈiːvn]
Sohn son [sʌn]
so(lch) (ein/e) such a [sʌtʃ]
Sommer summer [ˈsʌmə]
Sonne sun [sʌn] **Die Sonne scheint.** It's sunny. [ˈsʌni]
Sonnenaufgang sunrise [ˈsʌnraɪz]
sonnenbaden sunbathe [ˈsʌnbeɪð]
sonnig sunny [ˈsʌni]
Sonntag Sunday [ˈsʌndeɪ], [ˈsʌndi]
sonst or [ɔː]
Sorte (von) kind (of) [kaɪnd]
Soße sauce [sɔːs]
Spaghetti spaghetti [spəˈgeti]
sparen save [seɪv]
Sparkonto savings account [ˈseɪvɪŋz əkaʊnt]
Sparschwein piggy bank [ˈpɪgi bæŋk]
Spaß fun [fʌn] **Spaß haben** have fun [hæv] **Spaß machen** be fun [biː]
spät: (zu) spät late [leɪt]
später later [ˈleɪtə]
Spaziergang walk [wɔːk]
Speisekarte menu [ˈmenjuː]
Spiegel mirror [ˈmɪrə]
Spiel game [geɪm]; match [mætʃ]
spielen play [pleɪ]
Spieler/in player [ˈpleɪə]
Spielkarte playing card [ˈpleɪɪŋ kɑːd]
Spielstand score [skɔː]
Spielzeug toy [tɔɪ]
Spitze top [tɒp] **an der Spitze (von)** at the top (of) [æt], [ət]
Sport sport [spɔːt]; *(Schulsport)* PE (= physical education) [piː ˈiː], [fɪzɪkl edʒuˈkeɪʃn]
Sportart sport [spɔːt]
Sporthalle sports hall [ˈspɔːts hɔːl]
Sportler/in sportsperson [ˈspɔːtspɜːsn]
sportlich sporty [ˈspɔːti]
Sprechen speaking [ˈspiːkɪŋ]
sprechen (mit) speak (to) [spiːk] **deutlich sprechen** speak clearly [ˈklɪəli] **lauter sprechen** speak more loudly [mɔː] **sprechen über** speak about [əˈbaʊt]
springen jump [dʒʌmp]
Staatsbürger/in citizen [ˈsɪtɪzn]
Stadion stadium [ˈsteɪdiəm]
Stadt city [ˈsɪti]; town [taʊn]
Stadtplan map [mæp]
Stadtzentrum town centre [taʊn ˈsentə]
Standuhr clock [klɒk]
Star star [stɑː]
stark strong [strɒŋ]
Stärke strength [streŋθ]
Start start [stɑːt]
stattfinden take place [teɪk pleɪs]; be on [biː ɒn]
Staub saugen vacuum [ˈvækjuəm]
stecken: (etwas wohin) stecken put [pʊt]
stehen stand [stænd]
stehlen steal [stiːl]
stellen: (etwas wohin) stellen put [pʊt] **sich (hin)stellen** stand [stænd] **stellen, legen, setzen** set [set]
Sternzeichen star sign [ˈstɑː saɪn]
Stichwort keyword [ˈkiːwɜːd]
Stiefbruder stepbrother [ˈstepbrʌðə]
Stiefel boot [buːt]
Stiefmutter stepmother [ˈstepmʌðə]; stepmum [ˈstepmʌm]
Stiefschwester stepsister [ˈstepsɪstə]
Stiefsohn stepson [ˈstepsʌn]
Stieftochter stepdaughter [ˈstepdɔːtə]
Stiefvater stepdad [ˈstepdæd]; stepfather [ˈstepfɑːðə]
Stift pen [pen]
still quiet [ˈkwaɪət]; *(lautlos)* silent [ˈsaɪlənt]
Stock(werk) floor [flɔː] **das oberste Stockwerk** top floor [tɒp ˈflɔː]
Stolz pride [praɪd]
stoßen knock [nɒk]
Strand beach [biːtʃ] **an den/zum Strand** to the beach [tu], [tə]
Straße *(in Ortschaften)* street [striːt]
Straßenmusik street music [ˈstriːt mjuːzɪk]
Streetdance *(Tanzstil)* street dance [ˈstriːt dɑːns]
stricken knit [nɪt]
Stück piece [piːs] **Stück Papier** piece of paper [ˈpeɪpə]
Struktur structure [ˈstrʌktʃə]
Student/in student [ˈstjuːdnt]
studieren study [ˈstʌdi]
Stufe step [step]
Stuhl chair [tʃeə]
Stunde hour [ˈaʊə]; *(Unterrichtsstunde)* lesson [ˈlesn] **pro Stunde** per hour [pɜː], [pə]
stundenlang for hours [fɔː ˈaʊəs]
Stundenplan timetable [ˈtaɪmteɪbl]

suchen, Ausschau halten nach look for [lʊk fɔː]
Superheld/in superhero, *(pl)* superheroes [ˈsuːpəhɪərəʊ]
Supermarkt supermarket [ˈsuːpəmɑːkɪt]
Suppe soup [suːp]
Surfing surfing [ˈsɜːfɪŋ]
süß cute [kjuːt]; sweet [swiːt]
Süßigkeiten sweets *(pl)* [swiːts]
Sweatshirt sweatshirt [ˈswetʃɜːt]

T

Tag day [deɪ]
Tageszeitung newspaper [ˈnjuːspeɪpə]; paper [ˈpeɪpə]
Talent gift [gɪft]
Tante aunt [ɑːnt]
Tanz dance [dɑːns]
Tanzen dancing [ˈdɑːnsɪŋ]
tanzen dance [dɑːns]
Tänzer/in dancer [ˈdɑːnsə]
Tapferkeit bravery [ˈbreɪvəri]
Tasche bag [bæg]
Tätigkeit activity [ækˈtɪvəti]
Tatsache fact [fækt]
Taufe christening [ˈkrɪsnɪŋ]
Tausch swap [swɒp]
tauschen swap [swɒp]
tausend thousand [ˈθaʊznd]
Technik technology [tekˈnɒlədʒi], *(infml auch)* tech
Technikunterricht technology [tekˈnɒlədʒi], *(infml auch)* tech
Technologie technology [tekˈnɒlədʒi], *(infml auch)* tech
Tee tea [tiː]
Teelöffel teaspoon [ˈtiːspuːn]
Teil part (of) [pɑːt]; piece [piːs]; share [ʃeə]
teilen share [ʃeə]
Telefon phone [fəʊn] **am Telefon** on the phone [ɒn]
Telefonanruf (phone) call [ˈfəʊn kɔːl]
telefonieren phone [fəʊn]
Telefonnummer phone number [ˈfəʊn nʌmbə]
Tennis tennis [ˈtenɪs]
Terrarium terrarium [teˈreəriəm]
Test test [test]; quiz, *(pl)* quizzes [kwɪz], [ˈkwɪzɪz] **einen Test machen** do a quiz [duː]
testen test [test]
teuer expensive [ɪkˈspensɪv]
Text text [tekst]
Theater theatre [ˈθɪətə]
Theater spielen act [ækt]
Thema topic [ˈtɒpɪk]
Ticket ticket [ˈtɪkɪt]
Tier animal [ˈænɪml]; *(Haustier)* pet [pet]; *(Bestie)* beast [biːst]
Tierarzt/Tierärztin vet [vet]
Tipp tip [tɪp]
Tisch table [ˈteɪbl]
Tischtennis table tennis [ˈteɪbl tenɪs]
Titel title [ˈtaɪtl]
Tochter daughter [ˈdɔːtə]
Toilette toilet [ˈtɔɪlət]
tolerant (gegenüber) tolerant (of) [ˈtɒlərənt]
toll great [greɪt]
Tomate tomato, *(pl)* tomatoes [təˈmɑːtəʊ]
Tomatensauce tomato sauce [təˈmɑːtəʊ sɔːs]
Topf pot [pɒt]
Torte cake [keɪk]
tot dead [ded]
töten kill [kɪl]
Tour tour [tʊə]
Tourist/in tourist [ˈtʊərɪst]
Touristeninformation tourist information centre [tʊərɪst ɪnfəˈmeɪʃn sentə]
Tradition tradition [trəˈdɪʃn]
traditionell traditional [trəˈdɪʃənl]
tragen wear [weə]
Trainer/in trainer [ˈtreɪnə]
Training training [ˈtreɪnɪŋ]
Trampolin trampoline [ˈtræmpəliːn]
Trampolinspringen/-turnen- trampolining [ˈtræmpəliːnɪŋ]
Traum dream [driːm]
träumen (von etwas) dream (of/about sth.) [driːm]
traurig sad [sæd]
treffen: treffen auf hit [hɪt] **(sich) treffen** meet [miːt]
Treppe stairs [steəz]
Tretroller scooter [ˈskuːtə]
Trick trick [trɪk]
Trifle *(englischer Nachtisch)* trifle [ˈtraɪfl]
trinken drink [drɪŋk]
Trophäe trophy [ˈtrəʊfi]
trotzdem still [stɪl]
Tschüs. Bye. [baɪ]; See you. [siː]; Speak later. [spiːk ˈleɪtə]
T-Shirt T-shirt [ˈtiː ʃɜːt]
tun do [duː] **(etwas wohin) tun** put [pʊt] **du hast (viel) zu tun** you're busy [ˈbɪzi] **es genießen, etwas zu tun** enjoy doing sth. [ɪnˈdʒɔɪ] **etwas dauernd/immer wieder tun** keep doing sth. **etwas tun müssen** have to do sth. **etwas weiterhin tun** continue to do sth. [kənˈtɪnjuː] **wie man etwas tut / tun kann / tun soll** how to do sth. [haʊ]
Tür door [dɔː]
Turmuhr clock [klɒk]
Tüte: Tüten voller Müll bags of rubbish [bægz]
Tyrann/in bully [ˈbʊli]
tyrannisieren bully [ˈbʊli]

U

üben practice [ˈpræktɪs]
über
1. *(räumlich)* over [ˈəʊvə]
2. *(mehr als)* **über 50** over 50
3. about [əˈbaʊt] **über mich/dich/...** about me/you/...

über eine Brücke/Straße ... across a bridge/street ... [əˈkrɒs]
über above [əˈbʌv]
überall everywhere [ˈevriweə]
überhaupt nicht(s) not ... at all [nɒt ət ɔːl]
überprüfen check [tʃek]
Überprüfung check [tʃek]
überraschen surprise [səˈpraɪz]
überrascht surprised [səˈpraɪzd]
Überraschung surprise [səˈpraɪz]
Überschrift heading [ˈhedɪŋ]; title [ˈtaɪtl]
Übung(en) exercise [ˈeksəsaɪz]; practice [ˈpræktɪs]
Übungsheft exercise book [ˈeksəsaɪz bʊk]
Uhr clock [klɒk]
Uhrzeit time [taɪm]
umarmen: (jn./einander) umarmen hug (sb.) [hʌg]
um: um 8 Uhr at 8 o'clock [æt], [ət]
umdrehen turn [tɜːn]
umhergehen (in) walk around [wɔːk əˈraʊnd]
Umkleideraum changing room [ˈtʃeɪndʒɪŋ ruːm]
umrühren stir [stɜː]
umsteigen change trains [tʃeɪndʒ treɪn]
umweltbewusst green [griːn]
umweltfreundlich werden go green [gəʊ griːn]
umziehen (nach) move to [muːv]
unabhängig (von) independent (of/from) [ɪndɪˈpendənt]
und and [ænd], [ənd] **Und du?** What about you? [əˈbaʊt]
Unfall; Zufall accident [ˈæksɪdənt]
unfreundlich unfriendly [ʌnˈfrendli]
unheimlich scary [ˈskeəri]
unhöflich rude [ruːd]
Uniform uniform [ˈjuːnɪfɔːm]
unordentlich messy [ˈmesi]
Unordnung mess [mes]
Unrecht: Unrecht haben be wrong [rɒŋ]
uns us [ʌs], [əs]
unser/e our [ˈaʊə]
unten: nach unten (die Treppe hinunter) downstairs [daʊnˈsteəz]
unter under [ˈʌndə] **unter der Erde** underground [ˈʌndəgraʊnd]
unterhalten: sich unterhalten (mit) chat [tʃæt]
unterirdisch underground [ˈʌndəgraʊnd]
Unterricht class [klɑːs] **im Unterricht** in class
unterrichten teach [tiːtʃ]
Unterrichtsstunde lesson [ˈlesn]
Unterschied difference [ˈdɪfrəns]
unterstreichen highlight [ˈhaɪlaɪt]
untersuchen research [rɪˈsɜːtʃ]
unter Wasser, Unterwasser- underwater [ʌndəˈwɔːtə]
Urlaub holiday [ˈhɒlədeɪ] **im/in den Urlaub** on holiday

V

Vanille vanilla [vəˈnɪlə]
Vampir vampire [ˈvæmpaɪə]
Vati dad [dæd]
vegan vegan [ˈviːgən]
Veganer/in vegan [ˈviːgən]
Vegetarier/in vegetarian [vedʒəˈteəriən], *(infml auch)* veggie [ˈvedʒi]
vegetarisch vegetarian [vedʒəˈteəriən], *(infml auch)* veggie [ˈvedʒi]
Verabredung date [deɪt]
verärgert upset [ʌpˈset]
verbinden (mit) link [lɪŋk]
verboten no [nəʊ]
verdienen *(Geld)* earn [ɜːn]
Verein club [klʌb]
Vereinigtes Königreich the United Kingdom (the UK) [junaɪtɪd ˈkɪŋdəm], [juː ˈkeɪ]
vergangene(r,s) past [pɑːst]
vergessen forget [fəˈget]
vergessen: nicht vergessen remember [rɪˈmembə]
verirren: Hast du dich verirrt? Are you lost? [lɒst]
verkaufen sell [sel]
Verkäufer, Verkäuferin shop assistant [ˈʃɒp əsɪstənt]
Verkaufsbude kiosk [ˈkiːɒsk]
Verkaufsstand kiosk [ˈkiːɒsk]
verkehrt herum upside down [ʌpsaɪd ˈdaʊn]
Verkleidung costume [ˈkɒstjuːm]
verlässlich reliable [rɪˈlaɪəbl]
verlaufen: Hast du dich verlaufen? Are you lost? [lɒst]
verletzen, wehtun hurt [hɜːt]
verlieren lose [luːz]
Verlies dungeon [ˈdʌndʒən]
vermischen mix [mɪks]
vermissen miss [mɪs]
vermisst missing [ˈmɪsɪŋ]
verpassen miss [mɪs]
verrückt crazy [ˈkreɪzi]
verschieden different [ˈdɪfrənt]
verschneit snowy [ˈsnəʊi]
verspäten: Ich habe mich verspätet. I'm late. [leɪt] **Verspäte dich nicht.** Don't be late.
Versprechen promise [ˈprɒmɪs]
verstehen understand [ʌndəˈstænd]
etwas verstehen work sth. out [wɜːk]
versuchen try [traɪ]
Vertrauensschüler/in head student [hed ˈstjuːdnt]
verwenden use [juːz]
verwundert puzzled [ˈpʌzld]
verzichten: auf etwas verzichten cut sth. out [kʌt]
Verzierung decoration [dekəˈreɪʃn]
Video; Video- video [ˈvɪdiəʊ]
viel/e a lot of [ə ˈlɒt əv], lots of [ˈlɒts əv]; many [ˈmæni]; much [mʌtʃ] **wie viele?** how many? [haʊ]
vielleicht maybe [ˈmeɪbi]
vier four [fɔː]
viertel nach 7 quarter past 7 [ˈkwɔːtə pɑːst ˈsevn]
viertel vor 7 quarter to 7 [ˈkwɔːtə tu ˈsevn]
vierzehn fourteen [fɔːˈtiːn]
vierzig forty [ˈfɔːti]
violett purple [ˈpɜːpl]
visuell visual [ˈvɪʒuəl]
Vogel bird [bɜːd]
Vokabelverzeichnis vocabulary [vəˈkæbjələri], *(infml auch)* vocab [ˈvəʊkæb]
Vokabular vocabulary [vəˈkæbjələri], *(infml auch)* vocab [ˈvəʊkæb]
voll(er) full (of ...) [fʊl]
völlig (still) perfectly (still) [ˈpɜːfɪktli]
von from [frɒm]; of [ɒv], [əv]
vor
1. *(zeitlich)* before [bɪˈfɔː]
vor der Schule / der Unterrichtsstunde before school / the lesson [skuːl], [ˈlesn] **vor langer Zeit** a long time ago [ə lɒŋ taɪm əˈgəʊ]
2. *(räumlich)* in front of [ɪn ˈfrʌnt əv]
vorbei an past [pɑːst]
vorbeikommen: vorbeischauen (bei jm.) come round (to sb.) [raʊnd]
vorbereiten: sich vorbereiten (auf) prepare (for) [prɪˈpeə]
Vorhersage prediction [prɪˈdɪkʃn]
vormittags: 9 Uhr vormittags 9 a.m. [eɪˈem]
Vorname first name [ˈfɜːst neɪm]
vorsichtig careful [ˈkeəfl]
vorstellen: (jm.) etwas vorstellen present sth. (to sb.) [prɪˈzent]
sich etwas vorstellen imagine sth. [ɪˈmædʒɪn]
Vortrag talk [tɔːk]
vorüber an past [pɑːst]
Voraussage prediction [prɪˈdɪkʃn]
Vorwahl(nummer) code [kəʊd]

W

wach awake [əˈweɪk]
Wackelpudding jelly [ˈdʒeli]
wählen choose [tʃuːz]
wahr true [truː]
wahr werden come true [kʌm truː]
während during [ˈdjʊərɪŋ]; as [æz], [əz]
Wald forest [ˈfɒrɪst]
Wand wall [wɔːl] **an der/die Wand** on the wall [ɒn]
Wandern hiking [ˈhaɪkɪŋ]; walking [ˈwɔːkɪŋ]
wandern hike [haɪk]; walk [wɔːk]
Wanduhr clock [klɒk]
wann when [wen]
warm hot [hɒt]; warm [wɔːm]
warm werden get warm [get]
warten (auf) wait (for) [weɪt]
warum why [waɪ]
was what [wɒt] **Was ist mit dir?** What about you? [əˈbaʊt]
Was (Wie viel) kostet ...? How much is...? [haʊ mʌtʃ ɪz]
Was (Wie viel) kosten ...? How much are ...? [haʊ mʌtʃ ɑː]
waschen: sich waschen wash [wɒʃ]
Wasser water [ˈwɔːtə]
Wassermelone water melon [ˈmelən]
Website website [ˈwebsaɪt]
Wechselgeld change [tʃeɪndʒ]
Weg journey [ˈdʒɜːni]; way [weɪ]
weg away [əˈweɪ]
weg von off [ɒf]
weglassen: etwas weglassen cut sth. out [kʌt]
wehen blow [bləʊ]
Weide field [fiːld] **auf der Weide** in the field
Weihnachten Christmas [ˈkrɪsməs]
Weihnachtstag Christmas Day [krɪsməs ˈdeɪ]
weil because [bɪˈkɒz]
Weise: Art und Weise way [weɪ]
auf diese Weise (in) this way
auf unterschiedliche Weise in different ways [ˈdɪfrənt]
weit (entfernt) far [fɑː]
weiß white [waɪt]
weitere more [mɔː] **drei weitere** three more [θriː]
weitermachen continue [kənˈtɪnjuː]
(mit) etwas weitermachen continue to do sth. [duː]
welche(r, s) which? [wɪtʃ]; what [wɒt]
Welt world [wɜːld]
Weltraum space [speɪs]
Wendung phrase [freɪz]
wen, wem who [huː]
wenn
1. **(falls)** if [ɪf] **Was wäre, wenn?** What if? [wɒt]
2. *(zeitlich)* when [wen]
wenigstens at least [æt liːst]
wer who [huː]
werden get [get]; become [bɪˈkʌm]
Werken design and technology [dɪzaɪn ən tekˈnɒlədʒi]
Werktag weekday [ˈwiːkdeɪ]
Werkunterricht design and technology [dɪzaɪn ən tekˈnɒlədʒi]
Wetter weather [ˈweðə]
Wettkampf competition [kɒmpəˈtɪʃn]; match [mætʃ]
wichtig important [ɪmˈpɔːtnt]
wichtigste(r, s) main [meɪn]
wie (ähnlich/so wie) like [laɪk]
wie how [haʊ] **Wie alt bist du?** How old are you? **Wie geht es dir/euch/Ihnen?** How are you?
Wie heißt du? What's your name? [wɒts] **Wie ist ...? / Wie sieht ... aus?** What's ... like? **wie viele?** how many?
Wie wäre es mit einer/einem ...? What about a ...?
Wie spät ist es? What time is it? [wɒt taɪm ɪz ɪt]
wiederholen repeat [rɪˈpiːt]
Willkommen in/an ... Welcome to ... [ˈwelkəm]
Wind wind [wɪnd]
windig windy [ˈwɪndi]
Windsurfen windsurfing [wɪndsɜːfɪŋ]

winken: (jm. zu)winken wave (to sb.) [weɪv]
Winter winter [ˈwɪntə]
wir we [wiː] **Es sind nur wir.** It's just us. [ʌs], [əs] **wir sind** we're (= we are) **wir sind nicht** we aren't **wir waren** we were [wɜː], [wə]
wirklich really [ˈriːəli], [ˈrɪəli]
Wirkung: Auswirkung (auf) effect (on) [ɪˈfekt]
wissen know [nəʊ]
Wissenschaftler/in scientist [ˈsaɪəntɪst]
Witterung weather [ˈweðə]
Witz joke [dʒəʊk]
witzig funny [ˈfʌni]
wo where [weə] **Wo kommst du her?** Where are you from?
Woche week [wiːk]
Wochenende weekend [wiːkˈend] **am Wochenende** at the weekend
Wochentag weekday [ˈwiːkdeɪ]
wohltätige Organisation charity [ˈtʃærəti]
wohnen live [lɪv]
Wohnsiedlung estate [ɪˈsteɪt]
Wohnung flat [flæt]; apartment [əˈpɑːtmənt]
Wohnzimmer living room [ˈlɪvɪŋ ruːm]
Wolke cloud [klaʊd]
wolkig cloudy [ˈklaʊdi]
wollen want [wɒnt] **etwas tun wollen** want to do sth. [duː]
Wort word [wɜːd]
Wörternetz mind map [ˈmaɪnd mæp]
Wortschatz vocabulary [vəˈkæbjələri], *(infml auch)* vocab [ˈvəʊkæb]
wunderbar wonderful [ˈwʌndəfl]
wünschen: sich wünschen wish [wɪʃ]
Wurst: Würstchen sausage [ˈsɒsɪdʒ]
würzig spicy [ˈspaɪsi]
wütend angry [ˈæŋgri]

Y

Yoga yoga [ˈjəʊgə]

Z

Zahl number [ˈnʌmbə]
zahlen: (etwas be)zahlen pay (for sth.) [peɪ]
Zahn tooth, *(pl)* teeth [tuːθ], [tiːθ]
Zahnspange: Zahnklammer braces [ˈbreɪsɪz]
Zauberei magic [ˈmædʒɪk]
Zauberkasten magic set [ˈmædʒɪk set]
zaubern do magic [duː ˈmædʒɪk]
Zaubertrick magic trick [ˈmædʒɪk trɪk]
zehn ten [ten]
Zeichen mark [mɑːk]
zeichnen draw [drɔː]
Zeichnen drawing [ˈdrɔːɪŋ]
zeigen show [ʃəʊ]
Zeile line [laɪn]
Zeit time [taɪm] **(für) eine lange Zeit** (for) a long time [lɒŋ]
Zeit verbringen (mit) / Geld ausgeben (für) spend time/money [spend taɪm], [spend ˈmʌni]
Zeitschrift magazine [mægəˈziːn]
Zeitung newspaper [ˈnjuːspeɪpə]; paper [ˈpeɪpə]
Zeitungshändler newsagent [ˈnjuːzeɪdʒənt]
Zensur mark [mɑːk]
Zentrum centre [ˈsentə]
zerbrechen: etwas zerbrechen break sth. [breɪk]
Zeremonie ceremony [ˈserəməni]
Zettel piece of paper [piːs ɒv ˈpeɪpə]
Ziege goat [gəʊt]
ziehen (nach) move to [muːv]
ziemlich quite [kwaɪt]
Ziel destination [destɪˈneɪʃn]
Ziffer number [ˈnʌmbə]
Zimmer room [ruːm]
Zirkus circus [ˈsɜːkəs]
Zitrone lemon [ˈlemən]
Zoo zoo [zuː]
zu: um zu to [tu], [tə]
zubereiten prepare (for) [prɪˈpeə]
Zucker sugar [ˈʃʊgə]
Zuckerguss icing [ˈaɪsɪŋ]
zuerst (at) first [fɜːst]
Zug train [treɪn]
Zuhause home [həʊm]
zuhören listen [ˈlɪsn]
Zuhörer/innen audience [ˈɔːdiəns]
Zukunft, zukünftige(r,s) future [ˈfjuːtʃə]
zumachen close [kləʊz]
zumindest at least [æt liːst]
zurück back [bæk]
zurzeit at the moment [ˈməʊmənt]
zusammen together [təˈgeðə]
Zuschauer/innen audience [ˈɔːdiəns]
zuverlässig reliable [rɪˈlaɪəbl]
zuversichtlich confident [ˈkɒnfɪdənt]
zu viel des Guten too much of a good thing [tuː mʌtʃ ɒv ə gʊd θɪŋ]
zwanzig twenty [ˈtwenti]
zwei two [tuː]
zweite(r, s) second (2nd) [ˈsekənd]
Zwiebel onion [ˈʌnjən]
zwischen between [bɪˈtwiːn]
zwölf twelve [twelv]
zwölfte(r, s) twelfth (12th) [twelfθ]

Ähnliche Wörter im Englischen und Deutschen

Viele englische Wörter ähneln deutschen Wörtern: *a cowboy* = ein Cowboy. Beachte aber die Unterschiede 1–3!

(1) Nomen werden im Deutschen großgeschrieben, aber im Englischen klein.
(2) Verben haben im Deutschen andere Endungen, aber einen ähnlichen Stamm, z. B. planen – *(to) plan*.
(3) Oft unterscheidet sich die Aussprache. Höre dir die blau markierten Wörter in der App an und sprich sie nach.

active / activity
address
allergic (to)
alphabet
app
April
article
August
badminton
balcony
ball
banana
band
barbecue
basketball
biology
bowling
box
(to) bring
British
browser
burger
bus
butter
cafe
camera
card
character
check
chocolate
circus
city
class
classroom
clever
club
coffee
cola
comic
computer
console
cool
corridor
cost / (to) cost
cousin
creative
culture
curry
dance / (to) dance
December
decoration
drama
drink / (to) drink
electric
elephant
end / (to) end
England / English
family
fan
February
feedback
film
(to) find
fish
football
friend / friendly
garden
gold
group
hamster
happy
Hello
highlight
hockey
hot dog
house
hungry
idea
information
internet
January
July
June
karaoke
kebab
kid
kilometre (km)
kiosk
lamp
market
maths
melon
milk
millilitre
mini
minute
modern
moment
Monday
museum
music
name
November
number
October
online
orange
park
parkour
partner
party
pasta
perfect
person
photo
picnic
plan / (to) plan
playlist
pool
popcorn
post
poster
problem
project
restaurant
ring
robot
room
rucksack
salad
sandwich
sauce
school
(to) send
September
shopping centre
silver
skateboard
skatepark
smart
snack
sofa
software
song
sport
star
stop
story
street dance
student
summer
Sunday
supermarket
surfing
sweatshirt
(to) swim
swimmer
test / (to) test
text / (to) text
ticket
tip
title
toilet
tomato
top
tourist
tradition
trainer / training
trick
T-shirt
uniform
vanilla
vegan
vegetarian / veggie
video
warm
website
wind
winner
winter
word
yoga
yoghurt
zoo

The English alphabet

a [eɪ]	h [eɪtʃ]	o [əʊ]	v [viː]
b [biː]	i [aɪ]	p [piː]	w ['dʌbljuː]
c [siː]	j [dʒeɪ]	q [kjuː]	x [eks]
d [diː]	k [keɪ]	r [ɑː]	y [waɪ]
e [iː]	l [el]	s [es]	z [zed]
f [ef]	m [em]	t [tiː]	
g [dʒiː]	n [en]	u [juː]	

English sounds

[iː] green, he, sea
[ɑː] ask, class, car, park
! [ɔː] or, ball, door, four, morning
[uː] ruler, blue, too, two, you
[ɜː] her, girl, work, T-shirt
[ɪ] in, big, expensive
[e] yes, bed, again, breakfast
[æ] animal, apple, black, cat
[ʌ] mum, bus, colour
[ɒ] song, on, dog, what
[ʊ] book, good, put, bully
[ə] again, today, a sister
[i] happy, monkey
[u] museum, you, to

[eɪ] name, eight, play, great
[aɪ] I, time, right, my
[ɔɪ] boy, toilet, noise
[əʊ] old, no, road, yellow
[aʊ] now, house
[eə] where, pair, share, their
[ɪə] here, material, really, year
[ʊə] tour

[b] bike, table, verb
[p] pen, paper, shop
[d] day, window, good
[t] ten, letter, at
[g] go, again, bag
[k] kitchen, car, back
[m] man, remember, mum
[n] no, one, ten
! [ŋ] wrong, young, uncle, thanks
[l] like, old, small
[r] ruler, friend, sorry
! [w] we, where, one
[j] yes, you, uniform
[f] family, after
! [v] very, seven, have
[s] six, poster, yes
! [z] zoo, quiz, his, music, please
[ʃ] she, station, English
[tʃ] teacher, watch
[dʒ] job, German, project, orange
! [θ] thing, three, bathroom, north
! [ð] the, weather, with
! [h] house, who, behind

Die Lautschrift zeigt dir die Aussprache von Wörtern und Lauten *(sounds)*.

!

Übe mit Hilfe der App besonders die Aussprache dieser Laute, denn sie kommen im Deutschen nicht vor oder werden anders geschrieben.

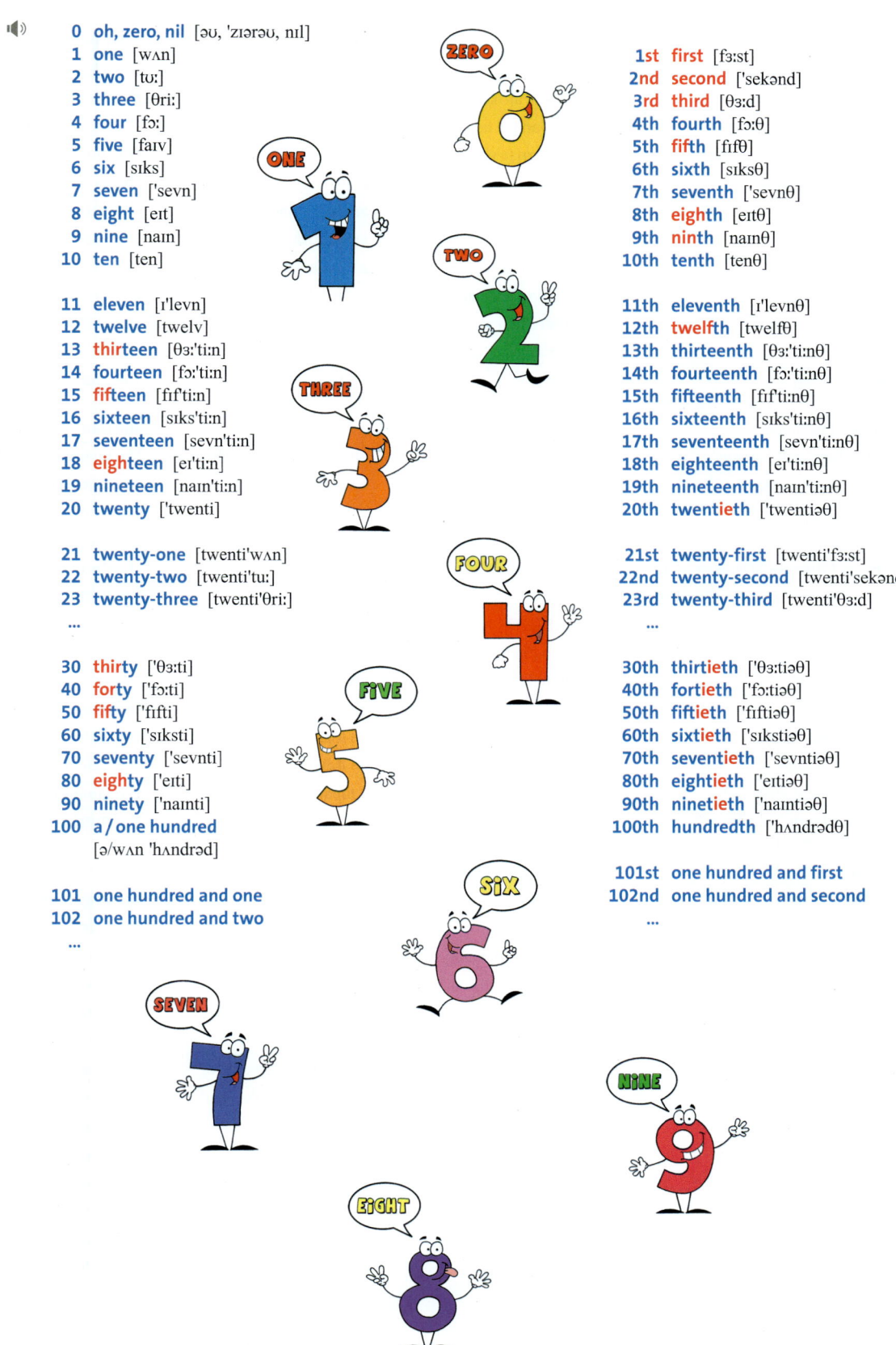

0 **oh, zero, nil** [əʊ, 'zɪərəʊ, nɪl]
1 **one** [wʌn]
2 **two** [tuː]
3 **three** [θriː]
4 **four** [fɔː]
5 **five** [faɪv]
6 **six** [sɪks]
7 **seven** ['sevn]
8 **eight** [eɪt]
9 **nine** [naɪn]
10 **ten** [ten]

11 **eleven** [ɪ'levn]
12 **twelve** [twelv]
13 **thirteen** [θɜː'tiːn]
14 **fourteen** [fɔː'tiːn]
15 **fifteen** [fɪf'tiːn]
16 **sixteen** [sɪks'tiːn]
17 **seventeen** [sevn'tiːn]
18 **eighteen** [eɪ'tiːn]
19 **nineteen** [naɪn'tiːn]
20 **twenty** ['twenti]

21 **twenty-one** [twenti'wʌn]
22 **twenty-two** [twenti'tuː]
23 **twenty-three** [twenti'θriː]
...

30 **thirty** ['θɜːti]
40 **forty** ['fɔːti]
50 **fifty** ['fɪfti]
60 **sixty** ['sɪksti]
70 **seventy** ['sevnti]
80 **eighty** ['eɪti]
90 **ninety** ['naɪnti]
100 **a / one hundred** [ə/wʌn 'hʌndrəd]

101 **one hundred and one**
102 **one hundred and two**
...

1st **first** [fɜːst]
2nd **second** ['sekənd]
3rd **third** [θɜːd]
4th **fourth** [fɔːθ]
5th **fifth** [fɪfθ]
6th **sixth** [sɪksθ]
7th **seventh** ['sevnθ]
8th **eighth** [eɪtθ]
9th **ninth** [naɪnθ]
10th **tenth** [tenθ]

11th **eleventh** [ɪ'levnθ]
12th **twelfth** [twelfθ]
13th **thirteenth** [θɜː'tiːnθ]
14th **fourteenth** [fɔː'tiːnθ]
15th **fifteenth** [fɪf'tiːnθ]
16th **sixteenth** [sɪks'tiːnθ]
17th **seventeenth** [sevn'tiːnθ]
18th **eighteenth** [eɪ'tiːnθ]
19th **nineteenth** [naɪn'tiːnθ]
20th **twentieth** ['twentiəθ]

21st **twenty-first** [twenti'fɜːst]
22nd **twenty-second** [twenti'sekənd]
23rd **twenty-third** [twenti'θɜːd]
...

30th **thirtieth** ['θɜːtiəθ]
40th **fortieth** ['fɔːtiəθ]
50th **fiftieth** ['fɪftiəθ]
60th **sixtieth** ['sɪkstiəθ]
70th **seventieth** ['sevntiəθ]
80th **eightieth** ['eɪtiəθ]
90th **ninetieth** ['naɪntiəθ]
100th **hundredth** ['hʌndrədθ]

101st **one hundred and first**
102nd **one hundred and second**
...

Country/Continent	Adjective	Person	People
Afghanistan [æfˈgænɪstan] *Afghanistan*	**Afghan** [ˈæfgæn]	**an Afghan**	**the Afghans**
Africa [ˈafrɪkə] *Afrika*	**African** [ˈafrɪkən]	**an African**	**the Africans**
Albania [ælˈbeɪniə] *Albanien*	**Albanian** [ælˈbeɪniən]	**an Albanian**	**the Albanians**
America [əˈmerɪkə] *Amerika*	**American** [əˈmerɪkən]	**an American**	**the Americans**
Asia [ˈeɪʃə, ˈeɪʒə] *Asien*	**Asian** [ˈeɪʃn, ˈeɪʒn]	**an Asian**	**the Asians**
Australia [ɒˈstreɪliə] *Australien*	**Australian** [ɒˈstreɪliən]	**an Australian**	**the Australians**
Austria [ˈɒstriə] *Österreich*	**Austrian** [ˈɒstriən]	**an Austrian**	**the Austrians**
Bulgaria [bʌlˈgeəriə] *Bulgarien*	**Bulgarian** [bʌlˈgeəriən]	**a Bulgarian**	**the Bulgarians**
Canada [ˈkanədə] *Kanada*	**Canadian** [kəˈneɪdiən]	**a Canadian**	**the Canadians**
China [ˈtʃaɪnə] *China*	**Chinese** [tʃaɪˈniːz]	**a Chinese**	**the Chinese**
Croatia [krəʊˈeɪʃə] *Kroatien*	**Croatian** [krəʊˈeɪʃn]	**a Croatian**	**the Croatians**
Czechia [ˌtʃekiə] *Tschechien, die Tschechische Republik*	**Czech** [tʃek]	**a Czech**	**the Czechs**
Denmark [ˈdenmɑːk]	**Danish** [ˈdeɪnɪʃ]	**a Dane** [deɪn]	**the Danes**
England [ˈɪŋglənd] *England*	**English** [ˈɪŋglɪʃ]	**an Englishman/-woman**	**the English**
Europe [ˈjʊərəp] *Europa*	**European** [ˌjʊərəˈpiːən]	**a European**	**the Europeans**
Finland [ˈfɪnlənd] *Finnland*	**Finnish** [ˈfɪnɪʃ]	**a Finn** [fɪn]	**the Finns**
France [frɑːns] *Frankreich*	**French** [frentʃ]	**a Frenchman/-woman**	**the French**
Germany [ˈdʒɜːməni] *Deutschland*	**German** [ˈdʒɜːmən]	**a German**	**the Germans**
(Great) Britain [ˈbrɪtn] *Großbritannien*	**British** [ˈbrɪtɪʃ]	**a Briton** [ˈbrɪtn]	**the British**
Greece [griːs] *Griechenland*	**Greek** [griːk]	**a Greek**	**the Greeks**
India [ˈɪndiə] *Indien*	**Indian** [ˈɪndiən]	**an Indian**	**the Indians**
Iran [ɪˈrɑːn] *Iran*	**Iranian** [ɪˈreɪniən]	**an Iranian**	**the Iranians**
Iraq [ɪˈrɑːk] *Irak*	**Iraqi** [ɪˈrɑːki]	**an Iraqi**	**the Iraqis**
Ireland [ˈaɪələnd] *Irland*	**Irish** [ˈaɪrɪʃ]	**an Irishman/-woman**	**the Irish**
Italy [ˈɪtəli] *Italien*	**Italian** [ɪˈtaliən]	**an Italian**	**the Italians**
Japan [dʒəpˈæn] *Japan*	**Japanese** [ˌdʒapəˈniːz]	**a Japanese**	**the Japanese**
the Netherlands [ˈnedələndz] *die Niederlande, Holland*	**Dutch** [dʌtʃ]	**a Dutchman/-woman**	**the Dutch**
Norway [ˈnɔːweɪ] *Norwegen*	**Norwegian** [nɔːˈwiːdʒən]	**a Norwegian**	**the Norwegians**
Pakistan [pakɪˈstæn] *Pakistan*	**Pakistani** [pakɪˈstæni]	**a Pakistani**	**the Pakistanis**
Poland [ˈpəʊlənd] *Polen*	**Polish** [ˈpəʊlɪʃ]	**a Pole** [pəʊl]	**the Poles**
Romania [ruˈmeɪniə] *Rumänien*	**Romanian** [ruˈmeɪniən]	**a Romanian**	**the Romanians**
Russia [ˈrʌʃə] *Russland*	**Russian** [ˈrʌʃn]	**a Russian**	**the Russians**
Scotland [ˈskɒtlənd] *Schottland*	**Scottish** [ˈskɒtɪʃ]	**a Scotsman/-woman**	**the Scots**
Serbia [ˈsɜːbiə] *Serbien*	**Serbian** [ˈsɜːbiən]	**a Serb** [sɜːb]	**the Serbs**
Slovakia [sləˈvakiə] *die Slowakei*	**Slovak** [ˈsləʊvak]	**a Slovakian** [sləˈvakiən]	**the Slovakians**
Slovenia [sləˈviːniə] *Slowenien*	**Slovene** [ˈsləʊviːn]	**a Slovenian** [sləˈviːniən]	**the Slovenians**
Spain [speɪn] *Spanien*	**Spanish** [ˈspanɪʃ]	**a Spaniard** [ˈspanɪəd]	**the Spaniards**
Sweden [ˈswiːdn] *Schweden*	**Swedish** [ˈswiːdɪʃ]	**a Swede** [swiːd]	**the Swedes**
Switzerland [ˈswɪtsələnd] *die Schweiz*	**Swiss** [swɪs]	**a Swiss**	**the Swiss**
Syria [ˈsɪriə] *Syrien*	**Syrian** [ˈsɪriən]	**a Syrian**	**the Syrians**
Thailand [ˈtaɪlænd, ˈtaɪlənd,] *Thailand*	**Thai** [taɪ]	**a Thai**	**the Thai**
Turkey [ˈtɜːki] *die Türkei*	**Turkish** [ˈtɜːkɪʃ]	**a Turk**	**the Turks**
the United Kingdom (the UK) [juˌnaɪtɪd ˈkɪŋdəm, ˌjuːˈkeɪ] *das Vereinigte Königreich (Großbritannien und Nordirland)*	**British** [ˈbrɪtɪʃ]	**a Briton** [ˈbrɪtn]	**the British**
Wales [weɪlz] *Wales*	**Welsh** [welʃ]	**a Welshman/-woman**	**the Welsh**

Titelbild
Cornelsen/Personen am Strand: Anja Poehlmann, Strandhäuschen: Shutterstock.com/JoolsW

Illustrationen
Cornelsen/**Harald Ardeias**: S. 5 mi.; S. 15 mi. re.; S. 16 ob. re.; S. 18 mi. re.; S. 23 A–F; S. 24 ob. + un. re.; S. 25 ob. re. + un. li.; S. 28 mi. re.; S. 31 1–6; S. 33 un. re.; S. 34 mi. li. + re.; S. 35 un. re.; S. 36 1–6; S. 46 ob.; S. 47 un. re.; S. 52–53 1–7; S. 58 un. A–D; S. 66 ob. re.; S. 67 un.; S. 68 ob. re.; S. 72 ob. li.; S. 78 A–C; S. 80 mi.; S. 81 ob. re.; S. 82 mi. re + un. re.; S. 83 re.; S. 90 A–D, 1–6; S. 94–95 alle; S. 96 1–6; S. 100 ob. re.; S. 104 un. re.; S. 105 ob. re.; S. 108 ob.; S. 110–111 alle; S. 112 mi.; S. 116 ob. re.; S. 122 ob. re.; S. 126 mi. re.; S. 134 ob.; S. 138 un. re.; S. 139 ob. re.; S. 153 un. re.; S. 188 mi.; Cornelsen/Inhouse/**Josephine Bienert-Köhler**: S. 50 A–D; S. 51 ob. li. + re.; S. 60 ob. re.; S. 62 mi.; S. 152 ob. re.; S. 163 ob. re.; S. 166 mi. re.; S. 169 re.; Cornelsen/**Carlos Borrell Eiköter**: Karte Umschlaginnenseite hinten (U3); Cornelsen/**Julie Colthorpe**: S. 157 mi. re.; Cornelsen/**Michael Fleischmann**: S. 213 mi. re.; S. 229 mi. re.; Cornelsen/**Klara Luise Frankenberg**: S. 157 ob. re.; Cornelsen/**Irina Zinner**: S. 1 Möwe; S. 4 Möwe; S. 5 Möwe; S. 6 Möwe; S. 7 Möwe; S. 8 Möwe; S. 9 Möwe; S. 10; S. 14 Möwe; S. 16 Möwe; S. 17 Möwe; S. 19 Möwe; S. 19 ob. li. + un.; S. 21 Möwe; S. 23 Möwe; S. 28 Möwe; S. 29 Möwen; S. 38 Möwen; S. 45 Möwe; S. 46 Möwe; S. 48 Möwen; S. 49 Möwe; S. 51 Möwe; S. 56–57 Möwen; S. 65 Möwen; S. 66 Möwe; S. 67 Möwe; S. 74 Möwe; S. 75 Möwe; S. 77 Möwe; S. 78 Möwe; S. 79 Möwen; S. 81 Möwe; S. 87 Möwe; S. 96 ob. re.; S. 101 Möwe; S. 103 Möwe; S. 107 Möwe; S. 109 Möwe; S. 112 Möwe; S. 114 Möwe; S. 115 Möwe; S. 124 mi.; S. 126 Möwe; S. 127 Möwen; S. 132 Möwe; S. 133 Möwe; S. 135 Möwe; S. 137 Möwe; S. 138 ob. re.; S. 139 Möwe; S. 145 Möwe; S. 151 Möwe; S. 156 Möwe; S. 167 Möwe; S. 170–177 Möwen; S. 179 Möwe; S. 180–183 Möwen; S. 192 Möwen; S. 195–201 Möwen; S. 263 Möwe.

Abbildungen
Umschlaginnenseite vorne (U2) bzw. Vorsatzseite 2: Siehe S. 12, 16 und 24; **S. 1 bzw. Vorsatzseite 3:** Siehe S. 28, 29 und 30; **S. 4** ob. li.: Cornelsen/Anja Poehlmann; **S. 5** ob. li.: Cornelsen/Anja Poehlmann; **S. 6** ob. li.: Cornelsen/Anja Poehlmann; **S. 7** ob. li.: Cornelsen/Anja Poehlmann; **S. 8** ob. li.: Cornelsen/Anja Poehlmann; **S. 10** mi. li.: Cornelsen/Anja Poehlmann; **S. 11** mi. li. + mi. re.: Cornelsen/Anja Poehlmann; **S. 12** ob. mi.: Shutterstock.com/Maksim Zaytsev, mi. li.: Shutterstock.com/wavebreakmedia, mi.: Cornelsen/Anja Poehlmann, mi. re.: Shutterstock.com/Bobo Ling; **S. 13** ob. mi.: Shutterstock.com/A_Lein, mi. li.: Shutterstock.com/Linda George, mi.: Cornelsen/Anja Poehlmann, mi. re.: Shutterstock.com/malik965, Emoticons: Shutterstock.com/Yefym Turkin; **S. 14** ob. re.: Shutterstock.com/vovidzha, un. re.: Shutterstock.com/fizkes; **S. 15** mi. re.: Cornelsen/Anja Poehlmann; **S. 17** mi. re.: Shutterstock.com/Radha Design; **S. 18** ob. re.: mauritius images/alamy stock photo/Lloyd Lane; **S. 19** ob. re.: Cornelsen/Grasshopper Films; **S. 20** ob. re. + mi. re.: Cornelsen/Anja Poehlmann, mi. re.: mauritius images/alamy stock photo/Benedicte Desrus, Emoticons: Shutterstock.com/Yefym Turkin, Regenbogenflagge: Shutterstock.com/sebastian ignacio coll, Kopfhörer: Shutterstock.com/M_Videous, Herzen: Shutterstock.com/Turkan Rahimli, Regenbogen: Shutterstock.com/Carboxylase, Kuchen: Shutterstock.com/JosepPerianes, Gitarre: Shutterstock.com/orbitoclast; **S. 21** un. re.: Shutterstock.com/UfaBizPhoto; **S. 22** ob. re.: Cornelsen/Anja Poehlmann, mi. li.: Shutterstock.com/daizuoxin, mi.: Shutterstock.com/rangsan lerkngam, mi. re.: Shutterstock.com/Chekyravaa, un. re.: Junge (li.): Anja Poehlmann, Frau (re.): Shutterstock.com/SpeedKingz, **S. 27** ob. re.: Cornelsen/Inhouse/Mara Leibowitz, A–F: Cornelsen/Grasshopper Films; **S. 30** ob. li.: Cornelsen/Anja Poehlmann, mi.: Shutterstock.com/Rainer Lesniewski, ob. re.: Shutterstock.com/FotoAndalucia, mi. li.: Shutterstock.com/Naypong Studio, mi.: Shutterstock.com/Laenz, mi. re. holidays: Shutterstock.com/Arsenie Krasnevsky, journey: Shutterstock.com/XXLPhoto, Emoticons: Shutterstock.com/Cosmic_Design; **S. 31** ob. re.: Cornelsen/Anja Poehlmann; **S. 32** ob. re.: Shutterstock.com/Dubova; **S. 33** ob. re.: Cornelsen/Anja Poehlmann; **S. 34** un. re.: Cornelsen/Anja Poehlmann; **S. 40–41** A–D: Cornelsen/Anja Poehlmann; **S. 42** mi. li.: Shutterstock.com/Le_Mon, mi. re.: Shutterstock.com/ngaga; **S. 43** ob. mi.: Shutterstock.com/CREATISTA, un. mi.: Shutterstock.com/TommyStockProject; **S. 44** ob. li. + ob. re.: Cornelsen/Anja Poehlmann, Emoticons: Shutterstock.com/Yefym Turkin; **S. 45** ob. li. + ob. mi. re.: Cornelsen/Anja Poehlmann, Emoticons: Shutterstock.com/Yefym Turkin, Hund: Shutterstock.com/Jaaak; **S. 48** A: Shutterstock.com/Dragon Images, B: Shutterstock.com/Kostiantyn Voitenko, C: Shutterstock.com/Rawpixel.com, D: Shutterstock.com/Krakenimages.com; **S. 49** ob. re.: Shutterstock.com/Gleb Usovich, un. li.: Shutterstock.com/Dean Drobot; **S. 54** 1–8: Shutterstock.com/Spreadthesign; **S. 55** alle: Cornelsen/Grasshopper Films; **S. 58** ob. li. A–H: Cornelsen/Anja Poehlmann; **S. 59** ob. + mi. li.: Cornelsen/Anja Poehlmann, un. mi.: Shutterstock.com/Laugesen Mateo; **S. 61** ob. re.: Cornelsen/Anja Poehlmann; **S. 62** un. li: Shutterstock.com/Sofya_Iva; **S. 63** ob. li.: Imago Stock & People GmbH/PA Images/Doug Peters/EMPICS Entertainment 35529208, ob. re.: mauritius images/alamy stock photo/michael melia, USA-Landkarte: stock.adobe.com/Racer57, USA-Flagge: stock.adobe.com/M-KOS, un. re.: Shutterstock.com/Pixel-Shot; **S. 64** mi. re.: Shutterstock.com/AnnGaysorn; **S. 65** un. re.: Shutterstock.com/Verina Marina Valerevna; **S. 69** mi. li.: interfoto e.k./Granger, NYC, mi. re.: interfoto e.k./IFPAD, un. li.: Bridgeman Images/Astrid Lindgren (1907–2002) Swedish author, un. re.: interfoto e.k./Friedrich; **S. 70** A: Shutterstock.com/delcarmat, B: mauritius images/alamy stock photo/Paul Briden; **S. 71** C: Shutterstock.com/Kiian Oksana, D: Shutterstock.com/JurateBuiviene; **S. 72** Knitting: Shutterstock.com/Mr.Alex M, Football club: Shutterstock.com/SpeedKingz, Karate: Shutterstock.com/Aleksandr Rybalko, Goats and other animals: mauritius

images/alamy stock photo/Nigel Cattlin, Photography: Shutterstock.com/michelangeloop, History in Brighton: Shutterstock.com/FenlioQ, Tea party and show: Shutterstock.com/CKP1001; **S. 73** mi. re.: Cornelsen/Anja Poehlmann, un.: Cornelsen/Oliver Meibert; **S. 74** ob. re.: Cornelsen/Anja Poehlmann, mi. li.: Shutterstock.com/Anton Brehov, 1–5: Shutterstock.com/RainiKandi, **S. 75** mi. re.: Depositphotos/Ian Allenden; **S. 76** mi. re.: Cornelsen/Anja Poehlmann; **S. 78** mi.: Cornelsen/Anja Poehlmann; **S. 79** ob. re.: Shutterstock.com/Phonlamai Photo; **S. 80** ob.mi. re.: Cornelsen/Anja Poehlmann; **S. 81** Emoticons: Shutterstock.com/Yefym Turkin; **S. 85** gardening: Shutterstock.com/Halfpoint, photography: Shutterstock.com/Quality Stock Arts, sewing: Shutterstock.com/BAZA Production, street dancing: Shutterstock.com/Rawpixel.com, A–D: Grasshopper Films LTD; **S. 86** mi. li.: stock.adobe.com/pairhandmade, mi. re.: Shutterstock.com/Monkey Business Images; **S. 87** mi. re.: Shutterstock.com/Duda Vasilii, un. li.: Shutterstock.com/MicroOne; **S. 88** mi. re.: Cornelsen/Anja Poehlmann; **S. 89** Emoticons: Shutterstock.com/Yefym Turkin; **S. 91** Emoticons: Shutterstock.com/Teguh Mujiono, Daumen hoch: Shutterstock.com/Yayayoyo, ob. re.: Cornelsen/Anja Poehlmann; **S. 97** ob.: Shutterstock.com/QatlasMaps, smile: Shutterstock.com/Rido, headache: Shutterstock.com/Nikodash, study: Shutterstock.com/fizkes, cough: Shutterstock.com/Kleber Cordeiro, screen: Shutterstock.com/Can Yesil, calendar: Shutterstock.com/Iconic Bestiary, click: Shutterstock.com/airdone, brunch: Shutterstock.com/Sara Winter; **S. 98** A: stock.adobe.com/Fevziie, B: stock.adobe.com/Katarzyna Leszczynsk; **S. 99** C: stock.adobe.com/JOHN LEIGH/thecoach1, D: mauritius images/Steve Vidler; **S. 102** un. re.: Cornelsen/Anja Poehlmann; **S. 104** ob. re.: Cornelsen/Anja Poehlmann; **S. 105** un. re.: Shutterstock.com/BearFotos; **S. 107** ob. re.: Shutterstock.com/JacquiMoore; **S. 109** ob. li.: Cornelsen/Anja Poehlmann, Emoticons: Shutterstock.com/Yefym Turkin; **S. 113** A–F: Grasshopper Films LTD; **S. 114** 1: Shutterstock.com/LianeM, 2: Imago Stock & People GmbH/Sylvio Dittrich; **S. 116** mi.: stock.adobe.com/grafikplusfoto; **S. 117** Emoticons: Shutterstock.com/Yefym Turkin; **S. 118** 1: Shutterstock.com/Rawpixel.com, Emoticons: Shutterstock.com/Yefym Turkin; **S. 119** mi.: Shutterstock.com/Ground Picture, Daumen: Shutterstock.com/Cosmic_Design; **S. 120** ob.mi.: dpa Picture-Alliance/ZUMAPRESS.com/London News Pictures via ZUMA/Hugo Michiels, un. li.: Cornelsen/Anja Poehlmann; **S. 121** ob. li.: stock.adobe.com/vm2002, mi. li.: stock.adobe.com/Ildi Papp/Ildi, USA-Flagge: stock.adobe.com/M-KOS, un. re.: StockFood/Lawton, Becky/PhotoCuisine; **S. 123** A: Shutterstock.com/GCapture, B: Shutterstock.com/Irina Yusupova, C: www.coulorbox.de, D: Shutterstock.com/Erik J, E: Shutterstock.com/F Armstrong Photography, F: Shutterstock.com/Botond Horvath, G: Shutterstock.com/Pressmaster, H: Shutterstock.com/Kimberly Shavender; **S. 125** un.: Shutterstock.com/Monkey Business Images; **S. 127** mi. li.: Cornelsen/Anja Poehlmann; **S. 128** A: Depositphotos/Ian Allenden, B: Shutterstock.com/Basyn, C: Depositphotos/VOLODYMYR VAKSMAN, D: Shutterstock.com/Gorodenkoff; **S. 129** E: Shutterstock.com/Gorodenkoff, F: Shutterstock.com/Roman Chazov, G: Shutterstock.com/Jacob Lund, H: stock.adobe.com/hedgehog94; **S. 130** ob. re.: Cornelsen/Anja Poehlmann; **S. 131** 1: Shutterstock.com/GzP_Design, 2: Shutterstock.com/Mr. Rashad, 3: Shutterstock.com/Skeleton Icon, 4: Shutterstock.com/M.Style, 5: Shutterstock.com/spiral media, 6: Shutterstock.com/Skeleton Icon, mi.: Shutterstock.com/Pinkcandy, un. li.: Shutterstock.com/serhii.suravikin; **S. 132** un. re.: Shutterstock.com/Monkey Business Images; **S. 133** A: Shutterstock.com/Simple Line, B: Shutterstock.com/samui, C: Shutterstock.com/Gigonthebeach, D: Shutterstock.com/Simple Line, E: Shutterstock.com/lineartestpilot; **S. 134** 1: Shutterstock.com/Lopolo, 2: Shutterstock.com/Dean Drobot, 3: Shutterstock.com/Drazen Zigic, 4: Shutterstock.com/JacZia, 5: Shutterstock.com/Atitaph_StockPHoTo; **S. 136** video/online games: Shutterstock.com/yudha satia, sweets & chocolates: Shutterstock.com/Natykach Nataliia, books and magazines: Shutterstock.com/IhorZigor, Diagramm: Shutterstock.com/Jacek Fulawka, pig: Shutterstock.com/ADragan, Molly: Shutterstock.com/ViDI Studio; **S. 137** 1: Shutterstock.com/Konstantin Zibert, 2: Shutterstock.com/Tupungato, 3: stock.adobe.com/highwaystarz, 4: stock.adobe.com/Federico Rostagno, 5: Shutterstock.com/fotoinfot, 6: stock.adobe.com/RossandHelen photographers/rh2010; **S. 138** mi. re.: Cornelsen/Grasshopper Films LTD; **S. 139** un. re.: Shutterstock.com/Monkey Business Images; **S. 140–142** alle: Cornelsen/Anja Poehlmann; **S. 143** ob. re.: Cornelsen/Grasshopper Films LTD; **S. 145** ob. re.: Shutterstock.com/Tom K Photo; **S. 146** un. re.: Shutterstock.com/Franck Boston; **S. 147** mi. re. + 1–6: Cornelsen/Anja Poehlmann; **S. 148** A: stock.adobe.com/Iakov Filimonov/JackF, B: Shutterstock.com/LADO, C: Shutterstock.com/ORION PRODUCTION, D: stock.adobe.com/Production/M/M-Production, E: stock.adobe.com/Dragana Gordic, trainers: Shutterstock.com/Penny Hillcrest, jacket: Shutterstock.com/Landscapemania, skateboard: Shutterstock.com/Krakenimages.com, hoodie: Shutterstock.com/Tarzhanovam, headphones: Shutterstock.com/Jiri Hera, rucksack: Shutterstock.com/burnel1, basketball: Shutterstock.com/Ronnie Chua, helmet: Shutterstock.com/Cullen Macias, robot: Shutterstock.com/Mauro Rodrigues, **S. 149** ob. re.: Cornelsen/Anja Poehlmann, Emoticon: Shutterstock.com/Yefym Turkin; **S. 150** mi. re.: Shutterstock.com/Monkey Business Images; **S. 151** 1 + 6: Shutterstock.com/Nadiinko, 2: Shutterstock.com/davooda, 3: Shutterstock.com/kuroksta, 4: Shutterstock.com/MAKSIM ANKUDA, 5: Shutterstock.com/ksenvitaln; **S. 152** 1: Shutterstock.com/Image Source Collection, 2: stock.adobe.com/lev dolgachov/Syda Productions, 3: Shutterstock.com/New Africa, 4: Shutterstock.com/Rachata Teyparsit, 5: Shutterstock.com/Ronald Sumners, 6: Shutterstock.com/Iryna Dincer, 7: Shutterstock.com/PR Image Factory, 8: Shutterstock.com/Monkey Business Images, 9: Shutterstock.com/Krasula; **S. 158** ob. re.: Shutterstock/Mona Makela, mi. re.: Shutterstock.com/ONYXprj, un. re.: stock.adobe.com/Mojzes Igor/luckybusiness; **S. 160** Laptop: Shutterstock.com/Passatic,

Bildschirm: Shutterstock.com/I000s_pixels; **S. 161** Daumen: Shutterstock.com/matsabe; **S. 164** Flaggen: Shutterstock.com/ONYXprj; **S. 165** ob. re.: mauritius images/alamy stock photo/keith morris; **S. 166** Laptop: Shutterstock.com/Passatic, Möwe: mauritius images/Nature in Stock; **S. 179** mi. li.: Shutterstock.com/owatta; **S. 182** un. re.: Shutterstock.com/autovector; **S. 184** ob. re.: Shutterstock.com/greenpic.studio, un. li.: Shutterstock.com/Laurie Barr; **S. 185** rafting: Shutterstock.com/Aleksandr Lupin, snorkelling: Shutterstock.com/Denis Moskvinov, a treetop walk: stock.adobe.com/Simon Dannhauer, ride an alpine slide: stock.adobe.com/Fotolia RAW, have a sleepover: Shutterstock.com/Darrin Henry, go on a zipline: stock.adobe.com/shiyana, paint my room: Shutterstock.com/Neirfy, do origami: Shutterstock.com/AnastasiaNi, play crazy golf: Shutterstock.com/Jana Vackova-Vesela, have a water fight: Shutterstock.com/kryzhov; **S. 186** a crew cut: stock.adobe.com/schankz, gelled hair: Shutterstock.com/Phovoir, a ponytail: Shutterstock.com/Prostock-studio, a fringe: Shutterstock.com/Gelpi, braided hair: Shutterstock.com/Nataliya Turpitko, a beard: Shutterstock.com/Roman Samborskyi, freckles: Shutterstock.com/PinkCoffee Studio, nail varnish: Shutterstock.com/Subbotina Anna, airbrushed nails: Shutterstock.com/Innger_Nails, a piercing: Shutterstock.com/Ludmila Ivashchenko, a tattoo: Shutterstock.com/New Africa, a scar: Shutterstock.com/BLACKDAY; **S. 187** jacket: Shutterstock.com/Pixel-Shot, hoodie: Shutterstock.com/way.uy, jumper: Shutterstock.com/Magdalena Wielobob, shirt: Shutterstock.com/elenovsky, socks: Shutterstock.com/koraypolat, skirt: Shutterstock.com/Maffi, tights: Shutterstock.com/Africa Studio, underwear: Shutterstock.com/Africa Studio, shorts: Shutterstock.com/Anna Chelnokova, trainers: Shutterstock.com/Den Rozhnovsky, sandals: Shutterstock.com/Chiyacat, jewellery: Shutterstock.com/Roma Borman, gloves: Shutterstock.com/NsdPower, scarf: Shutterstock.com/Adisa, belt: Shutterstock.com/In Green, sunglasses: Shutterstock.com/Jin young-in; **S. 189** action film: Shutterstock.com/FlashMovie, cartoon: Shutterstock.com/Macrovector, comedy: Shutterstock.com/Anneka, cooking show: Shutterstock.com/Supamotion, disaster film: Shutterstock.com/Regina Erofeeva, documentary: Shutterstock.com/Wirestock Creators, fantasy film: Shutterstock.com/Nejron Photo, game show: Shutterstock.com/Frame Stock Footage, horror film: Shutterstock.com/Jeff Cameron Collingwood, reality show: Shutterstock.com/Amy Lutz, romance: Shutterstock.com/chainarong06, science fiction (sci-fi) film: Shutterstock.com/ktsdesign, soap: Shutterstock.com/oneinchpunch, sports show: Shutterstock.com/Eugene Onischenko, thriller: Shutterstock.com/DedMityay; **S. 190** re.: Shutterstock.com/Rashad Ashur; **S. 191** chicken: Shutterstock.com/JIANG HONGYAN, fish: Shutterstock.com/MaraZe, sausage: Shutterstock.com/Einsteinstudio, eggs: Shutterstock.com/Nattika, lamb: Shutterstock.com/TheBusinessMan, pork: Shutterstock.com/GSDesign, beef: Shutterstock.com/MaraZe, strawberry: Shutterstock.com/Tim UR, apple: Shutterstock.com/Roman Samokhin, melon: Shutterstock.com/Boonchuay1970, raspberry: Shutterstock.com/Andriy Lipkan, orange: Shutterstock.com/Valentyn Volkov, mango: Shutterstock.com/Valentyn Volkov, banana: Shutterstock.com/bergamont, lemon: Shutterstock.com/Maks Narodenko, cherry: Shutterstock.com/Serg64, popcorn: Shutterstock.com/Jiri Hera, cupcakes: Shutterstock.com/Wealthylady, muffins: Shutterstock.com/Binh Thanh Bui, ice cream: Shutterstock.com/stockcreations, donuts: Shutterstock.com/Sergey Skleznev, jelly: Shutterstock.com/cigdem, butter: Shutterstock.com/bigacis, cheese: Shutterstock.com/Tanya Sid, joghurt: Shutterstock.com/pogonici, milk: Shutterstock.com/New Africa, cream: Shutterstock.com/grey_and, aubergine+ chili: Shutterstock.com/PixaHub, broccoli: Shutterstock.com/smspsy, carrot: Shutterstock.com/Valentina Razumova, cabbage: Shutterstock.com/JIANG HONGYAN, cucumber: Shutterstock.com/Maks Narodenko, garlic: Shutterstock.com/Maks Narodenko, peas: Shutterstock.com/WIPHARAT CHAINUPAPHA, peppers: Shutterstock.com/DronG, onion: Shutterstock.com/Yeti studio, lettuce: Shutterstock.com/PotaeRin, potatoes: Shutterstock.com/Anna Kucherova, tomato: Shutterstock.com/Tim UR; **S. 193** beautician: Shutterstock.com/Rido, builder: Shutterstock.com/megaflopp, care worker: Shutterstock.com/Pixel-Shot, call centre agent: Shutterstock.com/Bojan Milinkov, cashier: Shutterstock.com/hedgehog94, dentist: Shutterstock.com/Drazen Zigic, electrician: Shutterstock.com/Phovoir, engineer: Shutterstock.com/Chaosamran_Studio, lawyer+ paramedic+garage+factory+ laboratory: Shutterstock.com/Gorodenkoff, salesperson: Shutterstock.com/George Rudy, secretary: Shutterstock.com/DC Studio, farm: Shutterstock.com/Fotokostic; **S. 194** Cleaning: 1 Shutterstock.com/Dean Clarke, 2 Shutterstock.com/gabriel12, 3 stock.adobe.com/dusanpetkovic1, Meals: 1 Shutterstock.com/Monkey Business Images, 2 Shutterstock.com/Christian Mueller, 3 stock.adobe.com/Heliosphile, Clothes 1 stock.adobe.com/nowaczykfoto.pl/Mirek, 2 stock.adobe.com/Mihail, 3 Shutterstock.com/Bacho; **S. 203** mi. re.: Shutterstock.com/Isometrixus; **S. 204** jump: Shutterstock.com/NicoElNino, river: Shutterstock.com/Zoa.Arts, castle: Shutterstock.com/meunierd; **S. 206** flag: Shutterstock.com/Magcom, rainbow: Shutterstock.com/spline_x, glove: Shutterstock.com/Tung Phan; **S. 207** bus: Shutterstock.com/BlueRingMedia, thunderstorm: stock.adobe.com/firewings; **S. 208** un. re.: stock.adobe.com/demimerzie; **S. 209** ob. re.: Shutterstock.com/Maria Shalamova; **S. 210** un. re.: stock.adobe.com/Krakenimages.com; **S. 211** planet: NASA/NOAA/DSCOVR, boot: Shutterstock.com/forest badger; silver: Shutterstock.com/Paket, helmet: Shutterstock.com/Rvector; **S. 212** dolphin: Shutterstock.com/Pannochka, strong: Shutterstock.com/kristinblack, mask: Shutterstock.com/rawf8, **S. 213** dress: Shutterstock.com/Yuyula, face: Shutterstock.com/dean bertoncelj, ankle: stock.adobe.com/Csaba Deli, ambulance: stock.adobe.com/nspooner; **S. 214** blanket: stock.adobe.com/rgvc, fall asleep: Shutterstock.com/Ollyy, broken: stock.adobe.com/Алексей Синельников; **S. 215** ob. re.: Shutterstock.com/mdd; **S. 216** un. re.: stock.adobe.com/yevgeniy11; **S. 217** camera: Shutterstock.com/Skylines, clocks: Shutterstock.com/wongstock; **S. 218** bridge: stock.adobe.com/The Nico Studio, mountain: Shutterstock.com/Modvector, key: stock.adobe.com/vectorfusionart; **S. 219** ob. re.: Shutterstock.com/Andramin, sea: Shutterstock.com/Ron Mertens, trophy: stock.adobe.com/Tartila; **S. 220** screen: Shutterstock.com/A-R-T; **S. 221** mi. re.: Shutterstock.com/solarseven; **S. 222** candle: Shutterstock.com/irin-k, mosque: Shutterstock.com/naulicrea, yoghurt: Shutterstock.com/oksana2010, onion: Shutterstock.com/Lubava; **S. 224** ob. re.: Shutterstock.com/Sherbak_photo, un. re.: Shutterstock.com/Snap2Art; **S. 225** mi. re.: Shutterstock.com/Bildagentur Zoonar GmbH, un. re.: stock.adobe.com/Coprid; **S. 226** rain jacket: Shutterstock.com/gopfaster, jacket: stock.adobe.com/Olga, scarf: Shutterstock.com/Yury Gulakov, church: Shutterstock/KannaA, mirror: Shutterstock.com/Pavel Adashkevich; **S. 227** firefighter: stock.adobe.com/toa555, nurse: Shutterstock.com/Minerva Studio; **S. 230** magazine: stock.adobe.com/BillionPhotos.com, piggy bank: stock.adobe.com/Victor Moussa, electronics: Shutterstock.com/NosorogUA; **S. 232** mi. re.: Shutterstock.com/Iris vector; **S. 233** mi. re.: Shutterstock.com/Blue.Poppy.Art; **S. 264** ob. li.: Shutterstock.com/Laurie Barr; **S. 265** alle: Shutterstock.com/HitToon.

Fremdtext
S. 62 ob. li. (poem): Shel Silverstein: *Hug O'War*, in: 'Where the Sidewalk Ends' (the poems and drawings of Shel Silverstein). New York: Harper Collins Publishers 1974

Liedquelle
S. 126: Long-Legged Sailor: traditionell und gemeinfrei

(to) **be**	**was/were**	**been**	sein
(to) **become**	**became**	**become**	werden
(to) **break**	**broke**	**broken**	brechen
(to) **buy**	**bought**	**bought**	kaufen
(to) **choose**	**chose**	**chosen**	wählen, auswählen
(to) **come**	**came**	**come**	kommen
(to) **do**	**did**	**done** [ʌ]	tun, machen
(to) **eat** [iː]	**ate** [et, eɪt]	**eaten** [iː]	essen
(to) **fall**	**fell**	**fell**	fallen
(to) **feel**	**felt**	**felt**	fühlen, sich fühlen
(to) **fight**	**fought**	**fought**	kämpfen, bekämpfen
(to) **find**	**found**	**found**	finden
(to) **fly**	**flew**	**flown**	fliegen
(to) **get**	**got**	**got**	bekommen; (sich etw.) besorgen, holen
(to) **give** [ɪ]	**gave**	**given** [ɪ]	geben
(to) **go**	**went**	**gone**	gehen, fahren
(to) **hang**	**hung** [ʌ]	**hung**	hängen
(to) **have**	**had**	**had**	haben
(to) **hurt**	**hurt**	**hurt**	verletzen; wehtun
(to) **keep**	**kept**	**kept**	halten, behalten
(to) **know** [nəʊ]	**knew** [njuː]	**known** [nəʊn]	wissen; kennen
(to) **leave**	**left**	**left**	lassen, zurücklassen, verlassen
(to) **make**	**made**	**made**	machen, herstellen
(to) **meet**	**met**	**met**	treffen
(to) **put**	**put**	**put**	setzen, legen, stecken
(to) **ride** [aɪ]	**rode**	**ridden** [ɪ]	reiten; *(Rad)*fahren
(to) **say**	**said** [sed]	**said** [sed]	sagen
(to) **see**	**saw**	**seen**	sehen
(to) **sell**	**sold**	**sold**	verkaufen
(to) **set**	**set**	**set**	stellen, legen, setzen
(to) **show**	**showed**	**shown**	zeigen
(to) **sing**	**sang**	**sung**	singen
(to) **spend**	**spent**	**spent**	*(Geld)* ausgeben, *(Zeit)* verbringen
(to) **stand**	**stood**	**stood**	stehen
(to) **swim**	**swam**	**swum**	schwimmen
(to) **take**	**took**	**taken**	(mit)nehmen; bringen
(to) **teach** [iː]	**taught** [ɔː]	**taught** [ɔː]	lehren, unterrichten
(to) **tell**	**told**	**told**	sagen; erzählen, berichten
(to) **think**	**thought**	**thought**	denken, glauben, meinen
(to) **throw**	**threw**	**thrown**	werfen
(to) **understand**	**understood**	**understood**	verstehen
(to) **wear** [eə]	**wore** [ɔː]	**worn** [ɔː]	tragen *(Kleidung)*
(to) **win**	**won** [ʌ]	**won** [ʌ]	gewinnen
(to) **write**	**wrote**	**written**	schreiben

Typical tasks	Häufige Arbeitsanweisungen
Act out the conversation / song / story.	Führt das Gespräch / das Lied / die Geschichte vor.
Answer the questions / partner B's questions.	Beantworte die Fragen / Partner Bs Fragen.
Before you read / listen / watch	Bevor du liest / (zu-)hörst / anschaust ...
Check the spelling / your answers / ideas (with a partner).	Überprüfe deine Rechtschreibung / Antworten / Ideen (mit einem/r Partner/in).
Choose the correct answer / word.	Wähle die richtige Antwort / das richtige Wort aus.
Compare the pictures / your answers / ... with a partner.	Vergleiche die Bilder / deine Antworten / ... mit einem/r Partner/in.
Complete the table / list / sentences / ...	Vervollständige die Tabelle / Liste / Sätze / ...
Copy the table / list / notes.	Schreibe die Tabelle / die Liste / Notizen ab.
Correct the false / wrong sentences / answers.	Berichtige die falschen Sätze / Antworten.
Describe the picture / your room / ...	Beschreibe das Bild / dein Zimmer / ...
Draw pictures.	Male / Zeichne Bilder.
Find the answers / the correct / right / wrong words.	Finde die Antworten / die richtigen / falschen Wörter.
Finish the sentences.	Vervollständige die Sätze.
Give feedback.	Gib Feedback / eine Einschätzung.
Interview your partner.	Stelle deinem/r Partner/in Fragen.
Look at the board / at page ...	Schaue an die Tafel / auf Seite ...
Look at the photos / pictures /map / title.	Sieh dir die Fotos / Bilder / Karte / die Überschrift an.
Listen and check / practise / repeat / guess.	Höre zu und überprüfe / übe / wiederhole / rate.
Listen again.	Höre nochmals zu.
Listen to the story / conversation / dialogue.	Höre dir die Geschichte / das Gespräch / den Dialog an.
Make groups (of six / ... students).	Bildet Gruppen (zu je sechs / ... Schüler/innen).
Make sentences / notes / lists / a mind map.	Fertige Sätze / Notizen / Listen / eine Mindmap an.
Match the sentence parts / what the friends say.	Verbinde die Satzhälften / das, was die Freunde sagen.
Practise with a partner.	Übe mit einem/r Partner/in.
Put it in you DOSSIER.	Hefte es in deinem DOSSIER ab.
Put the sentences / dialogue in the correct order.	Bringe die Sätze / den Dialog in die richtige Reihenfolge.
Read about ...	Lies über ...
Read the conversation / text / story / article.	Lies den Dialog / Text / die Geschichte / den Artikel.
Stand up when you hear ...	Wenn du ... hörst, stehe auf.
Swap (cards) with a partner.	Tausche (die Karten) mit einem/r Partner/in.
Take turns.	Wechselt euch ab.
Talk about ...	Sprich / Sprecht über ...
Talk to a partner.	Sprich mit einem/r Partner/in.
Tell your partner / the class.	Erzähle / Sage es deinem/r Partner/in / der Klasse.
True or false? / True, false or not in the text?	Wahr oder falsch? / Wahr, falsch oder nicht im Text?
Say the four / ... sentences.	Sage die vier / ... Sätze.
Use your notes / the words in a).	Benutze deine Notizen / die Wörter aus Aufgabe a).
Walk around.	Gehe (im Raum) herum.
Watch part / scene 1 / all the film.	Sieh dir Teil / Szene 1 / den ganzen Film an.
Watch again.	Sieh es / sie / ihn nochmals an.
Work alone / with a partner / in groups.	Arbeite allein / mit einem/r Partner/in / in Gruppen.
Write the correct answers / sentences / words.	Schreibe die richtigen Antworten / Sätze / Wörter (auf).
Write (more) about ...	Schreibe (mehr) über ...